DATE DUE

TALKING HEADS
AND THE SUPREMES

The Canadian Production
of Constitutional Review

David M. Beatty

CARSWELL

Toronto • Calgary • Vancouver

1990

Canadian Cataloguing in Publication Data

Beatty, David M.
 The Canadian production of constitutional review : talking heads and the supremes

ISBN 0-459-34651-2

1. Judicial review — Canada.   2. Judicial power — Canada.   3. Canada. Supreme Court.   4. Canada — Constitutional law.   I. Title.

KE4248.B42 1990   347.71012   C90-094994-5
KF4575.B42 1990

© 1990 Carswell — A Division of Thomson Canada Limited.

Preface

Over the course of the past five years the subject of the Charter of Rights and Freedoms has come to dominate discussion in Canadian legal academe. In law schools, perhaps more than anywhere else, the Charter is surrounded in controversy; its very legitimacy debated daily in classrooms and corridors alike. Conferences are organized around, books are written about, and the pages of law reviews are filled with essays about every imaginable topic concerning the Charter and the role that judges have been asked to play in our liberal-democratic system of government. Amidst all of this clamour, in proposing to add to what many consider an already overcrowded field, one must be sensitive to the risk of raising the din to a level in which no one will be heard.

The original plan of the book was very different from the one that is set out in the pages that follow. When I started out on this project, my idea was to address a range of practical issues surrounding the procedural and institutional aspects of the Charter and the process by which the courts, and in particular the Supreme Court, review the constitutionality of Canadian law. I intended to look at very pragmatic questions, such as who can initiate a Charter challenge (what lawyers call standing); who can participate in a case (intervention); what kinds of evidence can be used, and remedies sought; as well as what qualifications should be demanded of the people who aspire to sit on the Bench.

The procedural and institutional aspects of constitutional review seemed to me to be a subject which was ripe for study. Over the years respected scholars (such as Paul Weiler and Peter Russell, to name only two), who were critical or at least sceptical about the prospect of the third branch of government reviewing action taken by the other two, had highlighted various institutional and structural characteristics of the courts which, in their minds, rendered judges ill-equipped to perform such a task.

Although a good deal had been written on many of these questions, there had not been a general, sustained attempt to address the concerns of these critics in a systematic way. For the most part, debates about the Charter were preoccupied with the larger, and more basic, theoretical question of whether constitutional review was consistent with our theories and tradition of democratic government — indeed with whether it was legitimate at all. It seemed to me that a down-to-earth book about how constitutional litigation actually is, and might better be conducted in the future, would fill a gap in the existing literature.

To carry off this project, I recognized that it would still be necessary to come to grips with the legitimacy issue and to address the question of how it could be that a small group of unelected persons could be given the task of telling the elected representatives of the people what they could or could not do. It would be impossible to write about how Charter challenges might be initiated and processed by the Supreme Court without being very clear about what the nature and scope of the judges' role in our system of government should be. None of the questions about the organization and methods of decision-making of the Court could be answered without first establishing that there was some legitimate part for the Court to play and being very specific about what the nine persons appointed to the Court were being asked to do.

Naively perhaps, my initial expectation was that delivering a clear picture about what role the entrenchment of the Charter had created for the Court would be a relatively simple and straightforward task. As a matter of legal fact, it seemed likely that, however heated the theoretical debates about whether the Court had any legitimate role to play at all had become, the members of the Court would have worked out a pretty clear idea of what their new job was all about. When I started this project the Supreme Court was in its fifth year of writing judgments about the Charter and with a relatively stable membership over that period, it seemed, (at least at the time), reasonable to assume that the Court's own performance would give a fairly clear picture of the sorts of functions in which the Court was now engaged.

As often happens with projects of this kind, initial assumptions proved to be overly optimistic, and very quickly the enterprise took on a life of its own. Rather than a book about procedures and institutional structures, the final product remains preoccuppied with the prior question of what, if any, role a group of unelected judges can legitimately play in supervising the affairs of the other two branches of government. What happened, as anyone familiar with the decisions of the Court could have forewarned, was that very quickly I discovered that there was no consensus among the members of the Court as to what their role should be. Although, at the beginning, there was a considerable degree of harmony and unanimity, gradually each of the judges began to articulate very definite and very different points of view as to what their role should ultimately be. Rather than a common and coherent characterization of what the process of constitutional review was all about, increasingly each of the judges developed his or her own ideas about the kind of performance the Charter called on them to play.

In discovering this diversity of opinion among the members of the Court, I was not, of course, making an original find. As described in the text, a number of commentators had been quite sensitive to the divisions that had built up in the Court almost from the moment they first appeared. However, the position in which I found myself was unique in that, while other observers were very sensitive to the competing ideas and theories about the Charter that had taken hold in the Court, for the most part they made no effort to evaluate their relative strengths. They were content to describe and analyse the competing approaches without addressing the question of whether one or other of them was stronger or weaker than the rest.

For my purposes, such a comparative assessment was unavoidable. To write a book about the procedural and institutional aspects of constitutional review meant that the divisions between the judges had to be resolved. Only if it could be established that one of the competing images of what judicial review was all about was superior to all of the rest, would there be any chance of resolving the institutional and procedural questions which initially motivated my inquiry. The judges' perceptions about the role of the Court were so different that, if it were accepted that all were to be valued equally, it would be practically impossible to design a set of procedures and organizational structures which could accomodate them all.

In this way, the shape and content that the book now has slowly began to take form. The whole first part of the book is intended to address the different approaches that the judges on the Court developed over the first five years that they worked with the Charter and to determine whether any one of them can claim a status of priority and legitimacy over the rest. In the second and third chapters, I describe in some detail the personalities of each of the judges on the Court in terms of their attitudes towards the Charter and the legal powers each of them thought they had acquired. As I have just indicated, there is nothing original in any of this. Commentators are generally agreed on the broad outlines of the philosophies held by each member of the Court. In these two chapters I have simply added details and examples to a picture whose general contours were already known.

In the final chapter of the first part I do, however, begin to cover new ground, and it is here that the focus of the book was ultimately fixed.

As I evaluated the strengths and weaknesses of the different theories of review which each of the judges espoused, patterns of decision-making became apparent which I had not noticed before. Eventually, after reading and re-reading each of the judgments written over the first five years, I realized that virtually every time one of the judges came to the conclusion that it was not appropriate to exercise his or her powers of review, he or she employed principles (the most important being one lawyers call "definitional balancing") and methods of reasoning (which I will call "avoidance" or "denial") that were inconsistent with and ultimately did violence to the most basic precepts and values on which the Charter rests. In effect, identifying the conceptual and analytical mistakes that had constrained the Court in the exercise of its powers of review revealed that there was *only one* approach to constitutional review that was consistent with the "inner logic" of the Charter, and that this, and *only this*, vision was constitutionally correct. Indeed, it was the sensitivity of Bertha Wilson, Antonio Lamer and Brian Dickson to this "liberal" understanding of what the power of constitutional review really entailed, that distinguished them from the five other more "conservative" judges on the Court who, characteristically, were more inclined to rely on one of the arguments that was constitutionally flawed.

Coming to the conclusion that there was only one correct approach to applying the Charter and understanding the role the Court should play in a system of liberal democratic government did not, as one might expect, mean that I could immediately turn my attention to the procedural and institutional questions as originally planned. Quite the contrary in fact. The position I had come to was one that I knew would be highly controversial and would be met with scepticism and resistance in all quarters. To say that certain principles or modes of analysis — like definitional balancing — were themselves constitutionally flawed was an embarrassingly strong claim to make. In effect I would be saying that every time the judges failed to embrace the "liberal" approach to judicial review they were themselves acting unconstitutionally. For those judges who insisted on reasoning in this way, it would even call into question their entitlement to continue to sit on the Court.

It was possible that the sharpness, or the edge, to the claim could be softened or muted to some degree by pointing out that the role which Wilson, Lamer and Dickson called on the judges to play was one which would be very familiar to lawyers and policymakers alike. Properly understood, the "liberal" approach to judicial review was really not very radical at all. Reduced to its essentials, the "liberal" approach could in fact be presented as a very straightforward application of two basic principles of justice or policy analysis. One of these principles is based on a simple, utilitarian or cost/benefit, method of analysis and focuses on the *purposes* which a law is said to promote. With this principle the Court evaluates a law's objectives by weighing them against the costs or effects (in terms of sacrificing entitlements which the constitution guarantees) which they impose. The second, and as it turns out more important, principle in this theory of constitutional review relates to the *means* lawmakers have chosen to accomplish their objectives. To test this aspect of a challenged law the Court relies on a standard measure of social welfare known as "Paretianism". With this principle, the Court asks whether there are alternative policies available to a Government by which the purposes of the law could have been realized, but in a way which would have compromised the guarantees embedded in the Charter less. (For a more detailed account of how the liberal model of judicial review can be reduced to these two principles, see my "The End of Law: . . . At Least As We Have Known It" in R. Devlin (ed.), *Canadian Perspectives on Legal Theory* (Emond Montgomery, 1990).

Still, as simple and attractive as the liberal model might be to describe, one could have no illusions that it would be appealing, either to those who are generally sceptical about claims of objectivity and determinacy in any legal regime, or to those who believe that constitutional rights and freedoms are qualitatively, and not just quantitatively, different from all other human interests and activities. For large numbers of people, I realized that the idea that there is a single, unifying theory of the Charter and the process of constitutional review would be highly problematic, both from an empirical and a normative point of view. At best, the claim that constitutional review was reducible to two "neutral principles" would strike many people knowledgeable in constitutional law as a futile attempt to revive an idea which had been thoroughly discredited generations ago. At worst it would be seen to be arrogant and provocative in the extreme.

Even for those with more faith in the objectivity and integrity of law, the role that the liberal understanding of the Charter requires the judges to play will seem odd and quite unconventional. It will certainly clash with the traditional teaching on constitutional review and the judicial protection of human rights. In contrast with conventional wisdom, the liberal method has relatively little to do with defining which interests and activities are protected by the rights and freedoms which the Charter guarantees. On the approach favoured by Wilson, Lamer, and Dickson, rather than the role of interpreter of a constitutional text, the Court's primary function is to evaluate the justifications offered by Governments and their supporters for why a particular social policy had been chosen to be enacted into law. Justification, not interpretation, it transpires, is what the Charter and judicial review is mostly about. Section 1, not the substantive sections in which the rights and freedoms are entrenched, is where all of the action takes place.

Given the controversial nature of the conclusions to which the analysis in Part One led, it seemed to me to be premature to begin to consider the procedural and institutional implications of this understanding of the liberal version of constitutional review. Both sides of the debate, I thought, could reasonably demand to know something more about the way constitutional review would actually work before being asked to concede its legitimacy. Something more needed to be said about how this method of review would actually be applied and the consequences to which it would lead before it would be appropriate to turn to the procedural and institutional questions which initially motivated this project.

Part Two has been organized with that purpose in mind. It is an attempt to allay the suspicions of those who might be inclined to doubt the claims in Part One, by showing that, conceived in this way, constitutional review can enhance both the democratic and progressive character of our system of government. Part Two builds on the model of the Charter identified in the first part by applying it to a variety of cases that are currently being litigated and that, in one shape or form, are destined to come to the Supreme Court. Challenges to laws regulating: religion in our schools; participation by various groups (including prisoners, public servants, trade unions and lobby groups etc.) in the political process; compulsory membership in unions; and the processes for determining whether a person is a genuine refugee, provide the framework for testing the integrity of the theory of review developed in the first part. In each example the decisions handed down by the lower courts that heard these cases are evaluated and compared to the result the Supreme Court should come to, assuming it remains faithful to the method of review which was favoured by the liberal judges and, indeed, required by the Constitution itself.

Only at the conclusion of the analysis of each of the cases considered in Part Two did I feel comfortable turning to the procedural and institutional questions which initially motivated this inquiry. Only by establishing that the method of reviewing the constitutionality of law, which was favoured by Bertha Wilson and her two liberal colleagues, was grounded on objective principles, and generally did lead to determinate and progressive results, could the institutional and structural features of the review process finally be addressed. Fortunately, with the function of the Court clearly defined, the procedural and institutional lessons turned out to be relatively simple and straightforward. Comparative analysis of how constitutional law is organized and practised in other free and democratic societies around the world pointed to alternative procedures and structures that can easily be adapted to the Canadian environment and that can ensure the Court can play its role more effectively and faithfully than it did over its first five years. Paradoxically, given the objectives this inquiry was intended to pursue, in the end it turns out that the institutional and procedural questions surrounding constitutional review are not as intractable as some people might have thought them to be. Once it is recognized that there is a single, unique theory of judicial review that is embedded in the Charter, and the issue of legitimacy is laid to rest, the institutional and procedural implications of that model fall rather easily into place. Major structural and institutional changes are not required to answer the concerns of those who are sceptical about the institutional and organizational capabilities of the Court and to ensure that the practice of constitutional review coincides with its underlying theory.

Having gone on at some length explaining the ultimate shape which the book has come to possess, I should add a note about my decision to make use of a musical metaphor in the title and in the organization of the book. In the first place I should stress that I see nothing in this style of presentation which in any way affects the merits of the argument (in the last chapter in Part One) on which the coherence of the book is based. It was meant strictly as a rhetorical device which I hope will enhance rather than detract from the reader's understanding of the text.

Nor should anyone think I am trying to play the role of an arts critic making claims about the quality of music performed by either of these musical groups. This is a book exclusively about constitutional review. The "Talking Heads" and "Supremes" were chosen primarily because their names had an obvious, independent meaning in a book about constitutional discourse and the process of judicial review. Moreover, as I point out in the text, there is a harmony in the style of the "Supremes" which makes the parallel with the work of the Court even more to the point. As for the "Talking Heads", it seemed to me that their recorded distrust of justice, freedom and common sense would make them an attractive counterbalance for legal scholars whose instincts were likely to be sceptical of the whole enterprise.

In the end, the musical metaphor was invoked to underscore my belief that discussion about and the practice of constitutional review can and should be brought down to earth and conducted in more humanistic and less conceptual terms. After all, if the argument of this book is correct, the principles of justice employed by the Court are neither particularly complex nor controversial. They are, in fact, simply part of a larger family of values in our community which finds constant expression in the contemporary musical and artistic world. Stripped of its legal jargon and arid conceptualism, in substance as well as in style, the difference between the judicial and an artistic performance is not as great as many in the legal and academic communities would have us believe.

That the book ends up on a relatively positive, up-beat note has made the prolonged effort, which is required to complete a project of this kind, much easier to endure. Other factors were even more influential in ensuring that the book was able to come to some sort of resolution within a reasonable period of time. The best part of the book was written in ideal circumstances, during the 1988-89 academic year, while I was on leave with my family, supported by a Connaught Research Fellowship. The SSHRC also contributed to the project with a grant to cover a substantial portion of the research and administrative expenses. For their support I am most grateful. During this time I was a visitor at the Institut Suisse de Droit Comparé in Lausanne, Switzerland. I cannot imagine a more supportive and congenial working environment in which to undertake a project of this kind.

As is the nature of these sorts of enterprises, numerous friends have been drawn into its production and have generously assisted me in ensuring its completion. Peter Hogg, Alan Hutchinson, Patrick Macklem, Ninette Kelley, and Michael Trebilcock all read an earlier draft of the manuscript and made helpful suggestions as to how it might be improved. Andrew Cunningham and Anne Sonnen did most of the initial digging for material at the beginning of the project and carried through to completing the footnotes at the end. Trudy Schmidt, Ninette Kelley, Joan McLeod, Tim Johnson, Don Sallis, Renate Pfluegl, Chris Black and Mary Ellen Yeomans looked after all of the technical and administrative details of turning transcript into text. Ken Mathies and Gary Rodriguez at Carswell could not have been more cooperative in ensuring a final manuscript was put in a publishable format as expeditiously as it is possible to do. To all of these people; to my students in Constitutional Law in 1987-88 and 1989-90 who provided a forum in which I was able to test these ideas; and to my sons Timothy, Colin and Adam for agreeing to being uprooted yet another time, my heartfelt thanks. To all of you I am indebted in ways I hope I can repay. The greatest debt I incurred in the completion of this project, and one it is doubtful I can ever discharge, is to Ninette. Her inspiration, collaboration and unwavering support, makes this as much her book as mine.

Table of Contents

Part III — Stage Production: The Procedure of Constitutional Review

Table of Cases

PART I

The Supremes:
The Possibility of Constitutional Review

1

Introduction

This is a book about the process by which judges decide whether a law — or some action by a Government agency or official — is constitutional or not.[1] In general terms it is about the role courts play in the formulation of social policy in a liberal democratic system of government. As a practical matter, however, most of the book concentrates on Canadian constitutional law and the Canadian Charter of Rights. This choice reflects my own lack of expertise with other countries' experiences with constitutional review rather than any flag-waving on my part. Moreover, the Canadian experience should be of interest to constitutional

---

1 Of the two functions of judges, reviewing Acts of a legislature as opposed to reviewing action taken by bureaucrats, administrative agencies and government officials (e.g., police), the first is clearly the most controversial and certainly the most novel. It is here where the tension between judicial review and our democratic tradition of Parliamentary sovereignty is greatest. By contrast, courts have always exercised a supervisory function over administrators, bureaucrats and government officials. What has changed is that the criteria against which courts measure the legitimacy of administrative action has been extended by the rights and freedoms which the Charter contains.

Given the novelty and controversy surrounding judges being given the power of deciding whether any Government has the authority to pass laws of certain kinds, the focus of the book will be on those cases in which the Court has been or will be asked to review the constitutionality of some rule or law. It is the judicial decision which tells a Government it cannot pass a particular law, not one relieving against bureaucratic excesses, that is most in need of explanation and defence. To the extent the cases involving challenges to action taken by administrative officials bear on that analysis, they will be canvassed as well. I will not, however, deal with issues which relate exclusively to such complaints. Nor will I consider remedial issues, such as what relief is available to individuals whose constitutional rights have been violated under s. 24 of the Charter and how that compares to the function the Court performs under section one. The focus of the book is addressed to the question of whether there is any legitimate role for the third branch of government to play in restricting the activities of the other two and if there is, what that role or function should be.

lawyers and students of government generally because it offers a rather pristine and very manageable body of material within which one can examine the function or role that the third branch of government performs when it reviews the constitutionality of law. Focusing on the Canadian experience allows one to examine the work of a group of nine judges,[2] struggling from first principles, without the use of prior cases to assist them, trying to make sense of and ascribe some meaning to a written, constitutional bill of rights. From their insights and their errors emerges a very clear, but so far little-acclaimed, theory of judicial review, which has implications beyond the Canadian borders.

The Charter of Rights and Freedoms was made part of Canada's Constitution on April 17, 1982. A little over two years later, on May 3, 1984, the Supreme Court of Canada handed down its first judgment evaluating a law under the Charter. In it the Court upheld the constitutionality of a section of the *Law Society of Upper Canada Act*, which required all lawyers in Ontario to be Canadian citizens. According to the Court, this legal requirement did not violate the "mobility rights", contained in section 6 of the Charter, of people (such as Americans) who, but for their citizenship, would have been fully qualified to practise law.

During the next five years[3] the Court issued rulings on over eighty additional challenges that were brought under the Charter.[4] Different aspects of law touching children's advertising, language rights, refugees, breathalizer tests, Sunday shopping, strikes and picketing, religious schools,

---

2 Although there are nine positions on the Supreme Court of Canada, at different times, during the period under review, there were only eight judges actively involved in the work of the Court. The death of Julien Chouinard, and the temporary secondment of Willard Estey to other Government duties, meant that for significant periods the Court was obliged to perform its role shorthanded.

    The focus of the book will centre on the eight judges who were most actively involved with the Charter over the course of its first five years. From left to right these include Bertha Wilson, Antonio Lamer, Brian Dickson, Willard Estey, Gerald Le Dain, Gerard La Forest, Jean Beetz, and William McIntyre. Although other judges were involved in one or two of the earliest cases, and a whole new group came on the scene during the course of the 1988-89 year, the work of these eight dominates the period under review and provides a sufficiently substantial, though still manageable, collection of judgments describing what they thought the Charter really meant.

3 In fact, the period under review extends slightly beyond the five-year mark in order to include several important cases such as *R. v. Turpin*, [1989] 1 S.C.R. 1296, and *Slaight Communications v. Davidson* (1989), 59 D.L.R. (4th) 416, and to pick up the final judgments of Le Dain, McIntyre and Beetz, who left the Court as the first five-year period came to a close.

4 The exact number of cases the Court decided in this period will vary depending on whether one considers various cases heard together and decided on common reasoning separately or as part of a group. Roughly, the breakdown of cases is: year 1 — 5; year 2 —10; year 3 — 15; year 4 — 21; year 5 — 32.

extradition, narcotics, dangerous offenders, drunk driving, constructive murder and abortion were all assessed for their constitutionality by the Court. In most of these cases, the Court found that the laws in question were constitutional, but in a substantial number of them one or more members of the Court concluded that certain aspects of some of these laws did violate the rights and freedoms that the Charter guaranteed. Indeed, near the end of this five-year period a plurality of the members of the Court actually struck down a section of British Columbia's *Barristers and Solicitors Act*, which paralleled the one they had considered in the *Law Society of Upper Canada* case, on the ground that it violated the equality rights that the Charter guaranteed in section 15 and which had not been in force when the latter case was decided.[5]

As might be expected, on various occasions, in the course of ruling on the constitutionality of these laws, each of the judges took the time and made an effort to explain what he or she understood the Charter to mean. In these first years there simply were no earlier cases which could assist the members of the Court in deciding how they should rule. First principles, and the logic that each of them saw in the Charter, were all that any of the judges had.

In the first part of this book I want to review the different understandings of each of the judges as to what the Charter is all about, and I want to do so in a way that will make sense to those who are not trained in the law. I think it is important that a book about constitutional review be written in this way. If non-lawyers could not understand what the Charter has been interpreted to mean and how it has been applied, there would be considerable force to the claim that adopting a process of constitutional review marks a profoundly anti-democratic turn in our system of government.[6] Human rights would be the exclusive domain of an intellectual and economic elite rather than an opportunity for the oppressed and disadvantaged to participate more effectively in the processes of politics. The Charter and judicial review would be available only to the very few

---

5 *Andrews v. Law Society of B.C.* (1989), 56 D.L.R. (4th) 1.

6 The concern that the Charter will result in a kind of legalization of politics, practised in a language and method unfamiliar and inaccessible to ordinary Canadians, has been raised by legal and political commentators alike. See, e.g., M. Mandel, *The Charter of Rights and the Legalization of Politics in Canada* (Toronto: Wall & Thompson, 1989); J. Bakan, "Constitutional Arguments: Interpretation and Legitimacy in Canadian Constitutional Thought" (1980), 27 Osgoode Hall L.J. 123; A. Petter, "Immaculate Deception: The Charter's Hidden Agenda" (1987), 45 Advocate 857; T. Ison, "The Sovereignty of the Judiciary" (1986), Cahiers de Droit 501; P. Russell, "The Political Purposes of the Canadian Charter of Rights and Freedoms" (1983), 61 Can. Bar Rev. 30; D. Schmeiser, "The Case Against Entrenchment of a Canadian Bill of Rights", 1 Dal. L.J. 15. For a more philosophical discussion of this tension, see Michael Walzer, "Philosophy and Democracy" (1981), 9 Pol. Theory 379.

"talking heads" fortunate enough to be born with and/or to have acquired sufficient resources to be able to learn and speak in its tongues.

To accomplish my purpose I propose therefore to depart from the style, though not the substance, of conventional legal analysis. Wherever possible I will avoid legal jargon and titles. So far as I can, I endeavour to keep discussions of technical points of law, that are of importance to lawyers, in the notes that are appended to the text. Throughout, I try to make use of a performance metaphor that is implicit in the title of the book, and I encourage the reader to think of the whole enterprise as being very similar to the task faced by an arts critic writing an "end-of-the-first-half-decade" piece on the work of a new rock or stage group that has made a very sudden and very spectacular debut on the cultural scene. Structurally, this first Part is organized as a review of a marathon concert or stage production with an intermission in the middle and a tentative evaluation at the end.

No one, I hope, will take offense at the more casual and familiar style this critical posture will take. Certainly none is intended. Increasingly, people have come to recognize the close connection that exists between law, literature, and social criticism.[7] The performance metaphor I realize is not perfect, but a strong parallel can, I think, be drawn. It has a number of advantages, not the least of which, I believe, is that it can help to demystify and to clarify the law for those who do not work with it on a daily basis. Calling judges "Honourable", "Mr. Justice", or "My Lord" cannot change the fact that the Supremes were nine individual Canadians struggling to learn a new and very daunting role. Titles cannot bestow infallibility.[8] Drawing connections to performances with which non-lawyers may be more familiar should make it easier for them to adjust to a production which it is unlikely they have frequently, if ever, encountered before.[9]

---

7 The connection has been drawn by lawyers and literary critics alike. Compare, e.g., Ronald Dworkin, *Law's Empire* (Cambridge: Harvard University Press, 1986), Chapter 7, with Stanley Fish, "Working on the Chain Gang: Interpretation in Law and Literature" (1982), 60 Texas Law Review 373. For a highly acclaimed integration of law and literary criticism in the field of American constitutional law, see James Boyd White, *When Words Lose Their Meaning*. See also S. Levenson and S. Mailloux (eds.), *Interpreting Law and Literature* (Evanston, Illinois: Northwestern University Press, 1988); and Michael Walzer, *Interpretation and Social Criticism* (Cambridge: Harvard University Press, 1987). A precedent for the musical metaphor can be found in Allan Hutchinson's "Democracy & Determinacy: An Essay in Legal Interpretation" (1989), 43 Miami L. Rev. 541

8 In the view of some, invoking titles of this kind can actually impede our understanding of law. See, e.g., William Conklin, *Images of a Constitution* (Toronto: University of Toronto Press, 1989), p. 44.

9 Although written in a way that should make the Court's work with the Charter more accessible to people not trained in law, I recognize there will be portions, particularly

The performance metaphor really is not as farfetched as it might initially seem. In fact, I think it can be quite helpful because it encourages us to think about things and in ways that are not always at the forefront of traditional legal analysis. In particular, it draws our attention as much to the individual performance of each of the judges as to the work of the Court as a whole.[10] In any review of a musical performance of a group such as "The Supremes", a critic would invariably focus some of his comments on the individual efforts of each member of the group, as well as on how well each of them coordinated their performance with the others. These would be important elements in any review of a concert or a theatrical performance. As we shall see, they can be very illuminating in our review of the Court's work with the Charter as well.

Indeed, in one sense, the question of how the judges interacted, in deciding the cases they heard under the Charter, is even more central than it would be in most musical reviews. In music, members of a group can interact either harmoniously or in ways that produce discordant sounds; although obviously the success of "The Supremes" lay partly in their choice to coordinate their efforts the first way rather than the second. In legal circles, by contrast, there is currently a very vigorous debate going on about the meaning of law in which a central question is whether, and/or the extent to which, either or both of these ways of personal interaction are legitimate among those who are judges on the same court.

The debate is between those who believe in the integrity of law and those who are sceptical of the role formal legal systems can play in the regulation of human affairs. The sceptics argue that, in the end, all law, including constitutional law, is "made up" or invented, by the judges. In their view, there never is only one "right answer" to any legal question, such as whether a piece of legislation prohibiting shopping on Sundays, or regulating the circumstances in which an abortion can be performed,

---

in Part One, where the doctrinal analysis will be heavy going. My hope is that I have been able to organize and synthesize this material so that those with the strength to plod through it will not be prejudiced by their lack of legal experience in understanding it. Non-lawyers should be on a much more equal footing in Parts Two and Three of the book, where traditional doctrinal analysis is kept to a minimum.

10 Traditionally, commentators have not focused attention on the performance of individual judges. See R. Martin, "Criticising the Judges", 28 McGill L.J. 1. For a notable exception, see S. Peck, "The Supreme Court of Canada 1958-1966: A Search For Policy Through Scalogram Analysis", 45 Can. Bar Rev. 666. Increasingly, however, as we shall see, academic commentators have paid a good deal of attention to the different personalities of each of the judges and how that has affected the work of the Court. At least one of the judges on the Court during this time — Willard Estey — is reported to have expressed concern that as ordinary Canadians come to learn how significant the personality of the judges is to the work of the Court, they may come to lose respect and faith in it. See *The Globe & Mail*, April 27, 1985, p. A5.

is constitutional or not. The sceptics claim that the legal principles which judges use to decide cases "march in pairs"[11] so that each judge can always find some principle which will allow him to justify any decision he wants. Because of its indeterminacy and malleability, the sceptics would say discordance rather than harmony is the natural language of law.

Believers reject the idea that law is so radically indeterminate and so much the subjective opinion of each judge. They think there is usually, if not always, only one right answer in each case.[12] They say objective rules do exist in law, including constitutional law, which can — and should — constrain the judges on a court. They do not believe that it is all up for grabs and just a matter of personal opinion as to whether, for example, Canada's abortion law is constitutional or not. In musical jargon, believers are committed to harmony. They say, against the sceptics, discordant opinions should have no validity in law. They would be inclined to think that the judicial branch of government is more like the cabinet than the legislature in the degree of solidarity and cohesion that should govern its deliberations.

In addition to drawing our attention to the group dimension of their work, invoking a parallel to a musical performance also encourages us to look for and applaud outstanding individual efforts on the Court. The performance metaphor reminds us that we need not, indeed should not, concentrate exclusively on the output of the group. In musical reviews, it is common to single out and applaud outstanding performances by individuals as well. In the eyes of virtually every reviewer, Diana Ross was, unambiguously, the most outstanding member of "The Supremes".

Being conscious of individual performances is as important in law as it is in music or theatre. In our review we should be alert to the possibility that one or two of the judges may have had insights about the Charter that stand out from all the rest. Great judges have distinguished themselves in the past. Duff, Rand and Laskin, to name only three, were persons whose ideas had a dominant influence in shaping the style and the jurisprudence of the Canadian Supreme Court.[13] Focusing on the individual efforts of

---

11   The phrase is borrowed from Paul Weiler, "The Supreme Court and the Law of Canadian Federalism" (1973), 23 U.T.L.J. 307, 364. Patrick Monahan makes the same point in *Politics and the Constitution* (Toronto: Carswell, 1987), p. 210, as does William Conklin in his book, *Images of a Constitution, supra*, note 8. The indeterminacy critique also features prominently in the writing of critical scholars such as Michael Mandel, Joel Bakan, Andrew Petter and Terry Ison — see *supra*, note 6.

12   See, e.g., Ronald Dworkin, *Taking Rights Seriously* (Cambridge: Harvard University Press, 1977); *A Matter of Principle* (Cambridge: Harvard University Press, 1985); *Law's Empire*, *supra*, note 7; and "No Right Answer" (1977), 53 N.Y.U. L. Rev. 1.

13   See D.R. Williams, *Duff: A Life in the Law*, (U.B.C. Press, 1984). Two other essays on Duff can be found in 12 Osgoode Hall L.J.; see W. Campbell, "The Right Honourable

each of the judges will allow us to determine whether, in its work with the Charter, the Court is more like those groups in which no one performer stands out or whether, as with "The Supremes", there were stronger and more illustrious members of the group.

Sir Lyman Duff: The Man As I Knew Him", p. 243; G. Le Dain, "Sir Lyman Duff and the Constitution", p. 261. See also R. Gosse, "The Four Courts of Lyman Duff" (1975), 53 Can. Bar Rev. 482. For a more penetrating and comprehensive evaluation of Laskin's work as a legal scholar and judge see "The Legacy", 35 U.T.L.J. 321. For a recent treatment of Rand's contribution to Canadian law, see W. Conklin, *Images of a Constitution*, *supra*, note 8. See also J.R. Cartwright, "Ivan Cleveland Rand: 1884-1969" (1969), 47 Can. Bar Rev. 155; E.M. Pollack, "Ivan Rand: The Talent is the Call" (1980), U.W.O. L. Rev. 115.

2

The First Set: 1984-1986

If one thinks of the first five years that the Court worked with the Charter as a marathon concert, the natural break for an intermission would occur around the end of year two. Specifically, I think most production managers would call for a pause shortly after the Court released its judgment in *R. v. Oakes*.[1] This decision, we shall see, pulls together much of the Court's work over the course of the first two years and is recognised by everyone as being a landmark, if not the most important, case the Court decided in its first five years.

Picture yourself then on February 28, 1986, the date the Court's decision in *Oakes* was handed down. You read the decision and you begin to reflect on what you have observed the Court to have done with the Charter over the previous two years. It would not surprise me if you said your initial reaction was that the Court had opened in a very bold and dramatic way.[2] Especially if one focused on the results of the cases, the Court's debut in Charterland might seem very vigorous indeed. In the four cases after its first decision in *Skapinker*[3] (the Law Society of Upper Canada case), the Court ruled that important sections of *Quebec's Language Code*,[4] the *Combines Investigation Act*,[5] the *Lord's Day Act*,[6] and the *Immigration Act*[7] were unconstitutional.

---

1 (1986), 26 D.L.R. (4th) 200.

2 At the time, this was not an uncommon reaction among commentators; see, e.g., F. Morton and M. Withey, "Charting the Charter, 1982-1985: A Statistical Analysis" (1987), 4 Can. Hum. Rts. Y.B. 65.

3 (1984), 9 D.L.R. (4th) 161.

4 *A.G. P.Q. v. Quebec Assn. of Protestant School Boards* (1984), 10 D.L.R. (4th) 321.

5 *Hunter v. Southam Inc.* (1984), 11 D.L.R. (4th) 641.

6 *R. v. Big M Drug Mart* (1985), 18 D.L.R. (4th) 321.

7 *Singh v. M.E.I.* (1985), 17 D.L.R. (4th) 422.

In year two, although the results were more evenly balanced, the Court declared parts of *B.C.'s Motor Vehicle Act*,[8] and the *Narcotics Control Act*[9] to be in violation of the Charter and ruled that the constitutional rights of individual Canadians had been violated by agents of the state (e.g., police) in four other cases as well.[10] In the two years following its first decision in *Skapinker*, only the federal cabinet's decision to permit the testing of unarmed cruise missiles in Canada,[11] a provision in the Criminal Code punishing persons who use firearms in the course of a robbery,[12] several sections in statutes governing the appointment, tenure and remuneration of Provincial Court judges,[13] and a common law rule of evidence[14] passed through the constitutional screen unscathed.

Although, collectively, these cases seem to suggest the Court opened its performance in a very daring way, upon further reflection, I am certain most reviewers would soon come to abandon that view. As so often is the case, a more critical appraisal can show initial impressions to be wrong. Rather than a daring and dramatic opening, the reality is that the first part of the Court's performance was overwhelmingly one of prudence and restraint. In every aspect of its work with the Charter the reviewer will see that the Court took great pains to proceed as carefully as it possibly could.[15]

Certainly the *pace* was one of caution. As we have noted, it was over two years after the entrenchment of the Charter before the Court handed down its first opinion on what the Charter meant. It issued only two more judgments in that year and it issued only fourteen judgments in the two years following its decision in *Skapinker*. Quantitatively, this was not a

---

8 *Ref. re s. 94(2) Motor Vehicle Act (B.C.)* (1985), 24 D.L.R. (4th) 536.

9 *R. v. Oakes, supra,* note 1.

10 *R. v. Therens* (1985), 18 D.L.R. (4th) 655; *R. v. Trask* (1985), 19 D.L.R. (4th) 123; *Rahn v. R.* (1985), 19 D.L.R. (4th) 126; *R. v. Dubois* (1985), 23 D.L.R. (4th) 503.

11 *Operation Dismantle Inc. v. R.* (1985), 18 D.L.R. (4th) 481.

12 *R. v. Krug* (1985), 21 D.L.R. (4th) 161.

13 *R. v. Valente* (1985), 24 D.L.R. (4th) 161.

14 *R. v. Spencer* (1985), 21 D.L.R. (4th) 756.

15 This view seems to be shared by sceptics and believers alike. Although noting the "overly activist posture" of the Court in the very first cases it heard, sceptics like Monahan and Petter conclude that the decisions handed down by the Court over the first two years were "not exactly . . . . earth-shattering". See P. Monahan and A. Petter, "Developments in Constitutional Law" (1987), 9 S. Ct. L. Rev. 69, 10 S. Ct. L. Rev. 61, 63; A. Petter, "The Politics of the Charter" (1986), 8 S. Ct. L. Rev. 473; T. Christian, "The Supreme Court of Canada and Section One — The Erosion of the Common Front", 12 Queens L.J. 277. For a similar assessment, see Peter Russell, "The First Three Years in Charterland" (1985), 28 Can. Pub. Admin. 367 ("It would be unrealistic to view these 'activist' Court decisions on legal rights as imposing the views of appointed judges on elected legislators. In a number of instances Charter decisions anticipate reforms whose time has come at the legislative level.").

performance a reviewer could describe as either activist or bold.

Even more than in its pace, the prudence of the Court can be seen in its *style*. Like a band experimenting with a new type of music, in the beginning the Court proceeded in a very cautious and conventional way. It chose harmony over discordance in virtually every judgment it wrote. Of the fifteen or so decisions it handed down in this two-year period, reviewers will find almost half of them were unanimous opinions.[16] In another five,[17] everyone who heard the case was agreed on what the outcome should be, but one or two of the judges wanted to add "concurring" reasons to explain additional or alternative grounds on which the decision could be supported. In another two, some members of the Court thought the case could be resolved without any reference to the Charter at all.[18] In only two cases in the first two years were dissenting judgments written,[19] and in only one of these[20] did the judges speak in a way that could be described as truly discordant.

From a performance of that kind it is apparent that in approaching their new role everyone on the Court put a lot of energy into ensuring that each of their individual contributions was subordinated to, and coordinated with, a larger symphonic whole. Reviewers will appreciate that not only did the Court not perform often over the course of its first two years, but when it did it tried very hard to address its audience in a single harmonious voice. Critics who are careful will also discover that the reason the judges were so successful maintaining such a collegial approach was largely because of the analytical approach they followed in virtually all of the judgments they wrote.

Essentially three different characteristics distinguish its judgments in this opening act.[21] Firstly, the Court spent a considerable amount of time defining, and securing agreement on, the basic structure and method of analysis that should be followed when the constitutionality of a law was being assessed. Secondly, and until these ground rules were worked out, the Court made a conscious effort to put off deciding the more complex

---

16 *Skapinker v. Law Society of Upper Canada, supra,* note 3; *P.Q. School Board v. A.G. P.Q., supra,* note 4; *Hunter v. Southam Inc., supra,* note 5; *R. v. Trask, supra,* note 10; *R. v. Rahn, supra* , note 10; *R. v. Valente, supra,* note 13.

17 *R. v. Big M Drug Mart, supra,* note 6; *Operation Dismantle v. R., supra,* note 11; *R. v. Spencer, supra,* note 14; *Reference re s. 94(2) Motor Vehicle Act (B.C.), supra,* note 8; *R. v. Oakes, supra,* note 1.

18 *Singh v. M.E.I., supra* , note 7; *R. v. Clarkson* (1986), 26 D.L.R. (4th) 493.

19 *R. v. Dubois, supra,* note 10; *R. v. Therens, supra,* note 10.

20 *R. v. Therens, ibid.*

21 A fourth characteristic noted by some observers about the judgments the Court handed down in the first two years is that substantively they are concerned primarily with procedural and formal rules of law rather than of policy issues of major public concern. See, e.g., Michael Mandel, *The Charter of Rights and the Legalization of Politics in Canada*

and controversial issues involved in judicial review for as long as it could. Finally, in those circumstances in which the Court decided it had no alternative but to exercise its new powers of review in a way which invalidated a piece of legislation or an administrative action, without exception it did so on the narrowest grounds possible.

Each of these strategies warrants some of the reviewer's attention. Of the three, unquestionably the Court devoted most of its efforts to the first. In the beginning almost all of the Court's energy was focused on the question of how the Charter should be read. Rules and principles were required in order to understand what the words of the Charter meant. It is commonplace to observe that words generally do not have one and only one meaning. The words "Keep Off the Grass", to use a favorite example, mean one thing if they are printed on a sign in a park; they mean something quite different when they are posted in a high school corridor.

The words in a constitution are no different. With the entrenchment of the Charter a new constitutional grammar was required. For example, how were words, such as "freedom of expression", to be understood? What kinds of behaviour constitutes expression: political speech making? picketing? advertising? slandering? mooning?[22] And what does "freedom" imply?[23] Does it, for example, include only the (negative) opportunity to speak one's mind freely without interference and censoring by others? Or does it also guarantee that the Government will make resources (such as access to public property) available to ensure that one's message will be heard?[24] In the same way that dictionaries alone cannot tell us which meaning we should give to the word "grass", so the Court had to settle on a method of interpretation that would allow it to understand what

---

(Toronto: Wall & Thompson, 1989). Mandel argues that the Court's most activist judgments occurred in cases challenging some aspect of criminal law or practice which were, for the most part, highly formal or procedural in nature. By contrast, when matters of substance, such as social and economic policies, were on the line, the Court tended to adopt a posture deferring to and thereby "legalizing" the status quo. For statistical confirmation of the criminal law bias of Charter litigation, see F. Morton and M. Withey, "Charting the Charter", *supra*, note 2. Morton and Withey also note that over the first three years, most Charter litigation was aimed at the action of public officials and/or decisions of administrative agencies rather than at the content of legislation itself.

22   Understood as exposing one's rectum in public for expressive purposes which are not intended to be erotic or sexual in any way. As to whether the latter constitutes expression within the meaning of s. 2(b), see *Koumoudouros v. Metro Toronto* (1984), 6 D.L.R. (4th) 523 (Ont. H.C.).

23   On the meaning of freedom generally, see P. Westen, " 'Freedom' and 'Coercion' — Virtue Words and Viċe Words" (1985), Duke L.J. 541.

24   See *Ref. re Alberta Public Service Employee Relations Act* (1987), 38 D.L.R. (4th) 161, 194, where Dickson contemplates other forms of Government assistance which may be implied in a constitutional guarantee of freedom of expression. For a general discussion of what obligations the Constitution imposes on Government to guarantee access to the

entitlements were guaranteed by words such as "freedom of expression".

From the outset the Court was clear about the general interpretive approach it would follow. The Charter, the Court said in its first judgment in *Skapinker*,[25] was part of the Constitution and as such it had to be read in a way which would allow it to grow and expand. In *Skapinker* and again in *Hunter v. Southam*,[26] the third decision it handed down, the Court distinguished a constitutional document such as the Charter from an ordinary statute passed by Parliament or a provincial legislature. The Court pointed out that ordinary legislation is usually written with much more specificity and in much greater detail than a constitutional document, and can be easily amended if a change is desired.

By contrast, a constitutional instrument such as the Charter is written in large and malleable terms and cannot be readily altered. For all the members of the Court, the permanence and sweeping language used in the text meant that if the Charter was to remain relevant it would have to be interpreted in a way which would allow for its "development over time to meet new social, political and historical realities often unimagined by its framers".[27]

A stricter method of interpretation, which might be used for legal documents such as statutes, was said not to be appropriate for constitutions, which have been "drafted with an eye to the future". In the Court's words such a method of interpretation would "stunt the growth [of the Charter] and hence the community it serves".[28] Recalling a famous remark of the American legal scholar, Paul Freund, the Court reminded itself "not to read the provisions of the Constitution like a last will and testament lest it become one".[29]

Referring to the above method as the "liberal" or "purposeful" approach, in four of the five cases it heard in its first year, the Court underscored that this was the proper interpretive methodology to employ.[30] Using this method, the meaning of rights and freedoms such as liberty,

---

most important means of communication, see Richard Moon, "Access to Public and Private Property Under Freedom of Expression" (1988), 20 Ottawa L. Rev. 339. On the more specific question of what rights of access members of political groups have to public property, such as airports, see Part Two, Chapter 6, *infra*.

25 *Supra*, note 3.

26 *Supra*, note 5.

27 *Hunter v. Southam, ibid.*, at 649.

28 *Skapinker v. Law Society of Upper Canada, supra*, note 3, at 168.

29 *Hunter v. Southam, supra*, note 5, at 649.

30 *Skapinker v. Law Society of Upper Canada, supra*, note 3, at 169-170; *Hunter v. Southam, supra*, note 5, at 649-650; *R. v. Big M Drug Mart, supra*, note 6; *Quebec Protestant School Board v. A.G. P.Q., supra*, note 4. The purposeful approach was also applied in *R. v. Therens, supra*, note 10, at 677; *Reference re s. 94(2) Motor Vehicle Act, supra*, note 8, at 547; *R. v. Dubois, supra*, note 10, at 521.

expression, association, and equality would be derived by analyzing the purpose of the constitutional guarantee. The Court would concentrate on the ends or the goals of the entitlements enumerated in the Charter. Each of the rights and freedoms guaranteed by the Charter would be defined by spelling out the interests and activities which furthered its purposes.[31]

There was nothing surprising or radical in the Court's decision to read the Charter in this way. It is entirely in accord with conventional legal analysis. This interpretative method is generally recognized as the most appropriate way to approach any legal document that uses words with very wide and general meanings.[32]

It is true that, like any legal rule or method of analysis, this interpretative approach is open to manipulation and abuse. Various legal scholars have questioned the integrity of this interpretative method precisely because it is feared that a judge can impose his or her values in deciding what purpose or purposes a right or freedom will be said to serve.[33] In practice, however, it is apparent that everyone on the Court was sensitive to this possibility and went to considerable lengths to ensure they would not succumb to such temptations. Reviewers will see that many of the most important parts of its earliest judgments were taken up with the task of distinguishing those sources which would assist them in identifying the purposes that a particular right or freedom could be said to serve from other sources that would not.

Over the course of the first two years, the Court identified four important sources from which the purpose of a right or freedom might be found and three others that it thought had little or no utility at all. The first and unquestionably most fundamental source of meaning for the Court lay in the larger objectives of the Charter itself.[34] Initially, the Court said that the ultimate purpose for which the Charter was entrenched in the Constitution was the "unremitting protection of individual rights and

---

31 R. v. Big M Drug Mart, supra, note 6, at 359-360.
32 See R. Dworkin, Law's Empire (Cambridge: Harvard University Press, 1986); J. Willis, "Statutory Interpretation in a Nutshell", 16 Can. Bar Rev. 1, 15-16; P. Hogg, "The Charter of Rights and American Theories of Interpretation", 25 Osgoode Hall L.J. 88.

The purposeful approach is also favoured by Courts in other countries with parallel powers of constitutional review. See D. Kommers, Judicial Politics in West Germany (Newbury Park, Cal.: Sage, 1976), p. 211; F. Jacobs, The European Court of Human Rights (New York: Oxford University Press, 1975), P 14. In the United States, the purposeful approach was embraced by the Supreme Court in the seminal case of McCulloch v. Maryland, 17 U.S. 316, 417.

33 P. Monahan and A. Petter, "Developments in Constitutional Law", supra, note 15, at p. 90; W. Conklin, Images of a Constitution (Toronto: University of Toronto Press, 1989), Chapter VII; P. Bobbitt, Constitutional Fate: Theory of the Constitution (Oxford University Press, 1982).

34 R. v. Big M Drug Mart, supra, note 6, at 359-360.

liberties".[35] Later, in *Oakes*, the Court refined this idea and rephrased it to embrace "respect for the values and principles required to maintain Canada as a 'free and democratic society' ".[36] As well, in *Oakes*, the Court identified some of these values to include, "respect for the inherent dignity of the human person, commitment to social justice and equality, accommodation of a wide variety of beliefs, respect for culture and group identity, and faith in social and political institutions which enhance the participation of individuals and groups in society". For the Court, these were the values and principles that underlie free and democratic societies and they were the "genesis of the rights and freedoms guaranteed by the Charter". In the end, the meaning of any of the fundamental freedoms such as expression, or religion, or association etc., or any of the other rights that the Charter guaranteed, was to be derived from the most basic values and principles that organize and distinguish societies that are free and democratic from those which are not.

In addition to the underlying values, principles and larger purposes of the Charter itself, the Court identified three other sources from which the purposes — and therefore the meaning — of each of the rights and freedoms guaranteed in the Charter might be revealed. Text, context and historical origins all could provide assistance, the Court said, in revealing what interests and activities each of the rights and freedoms guaranteed. Each of these sources proved useful to the Court in one or more of the decisions it handed down in its first two years. When, as in the first two cases it decided, the Court was concerned with less traditional and very precisely worded entitlements, such as freedom of movement within Canada or the right to be educated in the language of one's choice, textual language proved to be the determinative source of meaning.[37] In other cases, when the rights and freedoms at stake were more traditional and of much longer standing, such as freedom of religion or freedom from unreasonable search and seizure or the presumption of innocence, the Court made extensive analysis of the historical origins of these concepts.[38] Contextual analysis tended to be predominant when the claimed entitlements were, like the "legal rights", closely related to a number of other rights and freedoms that the Charter guaranteed.[39]

In exploring the meaning of the rights and freedoms entrenched in

---

35 *Hunter v. Southam, supra*, note 5.

36 *R. v. Oakes, supra*, note 1, at 225.

37 *Skapinker v. Law Society of Upper Canada, supra*, note 3; *P.Q. Protestant School Board v. A.G. P.Q., supra*, note 4.

38 *Hunter v. Southam, supra*, note 5; *R. v. Big M Drug Mart, supra*, note 6; *R. v. Valente, supra*, note 13; *R. v. Oakes, supra*, note 1.

39 *Ref. re s. 94(2) Motor Vehicle Act (B.C.), supra*, note 8; *R. v. Dubois, supra*, note 10; *R. v. Oakes, supra*, note 1; see also *R. v. Big M Drug Mart, supra*, note 6.

the Charter over the course of the first two years, it was these four sources
— the values and principles which characterize free and democratic
societies, the historical antecedents, the language by which they were
described and the context in which they were located — which the judges
turned to most consistently. At the same time that it was identifying the
interpretive aids that would be most helpful, there were other sources that
the Court singled out as especially problematic or which were simply
ignored. Three possibilities were earmarked by the Court as being
particularly inappropriate and of little or even no use at all. These were
its own earlier interpretations of corresponding entitlements in the old
Canadian Bill of Rights, parallel definitions by the U.S. Supreme Court
of the American Constitution, as well as the intentions of those who played
the most active role in drafting and organizing the entrenchment of the
Charter in the months leading up to April 17, 1982. For different reasons
each of these was rejected as providing much assistance in deciding what
interests and activities the Charter protected.

Of the three, in the Court's mind the Canadian Bill of Rights was
unquestionably the least helpful source of interpretation for the Charter.
In case after case, the Court cautioned that the definitions of the rights
and freedoms contained in the old Bill of Rights could not easily be
transferred to the Charter.[40] Again and again, the Court stressed that
Canada's first Bill of Rights was not a constitutional document. It was,
in reality, just an ordinary statute, and like any statute it had been read
with an eye to the past. Applying ordinary techniques of statutory
interpretation,[41] the Supreme Court had consistently defined the interests
and activities protected by the Bill of Rights as being limited to those which
existed at the moment the Bill of Rights was enacted. It had always been
interpreted as embracing a static or "frozen" conception of what human
rights Canadians might enjoy, rather than, as the Charter required, being
allowed to develop and grow to meet the changing social, political and
historical conditions it would confront.

Although the attitude of the Court toward American constitutional
law as a source of assistance in interpreting the Charter was not quite
so hostile, still it was decidedly cautious and tended, on the whole, to be
quite negative. On the one hand, the Court certainly thought that American
constitutional law supported the general purposive method of interpretation
it proposed to follow and it cited the leading American cases that argued

---

40 *Skapinker v. Law Society of Upper Canada, supra,* note 3; *Singh v. M.E.I., supra,* note
7; *R. v. Big M Drug Mart, supra,* note 6; *R. v. Therens, supra,* note 10; *Ref. re s. 94(2)
Motor Vehicle Act, supra,* note 8; *R. v. Oakes, supra,* note 1. This was a position it reaffirmed
in year five in *R. v. Whyte* (1988), 51 D.L.R. (4th) 481.

41 For a discussion of the difference between interpretation of constitutions and statutes,
see R. Dworkin, *Law's Empire, supra,* note 32

in favour of interpreting constitutions in this way.[42] As well, on several occasions, various members of the Court made reference to how American Courts had interpreted phrases such as "unreasonable search and seizure" or "liberty", which were common to both Constitutions.[43] On the whole, however, the Court cautioned against the transplantation of American constitutional law. Noting the different political, legal and social pasts of the two countries, the judges warned that much of the American jurisprudence, such as the political questions doctrine[44] or its definitions of traditional guarantees like freedom of religion and expression, could be translated to the Canadian Constitution only with the greatest care.[45] Although it would not be until after intermission, in year three,[46] before it would explain the reason why American definitions of rights and freedoms were not suited to the Canadian scene, during the course of the first two years the Court left no doubt that blindly following the decisions of the American Supreme Court was not an approach it would endorse.

The Court displayed a similar ambivalence about relying on the intention of those who drafted and entrenched the Charter in deciding what entitlements it guaranteed. Like its use of American constitutional law, in some of its earliest judgments the language of intention features prominently in the decisions of the Court.[47] In the *Quebec Protestant School Board* and *Skapinker* cases, for example, the Court thought it was clear, from the language of the rights at stake, that the "framers" or "makers" of the Constitution intended to protect the opportunity of English migrants to Quebec to have their children educated in their mother tongue in the first case but not the right of non-Canadians to practise law in the second. By the end of the second year, however, the Court had expressed strong doubts as to when, except in unusual situations, such as those in *Skapinker* and the *Quebec School Board Reference*, the intention of the "framers" of the Charter could really be helpful in defining what protection and

---

42 *Skapinker v. Law Society Of Upper Canada, supra,* note 3; *Hunter v. Southam, supra,* note 5.

43 *Hunter v. Southam, supra,* note 5; *Singh v. M.E.I., supra,* note 7. See also *R. v. Oakes, supra,* note 1.

44 *Operation Dismantle v. R., supra,* note 11.

45 *Hunter v. Southam, supra,* note 5; *R. v. Big M Drug Mart, supra,* note 6; *Ref. re s. 94(2) Motor Vehicle Act (B.C.), supra,* note 8; *Operation Dismantle v. R., supra,* note 11, *per* Wilson.

46 *R. v. Edwards Books & Art Ltd.* (1986), 35 D.L.R. (4th) 1; *Ref. re Alberta Public Service Employee Relations Act* (1987), 38 D.L.R. (4th) 161; *R. v. Turpin,* [1989] 1 S.C.R. 1296; *Andrews v. Law Society of B.C.* (1989), 56 D.L.R. (4th) 1. See Chapter 4 at pp. 82-83, *infra.*

47 *Skapinker v. Law Society of Upper Canada, supra,* note 3, at 176, 178; *Quebec Protestant School Board v. A.G. P.Q., supra,* note 4; *Operation Dismantle v. R., supra,* note 11, *per* Wilson, at 517; *R. v. Therens, supra,* note 10, at 674, 682-683.

entitlements each of the rights or freedoms guaranteed.[48] In the Court's mind there were at least two sets of difficulties in trying to define the meaning of the rights and freedoms entrenched in the Charter by discovering what interests or activities the framers intended to protect. Both, it turns out, are very serious problems, well known to students of constitutional law.[49]

The first is a pragmatic problem. As a practical matter, trying to uncover the intention of the framers of the Charter usually ends up as a search for a fact or a state of mind which simply does not exist. Except on rare occasions, to speak of there being a single, collective intention about what a right or freedom was meant to protect is to say something that is transparently false. In the first place, as the Court pointed out, those responsible for the drafting of the Charter could not have foreseen every

---

48 See *Ref. re s. 94(2) Motor Vehicle Act*, *supra*, note 8. Note that even in *Skapinker* the Court was wary of the evidence of the historical record concerning the intent of those most directly concerned with the entrenchment of s. 6.

49 The literature reviewing the problems in relying on the intention of those who participated in the drafting and entrenchment of a constitutional document, such as the Charter, as a basis for defining its meaning, is voluminous. In Canada, see P. Hogg, "The Charter of Rights and American Theories of Constitutional Law", 25 Osgoode Hall L.J. 88; P.C. Weiler, "Rights and Judges in a Democracy: A New Canadian Version" (1984), 18 Jnl. L. Reform 51, 62; D. Greschner, "Two Approaches to Section One of the Charter", 49 Sask. L. Rev. 336; W. Mackay, "Interpreting the Charter of Rights: Law, Politics and Poetry", in G. Beaudoin (ed.), *Charter Cases* (Yvon Blais, 1987), p. 347. See also J.A. Corry, "The Use of Legislative History in the Interpretation of Statutes" (1954), 32 Can. Bar Rev. 624; B. Wilson, "The Making of a Constitution: Approaches to Judicial Interpretation" (1988), Public Law 370, 374.

For more general critiques, see R. Dworkin, *Law's Empire*, *supra*, note 32; P. Brest, "The Misconceived Quest For the Original Understanding" (1980), 60 B.U.L. Rev. 204.

For arguments in favour of limited reference to intention as a source of meaning for constitutional laws see P. Monahan, *Politics and the Constitution* (Toronto: Carswell, 1987), and B. Strayer, "Constitutional Interpretation Based on Consent: Whose Consent and Measured When" in *Legal Theory Meets Legal Practice*, Bayefsky, ed. (Edmonton: Academic Printing & Publishing, 1988). For a vigorous defence of using intention to interpret the American Bill of Rights, see R. Bork, *The Tempting of America: The Political Seduction of The Law* (New York: Free Press, 1990).

In this literature, one finds reference to another difficulty of using "the intention of the framers" that was not explicitly referred to by the Court. The problem is caused by the fact that frequently the actual framers of large parts of the constitution were "intermediate level civil servants". See E. McWhinney, "The Canadian Charter of Rights and Freedoms: The Lessons of Comparative Jurisprudence", 61 Can. Bar Rev. 55. To the extent that it was these people, rather than the members of Parliament and the provincial legislatures, who were responsible for the way the Charter was drafted, attributing any significance to their objectives and agenda would be fundamentally at odds with our heritage of democratic rule. See generally, R. Simeon and K. Banting, "Federalism, Democracy and the Constitution", in Simeon and Banting (eds.), *And No One Cheered* (Toronto: Methuen, 1983).

constitutional issue that might arise. Certainly on the particular questions submitted to the Court, such as whether the Charter applied to extradition hearings, or whether the Constitution guaranteed francophone litigants that they would be understood in their mother tongue in the federal courts and the courts of New Brunswick, more often than not the framers would have had no intention at all. They simply wouldn't have thought at that level of detail and particularity.

In addition, even if the question of whether a particular interest or activity was covered by the Charter had been specifically considered, because of the "multiplicity of actors who played major roles in the negotiating, drafting and adoption of the Charter", the likelihood is that there were numerous different and conflicting ideas among those who were directly responsible for making the decision. Jean Chretien, Roy Romanow, and Roy McMurtry, to mention only three with the highest profiles in the days leading up to April 17, 1982, had radically different hopes and expectations for what the rights and freedoms entrenched in the Charter might achieve. Conscious of the political reality that gave birth to the Charter, the Court recognized that to try and establish a collective intention of the "multiplicity of individuals" in the federal Parliament and all of the provincial legislatures, who played a role in the entrenchment of the Charter, was an exercise in futility, if not fraud.[50] Except for sections such as 23 (Minority Language Educational Rights) and 6 (Mobility Rights), whose specificity in language and purpose set them apart, the Court clearly recognized that it would usually be impossible to speak of there being a single, collective intent as to what interests and activities a right or freedom was understood to protect.[51]

In addition to the practical problems that would be encountered trying to define the rights and freedoms by the intention of those who were responsible for their entrenchment in the Charter, the Court thought that such an interpretative approach suffered from a serious conceptual or methodological problem as well. Even if the practical and logical difficulties of speaking

---

50 Cf. J.A. Corry, "The Use of Legislative History", *ibid.*, "all reference to legislative history can do is help mask the judges' law-making".

51 The perception that the specificity of the language in a section such as s. 23 distinguishes it from the more generally worded rights and freedoms, and allows for some reference to the original intent of those who entrenched the Charter, is shared by Paul Weiler. See his "Rights and Judges in a Democracy: A Canadian Version" (1984), 18 Jnl. L. Reform 51, 62. See also Patrick Monahan, *Politics and the Constitution, supra,* note 49, Scott Fairley, "Developments in Constitutional Law: The 1983-84 Term" (1985), 7 Sup. Ct. L. Rev. 63. Cf. *Cornell v. R.*, [1988] 1 S.C.R. 460, and *Ref. re an Act to Amend the Education Act* (1987), 40 D.L.R. (4th) 18, where in the years following *Oakes*, the Court was also able to speak of a collective intention as to (i) when the equality provisions of the Charter should go into effect, and (ii) whether the Charter had any application to other sections of the Constitution.

of a very large group having a common, collective intent could be overcome, the Court questioned how appropriate it would be for the constitutionality of laws to be determined in this way. On reflection, the idea of focusing on the framers' intent to decide what protection a particular right or freedom would provide struck the judges as being inconsistent with the liberal, purposive method they had endorsed in year one. Searching for a common intention of those who were responsible for bringing the Charter into existence was seen to be more like the interpretive method used to read the Bill of Rights. It directed the Court's attention backwards in time. The judges worried that defining the rights and freedoms that the Charter guaranteed according to the "intention of the framers" would have a tendency to freeze their meaning. If the core of judicial review were to become a search for the intention of those who brought the Charter into existence, it would make it very unlikely that the protection provided by the Charter could ever expand to meet the changing social conditions it would face in the future. Recalling a metaphor well known in constitutional law, the Court cautioned itself that, to ensure that the Charter would be able to grow like "a living tree", as its constitutional character demanded, reference to the intention of the framers, like use of American legal doctrine, must be made only with the greatest caution and care.

We have now spent some time considering the interpretative methodology developed by the Court over the course of its first two years. The considerable time and attention which the Court paid to distinguishing good sources of meaning — good dictionaries, so to speak — from bad, underscores how carefully and cautiously it adjusted to its new role. For most reviewers, I suspect, this record would support the observation that, by and large, the members of the Court had been able to resist any temptation to read the Charter in a manipulative way. Moreover, reviewers who thought about the Court's interpretative methodology most carefully would discover that the Court was just as rigorous in how it applied the purposive approach, as it was in identifying the sources of meaning that ensured the objectivity and integrity of the whole enterprise.

The degree of caution and care exercised by the Court in its purposive approach can be seen most clearly in its treatment of section 1, although it shows itself in how it addressed other sections, such as section 7, as well.[52] Essentially the Court's strategy was to put off interpreting section 1 as long as it possibly could. Everyone recognized how crucial this section,

---

52 See, e.g., how Bertha Wilson refused to attempt a comprehensive definition of the principles of fundamental justice in *Operation Dismantle v. R.*, *supra*, note 11, and Antonio Lamer in *Ref. re Motor Vehicle Act*, *supra*, note 8, left unanswered the question of whether an absolute liability offence would violate s. 7 if it provided for a fine rather than a jail sentence.

which both guarantees the rights entrenched in the Charter and provides for the circumstances in which they can be limited or abridged, is, and no one was in a hurry to attempt an exhaustive definition of its terms. Time and again the Court cautioned itself about speculating on its meaning until it was absolutely necessary to do so.[53] Even when, in cases such as *Singh*, *Big M Drug Mart* and the *B.C. Motor Vehicle Act* reference, it was obliged to consider whether a law that limited a right or freedom could be justified under section 1, it went no further in plumbing its meaning than was absolutely required.

As a result it was almost two years after its initial decision in *Skapinker* before the Court attempted an extended analysis of what, both numerically and substantively, is unquestionably one of if not the most important section of the Charter. By the end of the second year, it had had repeated opportunities to apply the purposive method and to become familiar with the sources that would be of most assistance in defining what interests and activities each of the entitlements in the Charter guaranteed. Only then, apparently, did it feel comfortable and confident enough with the purposive methodology that it was ready to use it to discover the meaning of section 1 itself.

R. v. Oakes[54] is the case in which the Court finally acted out that part of its role from which it had shied away for so long. For many, *Oakes* is the most significant decision the Court has handed down so far. The facts of the case are themselves relatively unimportant. David Oakes had been charged with unlawful possession of hashish oil for the purpose of trafficking. By the terms of the *Narcotics Control Act*, if a person was shown to be in possession of a narcotic, they were obliged to prove that they were not in the business of trafficking. In Oakes' mind, and ultimately the Court's as well, that provision of the Act violated his right to be presumed innocent of having engaged in such illicit activities.

What makes *Oakes* such a significant case is that it was the first time the Court attempted to describe, in a coherent and comprehensive way, the principles it would use to determine if a law, such as the *Narcotics Control Act*, which limited constitutional guarantees, could be justified under section 1. *Oakes* was the first case in which the Court fully described and applied the idea that the rules which are implicit in section 1, and which specify when a law can legitimately limit a right or freedom, must themselves be fixed in light of the larger purposes the Charter was meant to serve. In essence, the Court said, the limits that section 1 allows

---

53 *Skapinker v. Law Society of Upper Canada, supra*, note 3, at 181; *Hunter v. Southam, supra*, note 5, at 660; *Singh v. M.E.I., supra*, note 7; *Operation Dismantle v. R., supra*, note 11, *per* Wilson J.
54 *Supra*, note 1.

Governments to impose must be derived from the same values and principles of free and democratic societies that underlie the rights and freedoms they constrain. The values it had described as characteristic of free and democratic societies — the inherent dignity and autonomy of the person, equality, pluralism, etc. — would be the same sources and premises from which the limits would be derived as the rights defined.[55]

Applied to section 1, the purposive approach yielded four "principles of justification" to the Court. Two of these related to the ends, or the public interest, that were promoted by a challenged law, and the other two related to the means by which those ends would be realized. With respect to the ends, the Court said that in order for a law to limit or to compromise rights and freedoms embedded in the Charter, it must, at minimum, serve the public interest in a way which is of "sufficient importance" to warrant overriding a constitutionally protected right or freedom.[56] To meet this "object test" a law must, the Court said, relate to concerns which are "pressing and substantial in a free and democratic society".[57] Beyond this initial threshold criterion the Court imposed a second requirement that the public interest which a law was designed to serve must not impinge on consitutional guarantees in ways and to degrees which were out of all proportion to the benefits it would achieve. In the Court's words, "the more severe the deleterious effects [of a law], the more important the objective must be if [it] is to be reasonable and demonstrably justified in a free and democratic society." The purposes and effects of any law had to satisfy a basic measure of proportionality which, for convenience, we might call the "balancing principle".

In addition to requiring that laws serve social objectives which outweigh whatever the negative effects they have on peoples' constitutional guarantees, the Court held that lawmakers must use means which are also "reasonable and demonstrably justified".[58] Specifically, the Court said that to be demonstrably justified in a free and democratic society, all laws which impinged on constitutional entitlements had to be drafted to meet two additional measures of "proportionality". According to the first of these principles it must be shown that a law is designed in a way which is rationally connected to the objectives which the law is trying to achieve. Known as the "rational connection" principle, the requirement is that the means a Government chooses to accomplish its objectives must not be

---

55 For a very different, and in my view erroneous, reading of the Court's judgment in *Oakes*, in which it is claimed Brian Dickson abandoned the purposeful (or, in his terms, teleogical) approach, see W. Conklin, *Images of a Constitution* (Toronto: University of Toronto Press, 1989), p. 146.

56 *R. v. Big M Drug Mart, supra*, note 6, at 366.

57 *R. v. Oakes, supra*, note 1, at 227.

58 *Ibid.*, at 227.

arbitrary. It must not be based on irrational considerations. Secondly, the Court said a law that limits a right or freedom should do so as little as possible. It should not limit rights and freedoms more broadly than is required to serve the objects the law is designed to secure. This is the principle of "alternative means", and it insists that if there were other policies available to a Government which could accomplish all of the objectives of the challenged law in a way that interfered with constitutional guarantees less, the latter must explain why it did not make use of them. It would be entirely inconsistent with liberal democratic values of respect for the inherent dignity of the human person, equality, pluralism, etc., if lawmakers could adopt social policies that needlessly — gratuitously — infringed the freedom of those they affected.

The way in which the Court approached the meaning of section 1 should reinforce a reviewer's sense of just how cautiously the judges moved into their new roles. Only with its decision in *Oakes* did the Court pull together all of the essentials in the method and structure of review it would use in future cases. By waiting until it was completely familiar with the interpretative approach it had embraced, the Court had taken two years until it was able to outline all of the major principles of interpretation and justification it would use to decide whether a challenged law was compatible with the Charter or whether it was constitutionally flawed. By proceeding slowly, from first principles, the Court was able to secure agreement from everyone on the Court as to how its powers of review would be exercised and, ultimately, on what the entrenchment of the Charter would mean.

For reviewers of the Court's performance, the model in *Oakes* could be described in very simple and straightforward terms. In a sense, constitutional review could be likened to a dialogue or debate between citizens and the State about the reasonableness of each law or action taken by a Government or one of its officials. Like any debate, the process could be divided into two phases which, as the Court stressed, are completely separate and analytically quite distinct. In the first stage, the person or persons challenging the law would try to persuade the Court that one of their rights and freedoms guaranteed by the Charter (religion, association, equality, etc.) had been infringed in some way. To accomplish this, the challengers would have to establish two separate things. First, they would have to show that the interest or activity which they asked the Court to protect was one which fell within one of the rights and freedoms which the Charter guaranteed. It would be at this point in the proceedings that interpretative questions about what interests and activities were protected by the Charter would be answered. Secondly, and assuming they had successfully surmounted the interpretative hurdle, the challengers would also have to prove that the law they were challenging really did constrain people in the ways that they claimed. They would have to prove, as a matter of fact, that their constitutional freedom had been burdened by the law they had attacked.

In contrast with the rules governing ordinary debates, the second stage of the review process was not automatic. It would only be undertaken where the person or persons complaining about a law were able to satisfy the Court of the validity of both the legal (interpretative) and factual bases of their claims. If the complainants failed in either of these tasks, their case would be dismissed and there would be no occasion for the Court to proceed to the second stage. Where, however, it could be shown that the challenged law did limit an interest or activity which fell within one of the guaranteed rights or freedoms, the Court would embark on the second, "justificatory" stage of the review process. In this phase of the debate it would be the Government's turn to talk. Using the principles the Court had summarized in *Oakes*, those defending the constitutionality of a law would endeavour to show that it was the kind of rule or regulation that could be demonstrably justified in a free and democratic society, even though it limited the rights and freedoms of some of its members. Like the burden which challengers must bear, there would be two distinct issues which a Government would have to address if it were to successfully defend the constitutionality of a challenged law. As we have just seen, it would have to establish not only the importance of the public interest which a challenged law was expected to promote, but the integrity of its particular approach — its means — as well. A Government would have to explain very clearly the advantages of the social policies which it had chosen to enact into law and why there were no other alternative means available which would have impinged on peoples' constitutional freedom less.

With this description of how the Court came to envisage its role in *Oakes*, we might pause for a moment just to remind ourselves of what we have been doing so far. Assuming the position of reviewers or critics of the Supreme Court's performance, we have been noting how tentatively the Court moved into its new role and how all of its initiatives were marked with considerable caution and prudence. First we have seen how it concentrated its attention on developing rules of grammar and sources of meaning which would allow it to read the Charter objectively and in a way that made most sense of its terms. Then we noticed how it waited until it had acquired considerable experience with its interpretative method before it plumbed the meaning of the most complex and vaguely worded sections of the Charter. The result was the simple but comprehensive model of review described in its decision in *Oakes*.

The way in which the Court developed its principles of interpretation, and then applied them to identify the principles of justification which were embedded in section 1, are two important reasons why all of the members of the Court were able to express their views as harmoniously as they did. In addition to these two strategies, consensus was also promoted by the way in which the Court actually exercised its powers of review when it ruled that a law was unconstitutional. Paralleling its general approach of avoiding issues until it was absolutely necessary to decide them, it is apparent that when the Court did strike down a law as being unconstitutional, the judges made a conscious effort to go no further than was absolutely required. All of the cases which, as we noted, initially might strike many reviewers as being so dramatic and bold were, in reality, decided upon the narrowest possible grounds.

In two of the decisions in which it ruled that a law was unconstitutional the Court really said nothing more than a legislature can not pass a law just for the purpose of limiting peoples' constitutional rights. In *Big M Drug Mart*, for example, the Court ruled that the Sunday closing section of the *Lord's Day Act* was unconstitutional because the only purposes the federal Government could validly claim to be persuing all were related to assisting the dominant religious groups to impose their religious and moral values on the rest of the community.[59] Similarly, in the *Quebec Protestant School Board* case, although Bill 101 had been passed before the Charter came into effect, the Court made it clear that its reasoning would have been the same even if the Charter had been entrenched first. Regardless of the order in which the Charter and Quebec's language law came into existence, the latter was unconstitutional because it was explicitly aimed at denying the constitutional entitlements of certain English speaking people to have their children educated in their mother tongue in Quebec. A law cannot have as its purpose the limitation of a constitutional right because, as the Court pointed out, what the Government would be endeavouring to accomplish would be an amendment of the Charter by a simple act of the legislature rather than by the much more complex amending procedure set out in the Constitution itself.[60]

In other cases in which the Court ruled that some part of a law was unconstitutional, it was not uncommon for it to make comments in the course of its judgment, setting limits on the reach of its decision and

---

59 The reason for this was the way in which ss. 91 and 92 of the *British North America Act* divided powers between the federal and provincial levels of Government. According to earlier decisions of the Court, it was well established that the federal Government could only justify its enactment of the *Lord's Day Act* as an exercise of its criminal law power to regulate and control the moral and religious life of the country. It could not try to justify the prohibition on Sunday shopping as an attempt to ensure as many workers as possible enjoyed a common day of recreational and community activity. On the generally accepted understanding of ss. 91 and 92, that was an objective only the provincial Governments had the authority to pursue.

60 *P.Q. Protestant School Board v. A.G. P.Q.*, *supra*, note 4, at 337.

indicating how the law might have been saved. For example, in the case in which the Court struck down a section of *B.C.'s Motor Vehicle Act* which provided for the automatic imprisonment of persons convicted while their licences were under suspension, the judges were at pains to make clear that their decision was not aimed at all absolute liability offences. The Court said it was singling out only those offences which, like the one under review, might result in automatic imprisonment. In his judgment, Antonio Lamer sent a very strong signal that the Court would likely regard quite differently absolute liability offences which resulted in fines rather than imprisonment, or strict liability offences which would allow defendants the possibility of pleading defences like due diligence.[61]

In *Oakes* itself, the Court limited the effect of its ruling in exactly the same way. There the Court made it clear that the "reverse onus" provisions of the *Narcotics Control Act*, which required an accused person found in possession of any quantity of drugs to prove he or she was not engaged in trafficking, could be saved if they were restricted to cases in which an accused was found in possession of significant amounts of illicit drugs.[62] Similarly, in both *Hunter v. Southam* and *Singh v. M.E.I.*,[63] the Court was quite explicit that, with the appropriate procedural safeguards attached, the search and seizure powers in the *Combines Investigation Act*, and the refugee determination process in the *Immigration Act* would be validated as well.

Justifying decisions that struck down different aspects of Government policy in this way obviously facilitated harmonious relations among members of the Court. Deciding cases on the narrowest possible grounds allowed the judges to avoid having to confront difficult and unknown legal issues before they were fully prepared. As well, adopting this style of reasoning was an effective way in which the Court could show maximum respect for our democratic traditions and the sovereignty of the popular will.

The tension between judicial review and democratic rule is one of the most divisive aspects of an entrenched bill of rights. It is without question the major reason why so many on the left politically are sceptical about judicial review.[64] As they are at such pains to stress, entrenching

---

61   *Reference re s. 94(2) Motor Vehicle Act, supra*, note 8, at 559.

62   *R. v. Oakes, supra*, note 1, at 229.

63   *Supra*, notes 5 and 7.

64   See, e.g., Michael Mandel, *The Charter of Rights and the Legalization of Politics in Canada, supra*, note 21; Andrew Petter, "The Politics of the Charter" (1986), 8 Sup. Ct. L.R. 473; Allan Hutchinson, "Toward a Democratic Theory of Law" (1985), Cambridge Lectures 39; T. Ison, "The Sovereignty of The Judiciary" (1986), 10 Adelaide L. Rev. 1. For a more detached treatment of the issue see John Whyte, "Legality and Legitimacy: The Problem of Judicial Review of Legislation", 12 Queen's L.J. 1. For one response to these concerns see Paul Weiler, "Of Judges and Rights, Or Should Canada Have a Constitutional Bill of Rights" (1980), 60 Dalhousie Review 205.

the Charter of Rights and Freedoms in our Constitution unavoidably carried with it the consequence that an unelected group of nine individuals will sit in judgment on the social policies that our democratically elected legislatures have chosen to enact into law. The inescapable corollary of protecting human rights by putting them in a Constitution is that the power of the judiciary *vis-à-vis* the other two branches of government is greatly enhanced. There is simply no denying the fact that the Charter imposes a limit or constraint on what previously was an absolute sovereignty of Parliament and provincial legislatures within their respective spheres of authority.[65]

From the beginning the Court showed an acute awareness of this tension and did everything it could to minimize its effect. Early and often the Court stressed that courts must allow the legislature and executive that degree of discretion which is necessary to enable them to perform their job properly. Repeatedly the Court emphasized that its role in evaluating the constitutionality of a law was different from reviewing the substance of a law on its merits. Judicial review, the Court said, did not involve the Court just second guessing the other two branches of government.[66] Restricting its reasons to the narrowest possible grounds was another very practical way the Court could show respect for our democratic traditions and permit the legislative and executive branches the discretion they needed to act. In each of these ways the Court was able to minimize, if not mute, the potential conflict between the constitutional protection of human rights and the sovereignty of the popular will and in doing so enhanced considerably the degree of consensus among the judges.

We have now gone on at some length examining how the Court came to understand what the words in the Charter really meant and what its

---

65 At least not for some members of the Court. Both Dickson and Wilson have noticed the check which the Constitution imposes on the absolute sovereignty of Parliament. See Brian Dickson, "The Democratic Character of the Charter of Rights in *Law, Politics and the Judicial Process in Canada*, Morton (ed.) (Calgary: University of Calgary Press, 1984); and "The Public Responsibility of Lawyers" (1983), 13 Manitoba L.J. 175, 184. And see Bertha Wilson, "The Making of a Constitution", *supra*, note 49. See also Roy Romanow, "And Justice for Whom" (1986), 16 Man. L.J. 102.

   Of course, with respect to the rights guaranteed in s. 2 and ss. 7-15, the Charter provides (in s. 33) a mechanism by which a legislature can override a decision of the Court and reassert the sovereignty of its will. On the whole, the Court has interpreted s. 33 in a way which has been facilitative of its use. See *Ford v. Quebec* (1988), 54 D.L.R. (4th) 577; and *Irwin Toy v. Quebec* (1989), 58 D.L.R. (4th) 577. See also L. Weinrib, "Learning to Live with the Override" (1990), 35 McGill L.J. 542.

66 See, e.g., *Skapinker v. Law Society of Upper Canada*, *supra*, note 3; Wilson in *Operation Dismantle v. R.*, *supra*, note 11, at 504; Lamer in *Reference re s. 94(2) Motor Vehicle Act (B.C.)*, *supra*, note 8, at 546; *Valente v. R.*, *supra*, note 13.

own role in the system of government used by free and democratic societies would become. If a reviewer was waiting in the intermission for the second half of the performance to start and she began to reflect on what she had seen so far, the Court's record should, I think, generate some enthusiasm even if she was instinctively sceptical of judicial review. Rather than a dramatic and aggressive opening act, in reality the judges' performance turns out to have been a very reasoned and careful analysis of how the Charter should be read and how their own powers in reviewing the constitutionality of a challenged law should be exercised. Although, as others have observed, there was not much cheering in the community at large when the Charter was initially included in the Constitution,[67] two years later there were good reasons to hope that the Charter could simultaneously enhance human freedom and the democratic character of the Canadian polity. The fact that the judges had been able to derive the broad outlines of a model of judicial review harmoniously, from first principles, was a performance which called for a positive review and demanded something more than just polite applause.

As strong as the first half of the Court's performance was, it would be misleading to suggest that it was perfect in every respect. Even at this stage, before one could be aware of the dramatically different performance that the Court would offer over the next three years, it would be apparent to a sensitive reviewer that the Court had experienced some difficulties mastering its new role. The performance was uneven in parts, and miscues could easily be spotted. Some of these points for which the Court's performance might be criticized were not particularly serious and were more understandable than others. They were of a kind one would anticipate any court making as it worked out and experimented with the method and the structure of the analysis it would use to evaluate the constitutionality of the laws it would be asked to review. These were a normal part of the learning process which could be expected to be remedied as the Court became more familiar and comfortable with its new role.

A good example of a difficulty of this kind was the Court's treatment of section 1. Given its conscious effort to defer a systematic analysis of this section until almost the end of year two, it is not surprising that, prior to its decision in *Oakes*, the Court did encounter some initial difficulties in working with this section and relating it to the other sections in which substantive rights and freedoms are guaranteed. In the *Quebec Protestant School Board* and *Big M Drug Mart* cases, for example, the Court suggested that laws which were passed for certain objectives would be ruled unconstitutional "without even considering whether such legislation could

---

67 K. Banting and R. Simeon, *And No One Cheered* (Toronto: Methuen, 1983).

be legitimised by section 1".[68] Implicitly the Court was saying that the objectives of a law would be evaluated as part of the interpretation of the rights and freedoms in the Charter rather than as one of the reference points of evaluation under section 1. After the Court's decision in *Oakes*, such an assertion would be impossible to sustain. As it would explicitly recognize near the end of the whole performance, on the structure outlined in *Oakes*, the question of legislative objectives falls squarely within the first (object test) and fourth (balancing) principles of justification in section 1.[69]

Similarly, in *Oakes* itself, some reviewers might want to criticize the Court for having invoked the wrong proportionality principle in striking down the reverse onus sections of the *Narcotics Control Act*. They might deny that there was no rational connection between the objectives of the legislation and the requirement that those in possession of illegal drugs must prove they were not engaged in trafficking. They would say deterring transport and trade in illicit drugs will be furthered by a law of this kind. The fact that the law may seem heavy handed and even draconian does not make it irrational.[70]

Although this is not a criticism of the Court's ultimate disposition of the case, it would undoubtedly have been preferable if the Court had based its decision squarely on the principle of alternate means. To say a law is guilty of "overkill" is to admit that the means that have been chosen are broader and more restrictive than necessary. It does seem more accurate to say that the defect of the law struck down in *Oakes* was that all of the Government's objectives of deterring trafficking in drugs could have been met just as effectively if, as the Court suggested, an exemption were made for those, like David Oakes, who were found with such small quantities that it was clear they were not engaged in the evil (trafficking) which the law was designed to address.[71] Creating an exception for people like Oakes would obviously show greater respect for their constitutional guarantees and it would do so without affecting the Government's

---

68   See *P.Q. Protestant School Board v. A.G. P.Q.*, *supra*, note 4, at 338. But see Wilson in *R. v. Big M Drug Mart*, *supra*, note 6, at 373.

69   *Ford v. Quebec* (1989), 54 D.L.R. (4th) 577; see also Bertha Wilson, in *R. v. Morgentaler* (1988), 44 D.L.R. (4th) 385. But see *Irwin Toy*, *supra*, note 65; Beetz in *A.G. Manitoba v. Metropolitan Stores* (1987), 38 D.L.R. (4th) 321 and La Forest in *R. v. Lyons* (1987), 44 D.L.R. (4th) 193. For a critique of the Court's reasoning in the *Quebec Protestant School Board* case, see P. Hogg. *Constitutional Law of Canada*, 2nd ed. (Toronto: Carswell, 1985), pp. 682-683. Cf. L. Weinrib, "The Supreme Court of Canada and Section One of the Charter" (1988), 10 S. Ct. L. Rev. 469, 479-483; T. Christian, "The Limited Operation of the Limits Clause" (1987), 35 Alberta L. Rev. 264.

70   P. Monahan, *Politics and the Constitution* (Toronto: Carswell, 1987), pp. 62ff.

71   To the same effect see R. Elliott, "The Supreme Court of Canada and Section One: The Erosion of the Common Front", 12 Queen's L.J. 277.

objectives of deterring trafficking in any way.

Unquestionably the most difficult problem that the Court experienced with section 1 was deciding how it would be integrated with the other substantive sections of the Charter where rights and freedoms are guaranteed. We have just noted the Court's slip up in the *Quebec Protestant School Board* case where it suggested that the objectives of a law would be evaluated in the definition of the right and freedom rather than as one of the principles of justification to be applied under section 1. Just as troublesome for the judges was the question of what the balancing of social benefits and constitutional costs was all about and how it should be done. Many would be instinctively sceptical of the Court's claim that in performing this role it was not "second guessing" the legislature on the merits of the law being reviewed.[72] Protestations of this kind would suggest to many either that the judges failed to understand or that they refused to admit what constitutional review really was all about.

Some reviewers might also be disturbed by the way the Court, on occasion, applied the balancing principle. In particular cases, reviewers might quarrel with the Court's judgment about the balance struck by a particular law.[73] More generally, they might perceive indecision and inconsistencies in the Court's mind as to where, in the process of review, the balancing principle should be invoked. In *Oakes* the Court was quite explicit that section 1 and the other substantive sections that described the rights and freedoms guaranteed by the Charter were "analytically distinct" and should be kept separate and apart. The Court was also clear that the balancing function was what the last proportionality principle was all about. Indeed, on at least two occasions prior to *Oakes*, the Court had anticipated this structure and had explicitly evaluated whether the public interest promoted by a law was sufficiently pressing that it outweighed

---

72 See, e.g., Monahan and Petter, "Developments in Constitutional Law", 9 S. Ct. L. Rev. 69; R. Elliott, "The Supreme Court of Canada and Section One: The Erosion of the Common Front", 12 Queen's L.J. 277, 296; M. Gold, "The Rhetoric of Rights: The Supreme Court and the Charter", 25 Osgoode Hall L.J. 375, 388; M. Mandel, *The Charter of Rights and the Legalization of Politics in Canada* (Toronto: Wall & Thompson, 1989); W. Conklin, *Images of a Constitution* (Toronto: University of Toronto Press, 1989), Chapter 7.

73 See, e.g., Monahan and Petter, *ibid*, critique the way the Court balanced the interests involved in *B.C. Motor Vehicle Act Reference* and *Hunter v. Southam*. Of the cases following *Oakes*, the two that, in my view, are most open to criticism of this kind are *R. v. Milne* (1987), 46 D.L.R. (4th) 487 and *B.C.G.E.U. v. A.G. B.C.* (1988), 53 D.L.R. (4th) 1. For a similar assessment of the Court's decision in *Milne*, see E. Colvin and T. Quigley "Developments in Criminal Law and Procedure: The 1987-88 Term", 11 S. Ct. L. Rev 165, 227. For a critical review of the Court's decision in *B.C.G.E.U.*, see Patrick Macklem, "Developments in Employment Law: 1988-89 Term", forthcoming in 12 S. Ct. L. Rev.

the interests of those whose rights and freedoms it violated under section 1.[74]

However, the Court did not always respect this division, and in other cases it seemed to perform the balancing function in the first phase of the review process in the course of defining what interests or activities were protected by the right or freedom for which protection was sought.[75] In *Hunter v. Southam*, for example, when it was decided that Southam's right to be free from unreasonable search and seizure had been infringed, virtually all of the Court's analysis of the State's interest in detecting and preventing crime and the individual's interest in his privacy was undertaken in the first, interpretive phase of the review process. Similarly, ruling that laws which impinge on a person's constitutional rights or freedoms only incidentally or in very trivial and insignificant ways are not subject to review, as Bertha Wilson did in her judgments in *Operation Dismantle* and the *B.C. Motor Vehicle Reference*, also involves doing some of the balancing function outside of section 1. It would not be unreasonable for reviewers to assume that after its decision in *Oakes*, the Court would no longer engage in balancing the social objectives of a law against the constitutional entitlements which it contains when it is engaged in the definitional or interpretive phase of the review process. The expectation would be that after *Oakes*, all of the balancing would be done at the end of the second stage of the review process under section 1.[76]

In the final analysis it is unlikely that any of these difficulties which the Court experienced as it worked out the principles and structure of the model it summarized in *Oakes* would cause many reviewers serious concern. All of them are precisely the kind of miscues most performers encounter working their way into a new role. All seem to be a natural part of the learning process and could be expected to be resolved over time. Because the Court had not finally settled the structure and principles of the second, justificatory stage of the review process until right at the end of year two, it is not surprising that the Court would experience some difficulties in defining its content and integrating it with other sections

---

74 *Reference re s. 94(2) Motor Vehicle Act (B.C.)*, *supra*, note 8; *Singh v. M.E.I.*, *supra*, note 7; see also *Jack and Charlie v. R.* (1985), 21 D.L.R. (4th) 641, 646.

75 *Hunter v. Southam*, *supra*, note 5; also *Krug v. R.* (1985), 21 D.L.R. (4th) 161, *Valente v. R.* (1985), 24 D.L.R. (4th) 161.

76 This would be especially true after its decision in *Ref. re s. 94(2) B.C. Motor Vehicle Act*, *supra*, note 8, at 561.

A parallel issue arose when the Court considered challenges by individuals to administrative action rather than to a legislative enactment. Here, however, the balancing of the public interest would be carried out in the remedial phase in s. 24. See, e.g., *R. v. Therens*, *supra*, note 10; *Clarkson v. R.* (1986), 26 D.L.R. (4th) 493. For a discussion of how balancing figures in the Court's consideration of what constitutes an appropriate remedy see Paul Gewirtz, "Remedies and Resistance", 92 Yale L.J. 585.

of the Charter. With the framework settled in *Oakes*, and with the Court being able to familiarize itself with repeated applications in the future, it could be reasonably expected that these sorts of problems would gradually disappear.

There were other parts of the Court's performance, however, that reviewers might have found more disturbing than the difficulties that the Court experienced in working out *how* its two-stage model of review would be applied. These were judgments in which various members of the Court seemed to suggest that there were occasions in which the Charter might have no application at all. Over the course of the first two years, one can identify two distinct situations which different members of the Court indicated were beyond the reach of, and unaffected by, the model they had constructed in *Oakes*. First the Court said that there were certain kinds of laws, such as foreign laws, which lay beyond its powers of review. If a law of a foreign nation threatened the liberty or security of a person, there was nothing, the Court said, it could do. The Court relied on this principle to dismiss a challenge brought by a businessman named Robert Spencer who had claimed that his right to liberty and the security of his person were being threatened by his being compelled to give evidence in a legal proceeding in Canada.[77] Spencer had been a manager in a bank in the Bahamas and, according to a Bahamian law, he could be jailed if he testified about anything relating to his job in the Bank even though his evidence was demanded by order of a court. In rejecting his claim the Court ruled that it was the Bahamian and not the Canadian law that threatened him with the loss of his liberty and Bahamian law was not within the authority of Canadian courts to review.

In addition to ruling that there were certain kinds of laws that were not subject to constitutional review, various members of the Court also suggested that they would not exercise their powers with respect to laws that either were not coercive in any way or, if they were, the restrictions they imposed were oblique and indirect. In *Spencer*, for example, the Court said not only that the Charter had no application to foreign law, but also that the Canadian law, under which Spencer was being compelled to testify (under pain of being found in contempt of court), "in no way deprive(d) him of his liberty or the security of his person". The threat to Spencer's constitutional rights, the Court ruled, came *solely* from the operation of Bahamian law. In *Operation Dismantle*, Bertha Wilson wrote a very similar judgment. In her mind, the claim of those protesting the testing of the cruise missile could not succeed because the executive order being challenged was not specifically aimed at any one member of the political community. Even though, unlike the other members of the Court, she was

---

77 *R. v. Spencer* (1985), 21 D.L.R. (4th) 756.

prepared to assume that the Cabinet's decision might increase the threat of nuclear war, and so the risk of death or injury that each of the claimants had to face, she thought the coercive character of the law was too attenuated and indirect to warrant review by the Court.

At this point it can be anticipated that some people may find it difficult to understand why these cases should be disturbing to a reviewer. After all, it seems rather evident that the Charter can have no effect on a law that is not Canadian and has no relevance to Canadian law that does not restrict anyone's freedom in any way. On reflection, however, the idea that there are limits which constrain the reach of the Charter seems increasingly problematic. Certainly, the idea that the Charter does not apply to all Canadian law requires an explanation. The Charter, after all, is part of the Constitution, and as such must be recognized as being the supreme law of the land. Constitutions, including the Charter, are the law against which the validity of all other laws are measured. That is what section 52 explicitly provides. And yet the idea that there exists law in Canada which lies beyond the Charter's reach seems to challenge the principle of constitutional supremacy directly. Once you say that there are laws or rules in Canada which fall beyond the reach of the Charter, the supremacy of the Constitution is unavoidably compromised. It is no longer supreme. By definition, there is a body of law to which it does not apply and which can be formulated and drafted in ways which ignore all of the principles and values which the Charter contains. The idea that some Canadian law operates alongside or even above the Charter seems to embrace principles and ways of reasoning that implicitly, if not explicitly, contradict the large and liberal approach the Court had said constitutional documents like the Charter required.

Even the idea that the Court may take into account and evaluate foreign law in the context of a Charter challenge is not as strange as it might initially seem. In fact, at least three of the judges on the Court had already recognized a claim which was based substantially on foreign law. In *Singh*, it will be recalled, Bertha Wilson, Antonio Lamer and Brian Dickson upheld a challenge to an earlier version of Canada's refugee law even though the threat to the challengers' lives, liberty and security of their persons came, in the final analysis, from foreign law. Even though Singh could not prove with certainty that he would be abused in a way which compromised his rights, and even though the Canadian law was involved only indirectly and did not impose a direct threat to his life, liberty or security of his person, these three members of the Court clearly understood that it was precisely the possibility that the foreign law involved in his case might fall so far short of the standards and principles contained in the Charter, which made his case so strong.

But we should not dwell any longer on the imperfections of the Court's opening act. Although there were moments in the Court's performance which would be cause for concern to reviewers, they represent a very small percentage of the Court's work over the first two years. On most, if not all, relevant criteria the Court's opening act was an impressive performance indeed. Assuming the position of a reviewer who had just witnessed the first half of the Court's performance and who was just about to return to her seat after intermission, I think most people would have a stronger sense of optimism and excitement about the process of judicial review than before the curtain was first raised on Charterland.

Certainly those who instinctively believed in the entrenchment of human rights into the constitutional framework of government would have every reason to be excited. It is true that, except for refugees and those caught in the criminal justice system, the Charter had not in fact made a substantial impact on the lives of those who traditionally have been ill-treated by the political process. Nevertheless, with its decision in *Oakes*, the Court had put in place a model of constitutional review which it had derived objectively from the most basic principles and values which underlie the Charter[78] and which had the potential of enhancing both the quality of social justice and political participation in the country.

In effect, with its decision in *Oakes*, the Court had defined for itself a new role, similar to that of a social critic,[79] or moral conscience,[80] in our system of government. All law, whether *Quebec's Language Code, B.C.'s Motor Vehicle Act*, or the federal Government's refugee determination procedure or the *Lord's Day Act*, would be screened against a series of principles or standards of justice. Governments intent on enacting laws which impinged on the freedom of any individual or group would be required to show that their policies were rational, reasonable, and intruded as little as possible on the freedom of those constrained if they were to be certified as being constitutionally valid. Laws which limited the rights or freedoms guaranteed in the Charter would have to be shown to be derived from and to be consistent with the same values and principles which underlie the rights and freedoms themselves. The Court had developed a theory of constitutional review in which its essential task was to assess how reasonably individuals "act" as legislators when they gain control of the powers of the State. In a sense the Court had crafted a role for itself which was the same as, or very similar to, the one it performs when it measures the reasonableness of the conduct of individuals against the

---

78 See *supra*, pp. 23-25.
79 See Michael Walzer, *Interpretation and Social Criticism* (Cambridge: Harvard University Press, 1987).
80 Certainly where Government is given the power under s. 33 of the Charter to override a judgment of the Court, the latter's role is purely advisory.

principles of tort law (such as negligence or defamation) or the job arbitrators do when they evaluate how management exercises its discretion under a collective agreement against principles of fairness and reasonableness.[81]

On this model or theory of judicial review, constitutional review can fairly be described as offering groups in society, who traditionally have not had much influence in politics, a way of participating directly in the processes by which social policy is transformed into law. Even though the Court had not heard from many people in its first two years who could be considered disadvantaged, the claimants in *Singh* had shown that the entrenchment of the Charter created a process in which interest group politics could be practised more effectively than ever before. Groups that were practically, if not, as with the refugees, legally disenfranchised, and which Governments have been traditionally inclined to ignore, now had a place where their voices would be heard and the means to enrich the quality of discussion and debate in the community as a whole. Now, when a group felt that social policies were being enacted which did not weight their interests fairly or reasonably, they could insist that the Government engage in dialogue with them and establish by "clear and convincing evidence" that its policies did in fact satisfy the principles of justification which lay at the core of constitutional review. By providing a forum in which laws could be tested against principles of social justice, the Charter made it possible for our system of government to become both more progressive and more democratic at one and the same time.

It seems certain then, that reviewers who were inclined to believe in the Supremes from the beginning would be returning to their seats with a sense of excitement and anticipation. They would know that linguistic and religious minorities, numerous groups of workers, women, as well as many individuals caught up in the criminal justice system, had already filed challenges against a host of laws which they felt unfairly and unreasonably prejudiced their interests and which would soon be heard by the Supremes. There would be an expectation that in the second half of the Court's performance we would witness the realization of the potential of the model which the Court had laid out at the end of the first Act.

---

81 The similarities between the Court's role in Charter and non-Charter cases is touched on in B. Hoffmaster, "Judicial Review of the Charter of Rights and Freedoms: What Are the Limits of Judging", in A. Bayefsky (ed.), *Legal Theory Meets Legal Practice*, (Edmonton: Academic Press & Publishing, 1988).

In the principles and doctrines they use to measure the reasonableness of disciplinary sanctions (e.g., on the principle of progressive discipline) and plant rules (principle of fairness) arbitrators will see a direct parallel to the last two proportionality principles in *Oakes*. See Brown and Beatty, *Canadian Labour Arbitration*, 3rd ed. (Toronto: Canada Law Book, 1989), Topics 4:1500, 2310, 2320; Topic 7: 4416.

Even reviewers whose instincts would incline them to be sceptical about entrenching individual rights and freedoms into the constitutional framework should, I believe, be cautiously sanguine about the possibilities of judicial review, at least more optimistic than when the performance began. Although one could anticipate that they would be critical of the deficiencies in the Court's performance, nevertheless one would also expect that they would be encouraged by how cautiously and prudently the Court had crafted its new role. Even with the concern about the uncertainties and apparent confusions in the Court's understanding of its own role,[82] the judges had shown they were highly sensitive to the tension between judicial review and our democratic traditions which, it will be recalled, is what worries many sceptics the most. On balance, sceptics should recognize and be encouraged by the Court's conscious effort to interfere with, and constrain, the sovereignty of Parliament and the legislative will as little as it possibly could.

---

82 *Supra*, note 72.

3

The Second Set: 1986-1989

Even if my sense about how reviewers are likely to react to the "Supremes in Charterland" could be criticized as being more sanguine than the Court's performance over the first two years justifies, I doubt anyone really anticipated the performance that unfolded over the course of the next three years. Almost everything was turned on its head. Stylistically as well as substantively the Court's performance was completely transformed. On both dimensions, the Court shifted its approach one hundred and eighty degrees, and a radically new method of judging was introduced. Stylistically, a new tempo and mode of expression were employed. The pace at which the Court issued its judgments increased exponentially. Each succeeding year the Court decided almost as many cases as it had in all of the previous years combined.[1] In place of the single voice in which the Court initially spoke, all of a sudden three and sometimes four opinions might be heard in a single case.[2] Instead of

---

1 See the numbers reported in Chapter 1, *supra*, note 4. For a similar observation, see Andrew Petter and Patrick Monahan, "Developments in Constitutional Law: The 1986-87 Term" (1988), 10 S. Ct. L. Rev. 61, 62.

2 Cases in which three or four separate opinions were written include: *Société des Acadiens du Nouveau-Brunswick v. Assn. of Parents for Fairness in Education* (1986), 27 D.L.R. (4th) 406 (hereinafter "Les Acadiens"); *R. v. Mills* (1986), 29 D.L.R. (4th) 161; *R. v. Jones* (1986), 31 D.L.R. (4th) 569; *Edwards Books and Art Ltd. v. R.* (1986), 35 D.L.R. (4th). 1; *Ref. re Alberta Public Service Employee Relations Act* (1987), 38 D.L.R. (4th) 161; *Public Service Alliance v. Canada* (1987), 38 D.L.R. (4th) 249; *Saskatchewan v. RWDSU* (1987), 38 D.L.R. (4th) 277 (hereinafter, *Labour trilogy*); *R. v. Rahey* (1987), 39 D.L.R. (4th) 481; *R. v. Schmidt* (1987), 39 D.L.R. (4th) 19; *Argentina v. Mellino* (1987), 40 D.L.R. (4th) 74; *U.S.A. v. Allard and Charette* (1987), 40 D.L.R. (4th) 102 (hereinafter *Extradition trilogy*); *R. v. Smith* (1987), 40 D.L.R. (4th) 435; *Ref. re an Act to Amend the Education Act* (1987), 40 D.L.R. (4th) 18; *R. v. Lyons* (1987), 44 D.L.R. (4th) 193; *R. v. Vaillancourt* (1987), 47 D.L.R. (4th) 400; *R. v. Morgentaler* (1988), 44 D.L.R. (4th)

applying the model they outlined in *Oakes* harmoniously, in the style they had developed over the first two years, and to which they frequently returned in year five,[3] over the course of the next three years, more often than not, the judges differed sharply amongst themselves as to *how* and even *if* the model should be applied to the laws they had been asked to review.

The shift in the Court's method was spearheaded by five judges: Jean Beetz, William McIntyre, Gerard La Forest, Gerald Le Dain and Willard Estey. These five adopted an extremely cautious and very conservative attitude towards the Charter and their own powers of review. Based on the ideas favoured by these five — and in particular by William McIntyre and Jean Beetz — the Court began to reason in ways which imposed very substantial constraints on the circumstances in which, and the ways in which, the object test and the proportionality principles would be used to measure the constitutionality of State action. Except for a few individuals caught up in the criminal justice system,[4] the Anglophones in Quebec,[5] several groups of lawyers and related professionals,[6] and the women who were the ultimate winners in Henry Morgentaler's successful challenge to

---

385; *R. v. Corbett*, [1988] 1 S.C.R. 670; *R. v. Holmes* (1988), 50 D.L.R. (4th) 680; *R. v. Dyment* (1988), 55 D.L.R. (4th) 503; *R. v. Simmons* (1988), 55 D.L.R. (4th) 673; *R. v. Schwartz* (1988), 55 D.L.R. (4th) 1; *Andrews v. Law Society of B.C.* (1989), 56 D.L.R. (4th) 1; *R. v. Strachan* (1989), 56 D.L.R. (4th) 673; *Slaight Communications v. Davidson* (1989), 59 D.L.R. (4th) 416.

3   The cases decided in 1988-89 in which the Court was unanimous include: *R. v. Whyte* (1988), 51 D.L.R. (4th) 481; *R. v. Canadian Newspapers* (1988), 52 D.L.R. (4th) 690; *R. v. Thomsen*, [1988] 1 S.C.R. 640; *R. v. Hufsky*, [1988] 1 S.C.R. 621; *R. v. Thibault*, [1988] 1 S.C.R. 1033; *R. v. Cornell*, [1988] 1 S.C.R. 461; *R. v. Upston*, [1988] 1 S.C.R. 1083; *Ford v. Quebec* (1988), 54 D.L.R. (4th) 577; *Devine v. Quebec* (1988), 55 D.L.R. (4th) 641; *Ref. re Workers' Compensation Act* (1989), 56 D.L.R. (4th) 765; *R. v. Amway Corp.* (1989), 56 D.L.R. (4th) 309; *Borowski v. Canada* (1989), 57 D.L.R. (4th) 231; *Gauthier v. Québec*, [1989] 1 S.C.R. 859; *R. v. Turpin*, [1989] 1 S.C.R. 1296; *R. v. Beare (Higgins)* (1989), 55 D.L.R. (4th) 481; *R. v. Genest* [1989], 1 S.C.R. 59; *R. v. Duguay* (1989), 56 D.L.R. (4th) 46; and *Air Canada v. British Columbia* (1989), 59 D.L.R. (4th) 161.

4   Most successful challenges were aimed at specific administrative abuses individuals had endured rather than at the constitutionality of some part of the Criminal Code. Even in the latter cases the offences in issue make the challengers a relatively narrow and select group. See, e.g., *R. v. Smith*, *R. v. Vaillancourt* and *R. v. Dyment*, *supra*, note 2; *R. v. Duguay*, *supra*, note 3; *R. v. Genest*, *supra*, note 3. For a general review of the Court's disposition of Charter challenges to different parts of the Criminal Law during the 1987-88 term. See E. Colvin and T. Quigley, *Developments in Criminal Law and Procedure: the 1987-88 Term*, 11 S. Ct. L. Rev 165.

5   See *Ford v. Quebec*, *Devine v. Quebec*, *supra*, note 3.

6   See *Andrews v. Law Society of B.C.*, *supra*, note 2; *R. v. Thibault*, *supra*, note 3; *Black v. Law Society of Alberta* (1989), 58 D.L.R. (4th) 317.

Canada's abortion laws,[7] none of the other individuals and groups who had looked to the Charter to enhance the quality of their lives had their expectations fulfilled. Reviewers will discover that the workers, members of oppressed linguistic and religious minorities, persons facing extradition and preventive detention, etc. who had brought their pleas to the Court were, almost without exception, told that the injustices they perceived in the various laws that regulated their lives were beyond the authority and competence of the judges to review. It would be sixteen months after its decision in *Oakes* before the Court would apply the model again to strike down another law; and then it would be to rule invalid another section of the *Narcotics Control Act*.[8] Between these two decisions only four Canadians, all caught up in various ways with the criminal justice system,[9] would successfully claim the benefit and protection of the principles of justice that the Court had identified in *Oakes*. Even though it heard ten times more cases over the course of the three years following its decision in *Oakes*, the Court invalidated only slightly more laws than it had in the two years preceding it.[10] Moreover, in the majority of cases in which the Court could be persuaded to exercise its powers of review it was either to correct excesses by individual government agents (e.g., the police)[11] or to remedy some formal or procedural rather than a substantive deficiency in a law.[12] It is also striking that in the few cases when a challenge was successful in invalidating some substantive rule or section of an Act, more often than not it was brought by an individual or group already among the economic and political elite.[13]

For most reviewers, the ways in which the Court's performance was

---

7 See *R. v. Morgentaler, supra*, note 2.

8 *R. v. Smith, supra*, note 2. For a clear exposition of both the constitutional law and criminal law dimensions of this case, see K. Roach, "Smith and the Supreme Court: Implications for Sentencing Policy and Reform" (1989), 11 S. Ct. L. Rev. 433.

9 *Clarkson v. R.* (1986), 26 D.L.R. (4th) 493; *R. v. Mannion* (1986), 31 D.L.R. (4th) 712; *Collins v. R.* (1987), 38 D.L.R. (4th) 508; *Rahey v. R.* (1987), 39 D.L.R. (4th) 481.

10 Peter Russell reports a similar falling off in the success rate of Charter challenges in his "Canada's Charter of Rights and Freedoms: A Political Report" (1988), Public Law 388-391. See also A. Petter and P. Monahan, "Developments in Constitutional Law" *supra*, note 1.

11 See, e.g., *Pohoretsky v. R.* (1987), 39 D.L.R. (4th) 699; *R. v. Manninen* (1987), 41 D.L.R. (4th) 301; *R. v. Dyment, supra*, note 2; *R. v. Genest, supra*, note 3; *R. v. Duguay, supra*, note 3. For a statistical account of the extent to which these cases dominated Charter litigation in general, see F. Morton and J. Withey, *Charting the Charter 1982-85: A Statistical Analysis* (1987), 4 Can. Hum. Rts. Y.B. 65. See also A. Petter and P. Monahan, "Developments in Constitutional Law", *supra*, note 1.

12 See, e.g., *R. v. Vaillancourt* and *R. v. Morgentaler, supra*, note 2; *R. v. Thibault, supra*, note 3.

13 *Ford v. Quebec, supra*, note 3; *Andrews v. Law Society of B.C., supra*, note 2; *Black v. Law Society of Alberta, supra*, note 6; *R. v. Thibault, supra*, note 3. See also McIntyre's

transformed should be easy to identify. Especially in the two years immediately following its decision in *Oakes*, the Court showed a strong inclination to put restrictions on *when* and *how* thè principles it had articulated in that case would be applied. With respect to the circumstances in which it would exercise its powers of review, the Court took the position that the principles it had summarized in *Oakes* should only be applied to laws: (i) emanating from or embraced by either the federal Parliament, or its executive, or one of their provincial counterparts, which (ii) either constrained or threatened, in a sufficiently coercive way, (iii) those interests and activities which were covered by one of the rights and freedoms which the Charter guaranteed. Laws that did not meet all three of these conditions were said to be beyond the Court's power of review.[14] Other sorts of law, for example foreign law, or laws that did not affect a protected interest or activity, or common law rules regulating purely private relations, or that only marginally affected a constitutional right or freedom, were said either to be completely outside the reach of the Charter or subject only to a modified and much more superficial form of review.[15]

It is true that none of these limitations was entirely novel. Reviewers will know that, even if these limitations had played only a minor role, all of them had been raised and used by one or more members of the Court in the two years leading up to *Oakes*. In *Spencer*, the Bahamian bank case, it will be recalled, everyone on the Court was of one mind that the Charter did not provide any protection against threats to a person's constitutional entitlements that emanated from a foreign Government. Equally, at one time or another all of the judges had shown a willingness

---

dissent in *Andrews* and *Irwin Toy v. Quebec* (1988), 58 D.L.R. (4th) 577, and Beetz's dissent in *Irwin Toy* and *Slaight Communications v. Davidson, supra*, note 2.

For radical sceptics on the left, there is of course nothing coincidental in outcomes such as these. See Michael Mandel, *The Charter of Rights and the Legalization of Politics in Canada*, (Toronto: Wall & Thompson, 1989); Harry Glasbeek, *Workers of the World*, "Avoid the Charter of Rights", 21 Canadian Dimension (April 1987). In Mandel's view, not only does the record show that those who are already powerful and influential have been able to make use of the Charter to fortify their positions, but also that even when individual claimants who were from disadvantaged groups scored victories with the Charter, in most cases, these were purely formalistic and procedural claims which did little to rectify the most repressive aspects of our legal system and indeed which contributed to its legitimation.

14 On several occasions the Court also imposed a temporal restriction on how far the Charter could reach back and affect events that arose before it was entrenched. See *R. v. Stevens* (1988), 51 D.L.R. (4th) 394; *Re Irvine and RTPC* (1987), 41 D.L.R. (4th) 429. See also *Jack and Charlie v. R.* (1985), 21 D.L.R. (4th) 641; cf. *R. v. Gamble*, [1988] 2 S.C.R. 595; *Dubois v. R.* (1986), 23 D.L.R. (4th) 503 ; *R. v. Thibault, supra*, note 3.

15 The Court also held that it would not exercise its powers of review and provide an interpretation of the Charter in a case in which there was no law or Government action in force which could be evaluated. See *Borowski v. Canada* (1989), 57 D.L.R. (4th) 231.

to dismiss a challenge on the basis that the law or Government action under challenge did not actually coerce or threaten the complainants in any way. In *Operation Dismantle*, for example, the majority of the Court dismissed the anti-nuclear group's challenge on this basis, and in *Skapinker*, the Court spoke in one voice when it ruled that a free-standing right to work was not an interest or activity that was protected by the mobility rights that were entrenched in section 6.

What was new after *Oakes* was that the harmony and unity that characterised the first two years gave way to sharp disagreements within the Court as to when and how these limitations on the model should be applied. Broadly speaking, the judges split into two distinct groups. On one side, stood William McIntyre, Jean Beetz, Gerard La Forest, Gerald Le Dain, and Willard Estey.[16] More than the other three members of the Court, these five manifested a strong inclination to recognize one or more of these qualifications to limit the Charter's reach and their own powers of review. Without saying so explicitly they seemed to tap into and endorse a typically Canadian, populist and conservative concern that the Charter and the Court's powers of review should not be allowed to penetrate too deeply our democratic heritage and our commitment to the sovereignty of the people.[17] The other three judges, Bertha Wilson, Antonio Lamer,

---

16 Although there are slight variations in their analyses, by and large the academic commentators are agreed on the broad contours of the split that developed within the Court and the assignment of individual judges to either side of the liberal/conservative divide. See, e.g., R. Elliott, "The Supreme Court of Canada and Section One: The Erosion of the Common Front," 12 Queen's L.J. 277; A. Petter and P. Monahan, "Developments in Constitutional Law", *supra*, note 1; see Marc Gold, "Of Rights and Roles: The Supreme Court and the Charter" (1989) 23 U.B.C. L. Rev 507; L. Weinrib, "The Supreme Court of Canada and Section One of the Charter", *supra*, Chapter 2, note 69; Peter Russell, *The Judiciary in Canada* (Toronto: McGraw-Hill, 1988), p. 362; cf. the characterization of William Conklin in *Images of Constitution* (Toronto: U. of T. Press, 1989), Chapter 7.

The most striking difference between Conklin's characterization and my own would be in our reading of Antonio Lamer. In my view, Conklin's failure to recognize the essentially "liberal" position favoured by Lamer can be accounted for by his concentration on a single judgment which Lamer authored early in the life of the Charter and failing to consider the whole range of judgments he wrote and concurred in over the course of the entire five years. For a parallel criticism of Conklin's characterization of Bertha Wilson's performance, see notes 18 and 81, *infra*. Apart from these differences, the approach I have labelled conservative tends to coincide with his rule-rationalist image, and the liberal or purposeful with what he calls a teleogical image of a constitution.

17 Certainly the most well known essay in this tradition is George Grant's *Lament for a Nation* (Ottawa: Carleton University Press, 1965). See also Patrick Macklem, "Constitutional Ideologies" 20 Ottawa L. Rev. 117. Within this conservative tradition, the role of the Court would generally be understood to be passive and deferential to the wishes of the legislature. See Mandel, *The Charter of Rights and the Legalization of Politics in Canada*, *supra*, note 13, at 54.

and Brian Dickson, by contrast, remained more committed to the liberal approach that had produced the model in *Oakes*. These three judges were much less likely to invoke one of these limiting principles in responding to a challenge, although on several noteworthy occasions they showed a willingness to embrace them as well.[18]

The division between these two groups was anything but airtight. As we shall see, there were a significant number of cases, especially in year five, in which everyone on the Court was agreed not only that the model in *Oakes* was applicable, but also on the outcome that it would yield.[19] The conservatives certainly did not reject the model in every case. As well, as we have just noted, to varying degrees, the "liberal" judges did occasionally embrace the more "conservative" approach. Overall, there was, unquestionably, a good deal of crossover between the two groups. In addition, there were important differences between the judges in each camp. Not infrequently liberals and conservatives differed amongst them-

---

18 Each of the "liberal" judges, on different occasions, recognized one or the other of these limits on the Charter's reach. See, for example, the decisions of Bertha Wilson in *R. v. Jones, supra*, note 2, and *R. v. Vermette* (1988), 50 D.L.R. (4th) 385; Antonio Lamer in *Les Acadiens, supra*, note 2, and *Andrews v. Law Society of B.C., supra*, note 2; and Brian Dickson in the *Extradition trilogy, R. v. Jones, R. v. Corbett* and *R. v. Simmons, supra*, note 2, *R. v. Stevens, supra*, note 14, *R. v. Gamble*, [1988] 2 S.C.R. 595, and *R. v. Strachan* (1988), 56 D.L.R. (4th) 673. As well, all three of them embraced the conservative method in *Retail, Wholesale & Department Store Union, Local 580 v. Dolphin Delivery* (1986), 33 D.L.R. (4th) 174.

It might also be noted that in several cases in which the constitutionality of a law was not challenged directly (see, e.g., *R. v. Mills* and *R. v. Rahey, supra*, note 2), these judges allowed their liberal instincts to carry them too far. In these cases, the liberals ruled that no justification could ever be put forward to legitimate unreasonable delay in a trial.

Bertha Wilson pursued a similar line of analysis much earlier in the *B.C. Motor Vehicle Reference, supra*, Chapter 2, note 8, when she argued that a law which threatened a person's life, liberty or the security of the person in ways which offended the principles of fundamental justice could not be justified under s. 1. This absolutist view had some support in the academic literature: see P. Bender, "Some Remarks About the Proper Role of Section One of the Canadian Charter", (1983) 13 Man. L.J. 669. Subsequently, as we shall see, in *R. v. Morgentaler, supra*, note 2, she abandoned this position and accepted the position advocated by the rest of her colleagues of the relevance of s. 1 to all of the rights and freedoms guaranteed by the Charter. (By failing to acknowledge her change of heart in *Morgentaler* and the record of her judgments thereafter, Bill Conklin unfairly, in my opinion, characterizes Bertha Wilson as having rejected the view that the Charter entails an element of utilitarian balancing). See *Images of a Constitution* (Toronto: U. of T. Press, 1989), p. 149ff.

In addition to the liberals, on occasion the conservatives embraced a similar "absolutist" approach. See, e.g., McIntyre (and Le Dain) in *R. v. Smith, supra*, note 2, and Estey in *R. v. Wigglesworth* (1987), 45 D.L.R. (4th) 235.

19 See note 3, *supra*.

selves and wrote more than one opinion in disposing of a case.[20]

The difference in the approaches of the two groups of judges can be seen in each of the limits which figure so prominently in the Court's decisions in the years immediately following *Oakes*. Even with respect to the first threshold, which limited the application of the Charter to laws enacted or embraced by the legislative or executive branch of the federal or one of the provincial governments, and where there was a good deal of consensus on the Court, the conservatives showed they were prepared to invoke this doctrine in circumstances in which at least two of the more liberal judges demurred.

On the first occasion in which the Court addressed this question after its decision in *Oakes*, all seven of the judges who sat on the case were agreed that the Charter had no application to that body of law, known as the "common law" or judge made law, when only the "private relations of individuals" were involved. In this case, known as *Dolphin Delivery*,[21] the Retail, Wholesale and Department Store Union had sought to have a common law rule which limited their freedom to picket that company struck down on the ground that it infringed their members' freedom of expression. All seven members of the Court who sat on that case responded that the protection of the Charter was not available to the picketers because, in their minds, the law which judges make to govern the relations of individuals and groups in their private affairs was not the kind of law which the Court was authorized to review.

Another body of law, which all members of the Court were agreed lay beyond the reach of the Charter, was the Constitution itself. No one had any doubt that judicial review, under the Charter, was to measure laws enacted by the federal or one of the provincial governmental authorities which had been endowed with the power to pass such laws. Constitutional review was not designed to scrutinize the other terms of the Constitution itself. To change the terms of the Constitution was a matter requiring formal amendment, and for that task, a special procedure was spelled out in other sections of the new Constitution. On the basis of this understanding, all seven members of the Court who considered the issue were agreed that a provision in the original Constitutional agreement of

---

20 One can find two or more "conservative" judgments written in *R. v. Mills, R. v. Rahey, R. v. Smith, Edwards Book Stores, R. v. Morgentaler, R. v. Holmes, R. v. Corbett, supra,* note 2, and two or more "liberal" judgments in *Les Acadiens; R. v. Mills, Edwards Books, R. v. Lyons, R. v. Morgentaler,* the *Labour* and *Extradition* trilogies, *R. v. Schwartz* and *R. v. Simmons, supra,* note 2. See also *Andrews v. Law Society of B.C., supra,* note 2, where there were three different judgments as to how a citizenship requirement in B.C.'s *Barristers and Solicitors Act* fared under the proportionality principles in s. 1.

21 *Retail, Wholesale & Department Store Union, Local 580 v. Dolphin Delivery Ltd.* (1986), 33 D.L.R. (4th) 174.

1867, the old BNA Act, which provided for special funding for Catholic schools in Ontario, could not be reviewed under the equality section (15) of the Charter. Even though laws passed under section 93 of the BNA Act might be inconsistent with the Charter's guarantee of equality, everyone was agreed that the constitutional document itself was not the kind of law which fell within the Charter's reach and the authority of the Court to review.[22]

Even though there was a good deal of consensus within the Court about the kinds of law to which the Charter applied and the kinds of law which lay outside the bounds of constitutional review, reviewers will find there were significant differences here as well. For example, in contrast with the unanimity which marked the Court's decision in *Spencer*, following *Oakes* the Court split sharply, essentially along liberal/conservative lines, on the extent to which foreign governments and their laws might be required to respect the rights and freedoms which Canadians were guaranteed in the Charter.[23] Led by Gerard La Forest, five members of the Court followed much the same reasoning that had been used in *Spencer* to dismiss three separate challenges to Canada's extradition laws. Writing for himself, Jean Beetz, William McIntyre, and Gerald Le Dain, and Brian Dickson,[24] La Forest actually made reference to the Court's earlier decision in *Spencer* to support his finding that none of the legal rights that are guaranteed in section 11 of the Charter to people "charged with an offence" had

---

22 *Reference re an Act to Amend the Education Act, supra,* note 2. For two comments on the Court's ruling in this case, see A. Petter and P. Monahan, "Developments in Constitutional Law: The 1986-87 Term" (1988), 10 S. Ct. L. Rev. 61, at 134-144; and Gordon Bale "Reference Re Funding For Roman Catholic High Schools — *Tiny* Convincingly Overruled but Equality Rights Needlessly Compromised" (1989), 11 S. Ct. L. Rev. 399. See also Brian Slattery, "The Constitutional Priority of the Charter", in Swinton and Rogerson (eds.), *Competing Constitutional Visions* (Toronto: Carswell, 1988), pp 81, 89.

The procedure for, and requirements of, amending the Constitution are set out in the *Constitution Act 1982,* Part. V, ss. 38-49. Some of these provisions, e.g., those dealing with amendments to the division of powers, the Senate, the Supreme Court, etc., would have been altered by the proposals contained in the Meech Lake Accord if the Accord had been ratified.

23 See *Schmidt v. R.; Argentina v. Mellino;* and *U.S.A. v. Allard and Charette, supra,* note 2.

24 Of the three liberal judges, we shall see that as time went on Dickson was increasingly more inclined than the other two to abandon the model in *Oakes*. The *Extradition trilogy* is only one of several occasions in which Dickson sided with his more conservative colleagues. For similar assessments of Dickson's performance relative to his liberal colleagues see L. Weinrib, "The Supreme Court of Canada and Section One of the Charter" (1988), 10 S. Ct. L. Rev. 469, at 509; M. Gold, "Of Rights and Roles: The Supreme Court and the Charter, *supra,* note 16; and Peter Russell, *The Judiciary in Canada, infra,* note 92.

any application to extradition hearings because, he said, that section only applies to offences created by a Canadian Government. It did not, these judges ruled, apply to charges initiated by a foreign Government. Accordingly, in their view, relief could not be given to persons whose rights — for example, to be presumed innocent or to be tried within a reasonable time, by a jury of their peers, etc. — might not be respected by the State to which they were resisting extradition. In their minds, just as in *Spencer*, the Charter had application only to Canadian laws that threatened the rights and freedoms guaranteed in the Charter. The fact that some foreign country's laws might not respect these fundamental legal rights was something they could do nothing about.[25]

Bertha Wilson and Antonio Lamer, the other two judges who sat on the extradition cases, disagreed with this view. They thought that it was unavoidable, in cases like these, that the Charter would have an impact abroad; although they could not agree on how far the effects would be felt. Antonio Lamer, who had not sat on the bench in *Spencer*, went the furthest. He said that a person facing an extradition hearing could claim all the legal rights guaranteed in section 11 that were relevant to his or her case. If, for example, the Canadian Government was being asked to extradite a person to be tried a second time for an offence for which he or she had already been acquitted, or to be tried after an unreasonable period of time, that person could properly claim the protection of section 11 in a judicial hearing convened to decide whether he or she ought to be extradited. Recalling her earlier judgment in the refugee case of *Singh*, in which she struck down the refugee determination procedure in Canada's *Immigration Act*, Bertha Wilson agreed with Lamer that, to the extent the Canadian Government was involved in the extradition of some person from Canada, protection of the Charter could be claimed and to that extent foreign law would avoidably be affected. On the question, however, of how far a foreign Government could be held accountable for delay in bringing a person to trial, she did not believe the Charter could be stretched as far as Lamer suggested it might. In her view, although the Charter might protect a person from unreasonable delay caused by the Canadian Government or one of its officials, it would provide no protection where the failure was the foreign Government's.

---

25 It might be noted that just one month after the five-year mark, the Court recognized that a person resisting extradition could claim the benefit of s. 6 — against being removed from Canada in a way that was not demonstrably justified. See *U.S.A. v. Cotroni*, [1989] 1 S.C.R. 1469. In this case however, Gerard La Forest adopted a very conservative position on how the Court should apply the proportionality principles set out in *Oakes* in reviewing a Government's policy on extradition. See note 56, *infra*. For an analysis of this and other cases decided by the Court after the period covered in this book, see my essay, "A Conservative's Court: The Politicization of Law" forthcoming in U.T.L.J.

The *Extradition trilogy* provides reviewers with a clear illustration of a set of cases in which the members of the Court followed two very different approaches to determine the extent to which the Charter would affect a law which has neither been enacted nor embraced by Parliament, one of the provincial legislatures or their executives. The extradition cases are also typical of cases in this period in that, when there was disagreement in the Court, the conservative view frequently prevailed. Similar observations can be made with respect to the second constraint, or limit, favoured by the Court in the years following *Oakes* to restrict the Charter's reach. According to this criterion, if a law did not impact coercively or only threatened personal freedom indirectly, it would not be subject to review. Here again, reviewers will see the conservative judges inclined to embrace this approach more than their liberal colleagues and, in several important cases, their approach carried the day.[26]

Two cases in particular show how the liberals and conservatives approached the question of whether a law was coercive very differently and how specific judges, in this case William McIntyre and Jean Beetz, could distinguish themselves by the consistency of their commitment to the latter point of view.[27] In one case, *Re Jones*,[28] the Court was asked by a "stiff necked parson" to consider the constitutionality of a section of the Alberta *School Act*, which required people, like him, who operated alternative (including religious) schools, to apply to the provincial authorities to have their institutions certified and accredited academically. In the other, *Edwards Books*,[29] the Court was asked to evaluate the constitutionality of Ontario's *Retail Business Holidays Act* which, with very limited exceptions, prohibited all retailers from doing business on Sunday.

In *Jones*, all seven judges who listened to the challenge to the constitutionality of the Alberta law rejected it. But they did so for radically different reasons. Three of them — Gerard La Forest, Brian Dickson, and Antonio Lamer — for the most part followed the standard two-stage approach the Court had summarized in *Oakes*. First, they accepted Jones' claim that the law was coercive and impinged on his religious freedom.

---

26 See *R. v. Jones, R. v. Holmes,* and *R. v. Schwartz, supra,* note 2; *R. v. Vermette* (1988), 50 D.L.R. (4th) 385; *B.C.G.E.U. v. A.G. B.C.* (1988), 53 D.L.R. (4th) 1 (on s. 11).

It might be noted that in two cases decided at the beginning of year six, the Court dismissed challenges essentially on the ground that no factual foundation for the claims had been made out. See *Moysa v. Labour Relations Board (Alta.)* (1989), 60 D.L.R. (4th) 1; *Mackay v. Manitoba* (1989), 61 D.L.R. (4th) 385. See also Chapter 4, notes 43 and 108, *infra.*

27 William McIntyre relied on similar rulings in at least two other cases in dismissing all or part of a claimant's challenge. See his judgments in *R. v. Morgentaler* and *Public Service Alliance v. R., supra,* note 2.

28 *R. v. Jones, supra,* note 2.

29 *Edwards Books and Art Ltd. v. R., supra,* note 2.

Jones had said that Alberta's law offended his religious beliefs because, in making him apply for permission to run his own school, he was being obliged to acknowledge that the Government rather than God, had the final authority over the education of his children. No matter how peculiar these views might seem, La Forest, Dickson, and Lamer said that the Court had to respect them as being honestly held.[30] In their view, in the absence of any evidence to the contrary, it was not proper for the Court to question the sincerity of his claim that the Alberta law interfered with his religious freedom. To do so would be completely at odds with the values of pluralism, and respect for the human dignity of each individual, on which the Charter itself is based. In the end, however, La Forest, Dickson and Lamer rejected Jones' claim because they thought it could be demonstrably justified as a reasonable law against the object test and the proportionality principles which the Court applied under section 1. Even though they recognized that the law interfered with Jones' freedom to live his life according to his religious beliefs, they had no doubt that the Government's interest in the education of children more than justified the constraint which the law imposed.

The other four judges reached the same result but they were not content with adopting the reasoning of La Forest and his two liberal colleagues. Writing for herself, Jean Beetz, William McIntyre and Gerald Le Dain, Bertha Wilson dealt with Jones' plea to respect his religious beliefs in a much more direct and perfunctory way.[31] In the view of these four, there was no need for the Court to enter on the second stage of review because Jones was unable to pass the first. Rather than dismiss his complaint on the ground that the Alberta law could be shown to satisfy the principles of review enunciated in *Oakes*, Wilson and her colleagues wrote that Jones could not succeed because the Alberta law did not constrain his religious freedom in any way, or if it did, the coercion was so trivial and insubstantial as not to warrant the protection of the Charter.

According to these four, in providing for the opportunity to establish alternate schools, Alberta's law should be seen as enhancing, not constraining, the religious freedom of people like Larry Jones. They said the only obligation this law imposed on Jones was to acknowledge the secular role

---

30 But see *Kerr v. R.*, March 24, 1987, where Brian Dickson and Gerard La Forest along with Jean Beetz denied leave to appeal to a challenger who was claiming that laws criminalizing the use of marijuana interfered with his religious freedom. Although no reasons are given to explain the Court's disposition of leave applications, one can only surmise that in this case the judges were concerned about the challenger's sincerity.

31 As we shall see, Wilson's performance in *Jones* was one of the very rare occasions on which she chose to ally herself with the conservative members of the Court rather than with her more liberal colleagues. However, it is important to stress that in its result, Wilson's judgment in Jones was still the most liberal on the Court. See note 32, *infra*.

of provincial authorities in the education of children in the province and that did not offend or impinge on his religious freedom at all. Alternatively, they said, even if the law did infringe on Jones' freedom of conscience and religion it was an extremely "formalistic and technical one" and so "trivial [and] insubstantial" as not to constitute a breach of his constitutional rights.

In the end, the difference of approaches did not affect the outcome of the case. The result turned out to be the same whichever approach was used.[32] The very fact that two separate judgments were written, however, should alert reviewers to the fact that some of the judges were more inclined to use a method or an approach which restricted the reach of the Charter and their own powers of review, while others remained more committed to the model in *Oakes*. Indeed, two months later when the Court handed down its decision in *Edwards Books*, two of the judges underscored their preference for the more restrictive approach. *Edwards Books* was the was the case in which Ontario's Sunday closing law had been challenged by various religious and secular groups. For many reviewers, the parallel between the way in which the judges approached this case and how they handled Jones' challenge will be striking. Once again, one finds one group of judges holding that although Ontario's law did impact coercively on the complainants' religious freedom, it could be justified on the model in *Oakes*, while the second group ruled that the law did not restrict the complainant's freedom in any way and so the principles embedded in section 1 had no application at all.

In this case, however, the positions of the majority and the minority were reversed. In *Edwards*, 5 of the 7 judges who sat on the case accepted the complainant's claim that the law had a coercive effect on their lives. They ruled that even though the law did not directly impinge on the complainants' religious freedom by, for example, requiring them to work on their sabbath, nevertheless, the law did constitute a major inducement to do so and so interfered with their religious freedom. In the same way La Forest and his two colleagues had accepted the sincerity and validity of Jones' beliefs, these five judges accepted the complainants' assertion that by requiring them to stay closed on Sunday, the law put pressure on them to compromise their religious principles by remaining open on Saturday so that they could remain competitive and claim their fair share of business. Even though the law's impact was economic and indirect,

---

32 That was the view of all of the judges except Bertha Wilson. She thought that if it was accepted that Alberta' school law did impinge on Jones' religious freedom in some way, the Government had failed to adduce the necessary evidence to justify it under s. 1. In this and, as we shall see, in her ruling on the s. 7 aspect of Jones' challenge, Wilson's position in this case was clearly the most liberal on the Court. See text, pp. 63-67.

it was, for these judges, coercive nonetheless.

In *Edwards*, only two judges dismissed the case on the basis that Ontario's *Retail Business Holidays Act* was not coercive or invasive of the claimants' religious freedom. Enter, stage right, Messrs. Beetz and McIntyre. On this occasion, the other two judges who had made a parallel finding with respect to Alberta's *School Act* in *Jones*, Bertha Wilson and Gerald Le Dain, had no difficulty recognizing the validity of the complainants' claim that their constitutional entitlement to be free from coercion by the State in matters of religion had been infringed.[33] Beetz and McIntyre saw the case differently. As in *Jones*, they insisted that no coercion had been effected by the State. While not denying that the complainants had felt pressure to remain open on Saturday, and compromise their religious beliefs in so doing, these two judges insisted that any pressure to abandon their religious values came from the complainant's own religious beliefs and had not been imposed by the State. Without saying so explicitly, Beetz and McIntyre told those opposed to the Legislature's prohibition on Sunday shopping that the *indirect* and *economic* pressure that the law exerted was not the kind of coercion to which the Court would or could give relief under the Charter.

When reviewers read the Court's decisions in *Jones* and *Edwards* together, the position of Jean Beetz and William McIntyre will stand out from the rest. In these two cases, their vision of the reach of the Charter is more limited than anyone else's. Indeed, when their judgments in these cases are coupled with their decisions to join with the majority of the Court in the *Extradition trilogy* and *Dolphin Delivery*, the method of Jean Beetz and William McIntyre quickly emerges as the most conservative on the Court. In their view, none of the laws governing alternate schooling, Sunday shopping, and extradition hearings, which they had been asked to review, stood to be evaluated against the principles of justification which the Court had established in *Oakes*. In these, and several other cases,[34] when there was a disagreement among the members of the Court whether the Charter applied to the law that had been challenged, they were more inclined to take a conservative approach than anyone else on the Court.[35]

As they continue to sift through the judgments the Court handed down in the years immediately following its decision in *Oakes*, reviewers will

33 The idea that the Charter protected the so called negative aspect of personal freedom — to be *free from* coercion and restraint — was never questioned by anyone on the Court and was repeatedly affirmed over the course of all five years. See, e.g., *R. v. Big M Drug Mart* (1985), 18 D.L.R. (4th) 321; *Ford v. Quebec, R. v. Turpin, supra*, note 3; and *Slaight Communications v. Davidson, supra*, note 2.

34 See especially the judgments written by McIntyre in *R. v. Holmes, R. v. Smith; R. v. Schwartz, R. v. Morgentaler* and *PSAC v. R., supra*, note 2.

35 As we shall see, in two cases near the end of year five, McIntyre and Beetz were inclined to protect the constitutional guarantee of freedom of expression in circumstances in which their more liberal colleagues were not. See *Irwin Toy v. Quebec* (1988), 58 D.L.R. (4th)

learn that Jean Beetz's and William McIntyre's very cautious approach to their new powers of review was also played out in those cases in which the members of the Court disagreed as to whether some interest or activity was protected by one of the rights and freedoms entrenched in the Charter. Here again, these two judges showed themselves to be especially inclined to dismiss a challenge on the ground that the law did not invade an interest or activity which was fully protected by, or included in, any of the rights and freedoms entrenched in the Charter. They showed just as strong an instinct for a conservative approach in identifying the interests and activities which were protected by the Charter as they did in deciding whether a law was of the kind, and impacted in sufficiently coercive ways, to fall within the scope of the Charter. In effect, Beetz and McIntyre insisted that in order to be subject to judicial review, the coercion which a law effected on personal freedom must meet not only a quantitative threshold, but a qualitative one as well.

It would be important for reviewers to stress that Jean Beetz and William McIntyre were not the only judges who thought that there were interests and activities affected by laws which did not warrant full protection under the Charter. Not infrequently in fact, everyone was of one mind that the Court should not exercise its powers of review because the interest for which the complainant sought protection was not guaranteed by one of the rights and freedoms in the Charter. We have already observed how in *Skapinker*, all of the members of the Court were agreed that the interests and activities protected by section 6 did not include a free-standing right to work.

After *Oakes*, there were several occasions when all of the judges were inclined to respond to a challenge in this way. For example, in a series of cases involving members of different police forces who claimed the benefit of a number of the legal rights guaranteed to "persons charged with an offence", everyone on the Court thought that these entitlements were only available to persons facing proceedings which, either by their nature, (*viz.*, by their purpose) or by the penalties that might be imposed, (*viz.*, by their effects) were truly penal. No one believed, for example, that the protections set out in section 11, to be tried within a reasonable time, to a trial by a jury, to be presumed innocent, etc., applied to people facing internal, administrative or professional proceedings and possible disciplinary sanctions.[36] Similarly, everyone was agreed that only sentencing laws

---

577, and *Slaight Communications v. Davidson, supra*, note 2. For sceptical reviewers it will seem more than coincidental that in the two cases where the members of the Court reverse roles, the interests of commercial, corporate enterprises were at stake.

36 *R. v. Wigglesworth* (1987), 45 D.L.R. (4th) 235. See also *Trimm v. Durham Municipal Police* (1987), 45 D.L.R. (4th) 276; *Burnham v. Toronto Police Force* (1987), 45 D.L.R. (4th) 309; *Trumbley and Pugh v. Toronto Police Force* (1987), 45 D.L.R. (4th) 318. See also *R. v. Shubley* (1990), 65 D.L.R. (4th) 193.

which were "grossly disproportionate" would attract review under the guarantee against "cruel and unusual treatment" that is contained in section 12. Simply showing a person suffered an excessive or disproportionate punishment was not, in anyone's mind, the kind of interest that section 12 protected.[37] On another occasion there was unanimity in the view that the right to a fair trial protected by the Charter was not infringed when a person accused of an offense was confronted with his or her prior convictions in the course of a trial.[38] As its first half-decade came to a close, the judges added to the list by denying the Charter guaranteed (i) people facing routine border questioning and personal searches of their baggage any of the legal rights contained in sections 7-14;[39] (ii) the freedom to engage in violent forms of expression;[40] (iii) any proprietary rights that were purely economic in nature;[41] and (iv) the right to refuse to produce a drivers licence and insurance certificate on request.[42]

On other occasions, however, the Court was divided on whether an interest or activity was covered by the Charter, and when that happened Jean Beetz and William McIntyre almost always followed the more conservative approach. In these cases, despite the objections of one or more of the liberal judges, one typically finds these two allying themselves with either Willard Estey, Gerald Le Dain and/or Gerard La Forest in ruling that the interest or activity for which protection was sought did not fall within one of the rights and freedoms of the Charter guarantees or, if it did, it was not entitled to the full protection of the model set out in *Oakes.*

The outlines of this broad division between the two groups on the Court would be visible to reviewers in the first major judgment the Court handed down, three months after its decision in *Oakes.* Jean Beetz, Willard Estey and Gerald Le Dain lined up on one side; Brian Dickson and Bertha Wilson on the other. Uncharacteristically, Antonio Lamer abandoned Brian Dickson, with whom he almost always agreed, and Bertha Wilson, and

---

37 *R. v. Smith, supra,* note 2.

38 *R. v. Corbett, supra,* note 2. For a critique of the Court's decision in this case, see M. MacCrimmon, "Developments in the Law of Evidence: The 1987-88 Term", S. Ct. L. Rev. 275, 299. See also *R. v. Staranchuk* (1985), 22 D.L.R. (4th) 480, where the Court was of one mind that the protection against "self incrimination" had no application to cases in which the accused had been charged with perjury or analogous offences.

39 *R. v. Simmons, supra,* note 2, at 697.

40 *Irwin Toy v. Quebec, supra,* note 35; see also *R.W.D.S.U. v. Dolphin Delivery, supra,* note 21.

41 *Irwin Toy v. Quebec, supra,* note 35. See also *Air Canada v. British Columbia* (1989), 59 D.L.R. (4th) 161, 184.

42 *R. v. Hufsky,* [1988] 1 S.C.R. 621, 638. See also *R. v. Potvin,* [1989] 1 S.C.R. 52, in which the Court ruled that an accused person does not have a right to have the demeanour of all witnesses evaluated by the trial judge.

joined in the judgment written by Jean Beetz.[43] The case involved a complaint by a group called La Societé des Acadiens du Nouveau-Brunswick who argued, amongst other things, that their constitutional rights in section 19(2) had been violated because a judge of the New Brunswick Supreme Court had continued to sit on a case in which they were involved even though he was not, in their view, able to understand fully the legal arguments that their counsel had made to him in French. Section 19(2) of the Charter guarantees every person the right to use either English or French in any court of New Brunswick.

Jean Beetz, Willard Estey, Gerald Le Dain, and Antonio Lamer all said the Acadiens' claim could not succeed on the basis of section 19(2), although they did say relief might be granted under New Brunswick's statutory, official languages law. Forming the majority of the Court, they ruled that the interest for which the Acadiens sought protection — the right to be *understood* in French — was not an interest which was protected by section 19(2). Incredibly, they held that the language rights guaranteed in that section only protected a person's right to speak in French or English but not the right to be understood.

Bertha Wilson and Brian Dickson wrote separate judgments in this case in which each flatly rejected the way Beetz and his colleagues read section 19(2). Although, in the end, both of them agreed with the majority that the case should be dismissed because the Acadiens had not adduced enough evidence to prove that the judge in question did not understand their counsel, both Wilson and Dickson were very clear that the interest of the Acadiens, in having their legal arguments fully understood, was at the "highest level of the Constitutional hierarchy" and fell squarely within section 19(2). Had the Acadiens been able to adduce that evidence, both Wilson and Dickson would have said that their constitutional entitlements had been violated and, unless the Government could have justified the judge's behaviour according the principles embedded in section 1, their concurring judgments would have been written as dissents.

The difference between Messrs. Beetz, McIntyre, La Forest and Le Dain on the one hand and Wilson and Dickson on the other, in specifying what interests attracted the protection of the Charter, and the principles of justice enumerated in *Oakes*, resurfaced a year later in what has come to be known as the *Labour trilogy*. These were three cases in which the Court was asked to evaluate the constitutionality of half a dozen different provincial and federal labour laws which, in one way or another, limited

---

43 Other major cases in which Dickson and Lamer signed or authored different judgments include the *Extradition trilogy, Andrews v. Law Society of B.C., R. v. Lyons, supra*, note 2, *R. v. Gamble*, [1988] 2 S.C.R. 595, and *R. v. Stevens* (1988), 51 D.L.R. (4th) 394 and *R. v. Potvin, ibid.*

the ability of thousands of workers to strike and to engage freely in collective bargaining. In each case the workers complained that one or other of the relevant laws limited their freedom to associate, which was guaranteed in section 2(d), and that this restriction on their freedom could not be demonstrably justified as being reasonable in a society which purported to be democratic and free.

At this stage no reviewer should be surprised by the response of the two groups. On the one side William McIntyre, Gerald Le Dain, Jean Beetz and Gerard La Forest dismissed the workers' challenges on the ground that the right to strike, and the related aspects of collective bargaining for which they sought protection, were not interests or activities that were guaranteed by section 2(d). Writing for himself, Beetz and La Forest, Gerald Le Dain said that the *only* interests protected by section 2(d) were the freedom to form and bring an association into existence, maintain it, and participate in its lawful activities as well as the right to exercise their individual constitutional entitlements in association with others. It did not protect, in his view (nor in the view of William McIntyre who wrote a separate judgment) the right to engage in a particular activity like strikes or collective bargaining, even where that activity was essential to the enterprise the association was meant to promote. Because none of these judges thought the activity which the law constrained was one which fell within the protection of the Charter, they ruled the Court had no basis on which to review these laws, and the workers' challenges were accordingly dismissed.

Once again Bertha Wilson and Brian Dickson took issue with virtually everything that Le Dain and McIntyre wrote. Their approach to section 2(d) mirrors exactly the way they read section 19(2) in *La Societé des Acadiens*. Using the large, liberal, "purposeful" interpretive methodology which the Court had established in its very first year, both Wilson and Dickson had little difficulty in characterizing the freedom of workers to strike, and to engage in meaningful collective bargaining, as precisely the kinds of interests and activities the Charter was designed to protect. Moreover, in these cases, where the complainants had no difficulty in surmounting the evidentiary hurdle, and establishing that the laws in question really did restrict their freedom to associate with their co-workers, both Wilson and Dickson went on to hold that in various ways and to various degrees the prohibitions against strikes could not satisfy the principles of justification enunciated in *Oakes*. In the result, in the *Labour trilogy*, the two liberal judges were of the view that different aspects of these anti-strike laws were unconstitutional and their judgments in these cases were written, for the most part, as dissents.[44]

In the language and collective bargaining cases, as well as in the

---

44 In *Saskatchewan v. R.W.D.S.U.* (1987), 38 D.L.R. (4th) 277, Brian Dickson ruled that

challenges concerning Canada's extradition[45] and burglary laws,[46] the conservative approach, of excluding a range of interests and activities from review under the Charter, was embraced by a majority of the judges who sat on those cases and the reach of the object test and the proportionality principles was diminished even further. This was not, however, the only scenario the Court wrote. As with the other two limitations we have considered, sometimes the liberal approach did prevail. Even on these occasions, however, when the rest of their colleagues were satisfied that the interest or activity for which the claimant sought protection was one which fell within the Charter's reach, reviewers will frequently find Jean Beetz and/or William McIntyre still holding out.[47] In *Dolphin Delivery* for example, Jean Beetz stood alone in his opinion that the workers' challenge in that case should be dismissed because the interest for which the protection was sought was not encompassed by one of the rights and freedoms which the Charter guarantees. The rest of the Court, it will be recalled, was of the view that the challenge to the common law rules governing picketing should be dismissed because that was not the kind of law to which the Charter applied. Although he agreed that the union's complaint could be dismissed on these grounds, Jean Beetz thought it necessary to issue a separate concurring judgment to make it clear that he did not even regard the picketing that was involved in the case as the kind of activity that qualified as expression within the meaning of section 2(d).

William McIntyre wrote or joined in similar "solo" judgments on several occasions, the most publicized, unquestionably, being his decision in *Morgentaler*.[48] In this case McIntyre wrote a judgment for himself and Gerard La Forest, dismissing Henry Morgentaler's challenge to Canada's abortion law. Of the seven judges who heard the case, they alone decided that there was not a single interest women have in terminating a pregnancy that falls within the Charter's protection. In their view, not even the very broad language in section 7, purporting to protect "the life, liberty and security of the person", guaranteed women the right to have an abortion when the security of their persons or their lives were threatened. While

---

Saskatchewan's law prohibiting a strike in the dairy industry could be justified under s. 1 and so his separate opinion was written as a concurrence rather than as a dissent.

45 *Schmidt v. R.*, *Argentina v. Mellino*, and *U.S.A. v. Allard and Charette*, *supra*, note 2.

46 *R. v. Holmes*, *supra*, note 2.

47 For a similar reading of Jean Beetz's approach, see Robin Elliott "The Supreme Court of Canada and Section One: The Erosion of the Common Front", 12 Queen's L.J. 277, 278.

48 See *R. v. Morgentaler, R. v. Simmons, R. v. Smith*, *supra*, note 2; *B.C.G.E.U. v. A.G. B.C.*, *supra* note 26; *R. v. Jacoy*, [1988] 2 S.C.R. 548. See also *R. v. Dubois* (1985), 23 D.L.R. (4th) 503, where he employed a narrower approach to s. 13 in a case the Court heard prior to *Oakes*.

recognizing that section 251 of the Criminal Code might well cause a woman much anxiety and stress, as in *Edwards* and in *Jones*, they held fast to their position that this was not the kind of interest or activity that section 7 was designed to protect.

In *Morgentaler*, as in *Dolphin Delivery*, the conservative approach of excluding various interests and activities from the scope of the Charter did not carry the day. The other five judges who heard *Morgentaler* followed the more liberal approach of *Oakes*. Each of them was able to identify some aspect of a woman's interest in having an abortion which was protected by the Charter and, collectively, they ruled that the limit which section 251 of the Criminal Code placed on that interest could not be justified against the proportionality principles outlined in section 1. It was this part of the Court's decision in *Morgentaler* which attracted all of the publicity in the media and almost certainly made it one of the constitutional cases which the public knows best. It is also the part of the judgment which is most interesting from the point of view of constitutional law.

So far we have been focusing our attention on the different approaches the liberals and the conservatives took to the question of *when* the Court should exercise its powers of constitutional review. It has been within that perspective that we have noticed how in *Morgentaler* it was two of the judges with the most conservative attitude towards their own powers — William McIntyre and Gerard La Forest — who pressed the idea that there were a range of interests and activities, in this case the procurement of an abortion, that the Charter did not protect. But the majority's decision in *Morgentaler* shows that the Court was just as divided on *how* the principles developed in *Oakes* should be applied as it was on the question of *when or whether* the Charter should be used at all. Although reviewers will find, once again, that there were numerous cases, especially in year five, when everyone on the Court was agreed on how the model should work,[49] in many others, like *Morgentaler*, the judges were badly divided. Not infrequently, two, three or even four opinions might be written by the judges as to how the model should be applied.[50] In these cases one can find even more evidence of the basic liberal-conservative division within the Court.

In *Morgentaler*, the majority actually divided three ways. Of the five judges who held that Canada's abortion laws violated some interest or activity which was protected under section 7, it will not be surprising to

---

49 *Supra*, note 3.
50 See, e.g., *Edwards Books v. R.*, *R. v. Mills*, *R. v. Rahey*, *R. v. Smith*, *R. v. Lyons*, *Andrews v. Law Society of B.C.*, *Slaight Communication v. Davidson*, *supra*, note 2; *Black v. Law Society of British Columbia* (1989), 58 D.L.R. (4th) 317; *Irwin Toy Ltd. v. Quebec* (1989), 58 D.L.R. (4th) 577. See also s. 24 cases such as *R. v. Simmons*, *supra*, note 2.

learn that Jean Beetz and Willard Estey took the most conservative approach. The interest that they said was protected by section 7 was a woman's claim to her life and to her physical and psychological well-being. In effect they read the Constitution as guaranteeing women the right to therapeutic abortions. Essentially, they said that interest was threatened by section 251 of the Criminal Code because of the manner in which the law was administered. Dickson and Lamer took a slightly broader, more liberal approach. They agreed with Beetz and Estey that section 7 protected a woman's interest in her physical and emotional well-being. However, they added that, apart from the physiological and psychological threats posed by Canada's abortion laws, simply forcing a woman to carry a foetus to term, for reasons that were not her own, was also an invasion of her bodily integrity and the security of her person. Like Beetz and Estey, Brian Dickson and Antonio Lamer thought that the administrative and regulatory procedures of the Act interfered with these constitutional guarantees.

Bertha Wilson, throughout most of this time the only woman on the Court, took the most expansive interpretation of all.[51] In addition to the interests her colleagues had identified, Wilson argued more generally that section 7 must be defined to protect the right of each person to make their own decisions on all matters of fundamental personal importance. Choosing whether a pregnancy will be terminated prematurely, or naturally with the birth of a child, was simply one example of a much wider protection embedded in section 7. Of the seven judges who sat on the case, she alone focused her attention on the substantive content of Canada's abortion law rather than its procedural inadequacies. Where all of the other judges thought that section 251 could be repaired with appropriate changes to the administrative and regulatory structure under which abortions were performed, Wilson alone argued that, to satisfy the proportionality principles set out in *Oakes*, any future abortion law would have to recognize some period in which the freedom of the woman to make such a fundamental personal decision would be paramount and unconstrained.

Reviewers will recognize that the alignment of the judges in *Morgentaler*, with Bertha Wilson at one end of the spectrum and William McIntyre, Gerard La Forest, Jean Beetz and Willard Estey at the other, is typical of the way the judges divided in the years following *Oakes*. It conforms precisely to the division in the Court we have already observed and, it turns out, it is also quite representative of how each of the judges approached the question of how the principles in *Oakes* should be applied.

---

51 For a similar reading of Wilson's judgment, see Marc Gold, "Of Rights and Roles", *supra*, note 16; and E. Colvin, "Section 7 of The Canadian Charter of Rights and Freedoms", 68 Can. Bar Rev. 560, 568-569.

Generally, those whom we have seen to be more inclined to take a conservative and cautious approach in deciding whether the Charter should be applied, favoured principles and methods of reasoning that further constrained the reach of the Charter.[52] Wilson, by contrast, maintained her position as the most liberal member of the Court and consistently exercised her powers of review more rigorously than anyone else.[53]

When the conservatives did apply the model in *Oakes* they frequently employed one of two principles, or lines of reasoning, in ways which substantially attenuated the force of the proportionality principles. One principle related to the extent to which the Court should defer to the sovereignty of the other two branches of government; the other to the way in which the public interest promoted by a law should be balanced and weighed. Both principles show up in many of the cases the reviewers will have already considered. Deference, for example, was central to the Court's reasoning in explaining why, in its view, the Charter had such a limited effect in the area of language, extradition and collective bargaining law. Gerard La Forest and William McIntyre seemed particularly inclined to an attitude of deference.[54] On questions of social and economic policy,[55] education, extradition,[56] abortion and sentencing,[57] La Forest explicitly appealed to his fellow judges to allow the other two branches of government a reasonable amount of discretion and room to manoeuvre. On a variety of occasions he adopted a posture of deference even when it could be shown the legislature or executive could have chosen a policy which would have realized all of its objectives but in a way which would interfere with peoples' constitutional entitlements even less.[58] By running all the proportionality principles together, and fusing them into a single standard of reasonableness, McIntyre adopted a similar posture and wrote parallel

---

52 The major exceptions are the judgments of McIntyre and Beetz in *Irwin Toy v. Quebec* and *Slaight Communications v. Davidson, supra*, note 35.

53 See, e.g., her judgments in *R. v. Jones, Edwards Books, R.W.D.S.U. v. Government of Saskatchewan, supra*, note 2. See also *U.S.A. v. Cotroni, supra*, note 25, a decision released shortly after the curtain fell down on the Court's first five years.

54 See Marc Gold, "Of Rights and Roles"; Robin Elliott, ". . . . The Erosion of the Common Front"; and L. Weinrib, "The Supreme Court of Canada and Section One of the Charter", *supra*, note 16, for a parallel characterization of La Forest's approach.

55 *Edwards Books; Andrews v. Law Society of B.C., supra*, note 2, at 38. See also his position in the *Labour trilogy, supra*, note 2.

56 *Schmidt v. R., Argentina v. Mellino, U.S.A. v. Charette, supra*, note 2. See also *U.S.A. v. Cotroni, supra*, note 25, one of the early cases in year six where La Forest purports to introduce an element of discretion and deference when he applies the second proportionality principle in his review of Canada's extradition laws.

57 *R. v. Lyons, supra*, note 2, at 225.

58 *Edwards Books, R. v. Lyons, R. v. Jones, supra*, note 2. See also *U.S.A. v. Cotroni, supra*, note 25, and his concurrence in the *Labour trilogy*. Cf. his judgment in *Andrews v. Law Society of B.C., supra*, note 2.

judgments in a number of important cases.[59]

For the more liberal members of the Court, deference was generally a much more focused idea. All liberals were agreed that on some matters — for example on what objectives legislatures can legitimately pursue — deference was entirely appropriate. In no case in the three years following its decision in *Oakes*, in which the liberal approach prevailed, was a law judged to be constitutionally flawed on account of the purposes it was designed to achieve.[60] Beyond this, however, the liberals on the Court were not always of one mind. Of the liberal group, once again Bertha Wilson was usually the one least inclined to defer to the choice of policies made by a legislature on grounds of Parliamentary sovereignty or institutional expertise. On several occasions she disassociated herself from judgments in which one or other of her liberal allies was prepared to defer to the will of the legislature in circumstances in which she was not.[61]

The full spectrum of opinion on the question of the extent to which the Court should defer to the legislature can be seen in the four separate judgments the Court issued in *Edwards*. In that case, a central concern of those challenging the Ontario's Sunday closing law was the exemption which allowed retailers who closed their business on Saturday to remain open on Sunday, if the businesses were small enough and employed seven or fewer employees. Bertha Wilson took the strongest position. She said the exemption was unconstitutional because it did not go far enough. She held that not only did the legislature have to provide an exemption for those who closed their businesses on Saturdays but it had to be available to everyone, regardless of the size of their operation, who fell within that class. Dickson, by contrast, was of the view that the Court should respect the balance of interests that the legislature had effected in the more limited exemption it had allowed. He went on to suggest, however, that he would not have been so deferential had the legislature provided no exemption at all. In his view, it would have been impossible to justify a law which insisted that even families which operated a store without any employees remain closed on Sundays when the tenets of their religion required them

---

59 See, e.g., *Andrews v. Law Society of B.C.*, *supra*, note 2, and *Black v. Law Society of Alberta*, *supra*, note 6. See also *R. v. Vaillancourt, R. v. Smith* and *R. v. Morgentaler*, *supra*, note 2. And see Chapter 4 note 74, *infra*.

60 See, e.g., *Edwards Books, R. v. Smith, R. v. Whyte, R. v. Vaillancourt, Andrews v. Law Society of B.C.*, *supra*, note 2; *R. v. Thomsen*, [1988] 1 S.C.R. 640; *R. v. Hufsky*, [1988] 1 S.C.R. 621; *Canadian Newspapers v. Ontario* (1988), 52 D.L.R. (4th) 690; *Ford v. Quebec*, *supra*, note 3; *Irwin Toy v. Quebec* (1989), 58 D.L.R. (4th) 577. Cf. Wilson and Beetz in *R. v. Morgentaler*, *supra*, note 2 and Lamer in *R. v. Schwartz*, *supra*, note 2; and see the cases in Chapter 4 at note 92, *infra*.

61 Compare her position with Lamer's in *Les Acadiens* and *Andrews v. Law Society of B.C.*, *supra*, note 2, and with Dickson's in *Edwards Books, Saskatchewan v. R.W.D.S.U., R. v. Lyons* and the *Extradition trilogy*, *supra*, note 2.

to close on another day. Reflecting his populist, tory approach to judicial review, Gerard La Forest embraced the most deferential position of all.[62] For reasons of both institutional competence and popular sovereignty he argued that a legislature must be given "reasonable room to manoeuvre" in drafting laws of this kind. In direct opposition to what Brian Dickson had said, he wrote that the Court should uphold the constitutionality of a Sunday closing law even if it provided no exemption at all.

Deference was without question one of the most important principles favoured by the conservatives and applied by the Court in exercising its powers of review after *Oakes*. Through it, the Court insulated large areas of policy making from any effective scrutiny by the Court. The other technique the Court used to qualify the proportionality principles it had set out in *Oakes* was to take account and do the balancing of the public interest promoted by a law in a way which further shielded the executive and legislative branches of government from review.

In theory, there were two approaches a judge might follow in reviewing how a law balanced the interests it affected.[63] The liberal approach, as outlined in *Oakes*, required the Court to balance the public interest which supported the enactment of the law at the very end of the second phase of the review process under section 1.[64] On the model in *Oakes*, balancing the public interest promoted by a law, against the constraints it imposed on the personal freedom of those it affected, was what the third proportionality principle was all about and it was there, on the liberal approach, where the real assessment of legislative objectives would be done.[65] The more conservative method was to weigh the public interest in the first phase of the review process in deciding whether a right or freedom had actually been infringed.[66]

Of the two approaches the first is clearly the more liberal. For one

---

62 Note that this is a position he reiterates in *Andrews v. Law Society of B.C.*, *supra*, note 2, at 38.

63 Some academic commentators have argued that, notwithstanding the language of the Court in *Oakes* and subsequent cases, balancing is a function the Court should never perform. See, e.g., L. Weinrib, "The Supreme Court of Canada and Section One of the Charter"(1988), 10 S. Ct. L. Rev. 489, 500-501.

64 See *Reference re s. 94(2) Motor Vehicle Act* (1985), 24 D.L.R. (4th) 536.

65 Note that where a complainant seeks a remedy under s. 24 in lieu of or in addition to a remedy under s. 52, the Court will be obliged to balance the public interest in the remedial stage. See Paul Gewirtz, "Remedies and Resistance", 92 Yale L.J. 585.

66 See *R. v. Jones* (La Forest); *Extradition trilogy* (La Forest); *R. v. Lyons* (La Forest); *R. v. Dyment* (La Forest); *R. v. Schwartz* (La Forest); *R. v. Smith* (McIntyre); *R. v. Simmons* (McIntyre); *R. v. Morgentaler* (McIntyre); *B.C.G.E.U. v. A.G. B.C.* (McIntyre, Dickson); *Labour trilogy* (Le Dain), *supra*, note 2; *R. v. Beare*, *supra*, note 3. It should be noted that even in the landmark case of *R. v. Oakes*, McIntyre and Estey indicated a preference for this approach.

thing, as a practical matter, doing the balancing in section 1 requires the State to bear the burden of gathering whatever evidence is necessary to establish that the public interest or purposes behind a law are substantial enough to justify the infringements of the rights and freedoms that it effects. The second method assigns that obligation to the person challenging the constitutionality of the law and so creates a very significant evidentiary and financial constraint on the availability of judicial review. It means, in effect, that challengers must satisfy a quantitative test by showing that the limit on their freedom outweighs the public interest the law seeks to protect. The significance of the difference can be seen in a case such as *Jones*, where the Court dismissed Jones' challenge even though the Government was never called upon to offer proof for its claim that the public interest in administrative efficiency justified the constitutional infringements it caused.

More broadly, reviewers can say that balancing at the end of the review process, rather than at the beginning, is more liberal because it ensures the principle of alternative means will play a more prominent role. On the model in *Oakes*, the balancing is done only after the Court is satisfied that there are no other alternative policies available to a Government to accomplish its purposes which would impinge on human freedom less. In a sense the two principles are ordered "lexically".[67] The Court weighs the public interest promoted by a law against the constraints it imposes on personal freedom only after it has passed the second proportionality principle of alternative means. When the Court fails to respect this ordering and does the balancing in the first, interpretative phase of the process, however, there is a very real possibility that laws will be validated that could not otherwise meet the second proportionality test. As the liberal judges went to such lengths to explain, that is the lesson of a long list of cases including the *Labour trilogy, Lyons, Holmes, Schwartz*, and *Smith*.[68]

Once again it will be important for reviewers to note that the attitude of each of the judges as to how the public interest underlying a law should be factored into the review process was anything but settled or fixed. In part, no doubt, reflecting the difficulty that all the judges seemed to have with the balancing principle from the beginning, no one on the Court adhered exclusively to one position or the other. As with each of the other limitations we have reviewed, there was a good deal of shifting by all of the judges on this issue. Not infrequently, those who instinctively favoured a conservative and cautious approach concurred in decisions where the interests affected by the law being challenged were balanced in the second

---

67 On the importance of lexical ordering to theories of justice, see J. Rawls, *A Theory of Justice* (Cambridge: Harvard University Press, 1971), p. 42ff.

68 *Supra*, note 2.

part of the review process under section 1. This was especially true in year five, and as a consequence, as often as not, in that year the liberal method prevailed.[69]

On other occasions, however, the instincts of some of the more conservative judges could not be suppressed and on several important occasions, when they could attract the support of more of their colleagues, they were able to carry the day.[70] The *de minimis* rule is perhaps the most widely recognized principle generated by the conservative approach. As we have already noted, on several occasions the failure to meet a quantitative threshold, to show a limitation was substantial enough, was given as a reason by one or other of the judges to dismiss a challenger's complaint.[71] Perhaps the most dramatic example of how the conservative position might carry a case was the Court's decision in *Re Jones*.

Jones was the case, it will be recalled, in which the constitutionality of Alberta's school law was challenged on the ground that it interfered with the rights and freedoms guaranteed in section 2(a) and section 7 of the Charter. We have already seen how the Court divided on the first part of Jones' claim. Both Bertha Wilson and Gerard La Forest wrote judgments dismissing the challenge with Wilson, uncharacteristically, adopting the more conservative approach. She ruled that the law did not in fact limit Jones' religious freedom in any way and even if it did, it was such a trivial and insubstantial restriction that it did not warrant protection under the Charter. In the latter ruling Wilson was, of course, doing the balancing in defining what interests and activities were protected by section 2(a). Essentially she was saying that if the interference with a constitutional guarantees is only minimal, if it is trivial, the Court should not exercise its powers of review.

Earlier we noticed how the conservative judges, Jean Beetz, William McIntyre and Gerald Le Dain sided with Wilson rather than La Forest in dealing with this aspect of Jones' complaint. When she performed the balancing function, in defining what entitlements the right to religious

---

69 See, e.g., *R. v. Thomsen, R. v. Whyte, R. v. Hufsky, Canadian Newspapers, Ford v. Quebec, R. v. Turpin*, supra, note 3; *B.C.G.E.U. v. A.G. B.C.*, supra, note 26 (on s. 2(b)); *Andrews v. Law Society of B.C.*, supra, note 2.

70 See, e.g., *R. v. Corbett, R. v. Simmons, R. v. Jones, R. v. Lyons*, Extradition trilogy, supra, note 2; *R. v. Beare/Higgins* (1988), 55 D.L.R. (4th) 481; *B.C.G.E.U. v. A.G. B.C.* (on s. 7), supra, note 26; *R. v. Potvin*, [1989] 1 S.C.R. 525; *R. v. Strachan* (1988), 56 D.L.R. (4th) 673.

71 See, e.g., *B.C.G.E.U. v. A.G. B.C.*, supra, note 26; *R. v. Simmons, R. v. Jones* and the Extradition trilogy, supra, note 2; *Irwin Toy v. Quebec*, supra, note 35; *R.W.D.S.U. v. Dolphin Delivery*, supra, note 21, holding that violent forms of expression are not protected by s. 2(b). See also Bertha Wilson in *Reference re s. 94(2) Motor Vehicle Act*, supra, note 64; and *Operation Dismantle* (1985), 18 D.L.R. (4th) 481; and Brian Dickson in *Edwards Books*, supra, note 2.

freedom guaranteed, she attracted their support. What we did not observe, however, is that when she abandoned that approach, as she did when she addressed Jones' section 7 complaint, the three conservative judges withdrew their endorsement and on this issue aligned themselves with Gerard La Forest.

On this part of Jones' claim, it was La Forest and not Wilson who invoked the balancing principle to define what entitlements section 7 guaranteed. Basically, La Forest rejected Jones' claim that his liberty had been violated because in his view the Province's interest, in creating the most effective administrative procedures to control its school system, was much more compelling and weighed much heavier in the balance than the very small infringement of Jones' liberty that was compromised by the Alberta law. Balancing the public interest in the first phase of the review process allowed La Forest to attract the support of Beetz, McIntyre, and Le Dain and on this issue it was his, not Bertha Wilson's judgment, which formed the majority decision. In the result, even though neither Beetz, McIntyre nor Le Dain wrote a judgment in the case, they were able to control the final decision of the Court simply by shifting their support according to which of the other two judges employed the more conservative approach.

Jones is an important case because it provides such a clear example of how, led by the more conservative judges, the Court embraced a line of reasoning which had the effect of constraining, rather than extending, the Charter's reach. As a matter of constitutional law, *Jones* stands for the proposition that the Charter offers no protection against limitations on personal freedom which, in the judgment of the Court, are trivial or insignificant compared to the public interest involved. *Jones* is also important because it reinforces Bertha Wilson's position as the most liberal member of the Court. Notwithstanding her treatment of Jones' claim, that his religious freedom had been infringed, the case actually shows that of all the judges on the Court, she was most committed to the Charter and the liberal approach.[72]

In the first place, in *Jones* Wilson shows again that she is the member of the Court most willing to define the rights and freedoms guaranteed in the Charter in a large and liberal way.[73] Anticipating her judgment in *Morgentaler*, Wilson ruled that section 7 protected a person's liberty to educate his or her children because that is a "matter central to the individual's sense of self and/or his place in the world". As well, in her

---

72 See note 32, *supra*.
73 For a similar assessment see Marc Gold, "Of Rights and Roles", *supra*, note 16. For an extra-judicial justification of this position, see her essay, "The Making of a Constitution — Approaches to Judicial Interpretation", 1988 Public Law 370.

judgment in *Jones*, she shows that in the second phase of the review process she is usually the most demanding. She was the only member of the Court, it will be recalled, who was prepared to sustain Jones' claim on the ground that the Government of Alberta had failed to adduce sufficient evidence to prove that the administrative powers adopted in the Act, and objected to by Jones, were necessary to accomplish its objectives.

Both lines of reasoning adopted by Wilson in her decision in *Jones* are typical of her approach to how the Court's powers of review should be applied. As reviewers will recall from their consideration of the *Morgentaler* case, it was not uncharacteristic of her to press for the most liberal and wide-ranging definition of the rights and freedoms which the Charter protected. Even at the end of the performance, when the Court first turned its mind to the equality guarantee in section 15, Wilson can be seen reminding her colleagues of the importance of reading the Charter in a way which will allow it to grow and be responsive to future needs.[74] Neither the conservatives nor even her fellow liberals were as vigilant in using the purposive approach to define the aspects of human freedom which the Charter guaranteed in the rights and freedoms it entrenched. In the two years following its decision in *Oakes*, the conservatives frequently abandoned the model.[75] In some of the cases we have reviewed, it was said that the purposeful method was either inappropriate,[76] or must not be taken too far.[77] In others it was simply ignored.[78] Even Dickson and Lamer had significant relapses and both, on occasion, read the rights and

---

74 *Andrews v. Law Society of B.C.*, *supra*, note 2. See also *U.S.A. v. Cotroni*, *supra*, note 25, where, in a case handed down early in year six, Wilson again distinguished herself by reading the mobility rights set out in s. 6 more liberally than anyone else.

75 To say the conservatives frequently abandoned the liberal method is not to say that they never returned to the model they helped develop in the first two years. In important cases such as *Ford v. Quebec*, *supra*, note 3, and *Black v. Law Society of Alberta* (1986), 58 D.L.R. (4th) 319, they unquestionably adhered to the purposeful approach. As well, on many other occasions they certainly mouthed allegiance. See, e.g., Beetz in *A.G. Manitoba v. Metropolitan Stores* (1987), 38 D.L.R. (4th) 321; McIntyre in *Andrews v. Law Society of B.C.*, *R. v. Morgentaler* and the *Labour trilogy*, *supra*, note 2. See also *R. v. Amway Corp.* (1989), 56 D.L.R. (4th) 311.

76 *Les Acadiens*, *supra*, note 2.

77 See, e.g., McIntyre in *Reference re Alberta Public Service Employee Relations Act* (p. 217), and *R. v. Morgentaler* (p. 467), *supra*, note 2.

78 See, e.g., *R. v. Mills*, and the *Labour* and *Extradition trilogies*, *supra*, note 2. See also *R.W.D.S.U. v. Dolphin Delivery*, *supra*, note 21. In *Dolphin Delivery*, the Court abandoned the purposeful approach in interpreting the word "government" in s. 32 of the Charter to exclude the judicial branch. Had the Court been vigilant in "ensuring the unremitting protection of human rights" there would be no doubt that word should be given the meaning it generally receives in political and legal circles. For a similar assessment of the Court's retreat from the purposeful approach, see A. Petter and P. Monahan, "Development in Constitutional Law", *supra*, note 1.

freedoms in the Charter in very illiberal and restrictive ways.[79]

Although her record was not perfect,[80] Bertha Wilson unquestionably was the member of the Court who remained most faithful to the idea that each of the rights and freedoms should be understood in terms of the larger purposes and values on which the Charter was based. She interpreted each of the entitlements entrenched in the Charter as ways of helping to ensure that each person enjoyed such freedoms as were necessary to allow him to "develop and realize his potential to the full, to plan his own life to suit his own character, to make his own choices for good or ill, to be non-conformist, idiosyncratic and even eccentric — to be, in today's parlance, 'his own person' and accountable as such".[81] Similarly, where Dickson and Lamer were inclined to see each of the rights and freedoms in the Charter as being independent and guaranteeing separate sets of interests and activities, she was more committed to a flexible approach which would allow for overlap and growth between the different rights and freedoms which the Charter guaranteed.[82] Finally, of all the judges she was the most rigorous in insisting that the two phases of the review be kept analytically distinct and that questions of justification and consideration of the public interest not limit the reach of the rights and freedoms which the Charter guarantees.[83]

As well as being inclined to read the rights and freedoms in the Charter more liberally than anyone else, Wilson also took the most rigorous position in stipulating how a law, which did impinge on a constitutional guarantee, could be justified against the proportionality principles in section 1. In

---

79 See the judgments of Antonio Lamer in *Les Acadiens* and Brian Dickson in *B.C.G.E.U. v. A.G. B.C.*, *supra*, note 26. Note also the concurring vote cast by Brian Dickson in the *Extradition trilogy* and *R. v. Lyons*. Cf. the joint opinions they authored in *R. v. Mills* and *R. v. Rahey*, *supra*, note 2.

80 Her most serious lapses, in my view, were in not completely disassociating herself from William McIntyre's judgment's in *Dolphin Delivery*, *supra*, note 21, and *Andrews v. Law Society of B.C.*, *supra*, note 2.

81 *R. v. Jones*, *supra*, note 2. Compare her position on economic interests in *R. v. Rahey*, *supra*, note 2, at 504, with Dickson in *Edwards Books; Public Service Alliance v. R.* and *Government of Saskatchewan v. R.*, *supra*, note 2. See also her article "The Making of a Constitution: Approaches to Judicial Interpretation", 1988 Public Law 370. For a different, and in my view incorrect, reading of Wilson's judgments and her commitment to a purposeful approach, see W. Conklin, *Images of a Constitution* (Toronto: University of Toronto Press, 1989), p. 149.

82 See, e.g., *R. v. Mills, R. v. Rahey, R. v. Smith*, *supra*, note 2, and *R. v. Carter* (1986), 29 D.L.R. (4th) 309. See also *R. v. Strachan* (1989), 56 D.L.R. (4th) 673, 696; *R. v. Simmons* (1988), 55 D.L.R. (4th) 673; *R. v. Jacoy*, [1988] 2 S.C.R. 548. In year six, Wilson again stood alone in advocating a flexible approach in *R. v. Debot*, [1989] 2 S.C.R. 1140.

83 See, e.g., *R. v. Big M Drug Mart*, *supra*, note 33, *Reference re s. 94(2) Motor Vehicle Act*, *supra*, note 64; *R. v. Strachan*, *supra*, note 70. See also her judgment for the Court in *R. v. Turpin*, [1989] 1 S.C.R. 1296. See also Chapter 4, note 71, *infra*.

addition to her judgment in *Jones*, there were several other occasions on which she stood alone, rejecting a Government's attempt to justify a law which had been found to interfere with some person's constitutional rights, for the reason that it had not given the Court enough evidence to support the claims it was making. For example, in *Edwards Books*, she was the one member of the Court to find Ontario's Sunday closing law unconstitutional because it only permitted retailers who closed on Saturday to open on Sunday if they had seven or fewer employees. In her view, the Government of Ontario had failed to adduce any evidence to support its position that extending the exemption to anyone who closed on another day of the week would have frustrated the purposes of the Act. As well, in one of the collective bargaining cases, she was the only one to rule that the Saskatchewan law, which had ordered dairy workers to remain on the job, was unconstitutional because it had not been established that an emergency would have been created in the industry if the law had not been passed.[84] In contrast with her position in both of these cases, liberals[85] and conservatives alike said, either that there was enough evidence before the Court to justify the law or, alternatively, as in *Jones*, that the point was so obvious that no evidence was necessary at all.[86]

When all of her judgments are read collectively, it would be impossible for a reviewer not to see that Bertha Wilson's position was unique on the Court. No one reviewing the performance of the Supremes could fail to notice how distinctive her commitment to the model in *Oakes* was from that taken by everyone else.[87] Unquestionably, the contrast is most striking with the method employed by William McIntyre and Jean Beetz. Juxtaposed against their judgments, Wilson's decisions show how widely the spectrum

---

84 She also ruled against the Government's position in *Public Service Alliance v. Canada*, *supra*, note 2, at 272, essentially on the same evidentiary basis. In addition, she wrote a separate concurring opinion in *R.W.D.S.U. v. Dolphin Delivery*, *supra*, note 21, disassociating herself from the majority's judgment in the application of s. 1. See also M. Gold, "Of Rights and Roles", *supra*, note 16.

85 E.g., Dickson in *Edwards Books* and *Government of Saskatchewan v. R.W.D.S.U.*, *supra*, note 2.

86 On at least two other occasions — *Ford v. Quebec*, *supra*, note 3, and *R. v. Thibault*, [1988] 1 S.C.R. 1033 — the whole Court rejected the Government's defence on the basis that no evidence had been put forward to justify its position under s. 1.

It bears repeating that almost immediately after the curtain went up on year six, Bertha Wilson once again had to divorce herself from her colleagues on the question of whether a law allowing for the extradition of a Canadian who could be prosecuted in Canada could be justified under s. 1. See *U.S.A. v. Cotroni*, *supra*, note 25.

87 It should also be noted that, along with Antonio Lamer, she took the most liberal position on the temporal reach of the Charter. See *R. v. Stevens* (1988), 51 D.L.R. (4th) 394; *R. v. Thibault*, [1988] 1 S.C.R. 1033; *R. v. Gamble*, [1988] 2 S.C.R. 595; *R. v. Dubois* (1985), 23 D.L.R. (4th) 503; *Irvine v. R.T.P.C.* (1987), 41 D.L.R. (4th) 429; *R. v. Jack and Charlie* (1985), 21 D.L.R. (4th) 641.

of opinion on the Court had spread and how highly individualistic its style of judging had become by the end of year five. The difference in their attitude towards the reach of the Charter and the scope of their own powers of review, and hers, was the most substantial division within the Court by far. Where she consistently adopted the most liberal and expansive approach to the Charter, and the Court's powers of review, McIntyre and Beetz invariably advanced the most conservative views as to when and how the principles of review outlined in *Oakes* should be applied.[88]

Although the difference between Wilson and the other members of the Court was less dramatic, it was very real nonetheless. No reviewer could fail to be struck by how frequently Wilson took the time and trouble to write a separate opinion in which she endeavoured to differentiate her position even from that of her traditional allies, Brian Dickson and Antonio Lamer. Focusing on Wilson's judgments in the way we have, underscores how, in the years following *Oakes*, each of the nine judges really began to formulate a very personal and particular theory about the Charter and the judicial role in constitutional review.

For the purpose of writing a review of the performance of the Supremes, it is unnecessary to go on at length and in detail about the different approaches developed by each of the judges. From the analysis of the cases we have undertaken so far, general characteristics can be identified in the manner and method of judging performed by each of the other members of the Court. Gerard La Forest, as we have seen, stands out as a conservative of a typically Canadian kind.[89] Like William McIntyre's, his judgments are distinguished by the frequency with which they call on the other members of the Court to adopt an attitude of deference to the other two branches of government. Perhaps more than anyone else, La Forest seemed bothered by the tension that exists between judicial review and our tradition of democracy and the sovereignty of the popular will.[90]

Gerald Le Dain and Willard Estey tended to be less expressive in the judgments they wrote and did not show such a strong affinity for one particular principle or doctrine. On balance, however, no reviewer could doubt their instinctive attraction to the conservative approach to the Charter and their own powers of review. Although, on occasion, they might embrace

---

88 But see note 35, *supra*.
89 On the link between conservatism and a deferential attitude to the political elite, see P. Macklem, "Constitutional Ideologies", *supra*, note 17.
90 The same characterization is made by Lorraine Weinrib in "The Supreme Court of Canada and Section One of the Charter" (1988), 10 S. Ct. L. Rev. 469, and by Marc Gold in his "Of Rights and Roles", *supra*, note 16. In the beginning of year six, La Forest underscored his commitment to a posture of deference by employing it in the application of the second proportionality principle in *Oakes*. See *U.S.A. v. Cotroni*, *supra*, note 25. See generally the text, pp. 59-60, *supra*.

a more liberal approach, or join a judgment with one of their more liberal colleagues,[91] more often than not they could be found adding their signatures to a decision which had the effect of limiting the Charter's reach.

The other two judges, Antonio Lamer and Brian Dickson, we have already noticed generally remained true to the liberal approach although Brian Dickson's commitment seems to have fallen off somewhat towards the end of the performance.[92] More than any other members of the Court, these two shared a common philosophy about judicial review and, in an extraordinary number of cases, signed a common judgment.[93] Although, as we have noticed, each of them abandoned the liberal approach on several important occasions,[94] generally one or both of them could be found allied with Bertha Wilson in trying to extend the model of review the Court had established in *Oakes*.[95] In the challenge initiated by the Societé des Acadiens, and in the freedom of association trilogy, for example, Dickson joined cause with Wilson in arguing for the large and liberal purposive approach that the Court had developed in its first two years. Similarly, Antonio Lamer aligned himself with her in the *Extradition trilogy*, on the question of the retrospective effect of the Charter,[96] and again in a case called *Re Lyons*[97] in which, over their dissents, the rest of the Court upheld the constitutionality of Canada's dangerous offender law. All three were united in pressing the liberal approach against McIntyre, Beetz, Estey, La Forest and Le Dain in arguing, unsuccessfully, for a flexible set of procedures that would allow constitutional challenges to be easily initiated and expeditiously resolved.[98]

---

91 See, e.g., Le Dain in *Edwards Books*, or Estey in *R. v. Spencer* (1983), 21 D.L.R. (4th) 756; *R. v. Milne* (1987), 46 D.L.R. (4th) 487.

92 Once again this positioning on the spectrum seems generally shared by academic commentators. See M. Gold, "Of Rights and Roles", *supra*, note 16; L. Weinrib, "The Supreme Court of Canada and Section One of The Charter", Chapter 2, *supra*, note 69; Peter Russell, *The Judiciary in Canada* (Toronto: McGraw-Hill, 1988), p. 362.

93 But see note 43, *supra*.

94 *Supra*, note 18.

95 On occasion, when Wilson was not assigned to the case, Dickson and Lamer were obliged to carry the liberal banner on their own. See, e.g., *R. v. Holmes*, *R. v. Schwartz*, *supra*, note 2.

96 See, e.g., *R. v. Gamble*, *R. v. Stevens*, *supra*, note 87.

97 *Supra*, note 2.

98 See, e.g., *R. v. Mills*, *R. v. Rahey*, *supra*, note 2; see also *R. v. Smith*, *supra*, note 2.

4

The Review: A First Attempt

For anyone reflecting on what kind of review should be written about the Court's performance over the first five years, it is certain that the highly individualistic style of judging that dominated the Court's decisions in the years immediately following its decision in *Oakes* will be of paramount importance. For many it will be regarded as the most critical feature of the whole show. For everyone it will be hard, if not impossible, to exaggerate the significance of this highly personal approach to the Charter and the role of judicial review. Stylistically, years three and four especially represent a radically new method and philosophy of judging from what the Court used in the first two years and, to a lesser degree, again in year five. The identity of the individual judges was now quite distinct from, and in some sense paramount to that of the group. Individual voices and solo performances had become the norm. The dynamic of decision making within the group had been totally transformed. Pluralism and majority rule replaced collectivism and collegial decision making with, as we have seen, often very dramatic results.

Not only will the shift in the Court's approach to judging the constitutionality of challenged laws figure prominently in any review of the Court's performance of its first five years, it seems unavoidable that it will cast a very negative shadow over what any reviewer can say. The complete turnaround in the Court's style of judging seems certain to find disfavour with reviewers of all stripes. The position of the reviewer after the Court had completed five years working with the Charter seems exactly the opposite of what it was at intermission, at the end of year two. After the Court's decision in *Oakes*, it will be recalled, it seemed almost churlish not to be optimistic and generally positive about the process of judicial review even if one could be critical about the Court's occasional lack of self-awareness and the odd technical mistake. Three years later the situation seems completely the reverse.

Certainly those whose instincts are to believe that written Bills of Rights and judicial review generally enhance the democratic and progressive qualities of liberal democratic systems of government could not be encouraged by the new style of judging.[1] For them the Court's performance over the course of years 3-5 systematically undermines everything which seemed so encouraging in the Court's work up to, and including, its decision in *Oakes*. The Court's new pluralistic style of judging seems to provide uncontrovertible evidence that the sceptics are right. It offers strong support for the sceptics' claim that the meaning of the Charter really is highly subjective and that, in the end, each judge can do pretty much as she or he pleases in deciding whether a law is constitutional or not. As well, the Court's idea of judicial review, as a process in which those who are disadvantaged in the political arena might redress injustices inflicted upon them by and in the name of the State,[2] seemed to have been abandoned, shackled by doctrines and principles that limited its reach. Even though the Court was able to regain some of the cohesion at the very end of the performance,[3] for most believers the optimism which prevailed at the end of year two would be replaced at the end of year five with depression, if not despair. True believers would find it impossible to write rave reviews of the performance they had seen.

Similarly, for those who are instinctively sceptical that there is any merit in written, entrenched bills of rights, the Court's performance could only be described as scandalous. Although sceptics could fairly adopt an "I told you so" attitude in any reviews they wrote, they could only condemn what they had the prescience to foresee. The pluralistic style of judging embraced by the Court might be cause for self-congratulation among sceptics but it could never justify their applauding the Court. For sceptics of law and constitutional review, the fragmentation of views within the Court as to how the Charter should be interpreted and applied, could only offer additional proof of their assertion that law is very subjective and ultimately a matter of each of the judge's personal whim. On virtually every issue faced by the Court, the principles have indeed marched in pairs.[4] How principles like deference and balancing and interpretive rules and sources of meaning, like intention and American law, are used seems, in the end, to be a matter of purely personal choice. For sceptics reviewing

---

1 See, e.g., Lorraine Weinrib, "The Supreme Court of Canada and Section One of the Charter" (1988), 10 S. Ct. L. Rev. 469.

2 *Edwards Books v. R.*, *Slaight Communications v. Davidson*, Chapter 3, *supra*, note 2; *R. v. Turpin*, [1989] 1 S.C.R. 1296.

3 See Chapter 3, *supra*, note 3 and the text at pp. 73-74.

4 Chapter 1, *supra*, note 11.

the performance of the Court, the fragmentation and division among the judges argues for the abolition of, and not applause for, the Charter and the process of constitutional review.[5]

It is true that a reviewer who instinctively believed in the Charter would not have to be quite as negative as one whose gut feeling was to be distrustful of law and judicial review. She could emphasize the fact that in a significant number of decisions handed down in year five, the members of the Court were able to return to the harmonious style of the first two years. Year five could be interpreted as foresaging a return to happier times. In a large number of the cases it decided in that year the Court was able to speak in a single voice. As often as not, the judges did exercise their powers of review in the way the model prescribed. Once again we find the members of the Court stressing the importance of interpreting the Charter purposefully[6] and of keeping the two phases of the review process analytically distinct.[7] In addition, in every case in which it invalidated a law, the Court relied on the principle of alternative means.[8] By contrast, when it came to apply the balancing test against laws regulating drinking and driving or children's advertising, the Court was much more

---

5 Although there have been few calls for the outright abolition of the Charter many sceptics have called for its marginalization in the life of Canadian politics. See, e.g., Michael Mandel, *The Charter of Rights and the Legalization of Politics* (Toronto: Wall & Thompson, 1989); H. Glasbeek, "Workers of the World: Avoid the Charter of Rights" 21 Canadian Dimension (April, 1987), p. 12; A. Hutchinson, "Charter Litigation and Social Change", in R. Sharpe, (ed.) *Charter Litigation* (Toronto: Butterworths).

6 See, e.g., *Andrews v. Law Society of British Columbia* (1989), 56 D.L.R. (4th) 1; *Black v. Law Society of Alberta*, (1989), 58 D.L.R. (4th) 317, and *Ford v. Quebec*, (1988), 54 D.L.R. (4th) 577. It should be noted that although the members of the Court invoked the purposeful method in *Andrews* in interpreting the meaning of s. 15, it simultaneously abandoned this method at a critical juncture in its decision and in so doing rejected the "similarity situated" principle as part of its definition of s. 15. Although the principle is clearly consistent with and indeed a logical derivative of the purposeful approach, the Court treated it and applied it literally (see 56 D.L.R. (4th) 1 at 11-12). For a similar criticism of the *Andrews* case, see M. Gold "Comment: Andrews v. Law Society of British Columbia" (1989), 34 McGill L.J. 1063; W. Black and L. Smith, "Andrews v. Law Society of British Columbia" (1989), 68 Can. Bar Rev. 591, 600. For a description of the purposeful character of the principle, see J. Tussman and J. ten Broek, "The Equal Protection of Laws" (1949), 37 Calif. L. Rev. 341. It was the Court's failure to apply the similarly situated test purposefully that caused it to reject the challenger's claim in *Reference re Validity of Sections 32 and 34 of the Workers' Compensation Act* (1989), 56 D.L.R. (4th) 765.

7 In several important cases it decided toward the end of year five, the Court underscored the importance of keeping the two phases separate. See, e.g., *Andrews v. Law Society of B.C.*, supra, note 6; *Black v. Law Society of Alberta*, supra, note 6; *R. v. Turpin*, [1989] 1 S.C.R. 1296; *Ford v. Quebec*, supra, note 6.

8 *Andrews v. Law Society of B.C.*, *Black v. Law Society of Alberta*, *Ford v. Quebec*, ibid. See also *R. v. Thibault*, [1988] 1 S.C.R. 1033.

deferential to the other two branches of government and it confirmed the reasonableness of the choices that had been made.[9]

As well as the Court's performance in year five, a believer might also single out the performance of Bertha Wilson and the more liberal members of the Court for special mention and applause. Certainly, as we have seen, there is much in their performance to which a believer could point that supports the characterization of the Charter and judicial review as a process by which those who traditionally have not had much influence in the political process can ensure that their interests are given the attention and consideration they deserve. At a personal level, Bertha Wilson's performance was as striking as the role Diana Ross played with "The Supremes".

Had the liberal model of judicial review prevailed over the course of the first five years, members of traditionally disadvantaged linguistic minorities, the working class, as well as those facing extradition hearings and indefinite detention (under dangerous offender laws), all would have secured a measure of respect and justice from the courts that the politicians and their bureaucrats had refused to give.[10] On a liberal understanding of the Charter, litigants would have a constitutional right to be understood in either official language. Judges would have a constitutional duty to be bilingual.[11] If Dickson and Wilson had prevailed, workers would be guaranteed that their right to strike and bargain effectively would not be needlessly impaired.[12] No one would be extraditable by the Canadian Government to a country whose laws did not respect the constitutional entitlements that the Charter guaranteed.[13] Everyone would have the right to have a jury of their peers decide if they were dangerous offenders and so liable to indefinite detention.[14] When the dissenting judgments of Wilson, Dickson, and Lamer are added to cases such as *Morgentaler, Hufsky, Thomsen, Canadian Newspapers, Vaillancourt, Smith, Ford, Andrews, Black*

---

9 *R. v. Hufsky*, [1988] 1 S.C.R. 621; *R. v. Thomsen*, [1988] 1 S.C.R. 640; *R. v. Whyte* (1988), 51 D.L.R. (4th) 581; *Irwin Toy v. Quebec* (1988), 58 D.L.R. (4th) 577. See also *R. v. Canadian Newspapers* (1988), 52 D.L.R. (4th) 690.

10 Persons charged with various criminal offences, including those charged with sexually assaulting children — see *R. v. Stevens* (1988), 51 D.L.R. (4th) 394; and those charged with various weapons offences — see, e.g., *R. v. Holmes* (1988), 50 D.L.R. (4th) 680, and *R. v. Schwartz* (1988), 55 D.L.R. (4th) 1 — would also have received some protection from the Charter had the liberal method prevailed.

11 See *Société des Acadiens du Nouveau-Brunswick v. Assn. of Parents for Fairness in Education* (1986), 27 D.L.R., (4th) 406.

12 See *Labour trilogy*, Chapter 3, *supra*, note 2.

13 See *Extradition trilogy*, Chapter 3, *supra*, note 2, and Wilson's dissent in *Cotroni*, [1989] 1 S.C.R. 1469.

14 See *R. v. Lyons* (1987), 44 D.L.R. (4th) 193.

and *Irwin Toy*,[15] in which their method of review carried the day, there is a good deal of support for the idea that the Charter can exert a progressive influence on our system of government which a believer, who was reviewing the performance, would want to applaud.

A reviewer who was sympathetic to the Charter could also praise Bertha Wilson and her two liberal allies for their sensitivity to the tension that exists when they assume the role of reviewing decisions made by the other two, popularly elected, branches of government. As we have already noted, the reasoning of the liberal judges is as distinctive for its respect of our democratic tradition as it is for its generally progressive effect. Consistent with the practice we observed in the Court's own performance in the first two years (and again in year five), time and again a decision of Wilson, Lamer or Dickson to strike down a portion of law was made on the narrowest possible grounds so as to leave the Canadian Parliament and provincial legislatures the widest possible room within which to fashion their social policies. In case after case the focus was always on means. *Never* did the Court put a limit on any of the objectives pursued by the legislators in the laws they reviewed. They acknowledged that guaranteeing essential services would always be available in the community, combatting house breaking, impaired driving, dangerous offenders, protecting the linguistic character of a community, regulating advertising, and access to abortion facilities or to practising a profession like law, all were legitimate subjects on which legislatures might formulate social policies. The only restriction was they could not be designed in a way which restricted the constitutional freedoms of those they affected more than necessary. On the liberal method, it was only when alternate policies could be identified which would allow legislators to accomplish their objectives in a way which respected human freedom more, that the judges questioned the sovereignty of Parliament. Beyond this, when they were discussing legislative objectives, and the balance of interests a particular law favoured, the three liberal judges consistently showed a considerable degree of deference to the decisions and choices that the legislators had made.[16] Whether their judgments were written as dissents or, as in year five, they carried the day, there was in fact never a case in which any of the liberal members of the Court questioned the constitutional validity of the law it had been asked to review solely on the basis of the balance of interests that it struck.

A review that concentrated on the decisions the Court handed down in the first two years, and again in year five, and that highlighted the

---

15 See Chapter 3, *supra*, notes 2-3.

16 As noted earlier, Chapter 3, *supra*, note 60, there were isolated instances in which one or other of the judges did seem to impose limits on the legitimate purposes a legislature might pursue — e.g., Wilson and Beetz in *Morgentaler*, Lamer in *Schwartz*.

performance of Bertha Wilson and her liberal allies, would undoubtedly appeal to readers whose instincts about written bills of rights were to believe. That is, after all, what happens when one preaches to the converted. To many readers, however, such a review would be wholly unconvincing and radically incomplete. It would be an exercise in evasion and avoidance. It would fail to address what would be regarded to be one of the most important aspects of the whole show. It would offer no explanation of why the "liberal" view of judicial review had not always prevailed, or why the reasoning favoured by the more conservative judges was not just as valid as the one believers preferred. More demanding and sceptical readers would not be moved unless and until it could be shown, not only that the liberal method of judicial review practised by Wilson, Lamer and Dickson promoted the progressive and democratic character of our system of government, but also that it was the *only* method any member of the Court should follow as a matter of constitutional law.

To write a positive review then, which was credible and could reasonably be expected to be taken seriously by people who were intuitively sceptical of both the law and the Court, a believer could not focus her attention exclusively on the performance of the liberals. She would have to come back and deal with the style and performance of the Supremes as a group. Beyond showing how the judgments of the more liberally inclined members of the Court consistently furthered the progressive and democratic character of our Government, the reviewer would also have to show why, when the Court was persuaded by one of the more conservative judges to abandon the model, it was making a major mistake. Until an effective critique was mounted against the way conservatives conceived of and exercised their powers of review, the sceptical reader could, with some justification, continue to insist on the subjectivity, indeterminacy and ultimately illegitimacy of the Charter and the whole idea of constitutional review.[17]

Unless the reviewer was able to discredit the conservative approach, sceptics would say that, like all law, constitutional review was inherently indeterminate. They would argue that if both the liberal and conservative

---

17 Obviously, to write a critical review, no similar, comparative assessment need be undertaken. Indeed it serves the (sceptical) purposes of such a review to assume that the approaches of each of the judges are equally valid (or more likely defective) as methods of approaching or understanding the Charter. It is this failure to undertake an evaluation of the competing theories of the judges which, in my view, detracts from the persuasiveness of what otherwise are perceptive analyses of the cases. Good examples of reviews of this kind include: Andrew Petter and Patrick Monahan, "Developments in Constitutional Law: The 1986-87 Term" (1988), 10 S. Ct. L. Rev. 61; and Joel Bakan "Constitutional Arguments: Interpretation and Legitimacy in Canadian Constitutional Thought", 27 Osgoode Hall L.J. 123.

approaches were equally valid understandings of what the Charter was all about, each would be available for the judges to use in any future case. It would be up to each judge to choose which method he or she would use to define what the words of the Constitution meant.

Moreover, in response to the rosy picture of the Court's performance in year five which believers would like to paint, sceptics would point out that as often as the Court applied the model in that year, at least one of the judges was prepared to invoke one of the doctrines or analytical techniques favoured by the conservatives to further limit the Charter's reach. Even in year five, the fact is that the earlier decisions in which the conservative approach prevailed were treated as being just as authoritative statements of what the Constitution meant as any the liberals had made. On more than one occasion in the course of year five, the Court ruled that various claims could be dismissed either because the interest for which protection was being sought had not been infringed (or if it had only to an insignificant degree) and/or because it was not the kind of interest or activity that fell within one of the rights or functions that the Charter guaranteed.[18]

In the face of such strong scepticism it would be understandable if, at this point, many reviewers despaired of ever being able to praise the performance of the Court over the first five years it worked with the Charter. It simply isn't true that the Court committed itself to a model of judicial review which generally furthered the progressive and democratic objectives of the system of government it was created to serve.[19] To write a positive, upbeat review in a manageable space would likely seem an impossible task. For many it would be difficult to know even how to begin.

Conceptually, the conservative method seems beyond reproach. As we have observed, at some level there is general agreement that there are limits on how far the Charter can reach. Everyone accepts that there are certain kinds of laws, like other provisions in the Constitution,[20] or those enacted by a foreign government, which cannot be rendered invalid by the process of judicial review. Equally, as the very first case the Court decided makes clear, each of the rights and freedoms entrenched in the

---

18 See, e.g., *R. v. Holmes* (1988), 50 D.L.R. (4th) 680; *R. v. Corbett*, [1988] 1 S.C.R. 670; *R. v. Simmons* (1988), 55 D.L.R. (4th) 673; *R. v. Vermette* (1988), 50 D.L.R. (4th) 385; *B.C.G.E.U. v. A.G. B.C.* (1988), 53 D.L.R. (4th) 1 (ss. 7 and 11); *R. v. Stevens* (1989), 51 D.L.R. (4th) 394; *R. v. Schwartz* (1989), 55 D.L.R. (4th) 1; *Irwin Toy v. Quebec* (1988), 58 D.L.R. (4th) 577 (violent expression). See also *R. v. Beare* (1988), 55 D.L.R. (4th) 481; and *Ref. re Workers' Compensation Act* (1988), 56 D.L.R. (4th) 765.

19 It bears repeating, as the Court pointed out in *R. v. Oakes*, that s. 1 makes the principles of free and democratic societies the ultimate value or "ground norm" on which the Charter is based.

20 See, e.g., *Ref. re an Act to Amend the Education Act, supra*, note 22.

Charter does not protect an unlimited range of interests and activities[21] and, on occasion, it may turn out to be the case that there is no factual basis to support a constitutional challenge.[22] As *Skapinker* illustrates, read purposefully, section 6 only guarantees people the right to move freely within Canada. It does not, either in language or purpose, provide every Canadian a free standing right to work. Interpreted liberally, it was plain that Skapinker had no cause to complain because, on the facts, it was undisputed that his freedom had not been restricted in this way. His physical presence in Ontario was conclusive evidence to the contrary.

There can be no doubt then that the conservatives are on firm ground in insisting that there are limits on how far the Charter can reach. As well, as we observed in the last chapter, everyone also concedes that the major principles, like deference and balancing, which the conservatives favoured when they exercised their powers of review, are integral parts of the model articulated by the Court in *Oakes*. The principles the conservatives relied on to perform their role are unquestionably important components of the method of review the Court endorsed in *Oakes*.

However, even though, at the level of principle, there does not appear to be anything wrong with the conservative approach, many reviewers, I suspect, will instinctively regard it with a sense of misgiving and unease. Certainly when believers reflect on all of the judgments in which the conservative approach has been applied, many will be bothered by the fact that writ large, as it were, this understanding of constitutional review has put an enormous range of law beyond the reach of the Charter. Collectively, the logic of the conservative method would exempt, or substantially shield, from review any law which (i) was not enacted or applied by the legislative or executive branch of the federal or one of the provincial governments; (ii) did not impact directly or in a sufficiently substantial way and/or; (iii) did not affect an interest or activity which the Charter protected. Substantively all foreign law, all common law rules governing the purely private affairs of individuals, as well as some of the most important parts of our laws governing collective bargaining, language, extradition, customs, and sentencing would be insulated from review to a greater or lesser degree.

Even though, at a level of principle, each of these judgments may appear to be on sound footing, collectively, by exempting all of these different areas and types of laws, they would strike many believers as constituting a major compromise of the basic rule that a constitution is

---

21 *Skapinker v. Law Society of Upper Canada* (1984), 9 D.L.R. (4th) 161. See also *R. v. Wigglesworth* (1987), 45 D.L.R. (4th) 235; and *Trimm v. Durham Municipal Police* (1987), 45 D.L.R. (4th) 276.

22 See, e.g., *Les Acadiens, supra,* note 11.

the supreme law in any land.[23] As we have already observed, to say certain kinds or bodies of law do not fall within the reach of the Charter is to place them beyond or above the Constitution itself. Practically, it means that some laws do not have to conform with the principles of justice which the Court identified in *Oakes*. It means that when those with the power to enact, declare and apply laws of these kinds exercise their legal authority, they enjoy a certain immunity from the Constitution and the principles of review it contains.

For most believers, I suspect the most distressing consequence of the conservative understanding of the Court's new role would be that it enables laws to be passed and enforced which needlessly — gratuitously — impair some of the most basic interests and activities in which humans engage. As we saw in the last chapter, on the reasoning of the conservative judges, people could be extradited, or denied the freedom to strike, or the right to have their legal arguments understood in English or French by the person judging their case, or the right to have a jury determine their status as dangerous offenders even though it was not necessary for Governments to limit their rights and freedoms in this way in order to accomplish their policy objectives.

If a reviewer reflects long enough on the cases in which the Court failed or refused to exercise its powers of review, sooner or later she will come to understand how it is that the conservative approach leads to such disturbing results. Eventually all reviewers should be able to see that on virtually every occasion on which the Court, or any individual judge, ruled that the Charter had no application to a challenger's complaint one or other very simple, but in the end quite fatal, mistake was made.[24] Broadly speaking, two kinds of errors can be identified; one interpretive, the other

---

23 In various cases the Court has explicitly referred to and underscored s. 52 of the Charter and the rule of constitutional supremacy. See, e.g., *Hunter v. Southam Inc.* (1985), 11 D.L.R. (4th) 641; *R. v. Big M Drug Mart* (1985), 18 D.L.R. (4th) 321 at 336; *Andrews v. Law Society of B.C.* (1989), 56 D.L.R. (4th) 1; *R. v. Holmes, supra*, note 10; *Ref. re Alberta Public Service Employee and Relations Act* (1987), 38 D.L.R. (4th) 161 (*per* Dickson, p. 193). See also P. Hogg, *Constitutional Law of Canada*, 2nd ed. (Toronto: Carswell, 1985).

24 A few cases, such as *R. v. Turpin*, [1989] 1 S.C.R. 1296, or *Ref. re Workers' Compensation Act, supra*, note 18, might more accurately be described as erroneous because the Court relied on an earlier precedent which was flawed in some way.

In the *Workers' Compensation* case, for example, the Court based its judgment on a finding that blue collar workers and their dependants could not be characterized as a disadvantaged class within the meaning of s. 15, even though in *Andrews* it had held that lawyers who are not landed immigrants or citizens of Canada could be so described. For brief comments on both the *Turpin* and *Workers' Compensation* decisions, see W. Black and L. Smith, "Andrews, "Law Society of British Columbia", 68 Can. Bar Rev. 591, 605.

analytical. If a reviewer reads the cases in which the conservative view held sway carefully enough, she will find one or both of these flaws underlies each judgment in which the Court, or one of its members, ruled that the Charter has no application and frequently she will find both.

The interpretive mistakes all relate to a tendency, especially on the part of the more conservative judges, to abandon the principle of purposeful interpretation and, simultaneously, to have recourse to the sources of meaning which, in the first two years, the Court had identified as being very problematic and of little assistance in helping to understand what the rights and freedoms entrenched in the Charter really meant. In some of the most important cases we reviewed in the last chapter there is simply no reference to the purposeful method of reading the rights and freedoms which were at stake. In several cases, such as *La Societé des Acadiens*[25] and the *Labour trilogy*, a majority of the Court was persuaded to abandon the purposeful approach even when one or more of their more liberal colleagues showed how it should be applied. In other cases, like *Dolphin Delivery*,[26] everyone on the Court simply seemed to forget the method and principles the Court had developed to read the Charter in the first two years. In *Dolphin Delivery*, by completely ignoring the purposeful method of interpretation and the sources of meaning on which it is based, the Court allowed itself to read the word "government" in section 32 of the Charter to mean that the Charter only applied to the legislative and executive branches. Incredibly, it accepted this definition even though it acknowledged that conventionally, both in politics[27] and in law[28] the word "government", at least when it is written in the lower case,[29] is generally understood to embrace the Court — as the third branch of government — as well.[30]

---

25 (1986), 27 D.L.R. (4th) 406.

26 (1987), 33 D.L.R. (4th) 174.

27 See, e.g., Peter Russell, *The Judiciary in Canada: The Third Branch of Government* (Toronto: McGraw-Hill, 1988).

28 See, e.g., P. Hogg, *Constitutional Law of Canada*, 2nd ed. (Toronto: Carswell, 1985), p. 672; D. Gibson, *The Law of the Charter — General Principles* (Toronto: Carswell, 1986), pp. 93-96.

29 Note that in his judgment McIntyre shows he was sensitive to the different meanings implied by the word "government", depending on whether the "g" is capitalized or left in the lower case. He consistently capitalizes the word when he is referring to the executive branch but then fails to pick up on the fact that the Charter uses the word "government" in the lower case (p. 194). See also D. Gibson, *The Law of the Charter, ibid* .

30 It might be noted that even if one interpreted "government" to refer only to the executive branch, the common law rules which govern the affairs of private persons would still fall within the terms of s. 32 because all of the rules devised by judges derive their authority from "Acts of Incorporation", enacted by each of the legislatures across the country. See Brian Slattery, "The Charter's Relevance to Private Litigation: Does Dolphin Deliver" (1986), 32 McGill Law J. 905.

Almost without exception, in every case when the judges moved away from interpreting the Constitution purposefully, they simultaneously turned to the sources of meaning which the Court had stressed were highly problematic in its decisions leading up to *Oakes*. At pivotal points in many of these judgments reference is made to the people who drafted the Charter to support a conclusion that the Charter was not applicable to the law being challenged.[31] In the minds of the conservatives there was no tension in decisions which said that the Charter was not applicable to foreign law, collective bargaining law, common law affecting the purely private affairs of individuals etc., and the rule of constitutional supremacy because, it was said, it was not the intention of those who entrenched the Charter in the Constitution that it should apply to these bodies of law. Almost as frequently, decisions of the American Supreme Court, interpreting parallel provisions of the American Bill of Rights[32] and/or some ordinary rule or regulation of Canadian law[33] were used by the Court to support its decisions that the Charter had no application to a challenger's complaint.[34]

On no occasion in which the Court turned to these alternative sources of meaning did anyone acknowledge, let alone grapple with, any of the difficulties which earlier it had said compromised their utility. Thus, in every one of the judgments in which the Court relied on the intention of the framers as one of the bases for shielding a law from the full force of constitutional review, it ignored all of the theoretical and conceptual

31 See, e.g., *Les Acadiens, supra*, note 25, and the *Labour* and *Extradition trilogies*, Chapter 3, *supra*, note 2; *Dolphin Delivery v. R.W.D.S.U.* (1987), 33 D.L.R. (4th) 174. See also *MacDonald v. City of Montreal* (1986), 27 D.L.R. (4th) 321. Intention was a source of meaning particularly attractive to William McIntyre. See his judgments in *R. v. Smith* (448), *R. v. Morgentaler* (469-470), *R. v. Simmons* and *Ref. re Alberta Public Service Employee Relations Act* (225, 231), Chapter 3, *supra*, note 2. Note also that intention featured prominently in the Court's treatment of the extent to which economic and corporate interests were protected by the Charter — see, e.g., *Irwin Toy v. Quebec* (1989), 58 D.L.R. (4th) 577; *R. v. Amway Corp.* (1989), 56 D.L.R. (4th) 309. For a similar analysis of the Court's treatment of intent as a source of meaning, see M. Gold "Of Rights and Roles": The Supreme Court and the Charter" (1989), 23 U.B.C.L. Rev. 507.

32 American case law played an important part in the Court's reasoning in the *Extradition trilogy, R. v. Jones, R. v. Lyons, R. v. Simmons*, Chapter 3, *supra*, note 2; *R. v. Potvin*, [1989] 1 S.C.R. 52; *R. v. Beare* (1989), 55 D.L.R. (4th) 481.

33 *R. v. Lyons, Extradition trilogy*, McIntyre and Beetz in *R. v. Morgentaler*, Chapter 3, *supra*, note 2; *R. v. Potvin, ibid.* See also M. Gold, "Of Rights and Roles: The Supreme Court and the Charter", *supra*, note 31. And see *R. v. Mills* (1986), 29 D.L.R. (4th) 161.

34 The source of meaning that received the most uniform treatment by the Court was the Canadian Bill of Rights. See, e.g., *Andrews v. Law Society of B.C., supra*, note 23; *R. v. Whyte* (1988), 51 D.L.R. (4th) 481, where, in applying model in *Oakes*, the Court reaffirmed the position it had taken in the first two years that the Canadian Bill of Rights was not a reliable guide to the interpretation of the Charter.

difficulties of using intention as a source of meaning which it had earlier recognized.[35] Compounding this inconsistency, in no case where intention was used as a source of meaning was a shred of evidence offered by anyone to substantiate the claim that those who negotiated, drafted and/or ratified the document really did intend the Charter to be circumscribed in the manner the Court proposed. Indeed, on two occasions the Court ignored or misinterpreted evidence of the "framer's intention" which flatly contradicted the Court's findings.[36]

In a similar fashion, when American authorities were cited to support an interpretation that the Charter, or one of its provisions, was inapplicable to a particular body of law, the Court simply ignored the fact, which it had earlier recognized, that American Courts are constrained to interpret the rights and freedoms in the American Bill of Rights as narrowly as they have because it does not contain a general limitation clause like our section 1.[37] As virtually everyone on the Court recognized, at one time or another,[38] it is on account of this structural difference in the American

---

35 See *Ref. re B.C. Motor Vehicle Act* (1986), 24 D.L.R. (4th) 536 . See text at Chapter 2, pp. 19-22. See also Wilson "The Making of a Constitution and Approaches to Judicial Interpretation", 1988 Public Law 370. Note that the Court appears to have reaffirmed this position at the beginning of year six in *U.S.A. v. Cotroni*, [1989] 1 S.C.R. 1469. But see *Cornell v. R.*, [1988] 1 S.C.R. 461, where the Court relied on the intention of the framers to rule that the principles of fundamental justice could not be interpreted to incorporate the equality guarantees prior to the entrenchment of s. 15.

36 See *Labour trilogy*, Chapter 3, *supra*, note 2; *Dolphin Delivery v. R.W.D.S.U.*, *supra* note 31. On the point at issue in the latter case see, *Proceedings* of Joint House of Commons — Senate Committee, Jan. 15, 1981, 38:50 (Tasse).

37 Most European constitutions are also different from Canada's Charter in this respect and characteristically build in specific limitation clauses to the description of each individual freedom and right. For an introduction to the European jurisprudence and its relevance to the Charter, see B. Hovius, "The Limitation Clauses of the European Convention on Human Rights: A Guide For the Application of Section One of the Charter" (1985), 17 Ottawa L. Rev. 213. See Also J. Claydon, "International Human Rights Law and The Interpretation of the Canadian Charter of Rights and Freedoms", in E. Beloba ba and E. Gertner (eds.), *The New Constitution and the Charter of Rights* (Toronto: Butterworths, 1983); June Ross, "Limitations on Human Rights in International Law: Their Relevance to the Canadian Charter of Rights and Freedoms", 6 Human Rights Quarterly 180. For a description of the work on the European Court generally see J.G. Merrills, *The Development of International Law By The European Court of Human Rights* (Manchester: Manchester University Press, 1988). The Court showed some sensitivity to the European method in *Andrews v. Law Society of B.C.*, *supra*, note 23, at 20.

38 See *Edwards Books, Reference re Alberta Public Service Employee Relations Act* (181), *per* Dickson; *Rahey v. R.*, *per* La Forest, *Andrews v. Law Society of B.C.* (20), *per* McIntyre, *supra* note 23; *R. v. Turpin*, *per* Wilson, *supra*, note 24. See also "The Making of a Constitution — Approaches to Judicial Interpretation", 1988 Public Law 370, 374. Cf. J. Cameron, "The Forgotten Half of Dolphin Delivery: A Comment on The Relationship Between the Substantive Guarantees and Section One of the Charter" (1988), 23 U.B.C.L. Rev. 147, 153.

Constitution that the U.S. Court must apply the equivalent of our proportionality principles when they interpret and define the parameters of the rights and freedoms guaranteed in their constitution.[39] American judges must do all the balancing and consideration of alternative policies available to a Government in deciding what interests or activities, like speech or religion, the Bill of Rights will protect. In the absence of a provision comparable to section 1 of the Charter, the American Court cannot separate the review process into two different parts. As a consequence, American definitions of rights and freedoms which are common to both constitutions will always be narrower and more restrictive than they need be in Canada. They will invariably contain qualitative and quantitative thresholds because there is nowhere else where the public interest can be balanced and weighed.[40]

The way in which the Court approached the interpretation of the Charter in the period immediately following its decision in *Oakes* was,

---

39 It should be noted that there is one other very important difference in how the American Supreme Court applies the proportionality principles. In contrast with the Canadian approach of uniform application, the Americans have created a three tiered system of review — strict, intermediate, and minimal scrutiny — which allows them to differentiate which proportionality principles will apply in any case. Roughly, minimal scrutiny involves an application of the first, rationality test while strict review entails an evaluation against all three measures set out in *Oakes*. In *Andrews v. Law Society of B.C.*, *supra*, note 23 the Court referred to the multi-standard American approach and contrasted it with approach to s. 1 it had developed in *Oakes*.

40 The fact that American constitutional law can be of little or no assistance in defining what interests and activities fall within the protection of the Canadian Charter does not mean it has no role to play whatsoever. Certainly, in the second, justificatory phase of the review process, the American experience of evaluating the constitutionality of laws which are substantially similar to those being reviewed by the Canadian Supreme Court could be of some assistance. As various members of the Court have recognized from time to time, at this stage of their deliberations, American decisions can prove useful in showing, implicitly or explicitly, how others have evaluated the reasonableness of their laws against the principles of proportionality that the Court identified in *Oakes*. A careful analysis of these decisions shows the factors which have been considered by American judges in evaluating whether an American law, which is similar to the one being reviewed by the Court, strikes a reasonable balance between the competing interests it affects. In addition, American case law can provide a source of alternative policies that might have been considered by Canadian legislators when the Court comes to apply the second proportionality principle in *Oakes*.

It should also be recalled that American authorities also provided valuable support for the Court's initial decision to embrace the method of purposeful interpretation. See Chapter 2, p. 18, *supra*. For a discussion of the relevance of other theories of interpretation in vogue in American constitutional law, see Peter Hogg, "The Charter of Rights and American Theories of Interpretation" (1987), 25 Osgoode Hall L.J. 88. For the transplantation of two American theories of constitutional interpretation see P. Monahan, *Politics and The Constitution* (Toronto: Carswell, 1987) and M. Gold, "The Rhetoric of Rights: The Supreme Court and The Charter", 25 Osgoode Hall L.J. 375.

undoubtedly, an important reason why it never confronted the tension between its decision to shield numerous laws from judicial review and the principle of constitutional supremacy. On the interpretive approach it was following, the constitutional supremacy of the Charter was not undermined by decisions which put various kinds of laws beyond any effective or meaningful form of review. A literal reading of the words of the Constitution, American authorities and the presumed intention of those who entrenched the Charter, all seemed to support the idea that these were the kinds of laws which were beyond, or not fully subject to, the Court's powers of review.

Interpretive method was not, however, the only, or even the most important reason why the Court drew the limits around the Charter as tightly as it did and why it failed to recognize the growing inconsistency between decisions which put more and more laws beyond the reach of the Charter and the principle of constitutional supremacy. In addition to its interpretive errors, the Court committed a series of factual and analytical mistakes as well. Flaws in its reasoning process, even more than its interpretive approach, caused the Court to impose much stricter limits on the reach of the Charter than its constitutional status warranted.

A close reading of all the decisions of the Court which employed the conservative approach shows that almost every one is afflicted by one (or more) of three different kinds of mistakes. Almost without exception, in every case in which the Court failed or refused to evaluate a law according to the principles it had established in *Oakes* the same mistakes are made again and again. In a small number of cases the Court committed an error which we might call "denial". Here reviewers will discover the Court asserting that there was no factual basis for a constitutional challenge even when there was no evidence to support such a ruling. In a second group of cases, the Court's mistake consisted in "avoiding" rather denying the factual basis of the challenger's claim. Here the Court will be found basing its decision that the Charter had no application to the case before it on irrelevant facts, as opposed to no facts at all. Finally, in the third and by far the largest set of cases, it is apparent that it was only because the Court failed to keep the two stages of the review process separate and analytically distinct that it concluded that a challenger's constitutional rights had not been limited by the law it had been asked to evaluate. For convenience we might refer to the mistake in these cases as the Court failing to exercise fully, or "abdicating", its powers of review.

1. DENIAL

Unquestionably "denial" was the most basic of the three different kinds of mistakes made by the Court. Denying that a claimant's constitutional rights had been infringed essentially involved the Court making a factual assertion that the laws being challenged did not interfere with the claimants' freedom in the way that they said. Now in principle, as we have observed, no one would dispute that in some circumstances it is perfectly proper for the Court to dismiss a challenge on this basis. We saw an example of this possibility in a case like *Skapinker*. There, it will be recalled, Skapinker could not make any claim that his physical mobility had been restricted by Ontario's *Law Society Act* because he was already living in Ontario and so it was perfectly proper for the Court to dismiss *his* challenge on the basis that *his* constitutional freedoms had not been limited in fact. Similarly it seems, from the report of the case, that the members of *La Societé des Acadiens* never did establish that their right to be understood by the judge hearing their case had been infringed.[41] On other occasions, however, the Court dismissed constitutional challenges on this basis when there was no evidence to support such a ruling and even when all the evidence before the Court was to the contrary. Although not a frequent occurrence, it can be seen that mistakes of this kind figured crucially in a number of the judgments which we have highlighted in the last chapter.

Perhaps the clearest example of where the Court moved from an assertion of fact that was patently false, to the conclusion that the Charter had no application to the law it had been asked to review, was its decision in *Jones*. In that case, it will be recalled, Bertha Wilson, along with three of the more conservative members of the Court, ruled that Jones' challenge under section 2(a) of the Charter could not be sustained because, in their view, Alberta's school law did not limit or impinge on his religious freedom in any way. They said the law enhanced, not constrained, religious freedom because it allowed for the creation of alternative and religious schools. For them, there was no question of Alberta's school law being in conflict with the Charter, or the principle of constitutional supremacy, because it simply did not interfere with Jones' religious freedom in any way.

It is not difficult to see why, both factually and constitutionally, it was wrong for these judges to deny that Alberta's school law did require Jones to compromise his religious beliefs. As a factual matter, a reviewer could only describe the majority's decision in *Jones* as grossly deficient. There was not a shred of evidence to which anyone on the Court could

---

41 See also *Canadian Newspapers v. R.* (1989), 52 D.L.R. (4th) 690, where the Court ruled that, on the facts of the case, it was impossible to say the accused was denied the right to have his guilt or innocence established in a public hearing and *Edwards Books and Art Ltd. v. R.* (1987), 35 D.L.R. (4th) 1, where the Court refused to rule whether Ontario's *Retail Business Holidays Act* infringed the religious freedom of Hindus or Muslims, due to the lack of cogent evidence that had been adduced on this aspect of the case.

point to support a finding that Alberta's law did not interfere with Jones' religious freedom in the way that he claimed. There was nothing that could cast doubt on the sincerity of his religious belief. The only evidence before the Court was Jones' own uncontested claim that, by requiring him to apply and secure the approval of the educational authorities, the Alberta law seriously interfered with his religious beliefs. In these circumstances, it was simply undeniable that, by forcing him to concede that the State, rather than God, had the final authority over the education of his children, he was acting contrary to his religious beliefs.

In writing a judgment that was not supported in any way by the evidence before the Court, Wilson and her colleagues committed more than a factual mistake. By reasoning this way, these judges caused the Court itself to act unconstitutionally. By rejecting the factual basis of his claim, when there was nothing before the Court to support such a ruling, the Court impugned his sincerity and failed to show him the kind of respect on which the Charter and free and democratic societies are built. For the Court to say that the procedure which required Jones to apply to the school authorities had no religious significance, was to deny him the very religious freedom which the Charter protects.[42]

This pattern of reasoning, of denying that a person's constitutional freedoms have been limited because of an erroneous finding or assumption of fact, is evident in several other judgments written by individual judges over the course of the first five years, and was adopted by the Court as a whole on a number of occasions in addition to its judgment in *Jones*.[43]

---

42 For a pre-Charter case in which the Ontario Court of Appeal avoided this posture see *Donald v. Hamilton Board of Education*, [1945] O.R. 518. Commenting favourably on this decision, Neil Finkelstein has written, "…. freedom of religion is always best preserved when the Courts accept a complainant's contention of religious principle at face value (assuming good faith) and move on to the next stage of weighing whatever conflicting public interest might be involved." See "The Relevance of Pre-Charter Case Law for Post-Charter Adjudication" in E. Belobaba and E. Gertner (eds.), *The New Constitution and The Charter of Rights* (Toronto: Butterworths, 1983).

43 *R. v. Vermette* (1988), 50 D.L.R. (4th) 385; *R. v. Holmes* (1988), 50 D.L.R. (4th) 680; *R. v. Corbett*, [1988] 1 S.C.R. 670; *R. v. Schwartz* (1988), 55 D.L.R. (4th) 1. See also McIntyre's judgment in *Public Service Alliance v. Canada* (1986), 38 D.L.R. (4th) 177 and *R. v. Morgentaler* (1988), 44 D.L.R. (4th) 385.

As noted, in two early decisions in year six, the Court grounded its decision to dismiss a challenge on erroneous findings of fact. In *Moysa v. Lab. Rel. Board* (1989), 60 D.L.R. (4th) 1, the Court ruled there was no factual basis for a journalist's claim that an order by a labour board compelling him to testify interfered with the freedom of the press, while in *Mackay v. Manitoba* (1989), 61 D.L.R. (4th) 385, the Court dismissed a challenge to the provisions in Manitoba's election financing law which compensated candidates and parties with a percentage of their election expenses from the public purse on the same basis. For a discussion of the merits of the ruling in the latter case, see *infra*, Part Two, Chapter 6, pp. 156-160.

Indeed, in one case the Court went even further than it did in *Jones*. In *Operation Dismantle* all of the judges, except Bertha Wilson, held not only that the members of the anti-nuclear coalition had failed to prove that the Government's decision to allow the testing of the cruise missiles would adversely affect their lives and the security of their persons, but also that it would *never* be possible for them to do so. According to the majority of the Court, if the claims put forward by Operation Dismantle were to succeed, it would have to be established that independent and sovereign nations, such as the USSR, would react to the testing of the cruise missiles in ways that would increase the risk of Canada's exposure to a nuclear war. In the view of the majority, that was a claim which was incapable of proof. Because, in their minds, the members of Operation Dismantle could *never* prove the factual basis of their case, the judges ruled that the challengers were not entitled to have even a day in Court.

As a statement of fact, the Court's position in *Operation Dismantle* is even more extreme and less tenable than its ruling in *Jones*. As others have already pointed out,[44] it is easy to imagine ways in which the members of Operation Dismantle might have gone about proving that the testing of cruise missiles in Canada would increase the risk of Canada's exposure to a nuclear attack and therefore represent an additional threat to their lives and to the security of their persons. They might, for example, have tried to call the Soviet Ambassador to Canada as a witness or attempted to secure documentary evidence from the Soviet Government and/or academic institutions to establish that the Soviet Union was, or would, consider responding to the testing of cruise missiles in Canada in ways that would increase the risk to Canada in the event of a nuclear war. Even though such evidence might be difficult to obtain and might eventually be discredited in Court, the *possibility* that credible evidence of that kind could be secured makes the Court's ruling that Operation Dismantle's claim was impossible to prove patently false.[45] The irony of the Court's decision in *Operation Dismantle* is that it dismissed the claim of the anti nuclear

---

44 M. Rankin and A. Roman, "A New Basis for Screening Constitutional Questions Under the Canadian Charter of Rights and Freedoms: Prejudging the Evidence?" (1987), 66 Can. Bar Rev. 365; Pat Monahan, *Politics and the Constitution, supra,* note 40, at 61. See also Michael Mandel, *Charter of Rights and the Legalization of Politics in Canada* (Toronto: Wall & Thompson, 1989), pp. 64-71. Bill Conklin, another critic of the Court's decision in *Operation Dismantle,* made the point by noting that "Dickson's delimitation of law to scientific fact logically compels him to wait for a nuclear 'accident'/holocaust before speculation, hypothesis or values transform into 'fact' and thereby become a ripe subject of constitutional investigation"; See *Images of a Constitution* (Toronto: University of Toronto Press, 1989), p. 148.

45 The fact that challengers might never be able to prove with absolute certainty that the risk to their persons would eventually materialize would not be fatal to their case. Early and often, the Court made it clear that showing a constitutional right was *threatened*

group on the ground that it could never prove the factual basis of its case even though in doing so the Court itself relied on an assertion which was incapable of proof.

2. AVOIDANCE

It was not a common occurrence for the Court simply to reject the factual basis of a challenger's claim without offering anything more than a flat denial. More commonly, whenever the Court dismissed a constitutional challenge on the ground that it had no basis in fact, it embellished its reasoning by what one might call a strategy of avoidance. In effect, in these cases, the Court distracted itself by concentrating on characteristics of the challenged law that were not strictly relevant to the claim being made. Rather than having no factual grounding, these decisions were based on facts that were not really responsive to the challenger's claim. Even in *Jones*, one can see how, by emphasizing the ways Alberta's school law actually promoted religious freedom in the province overall, the Court failed to see, and ultimately denied, that it could simultaneously restrict Jones' religious freedom in other ways. In other cases, by "reasoning" in this way, the Court, or one of its members, failed to see how a law could limit a person's constitutional freedom indirectly or indeed without any involvement by the executive or legislative branches of Government.[46]

---

was sufficient to establish a claim. See *Hunter v. Southam Inc.* (1985), 11 D.L.R. (4th) 641; *R. v. Big M Drug Mart, supra,* note 23, at 354; *Singh v. M.E.I.,* (1985) 17 D.L.R. (4th) 422, at 460; *Valente v. R.* (1986), 24 D.L.R. (4th) 161; *Ref. re s. 94(2) Motor Vehicle Act* (1986), 24 D.L.R. (4th) 536 at 554; *R. v. Thomsen,* [1988] 1 S.C.R. 640; *R. v. Morgentaler, supra,* note 43. See also *R. v. Smith* (1987), 40 D.L.R. (4th) 435; *Mills v. R.,* (1986), 29 D.L.R. (4th) 161; *Rahey v. R.* (1987), 39 D.L.R. (4th) 481.

In theory, it is possible that the Court might have relied on the difficulty the challengers would have in proving their case to dismiss their challenge in the second stage of the review process in s. 1. Here the argument would be that the time and resources needed by the challengers to make out their case were so extensive and the risk to their freedom so small that the Court should allocate its scarce resources on more pressing and substantial claims. Although considerations of administrative cost and convenience might provide a reason for the Court to come to the conclusion it did, it would provide no justification for the assertion that the challengers' constitutional guarantees had not been threatened in the way that they claimed.

46 In addition to the cases discussed in the text one can discern this technique being applied in *R. v. Simmons, supra,* note 18 where the Court relied on the fact that no one, in the circumstances of the challenger, would be surprised by being searched to avoid dealing with the complaint that the search was still unreasonable. (Cf. *R. v. Hufsky,* [1989] 1 S.C.R. 621). See also *R. v. Potvin, supra,* note 33, where the Court dismissed the challenger's claim that his interests were prejudiced by the trial judge not being able to assess a

Perhaps the clearest example of how a strategy of avoidance could cause a judge to miss the indirect coercion a law can impose can be seen in the concurring judgment Jean Beetz and William McIntyre wrote in *Edwards Books*. In this case, it will be recalled, the Court was faced with a claim by a number of retailers whose religious holiday fell on a Saturday and who claimed that, by prohibiting them from doing business on Sunday, Ontario's *Retail Business Holidays Act* put pressure on them to compromise an important tenet of their religious beliefs by remaining open on a day their religion said they should rest. They said that this law constituted a major inducement for them to work on their Sabbath because, if they didn't, they would be conceding a significant competitive advantage (and profits) to retailers whose philosophical and/or religious beliefs inclined them to treat Saturday no differently than any other day of the week. In prohibiting them from working on a day they would otherwise be free to sell, the Sunday closing law operated like an indirect tax. In the complainants' minds, the Act put them in the unfair and untenable position of having to choose between (i) renouncing their religious beliefs and staying open on Saturday, or (ii) renouncing their business interests and remaining closed on that day.

In dismissing their complaint, Jean Beetz and William McIntyre focused all of their attention on the second of the two choices the retailers said they faced. Concentrating on the situation that would occur if the retailers adhered to their religious beliefs and stayed closed on their sabbath, Beetz and McIntyre reasoned that in these circumstances whatever financial loss they suffered would be caused by their religious beliefs rather than any feature of Ontario's Sunday closing law. From this premise, Beetz and McIntyre moved directly to the conclusion that the retailers' complaint should be dismissed. Because the Ontario law did not impose any financial loss on the retailers, they said it was not coercive or limiting of the retailers' religious freedom and so not subject to review under the Charter.[47]

---

witness' credibility on the ground he might have benefitted from this circumstance. And see *Moysa v. Labour Relations Board* and *Mackay v. Manitoba, supra*, note 43.

Once again, even when the Court as a whole resisted adopting this approach, individual judges might succumb. Not surprisingly, William McIntyre seemed to follow this line of reasoning more frequently than anyone else. See his judgments in *R. v. Dyment* (1988), 55 D.L.R. (4th) 503; *R. v. Schwartz, R. v. Morgentaler, supra*, note 43; and *Black v. Law Society of Alberta* (1989), 58 D.L.R. (4th) 319. See also Gerald Le Dain in the *Labour trilogy* focuses his attention on two interests which s. 2(d) protects and fails to address the interests for which protection was being sought.

47 The inspiration for this line of reasoning was an essay written by Andrew Petter, " 'Not Never on a Sunday': *R. v. Video Flicks Ltd.*", 49 Sask. L. Rev. 96. It is repeated in A.

The fallacy in this reasoning is easy to see. It illustrates clearly how the method of avoidance works. At the base of their analysis, Beetz and McIntyre begin with an assumption with which there is little to quarrel. It seems unquestionably true that if any of the persons challenging Ontario's Sunday closing law chose to close their business on Saturday, any financial loss they suffered would be caused by their own decision to respect the tenets of their religious faith rather than by anything contained in the Ontario law. However, it seems equally obvious that the whole focus of Beetz and McIntyre's judgment is entirely irrelevant to the essence of the retailers' complaint. Their judgment focuses exclusively on the second half of the Hobson's choice the retailers faced from Ontario's law and ignores and avoids the first. The major thrust of the retailers' claim was that by forcing them to remain closed on Sunday, the Ontario law put enormous pressure on them to remain open — not closed — on Saturday and in so doing renounce practices that were central to the requirements of their religion. By focusing all of their attention on the choice of the retailers who decided to *stay closed* on Saturday, Messrs. Beetz and McIntyre never confronted, indeed they denied the existence of, the coercion Ontario's law exerted on the others who decided to subordinate their religious beliefs to their economic interests by *remaining open* and doing business on a day that their religion said should be set aside for matters of religious and spiritual contemplation.

In *Edwards Books* only Beetz and McIntyre were distracted by this line of reasoning and so it did not affect the outcome of the case.[48] A majority of the judges recognized that Ontario's law did put pressure on the retailers, whose religious day of rest was other than Sunday, to *stay open* on those days and to compromise their religious beliefs. Even though the pressure the law exerted was indirect, the majority had no doubt that it was just as real and coercive as if it had been applied directly. As Brian

---

Petter and P. Monahan, "Developments in Constitutional Law: The 1986-87 Term" (1988), 10 S. Ct. L. Rev. 61. As we shall see this phenomenon, of being led astray by arguments made by legal academics, features prominently in two other important decisions rendered by the Court in this period. See *Dolphin Delivery Ltd. v. R.W.D.S.U.* (1987), 33 D.L.R. (4th) 174 relying on articles by Kathy Swinton and Walter Tarnopolsky to aid in the interpretation of s. 32; and the *Labour trilogy*, Chapter 3, *supra*, note 2 (*per* McIntyre), relying on an essay by Peter Gall as to the scope of s. 2(d).

48 Note however that it did control the decision in *Robertson and Rosetanni v. R.* (1963), 41 D.L.R. (2d) 485 where the Court ruled Sunday closing laws did not violate the Canadian Bill of Rights. See N. Finkelstein, "The.Relevance of Pre-Charter Case Law for Post-Charter Adjudication" (1983), 4 S. Ct. L. Rev. 267, 272.

Dickson explained, given the purposes which the Charter is meant to serve, it simply does not matter whether the coercive burden of a law is direct or indirect, intentional or unintentional, foreseeable or unforeseeable. "All coercive burdens", he said, "fall to be evaluated against the principles and values which the Charter contained".[49]

On other occasions, however, the strategy of avoidance appealed to everyone on the Court and when that happened, it resulted in very serious limitations being imposed on the Charter's reach. The first time this happened was in the case of *Spencer v. R.* This, it will be recalled, was the case involving the Canadian who had formerly been a bank manager in the Bahamas and who had been called to give evidence about his dealings with one of the bank's clients who had been charged with violating Canada's *Income Tax Act.* Spencer claimed that he was confronted with the same kind of Hobson's choice faced by the retailers in *Edwards Books.* Either he could testify, thereby violating Bahamian law and risking criminal charges and possible imprisonment in the Bahamas, or he could refuse to testify and face the possibility of contempt proceedings in Canada.

As we noticed in the last chapter, the Court gave very short shrift to Mr. Spencer's counsel on this point.[50] The Court was unanimously of the view that it was really the Bahamas' bank laws and not Canada's evidence laws which threatened Spencer's liberty and the security of his person. In reaching this conclusion, however, the Court paid almost no attention to the Canadian law under which Spencer was being forced to testify. In one sentence, it dismissed the factual basis of his claim on the ground that, "The infringement of Mr. Spencer's liberty or security of the person, if any, does not result from the operation of Canadian law, but *solely* from the operation of Bahamian law in the Bahamas" (emphasis added).

---

49 This was a position the Court had adopted prior to *Oakes,* see *R. v. Big M Drug Mart, supra,* note 23, at 354, and which the liberals also embraced in *Singh v. M.E.I.* (1985), 17 D.L.R. (4th) 422. It was also embraced explicitly by La Forest in *Edwards Books, supra,* note 41, at 65, and in the *Extradition trilogy* when he considered the extent to which the Charter would apply to a decision of the Executive branch to actually extradite someone from the country.

50 Spencer's counsel was John Sopinka who was appointed to fill the vacancy left by the retirement of Gerald Le Dain at the end of year four. Having made the argument in *Spencer,* it would be reasonable to assume that Sopinka will not hesitate to exercise his powers of review in future cases in which the coercive effect of the law is indirect. But see *Moysa v. Labour Relations Board, supra,* note 43.

With its mind focused on the Bahamian law, the Court was naturally led to the conclusion that Spencer's complaint was completely unfounded. In the Court's mind, it was clear that the Charter offered no protection against threats made by foreign governments. As we noted in the last chapter, everyone on the Court was of one mind that only Canadian law was subject to review under the Charter and the principle of constitutional supremacy. As it would subsequently affirm in the *Extradition trilogy*, the Court had no doubt that the Charter did "not govern the actions of a foreign country",[51] nor could "our constitutional standards be imposed on other countries."[52] In the end, it was on this basis that Spencer's claim was dismissed.

Once again, at first blush, the Court seems to be on very firm ground in denying that the Charter has any application to foreign law. This claim seems quite uncontroversial in fact. Geographic borders unquestionably impose some kinds of restrictions on how far the Charter can reach. No one I know would take issue with the idea that the principle of constitutional supremacy is limited by the boundaries and the sovereignty of the Canadian State. No one thinks the Court could invalidate laws of a foreign State on the ground that they were inconsistent with the Canadian Charter of Rights and Freedoms.

On reflection, however, the assertion turns out to be quite problematic because, in two words, it is simply "not responsive" to the challenge that Spencer asked the Court to adjudicate. Spencer's challenge, after all, was to the constitutionality of the Canadian, not Bahamian law. In effect, by concentrating on the geographic limits that had no application to Spencer's claim, the Court distracted itself and allowed itself to make the factual error of saying his liberty had not been interfered with at all. The Court got itself off on a tangent, if you will. Focusing on the foreign law, which lay beyond the Charter's reach, caused the judges to lose sight of the way in which Canadian law was critically — albeit indirectly — involved in threatening Spencer's liberty and the security of his person. The Court made the same mistake as the one committed in by Jean Beetz and William McIntyre in *Edwards Books*. They focused exclusively on one aspect of the coercion about which the challenger complained.

As a factual matter, the Court's ruling in *Spencer* has no more foundation than its decisions in *Operation Dismantle* or in *Jones*. No matter what the judges might say, Canadian law did, unambiguously, put substantial pressure on Spencer to testify and in so doing it seriously threatened his liberty and the security of his person. Regardless of how he responded, Canadian evidence law presented him with exactly the same

---

51   *Schmidt v. R.* (1987), 39 D.L.R. (4th) 19, at 36.
52   *Ibid.*, at 43.

impossible dilemma about which the retailers in *Edwards Books* had complained. If Spencer refused to testify, out of fear perhaps that Bahamian officials might seek to have him extradited if he violated the Bahamian law, he could be cited for being in contempt of Court and liable to imprisonment in Canada. If, on the other hand, he chose to comply with Canadian law and testify in the proceedings to which he had been subpoenaed, he exposed himself to the risk that he would be prosecuted and liable to imprisonment in the Bahamas.

It is true that in either circumstance, the infringement of his constitutional freedom had not yet materialized. It was never certain he would lose his liberty. It is also true that Canada's evidence law did not *directly* threaten his liberty or the security of his person. Complying with the *Canada Evidence Act* only exposed Spencer to the possibility of being prosecuted and imprisoned under the laws of a foreign State. In the end, the threat imposed by Canadian law was both uncertain and indirect. Once again, however, neither of these characteristics of the coercion that the law exerted supports a finding that his rights were not violated at all.[53] As the Court's judgment in *Edwards Books* make clear, the fact that a law impacts on constitutional freedoms indirectly rather than directly does not shield it from judicial review. The underlying purposes of the Charter applies to laws of both kinds. Indirect threats to constitutional entitlements can be every bit as menacing and oppressive as those which bear directly on the individual.

On numerous occasions, in fact, the Court recognized that claims of this kind fell within the Charter's reach. *Singh* and *Morgentaler* are perhaps the two best known cases where the Court listened to challenges to laws which impinged on peoples' freedoms in these ways. The Court also posed a rather dramatic example in the *Extradition trilogy* in which it speculated about the constitutional duty of a Canadian Government asked to extradite a person to a foreign country in which it is known that torture is *sometimes* used in the criminal justice system. In circumstances of that kind, no one on the Court doubted for a moment that a law that permitted the Canadian Government's immigration officials to respond positively to such a request would be unconstitutional even though it was not certain that the person being extradited would be tortured in fact and even though, obviously, the Canadian Government was not inflicting the torture directly itself.[54] A case of that kind shows very clearly that it would be fundamentally inconsistent with the purposes that the Charter was meant to promote if the Court could not exercise its powers of review until after the infringement had actually occurred.

Spencer was the first case in which the strategy of avoidance was em-

---

53 See the cases cited in notes 45 and 49, *supra.*
54 See *Schmidt v. R., supra*, note 51, at 39.

braced by everyone on the Court. It was not, unfortunately, to be the last. Eighteen months later the Court committed precisely the same mistake, and on this occasion, the consequences for the vitality of the Charter and the principle of constitutional supremacy were considerably more grave.

The second occasion in which the involvement of a foreign Government confused and ultimately distracted the Court was the *Extradition trilogy*. Here, it will be recalled, a majority of the Court rejected the claims of various persons resisting being returned to the United States and Argentina. Reduced to its essentials, the reasoning of the Court was that section 11 of the Charter had no application to extradition hearings because all of the criminal proceedings faced by the challengers related to offences that occurred outside Canada. As in *Spencer*, in the *Extradition trilogy* the Court was preoccupied with the extent to which the threat to the challengers' constitutional rights came from a foreign Government and a foreign law to which the Charter had no application. The Court simply lost sight of, and in the end failed to address, the way in which the Canadian Government was inextricably — even if indirectly — involved in the threat that the challengers faced. Ignoring their earlier ruling in *Singh*, a majority of the Court simply avoided the challengers' complaint that it was the Canadian Government that was sending them back to a country where their constitutional rights (to life, liberty, etc.) would be jeopardized.

Although the flaw in the Court's reasoning was the same in both cases, the impact of the *Extradition trilogy* on the life of Charter, and the principle of constitutional supremacy, was considerably more severe. This time an entire procedure of law was affected. Extradition hearings were put completely beyond the reach of the Charter, and much of the rest of the extradition process was substantially shielded from the Court's powers of review. Avoidance in this case came at considerable cost.[55]

The involvement of foreign Governments in cases arising under the Charter was clearly a difficult problem for the Court. Their presence in a case was obviously distracting and accounts for why the Court avoided and failed to address the substance of the challengers' claims in both *Spencer* and the *Extradition trilogy*. However, more than foreign actors could confuse the Court in this way. In between *Spencer* and the *Extradition trilogy*, in fact the same day that it handed down its decision in *Edwards Books*, the Court handed down another landmark decision in which the method of avoidance played a critical part.[56] The case was *Dolphin Delivery*

---

55 Extradition proceedings were further insulated from judicial review in a judgment the Court handed down in the beginning of year six. See *U.S.A. v. Cotroni*, [1989] 1 S.C.R. 1469.

56 In addition to making this analytical mistake, as noted (text, *supra*, p. 80), the Court's decision in *Dolphin Delivery* was also undermined by its failure to read s. 32 of the Charter purposefully.

in which, it will be recalled, a group of workers in British Columbia challenged the constitutionality of a common law rule which limited their freedom to picket. As we saw in the last chapter, the Court refused to exercise its powers of review in this case essentially for the reason that, in its view, the common law rules that govern interaction in people's personal affairs lie beyond the reach of the Charter.

The parallel between the Court's judgment in *Dolphin Delivery* and those in which foreign Governments were involved is striking. As in the latter cases, in *Dolphin Delivery* the Court began with an idea with which few would take issue. In *Dolphin Delivery*, the critical idea from which the whole analysis proceeded was that the Charter does not regulate peoples' private affairs. In the same way that no one would seriously argue that the Charter could invalidate some rule or principle of foreign law, it is difficult to imagine anyone questioning the idea that the Charter does not regulate the behaviour of private individuals. As should now be clear, at its core the Charter is a set of principles, relating to ends and means, which measure the justice of law (or the acts of government officials), not the behaviour of individuals in their private lives. Once again, however, what is problematic about the Court's premise is that it is simply not relevant or responsive to the picketers' claim. Their complaint was that the common law rule that Dolphin Delivery was able to use to stop them from picketing was an unconstitutional limit on their freedom of speech. It was a common law rule which prohibited the workers from picketing, and not any behaviour on the part of the managers and shareholders of Dolphin Delivery, that the Court was asked to review.

The basis of the Court's mistake in *Dolphin Delivery* was the same as the one it committed in *Spencer* and the *Extradition trilogy*. In the same way the Court was confused in the latter two cases by the involvement of a foreign Government, the failure of the Court to respond to the picketers' challenge can be directly related to its preoccupation that the Charter was not meant to regulate relations between private individuals and groups. In *Dolphin Delivery*, the essence of the Court's reasoning was that the Charter had no place in the regulation of private relations because, in Canada at least, there already exists statutory Human Rights Codes to perform that task. Focusing on the behaviour of the individuals, rather than the common law rules about which the workers were complaining, the Court reasoned that Human Rights Codes were a more reasonable and flexible way than constitutional litigation to resolve disputes between private individuals.

Although the Court was distracted in all three cases by the involvement of actors who were thought to be immune to the Charter, the error committed in *Dolphin Delivery* was different in one respect. Whereas the mistakes made by the Court in *Spencer* and the *Extradition trilogy* were of a factual kind, in *Dolphin Delivery* the Court's reasoning was flawed analytically. In the first set of cases we have seen how the Court failed to recognize that indirectly the Canadian Government was critically involved in threatening the constitutional guarantees that were at stake. In *Dolphin Delivery*, by contrast, the Court's mistake was in thinking that Human Rights Codes and the Charter were, to some extent, substitutes for each other. The reality, of course, is that Human Rights Codes and the Charter operate at two very different levels in our legal system.[57] It is a mistake to think Human Rights Codes and the Charter are substitutes for one another.[58] Human Rights Codes regulate the behaviour of individuals towards their fellow citizens, in their homes, at work and at play. The Charter, by contrast regulates the content and quality of the law used by the State to coordinate those affairs including, as the Court itself recognized, the Human Rights Codes themselves.[59]

The fact Human Rights Codes have already been enacted to regulate private relations in the community provides no reason why all laws and rules that govern how each of us must interact with others in the community, (including the common law rules of contract, property and in the case of *Dolphin Delivery*, tort), should be excused from the process of judicial review and elevated to a status beyond or above the principle of constitutional supremacy. There is simply no logical connection between the idea that we already have Human Rights Codes to control how each of us must treat others in our daily affairs, and a ruling that all of the *law* we use to coordinate personal relations in the community does not have to conform to the principle of constitutional supremacy. To press the connection, as the Court does, is to commit a logical error — known to logicians and lawyers as a "non sequitur" — of the most basic and glaring kind. "Non sequitur", it simply does not follow, from the assumption that the Charter is not meant to control the behaviour of individuals in their private lives, that there is a body of rules devised by the third branch of government that stands above, or at least along side, the Constitution. Paralleling its impact on foreign Governments and the laws they enact, the Charter will also affect the private affairs of individuals and groups whenever they rely on a body of rules that limits the entitlements the Constitution guarantees.

It would be hard to exaggerate the magnitude of the Court's error in *Dolphin Delivery*. It is, without question, one of the most criticized

---

57 A point the Court eventually recognized in *Andrews v. Law Society of B.C.*, *supra*, note 23.

58 Note again how essays by legal academics played a crucial role in suggesting this line of analysis to the Court. See *supra*, note 47.

59 See, e.g., *Blainey v. Ontario Hockey Assn.* (1986), 26 D.L.R. (4th) 728.

judgments the Court has issued so far. Reviewers of all persuasions have commented how, in various ways, the Court's reasoning process is fundamentally flawed.[60] Incredibly, in a subsequent judgment upholding an injunction against the picketing of courthouses in British Columbia by provincial public servants, the Court ignored all of the criticism and, rather than overrule its decision in *Dolphin Delivery*, it endeavoured to distinguish its earlier ruling instead.[61]

---

60 See, e.g., P. Hogg, "The Dolphin Delivery Case: Applicability of the Charter to Private Action", 51 Sask. L. Rev. 273; E.R. Alexander, "The Canadian Charter of Rights and Freedoms in the Supreme Court of Canada (1989), 105 Law Q.R. 561; B. Slattery, "The Charter's Relevance to Private Litigation: Does Dolphin Deliver?", 32 McGill L.J. 905; A. Hutchinson and A. Petter, "Private Rights/Public Wrongs: The Liberal Lie of the Charter", 38 U.T.L.J. 278; J. Manwaring, "To The Bar of Justice: A Comment on the Decision in the Case of Dolphin Delivery", 19 Ottawa L.R. 413; D. Beatty, "Constitutional Conceits: The Coercive Authority of the Courts", 37 U.T.L.J. 183; R. Elliott and R. Grant, "The Charter's Application in Private Litigation" (1989), 23 U.B.C. L. Rev 3; E. Belobaba, "The Charter of Rights and Private Litigation: The Dilemma of Dolphin Delivery", in *Charter Issues in Civil Cases*, L.S.U.C. (Toronto: Carswell, 1988). For one of the few agnostic evaluations of *Dolphin Delivery*, see P. Cavalluzzo, "Freedom of Association: Its Effect Upon Collective Bargaining Trade Unions", in *Labour Law Under the Charter*, Queen's Law Journal, 1988.

61 It could be argued that even if the Court didn't intend to repudiate *Dolphin Delivery* in the *B.C. Government Employees* case, as a matter of law, it did. In *Dolphin Delivery* the Court was quite explicit that the common law would only fall within the scope of the Charter when the legislative, executive or administrative branches of government chose to rely on it in some way, and in the *B.C. Government Employees* case it is clear that neither the executive nor the legislative branches of government were involved in any way. Nor can it be argued, as the Court endeavoured to do, that the motivation of the Courts in the two cases is different. As a factual matter the distinction is impossible to maintain and constitutionally motivation is quite irrelevant to the reach of the Charter and the principle of constitutional supremacy. The inconsistency between these two cases is highlighted and criticized by Robin Elliott and Rob Grant in "The Charter's Application in Private Litigation", *ibid.*

In one of the final judgments the Court issued at the end of year five, *Slaight Communications v. Davidson* (1989), 59 D.L.R. (4th) 416, it implicitly undermined *Dolphin Delivery* even further by applying the Charter to a dispute between two private individuals. Although the Court was reviewing the statutory authority of an arbitrator in this case, as Brian Slattery has pointed out, the Court's authority to develop the common law is also grounded in a statutory grant of authority and so is indistinguishable in this respect. See B. Slattery, "The Charter's Relevance to Private Litigation", *ibid.*

As we have seen, the Court's decision in *B.C. Government Employees* can also be criticized for falling prey to the mistake of denying the factual basis of the picketers' complaint in the absence of any evidence to support such a finding. In *B.C. Government Employees*, the Court dismissed the challenger's s. 11 complaint on the ground no one had been charged with an offence. The mistake in such a ruling is that proof of an actual limitation is not required to establish a limitation of a right. As we have seen, the Court consistently has said the mere threat of a violation will suffice. See note 45, *supra*. In the *B.C. Government Employees* case, the Court recognized that the injunction

For a reviewer's purposes, the gravity of the Court's mistake in *Dolphin Delivery* lies in the vast body of law that it puts beyond the reach of the Charter and beyond the Court's powers of constitutional review. Focusing on a feature of the picketers' case that was irrelevant to the challenge, and thereby avoiding the merits of their claim, the Court effectively insulated all of the common law rules governing accidents, contracts, property and the like whenever the personal interests and affairs of individuals and groups were at stake. By a strategy of avoidance the judges effectively put themselves and their colleagues in lower courts above the Charter and the principle of constitutional supremacy.

In *Dolphin Delivery* the Court elevated a factor, relating to the identity of the litigants in the particular case, that should have been irrelevant, into a potentially very stringent limit on the reach of the Charter itself. When it is read alongside *Spencer* and the *Extradition trilogy*, *Dolphin Delivery* gives credence to the idea that it is the actor or person who seeks to enforce a law, as much as the law itself, which determines how supreme the Constitution really is.[62] It purports to read a limit on the scope of section 52 and the supremacy of the Constitution which has no legal or textual support.[63] Both in its purpose and in its language, section 52 is written in absolute terms. All Canadian law, not just laws that the federal and provincial Governments and/or their agents seek to enforce, is subordinated to the supremacy of the Charter and the principles of justice which it contains.

Avoidance, then, turns out to be a more serious error than its complementary strategy of denial. Beyond rejecting individual challenges to particular laws, avoidance led the Court to make mistakes that had an enormous impact on the system as a whole. Over the course of five years, it led the Court to impose restrictions on the reach of the Charter that excluded and/or substantially shielded huge areas of Canadian law from any independent and impartial review. By avoiding the core of a challenger's complaint, the Court seriously compromised the principle of constitutional supremacy and the status of the Charter in our hierarchy of law.

---

restraining the picketing did put the workers on notice that they would be punished if they persisted in exercising their constitutional freedom of expression. In purpose and effect, the restraining order issued by the Chief Justice of British Columbia threatened the picketers with criminal prosecution if they persisted in picketing the courthouses in the province.

62 *Dolphin Delivery, supra,* note 31, at 195.
63 See my "Constitutional Conceits", *supra,* note 60.

3. ABDICATION

Although at several critical points in its performance the Court faltered and failed to respond to a challenger's complaint, on the whole this was a relatively rare event. In the vast majority of cases, none of the judges was tempted simply to deny and/or avoid the factual basis of a challenger's claim. Invariably all, or most, of them would recognize that the challengers' freedom had been restricted in the ways in which they claimed. As a rule, the challenges which the Court heard over the course of its first five years were aimed at laws that were either enacted or embraced by one or other branch of the federal or one of the provincial Governments and that limited human freedom in very fundamental and obvious ways.

Even in these circumstances, however, there were times when the Court ruled that a challenger's constitutional rights had not been infringed. Even when there was no doubt that this was the kind of law to which the Charter applied or about the factual basis of a complaint, on a surprising number of occasions the judges refused to exercise their powers of review. In each of these cases, the reason given by the Court for refusing to evaluate the constitutionality of the law against all of the principles it had laid out in *Oakes* was essentially the same. The interest or activity for which protection was being sought was said by the Court not to fall within any of the rights or freedoms that the Charter guaranteed. Even if challengers could show that the law they were attacking did limit their freedom in some way, the Court would still dismiss their claims if they could not surmount the interpretative (or legal) hurdle that the model in *Oakes* required them to clear.

In distinguishing which interests and activities are protected by the Charter from those which are not, the Court invariably employed the same analytical method. Whether an interest or activity received the protection of the Charter turned directly on how the Court viewed the public interest that the challenged law was designed to promote. In some cases the Court pointed to the importance of the public interest that was promoted by the law they had been asked to review. In the *Extradition trilogy* and in its decision in *Jones*, that was certainly the case.[64] In the former, the Court stressed the benefits all countries derive from an effective system of extradition throughout the world and the importance of adhering to the principle of comity (respect) among independent States. In the latter, the Court underscored the compelling interest a community has in the quality of education its citizens receive. In both, the weight the Court put on the public interest advanced by each of those laws led it directly to the

---

64 See also *B.C.G.E.U. v. A.G. B.C.* (1989), 53 D.L.R. (4th) 1 (s. 7), at 57; *R. v. Beare, supra*, note 32; *R. v. Simmons, supra*, note 18; and *R. v. Corbett*, [1988] 1 S.C.R. 670.

conclusion that none of the challengers' constitutional rights had been infringed and so there was no occasion for it to evaluate these challenges against the principles set out in *Oakes*.

In other cases, the focus was more on the nature or the character of the law that had been challenged and the relative competence of the courts and the other two branches of government to formulate policies of that kind. The Court's decisions in *Les Acadiens*, and the *Labour trilogy*, are typical of judgments in which the Court reasoned in this way.[65] In each of these cases, laws regulating language and labour relations, were portrayed as being inherently matters of compromise and accommodation that in turn were said to be uniquely suited for resolution in the political, rather than judicial, process. Courts, by contrast, were characterized as institutions designed exclusively to resolve issues and make decisions of a more principled nature.

In a third group of cases the Court indirectly underscored the importance of the public interest in delineating the scope of its own powers of review, by emphasizing how trivial and insubstantial the limit on a challenger's freedom really was. As we have seen, *de minimis* complaints were not the kind any of the judges wanted to hear. There was a quantitative as well as a qualitative threshold all challengers had to meet before the powers of the Court would be activated. As we saw in the last chapter, the majority of the Court followed this approach in dismissing Larry Jones' complaint that Alberta's school law infringed his religious freedom. The principle carried the day in other cases as well,[66] and at one time or another all of the judges recognized it as establishing a legitimate limit on how far the Charter could reach.[67]

Now some reviewers might wonder what, if anything, the Court was doing wrong when it reasoned in this way. These cases seem entirely different from those in which the Court simply refused to address the factual basis of a challenger's complaint. After all, if it serves the public interest for the Court not to exercise its powers of review, that seems like a very good reason for the judges not to entertain a challenge. How, it might

---

65 See also *MacDonald v. City of Montreal* (1986), 27 D.L.R. (4th) 321; *Bilodean v. A.G. Manitoba* (1986), 27 D.L.R. (4th) 34; and La Forest in *Edwards Books, supra*, note 41.

66 See, e.g., *R. v. Simmons, supra*, note 18, *B.C.G.E.U. v. A.G. B.C.* (s. 7), *supra*, note 64; *R. v. Potvin, supra*, note 32. See also Chapter 3, *supra*, note 71.

67 Brian Dickson and Gerald Le Dain made use of it in *Edwards Books, supra*, note 41, at 34-35, 54; Bertha Wilson applied it in *R. v. Jones* (1986), 31 D.L.R. (4th) 569 (with McIntyre and Beetz), in *Ref. re B.C. Motor Vehicle Act, supra*, note 45, and in *Operation Dismantle v. R.* (1985), 18 D.L.R. (4th) 481, at 507-508; Gerard La Forest employed variations of the argument in *Edwards Books, supra*, note 41, and in the *Extradition trilogy*, Chapter 3, *supra*, note 2, *Spencer v. R.* (1986), 21 D.L.R. (4th) 756. Cf. *U.S.A. v. Cotroni, supra*, note 55.

be asked, could one find fault with this line of analysis? Building qualitative and quantitative thresholds into the application of the Charter seems to be a wise use of the Court's limited resources and to fit easily with the structure of review envisaged in *Oakes*.[68]

In many cases a reviewer might think that the text of the Charter explicitly directed the Court to evaluate the public interest promoted by a law in delineating which interests and activities were protected. Almost certainly she will have noticed that many of the rights and freedoms entrenched in the Charter are written in terms which strongly suggest that the public interest should be weighed as part of the process in which the rights and freedoms are defined. Section 8, for example, guarantees everyone shall be free from "unreasonable" searches and seizures. Similarly, section 11 guarantees any person charged with an offense the right to a "fair" hearing and to be tried within a "reasonable" time. Section 12 protects people from "cruel and unusual" treatment or punishment. Section 7, in turn, says that one can only be deprived of life, liberty or security of the person when it is in accordance with the "principles of fundamental justice" to do so. And, to claim the benefit of section 15's equality guarantee, a challenger must show that he has been treated "discriminatorily". In each of these entitlements the inclusion of words like fair and reasonable, cruel and unusual, fundamental justice and discrimination seems to instruct the Court to take account of the public interest promoted by a law in defining what particular interests and activities these entitlements protect. At the very least they make it clear that the interests and activities guaranteed by these entitlements are much more limited than those protected by rights and freedoms (like religion or expression, etc.) which are written in absolute terms. Unlike the latter, these sections explicitly seem to contemplate that laws can impose punishments, deprive people of their liberty and recognize inequalities, etc. without infringing the Charter if they are drawn in the proper way.

Other reviewers could be expected to point out that the reasoning process the Court used when it ruled that the interest or activity for which a challenger sought protection did not fall within any of the rights or freedoms entrenched in the Charter, was quite different from the analysis it followed when it simply denied or avoided the factual basis of a

---

68 Paul Weiler argues that the idea of institutional competence should be determinative in delineating those subjects (such as criminal law or laws governing law societies or the political activities of public servants) which it is appropriate for the Court to review and those (such as laws relating to employment, income policy, health care) which are not. See P. Weiler "The Charter at Work: Reflections on the Constitutionalizing of Labour and Employment Law" 40 U.T.L.J. 117. This is also discussed by Bob Sharpe in "Judicial Developments of Principles in Applying the Charter" in *Charter Issues in Civil Cases*, Law Society of Upper Canada (Toronto: Carswell, 1988).

challenger's claim. In these cases, unlike those we have just considered, the Court was able to cast its judgment in terms which seem to fit within the analytical framework of *Oakes*. In the preceding chapter we have seen that two principles were particularly important in leading the Court to erect qualitative and quantitative thresholds against the reach of the Charter and its own powers of review. The two principles were deference and balancing and what the Court did was to apply either or both of them in the first phase of the review process rather than the second. In almost every case in which it ruled that a challenger's constitutional rights had not been infringed by the law he or she sought to have reviewed, the Court can be seen using either or both of these principles as interpretative aids in determining what kinds of interests and activities the Charter guarantees.

Finally for many reviewers, I suspect, evaluating the public interest as part of the process in which the rights and freedoms entrenched in the Charter are defined will not seem nearly as offensive to the Charter and the principle of constitutional supremacy, as a technique like avoidance or denial, because it does not mean a law is completely immunized from review. After all, when the Court applies the balancing principle, in defining which interests and activities are protected by the rights and freedoms listed in the Charter, it is, to that extent at least, evaluating the proportionality that holds between the purposes and effects of the challenged law. In *Jones* for example, the majority of the Court ruled that Alberta's *School Act* did not interfere with the challenger's section 7 rights because they had no doubt that the community's interest in the efficient administration of its educational policies was more important than, and significantly outweighed, the very minor intrusion the law imposed on Larry Jones' freedom to educate his children in a way which was consistent with his religious beliefs. Similarly, in the *Extradition trilogy* the Court's ruling, that there was no violation of any of the claimants' section 7 rights, was made on the basis that any possible infringement of the life, liberty etc. of the complainants was more than outweighed by the principles of comity between the sovereign states and by the whole international system of extradition. In the *B.C. Government Employees* case no one on the Court had any doubt that the "massive disruption of the activities of the courts and consequent interference with the legal and constitutional rights of all citizens of British Columbia" provided ample justification for whatever "minimal" infringement of their liberties the challengers experienced as a result of the injunction that was at issue in that case.

Now even though, in these cases where the public interest is thought to substantially outweigh any constraint a law may impose on personal freedom, it may seem that when the Court "abdicates" its powers of review, it acts very differently than when it simply denies or avoids the factual basis of a challenger's claim, constitutionally its behaviour is just as flawed.

In fact the Court is on no firmer ground when it points to some aspect of the public interest to support a decision not to evaluate the constitutionality of a law under the two measures of proportionality embedded in section 1, than when it simply denies or avoids a challenger's claim.

Certainly as a matter of constitutional law the reasoning is just as defective. In fact, "definitional balancing", as this approach is sometimes called, is flawed in at least three different ways. In the first place, the consequences of this analytical approach are exactly the same as when the Court refuses to accept the factual basis of a challenger's claim. As we saw in our review of the cases in the last chapter, by abdicating its powers of review the Court has significantly compromised the principle of constitutional supremacy. The result of testing the constitutionality of laws in this way is that whole policy areas like foreign affairs, or social and economic policy have either been completely excluded or substantially shielded from any meaningful form of third party review. In the area of extradition the Court has said that it would only exercise its powers of review under section 7 in extreme and "compelling" situations. In other cases the Court systematically denied workers the protection of the Charter by putting virtually every important aspect of labour policy beyond its reach.[69] In *Jones*, the Court said legislatures must be given room, on matters of education policy, to make choices about the kinds of administrative structures that suit their needs and that it should only intervene when a legislature has acted in a way which is manifestly unfair.

In addition to being at odds with the principle of constitutional supremacy, defining which interests and activities are protected by the Charter by examining the public interest which a challenge law is expected to promote, is flawed as a method of interpretation. It relies on a source of meaning which the Court repeatedly rejected over the course of the first five years. Essentially, it purports to interpret the rights and freedoms

---

69 See *Dolphin Delivery v. R.W.D.S.U.*, *supra*, note 47; the *Labour trilogy*, Chapter 3, *supra*, note 2; *Reference re Workers' Compensation Act*, *supra*, note 18. The one exception to this otherwise consistent refusal to apply the Charter to labour policy is *Slaight Communications v. Davidson* (1989), 59 D.L.R. (4th) 416, where the Court ruled that arbitrators exercising legal powers under a statute (like providing remedies for people who have been unjustly dismissed) are subject to review under the Charter. To the extent that virtually all arbitrators in Canada derive their legal authority from a statute, the decision in *Slaight Communications* should bring all arbitral jurisprudence — all of the "common law of the shop" — within the Court's powers of review.

The importance of the Court's decision in *Slaight Communications* should extend even beyond the field of labour arbitration. As we have already noticed, *supra*, note 61, *Slaight Communications* is directly at odds with the earlier decision in *Dolphin Delivery*. Allowing the decisions in both of these cases to stand means that the law used to evaluate unjust dismissal will be subjected to review when applied by arbitrators, but not by Courts, even though as we have observed, both derive their powers from statutes.

which the Charter guarantees by reference to the purposes an ordinary law is enacted to promote. "Definitional balancing" is like an extreme rendition of the old (and discredited) "frozen concepts" approach, used to interpret the original Bill of Rights.[70] By defining which interests and activities the Charter protects, through an examination of the objectives which a Government wishes to pursue, the Court turns the hierarchical relationship which exists between constitutional and statutory documents on its head. Rather than using the Charter to evaluate the content of ordinary law, the latter is used to give meaning to the Constitution. As an interpretative method, "definitional balancing" is completely inconsistent with the Court's endorsement of the liberal, purposive approach.

Finally, and most importantly, in terms of the model in *Oakes*, the mistake the Court makes when it "abdicates" its powers of review, on the account of the public interest that is involved in a case, is that it fails to keep the two stages of the review process separate and analytically distinct.[71] Whenever the Court abdicates its review function it is using principles like deference and balancing in the first phase of the review process even though, on the logic of the Charter, both can only be used in the second. Principles like deference and balancing are principles of justification, not interpretation, and using them prematurely is inconsistent with and violates the Charter in at least two different ways. On the one hand, it leads directly to the Court upholding laws which otherwise offend the principle of alternative means. On the other, it makes challengers bear the burden of proving that their interests outweigh the benefits the public derives from the law that has been attacked, even though in *Oakes*, and in subsequent cases, all of the judges have stressed that it is the Government who should have to satisfy the Court on this point.

Whenever the Court adopted an attitude of deference towards, and/or balanced the public interest promoted by, a law in the first stage of the review process, there was a danger it would end up validating laws

---

70 The frozen concepts approach to the Canadian Bill of Rights can be seen in cases such as *Miller and Cockriell v. R.* (1976), 70 D.L.R. (3d) 324; *R. v. Burnshine* (1974), 44 D.L.R. (3d) 584. See generally, W. Tarnopolsky, *The Canadian Bill of Rights*, 2nd ed. (Toronto: McClelland & Stewart, 1975).

71 In numerous cases the Court stressed the importance, analytically, of keeping the two functions of interpretation and justification separate and distinct. See, e.g., *Ref. re B.C. Motor Vehicle Act, supra,* note 45; *Edwards Books* (p. 73), *supra,* note 41; *R. v. Smith, supra,* note 45; *Andrews v. Law Society of British Columbia, supra,* note 23; *Black v. Law Society of Alberta, supra,* note 46; *R. v. Turpin, supra,* note 24; *Ford v. Quebec* (1988), 54 D.L.R. (4th) 577; *U.S.A. v. Cotroni, supra,* note 55. See also Dickson in *R. v. Schwartz* (1988), 55 D.L.R. (4th) 503, and Wilson in *R. v. Strachan* (1989), 56 D.L.R. (4th) 673. Note that even when Bertha Wilson did not act on it, she was sensitive to the distinction between the two phases of review. See *R. v. Jones* (1986), 31 D.L.R. (4th) 569. And see her decisions in the cases noted in Chapter 3, *supra,* note 83.

which limited people's freedom more than was necessary to realize the objectives which the laws were designed to secure. By abdicating its powers of review, the Court permitted Government and its agents to use a sledgehammer to achieve their social objectives where a more precision instrument would have done the trick.[72] Perhaps the clearest example of how abdication could lead to such perverse results is the Court's decision in the *Labour trilogy*. There, it will be recalled, the majority of the Court adopted a very deferential posture in the first phase of the review process in defining what interests and activities were protected by the Charter's guarantee of freedom of association. The Court's explanation for why none of the challengers' constitutional rights had been violated was short and to the point. Strikes and collective bargaining were said to be activities that were notoriously subject to balancing and compromise and on which the elected branches of government had a good deal more expertise than the Court. Labour relations, said Gerald Le Dain, was a subject on which the judges were not comparatively well-equipped to review the merits of social policy and they should, therefore, defer on these issues to the legislature. Based on this assessment of its own relative lack of expertise, the Court interpreted the words "freedom of association" in a way which provided no protection to one of the most fundamental activities by which individuals can maintain some measure of control over their working lives.

Practically speaking, the effect of the Court's decision in the *Labour trilogy* was to put some of the most important parts of our labour policy beyond the Charter's reach[73]. In terms of the challenges they had been asked to hear, the result was that the Court affirmed the constitutional validity of half a dozen labour laws which prohibited, to varying degrees, different groups of workers from being able to strike and engage in collective bargaining even though it could be shown that the proscriptions were drawn more broadly than was required to accomplish the purposes of the Acts. For example, the majority ruled that a law passed by the Alberta legislature, prohibiting strikes by *all* public servants in order to ensure uninterrupted provision of essential services affecting lives, health and

---

72 In addition to the examples discussed in the text, other instances of the Court validating laws which gratuitously disregarded people's rights include: *R. v. Lyons* (sentencing), *supra*, note 14, *Les Acadiens* (language), *supra*, note 11, *R. v. Stevens, R. v. Holmes* and *R. v. Schwartz*, *supra*, note 10. In all of these cases, led by the conservatives, a majority of the Court upheld laws as constitutional even though they infringed personal freedom more than was necessary to accomplish the objectives which the legislature sought to achieve.

73 It bears repeating that in a judgment handed down just after the curtain fell on year five, the Court did rule that arbitral law — the so called common law of the shop — did fall within the scope of review. See *Slaight Communications v. Davidson*, *supra*, note 69.

safety in the community, was constitutional even though it applied to many people who did not perform emergency services of that kind. Similarly, a law limiting the freedom of federal public servants to strike and to engage in collective bargaining, passed as part of that Government's attempt to bring an inflationary economy under control, was judged to be constitutional even though it restricted the freedom of these workers to strike and bargain collectively with respect to important matters (like arbitration, seniority, or management rights) which had nothing to do with wages or compensation of any kind. Because deference was used as a tool of interpretation, rather than a principle of justification, the freedom of a large number of people was needlessly compromised. If the laws had been more carefully and sensitively drawn, the freedom of non-essential workers in the first case, and of all federal public servants in the second, could have been shown more respect without doing any violence to the objectives of the Government.

Bertha Wilson's judgment in *Jones* provides an equally clear example of why balancing the public interest in the first phase of the review process offends the principle of alternative means. In *Jones*, it will be recalled, Wilson, with the support of several of her more conservative colleagues, dismissed the challenger's complaint under section 2(a) of the Charter in the first stage of the review process. She ruled that, as a matter of fact, Alberta's school law did not impose any restriction on Jones' religious freedom and/or even if it had, it was too trivial and insignificant to count.

In dismissing Jones' complaint on this latter basis, Wilson and her colleagues never considered whether, even if it was "trivial", the restriction on his religious freedom was necessary at all; whether Alberta's law could meet the principle of alternative means. Indeed, Wilson quite candidly admitted, at the end of this part of her judgment, that had the Court not built a quantitative threshold into its interpretation of what interests and activities were protected in section 2(a), Jones would have been entitled to succeed. As she pointed out, the Government of Alberta had adduced no evidence to establish that making the parents apply for accreditation was more reasonable than alternative adjudicative and investigative means that the Government might have used to administer the scheme of the Act. In fact the evidence before the Court strongly suggested that there were alternative procedures the Alberta Government might have used that were just as efficient as the one they employed and that would have shown more respect for Jones' religious freedom. Again, by doing all of the balancing in the first stage of its inquiry, the Court came to validate a law that needlessly interfered with the constitutional rights of some, like Larry Jones, whose lives it touched.

Even when a right or freedom is not written in absolute terms the logic of the Charter requires the Court to put off balancing the public interest until the very end of the review process. On several occasions the Court failed to respect the analytical distinction between the two phases of the review process when such constitutional entitlements were involved and when it did it was led to validate laws which needlessly constrained the freedom of those they affected.[74] *Lyons* is a clear example of how this risk can materialize even when a right or freedom is written in qualified terms. In its judgment in this case, the Court spent a considerable amount of time evaluating (and ultimately deferring to) the public interest promoted by the rules of preventive detention contained in Canada's dangerous offender laws, in deciding whether the challenger's interests were protected by section 7. Largely as a result of its consideration of the public interest in the first phase of the review process, the Court was led to uphold laws which, among other things, denied people the right to have their status as dangerous offenders decided by a jury of their peers. Even though none of the purposes of the policy of preventive detention would be promoted by treating people like Lyons in this way, the Court ruled that his constitutional rights had not been infringed. Because, after it had performed the balancing function, the Court concluded that Canada's dangerous offender law did not violate section 7, it never evaluated the law against the principle of alternative means.[75]

Regardless of the right or freedom for which protection is being sought

---

74 See, e.g., *R. v. Jones, supra,* note 67; *Extradition trilogy,* Chapter 3, *supra,* note 2; *R. v. Lyons, supra,* note 14; *R. v. Holmes, supra,* note 10. For a similar analysis of *R. v. Jones,* see R. Elliott, "The Supreme Court of Canada and Section One — The Erosion of the Common Front", 12 Queens L.J. 277, 323.

It should be noted that frequently the Court did respect the analytical distinction between the two stages in the review process even when a qualified right or freedom was involved. See, e.g., *Ref. re s. 94(2) Motor Vehicle Act, supra,* note 45; *R. v. Smith, supra,* note 45; *Andrews v. Law Society of B.C., supra,* note 23; *Black v. Law Society of Alberta, supra,* note 46; *R. v. Turpin,* Chapter 3, *supra,* note 24; *U.S.A. v. Cotroni, supra,* note 55.

It should also be noted, however, that in several cases a second analytical distinction between the second (alternate means) and third (balancing) proportionality principles was not respected by one or more members of the Court and in these circumstances as well, there was a risk laws would be validated which could not meet the test of alternative means. See e.g. La Forest's judgments in *Edwards Books* and *Jones, supra,* note 2, and William McIntyre's judgments in *Andrews v. Law Society of B.C.,* and *Black v. Law Society of Alberta.* See also Chapter 3, pp. 59-60, and see note 98, *infra.*

At the beginning of year six, in *U.S.A. v. Cotroni, supra,* note 55, the Court sent a strong signal that it would be inclined to blur the distinction between these two principles even further by invoking the principle of deference when it applied the principle of alternate means, as well as when it performed the balancing role. See also *Irwin Toy v. Quebec, supra,* note 18, at 623, 625-626, where the majority ruled that the Court should allow for a margin of appreciation in its application of the principle of alternate means.

75 It might also be noted that in *R. v. Lyons,* the Court also deferred to Parliament's choice of means in its analysis of s. 12. See *supra,* note 14, at 221, 225. For a parallel criticism

then, doing the balancing of, and/or deferring to, the public interest when considering what aspects of human freedom the Charter protects is constitutionally defective because it is fundamentally antagonistic to the principle of alternative means. As well, reasoning in this way reverses how the burden of proof in constitutional cases should be assigned. In *Oakes* and in subsequent cases, the Court has stressed that the logic of recognizing two different stages in the review process requires that challengers bear the burden of proof in the first phase while those defending a challenged law are responsible for establishing their claims in the second. As we have seen, constitutional conversations are organized like any ordinary debate. In the first phase complainants must prove their constitutional entitlements have been limited or interfered with in some way. In the second it is the Government's and its supporters' turn. They are obliged to stand up and show that whatever limits the law imposes can be justified on the principles in section 1.

Consideration of the public interest in the first phase of the review process rather than the second reverses this order of proceeding. It results in the complainant, rather than the Government, having to establish how the competing interests affected by a law should be weighted. Deferring all consideration of the public interest until the second stage of the review process ensures it will be the Government, not the individual citizen, which is put to the time and expense of gathering and producing all of the material that supports its position. At a practical level, evaluating the public interest in the second phase frees those challenging the constitutionality of a law from having to gather all the evidence and affidavits that would be required to prove that the particular balance struck by a law is unreasonable. Spared what, experience so far suggests, can be a considerable expense, constitutional challenges would be considerably easier, although still far from costless to mount.[76] Saddling the Government with the burden of producing whatever evidence is required to establish the reasonableness of a law being reviewed has an unambiguously positive effect on the democratic quality of government as well. It ensures Governments will have to take seriously and show some minimum respect for the views of groups like workers, religious and linguistic minorities, individuals caught up in the criminal justice system, etc. whose cries of injustice all too often have been ignored in the past.

---

of the Court's judgment in *R. v. Lyons*, see M. Manning, "Lyons: A One Stage Approach to the Charter and Undue 'Constitutional Notice' " (1988), 60 Crim. Rep. 72. See Also K. Roach, "Smith and The Supreme Court: Implications for Sentencing Policy and Reform", 11 S. Ct. L. Rev 433.

76 Reports suggest the cost can range from $125,000 to $300,000, even on legal aid rates, at each level of the proceedings. For similar estimates, see Andrew Petter, "Immaculate Deception: The Charter's Hidden Agenda" (Nov. 1987), 45 *Advocate* 857, 860.

Contrary to claims of some people, that who bears the burden of proof really shouldn't matter in the end, the results of the cases show otherwise.[77] We know from our analysis of cases like the *Extradition trilogy* and *Jones* that where and/or how much of the public interest is evaluated in the first phase of the review process can be crucial to the outcome of the case. In neither of these cases were the Governments involved required to adduce any evidence to support their claims that the public interest in the enforcement of the laws being challenged outweighed the infringements of the claimants' freedom.[78] In the *Extradition trilogy*, without referring to any evidence, the Court simply accepted the Government's assertion that full review of Canada's extradition laws would be in "breach of the most elementary dictates of comity" between Canada and other sovereign nations and would "cripple the operation of our extradition arrangements".[79] Even when, as in a case like *Jones*, the limitation imposed by a law was not especially onerous or constraining, where the balancing was done could make a critical difference. As Bertha Wilson pointed out, the Government of Alberta never had to back up its claim that it would have frustrated the administration of the Act to allow a person like Larry Jones to establish that his school met the provincial standards before an impartial tribunal like a Court rather than before the education officials themselves. Indeed, the fact that other provinces have not seen fit to do so suggests the Alberta Government would have had some difficulty discharging the burden which the model in *Oakes* requires them to bear.

In both of these cases, by weighing the public interest promoted by a law in determining whether a challenger's constitutional entitlements had been limited, Governments were relieved of the responsibility of having to respond. The Governments involved never had to adduce any evidence to support their claims about the relative importance of the public interest served by the law and neither had to answer whether there were any more reasonable alternatives which would have suited their purposes just as well. In the result, in both cases, laws were validated which quite clearly limited important aspects of human freedom even though there was no reason or need for such restrictions to have been imposed.

Had the Court been more patient, and refrained from evaluating how the public interest promoted by these laws affected the challengers' claims

---

77 S.R. Peck, "An Analytical Framework for the Application of the Canadian Charter of Rights and Freedoms" (1987), 25 Osgoode Hall L.J. 1. See also J. Cameron, "The Forgotten Half of Dolphin Delivery: A Comment on the Relationship Between the Substantive Guarantees and Section One of the Charter", 22 U.B.C. L. Rev 147.

78 For another case in which it made a difference as to who was required to bear the burden of proof see *R. v. Smith, supra*, note 45.

79 *Argentina v. Mellino* (1987), 40 D.L.R. (4th) 74, at 237. See also *U.S.A. v. Cotroni, supra*, note 55.

until the second phase of the review process, these results would have been reversed. Failure to adduce evidence to support their claims about the relative importance of the public interest involved would have been fatal to the Government's case. That certainly was the conclusion of the Court in the *Ford* case when it remained faithful to the model in *Oakes* and kept the two phases of the review process analytically distinct. In that case, the Court struck down those provisions of Quebec's language laws which severely restricted the use of English in the commercial life of the province precisely because the Government of the day chose not to offer any evidence to show that such a substantial limitation on the freedom of a linguistic minority was necessary to guarantee the kind of community it wanted to create.[80]

So, in the end, reviewers should see that despite initial appearances, "abdication" is just as serious a mistake as those we have labelled as denial and avoidance. It is equally offensive to the principle of constitutional supremacy, and the logic of the Charter, for the Court to refuse to exercise its powers of review because of the public interest a challenged law is designed to promote, as it is simply to ignore and/or deny the factual basis of a challenger's claim. All three strategies involve fatal lapses in the judges' own duty to exercise their powers of review in a manner which conforms with the principles and values on which the Charter is based. All three undermine the Court's own self-styled responsibility, as "guardian of the constitution", to guarantee that lawmakers respect "the unremitting protection of human rights". Being deferential and doing the balancing in the first phase of the review process causes the judges to abdicate their powers precisely in those circumstances in which the Charter should be providing relief.

It is not possible to try to salvage the Court's analysis in these cases by arguing that each member of the Court had a choice in deciding how principles like deference and balancing might be employed. As a matter of constitutional law judges do not have a free and unfettered rein to use principles like deference or balancing however they please. Rules of constitutional review, like balancing and deference, are no different than rules governing shopping on Sunday, or abortion, or how people must behave in the marketplace. All are pieces of subordinate law and must conform to the principle of constitutional supremacy. As we have noted, section 52 of the Charter is absolute in its assertion of the primacy of the Constitution against all other forms and principles of law.[81] Applied

---

80   For a "Machiavellian" explanation for why the Government of Quebec approached the case in this way, see Michael Mandel, *The Charter of Rights and the Legalization of Politics in Canada* (Toronto: Wall & Thompson, 1989), p. 123.

81   *Supra*, note 23.

to the rules of constitutional law, section 52 requires that all of the principles and doctrines used by the Court in the interpretation and application of the Charter must themselves be derived from, and be consistent with, the principles and values which underlie the Charter.[82] Principles like deference and balancing are not exceptions to this rule. In choosing whether to be deferential to and/or do the balancing of the public interest in the first or second stages of the review process, the Court is obligated by the Constitution to act in a way which is consistent with the principles and values, on which the Charter itself is based.

In terms of the model in *Oakes*, we have seen how using principles like deference and balancing in the interpretive phase of review process is fundamentally at odds with the model of review envisaged in that case. In the language of *Oakes*, using deference as a principle of justification is always the more reasonable alternative.[83] Invariably it reconciles the tension between our commitment to our democratic tradition and to the protection of human rights in a much more sensitive and sensible way. Being deferential, and doing the balancing in the second phase of the review process, permits a judge to show the proper degree of respect for the legislative objectives a Government may wish to pursue, and the trade-offs it wants to make, while at the same time preventing unnecessary restrictions on the protection which the Charter can provide.[84]

The method of the more liberal judges makes this clear. Wilson, Dickson and Lamer were always highly deferential when it came to evaluating the purposes for which these laws were enacted and the balance of interests they effected. They recognized that setting the agenda of social policy, and reconciling the competing interests that are affected by those policies which are selected to be enacted into law, are the core function

---

82 A point it will be recalled that the Court repeatedly affirmed in its first two years in its application of the liberal and purposeful approach to constitutional interpretation. See generally L. Weinrib, "The Supreme Court of Canada and Section One of the Charter" (1988), 10 S. Ct. L. Rev. 469.

83 For the sceptical claim that "there is no uncontroversial way to draw a line between those cases where deference is appropriate and those where it is not" see Joel Bakan, "Constitutional Arguments: Interpretation and Legitimacy in Canadian Constitutional Thought", 27 Osgoode H.L.J. 123, 180 and ff. Bakan's mistake is in thinking that the line is to be drawn between the interests and activities being regulated by law rather than between the different stages of review.

84 Note at the beginning of year six the Court, led by Gerard La Forest, and over the dissenting opinion of Bertha Wilson, repeated its willingness to adopt a posture of deference in the application of the principle of alternative means thereby allowing for the needless compromise of constitutional entitlements. See *U.S.A. v. Cotroni, supra*, note 55. See also La Forest's judgment in *Black v. Law Society of Alberta* (1989), 58 D.L.R. (4th) 318, 349; and *Edwards Books and Art Ltd. v. R.* (1986), 35 D.L.R. (4th) 1. See generally note 74, *supra*.

of the political and legislative process.[85] On these aspects of the review process a principle of deference can play a legitimate and useful role. To be more deferential, or to do the balancing earlier gains nothing, except the gratuitous restriction on human freedom and the exclusion of large areas of social policy from having to conform to one of the most important principles of justice which the Constitution contains. There is no reason to adopt a posture of deference when the Court evaluates whether the means chosen by a Government are the least oppressive way to accomplish its ends. Nothing is gained by reversing the sequence in which the principles of alternate means and balancing are applied. No purpose or tradition of free and democratic societies is served by validating laws which could be easily amended to show greater respect for the freedom and dignity of those they affect without compromising any of the social objectives they were enacted to achieve.

Once a reviewer recognizes that the Court's abdication of its powers of review is just as offensive to the Constitution as the other two mistakes that plague the conservative approach, she will be in a position where a positive review would not only be possible, it would be mandatory for anyone committed to a fair-minded and even-handed evaluation of the Court's performance. The conservative approach will have been completely discredited. In virtually every case in which the Court ruled that a law did not have to be evaluated against the principles it articulated in *Oakes*, either it avoided completely, and/or analyzed incorrectly a challenger's claim and in so doing, acted unconstitutionally itself.[86] Although a reviewer would have to concede that the performance of the judges as a group was uneven at best, she could quite properly write positively and optimistically about what the future could be expected to hold.

Rid of the errors committed by the conservatives and the Court in the years immediately following its decision in *Oakes*, a reviewer could fairly emphasize that a model of judicial review remained, which could be derived, objectively, from agreed upon values, and which could enhance the democratic and progressive character of our system of government in important and enduring ways. The logical implication of discrediting the cases in which the judges themselves behaved unconstitutionally would be for the Court to return and pick up where it had left off in *Oakes*. Indeed, as we have seen, a reviewer might take some optimism from the

---

85 See Chapter 3, *supra*, note 60. One of the clearest statements of this recognition is expressed in *Irwin Toy v. Quebec, supra*, note 18.

86 In some cases such as *B.C.G.E.U. v. A.G. B.C.* (1989), 53 D.L.R. (4th) 1, *R. v. Turpin*, [1989] 1 S.C.R. 1296, *Ref. re Workers' Compensation Act* (1989), 56 D.L.R. (4th) 765, or *R. v. Milne* (1988), 46 D.L.R. (4th) 487, the Court's mistake was in a sense derivative in that it relied heavily on an earlier precedent which had employed the conservative approach.

Court's performance in the fifth year of its work with the Charter when, in many cases, the judges were able to return to the principles of review they had agreed on in *Oakes* with a consistency and degree of consensus closer to that they had shown in the first two years.[87]

If, in the future, every complaint was reviewed on its merits and no one was tempted to use or apply doctrines and principles in ways which were constitutionally flawed, the result would be that most, if not all, Canadian law would be subject to being evaluated against the principles of justice enunciated in *Oakes.* Rid of the errors which plagued its performance in the years immediately following *Oakes*, in each case the Court would be expected to begin the review process by determining whether the challenged law impinged on or interfered with any of the rights and freedoms which the Charter guaranteed. In this task, the Constitution would be read purposefully and in a large and liberal way. Although, occasionally, certain interests or activities might not fall with the protection of one of the rights and freedoms entrenched in the Charter,[88] the expectation would be that most laws could be shown to impact adversely on some aspect of the constitutional freedom and/or equality of those they affected. All law coerces and puts some constraint on the freedom of some people to govern their lives by their own lights.

In most cases it would be expected that the first phase of the review process would be relatively short and straightforward. On the model in *Oakes*, normally the person challenging the constitutionality of a law should have little difficulty in meeting the burden of proof that she or he bears in the first phase of the review process. Normally neither the factual nor the interpretative components of establishing that a law limits a constitutional guarantee should be difficult to prove. Interpreted purposefully

---

87 A reviewer could not make too much of the Court's record in year five, however. As we have seen, as a practical matter, the Court's results in year five were decidedly mixed. See p. 77, *supra.* In some cases, all or most of the members of the Court applied the model in *Oakes* in a fairly conventional and uncontroversial way. See, e.g., *Canadian Newspapers v. R., R. v. Whyte, Ford v. Quebec, Andrews v. Law Society of B.C., Slaight Communications v. Davidson,* Chapter 3, *supra*, note 2; *Black v. Law Society of Alberta, supra*, note 46; *Irwin Toy v. Quebec, supra*, note 18. On too many other occasions, however, the Court continued with the practice it developed in years three and four and failed to evaluate the constitutionality of a law against the proportionality principles in s. 1. See, e.g., *R. v. Holmes, R. v. Simmons, R. v. Corbett,* Chapter 3, *supra*, note 2. *B.C.G.E.U. v. A.G. B.C.,* (1989), 53 D.L.R. (4th) 1; *R. v. Vermette, R. v. Beare/Higgins, Reference re Workers' Compensation Act, R. v. Hufsky* (s. 9). Chapter 3, *supra*, note 3. Note the Court also misapplied the model in *R. v. Turpin, supra*, note 7.

88 As for example in *R. v. Wigglesworth,* etc., Chapter 3, *supra*, note 36; *Skapinker v. Law Society of Upper Canada* (1984) 9 D.L.R. (4th) 161; *R. v. Staranchuk* (1986), 22 D.L.R. (4th) 480. And see generally Chapter 4, p. 85.

most aspects of human freedom will fall within one or other of the entitlements entrenched in the Charter. As well, challengers can establish the factual basis of their claims just by showing the laws they attack pose some kind of threat — large or small, direct or indirect — to their freedom to organize their own lives. In most cases, most of the action would take place in the second phase of the dialogue or debate. It would be the Government and others defending the constitutionality of a challenged law who would have to do most of the talking.[89]

A reviewer could be even more particular than that. If the model in *Oakes* were applied consistently the Government's energy would, almost without exception, be directed to justifying a challenged law against the last two principles in *Oakes*. Logically, as well as practically, the object test and three proportionality principles can be reduced to these two criteria of review.[90] These two principles, of alternate means and balancing, constitute the 'inner morality' or the 'neutral principles', of Canadian constitutional law.[91] From our review of the cases decided by the Court over its first five years a reviewer would not expect Governments and their supporters would have any difficulty in establishing that a law under review was enacted for legitimate social objectives. As we have seen, in no case after its decision in *Oakes* did the Court strike down a law on this ground and, as others have pointed out, it is unlikely that many laws will be enacted in the future which do not, in some way, serve some aspect of the public interest.[92]

---

89 "Talking" is used figuratively. In fact, increasingly the most important part of the debate is conducted by the written word. Oral presentation is now substantially limited. Cf. the practice of constitutional litigation in Western Europe and the United States where oral proceedings play an even smaller role. For an introduction to some of the more important institutional and procedural features of these sytems, see Chapters 9 to 11, *infra*.

90 Logically the first proportionality principle — the rational connection test — is contained within the second criterion of alternative means and the object test is simply an extreme application of the third. Any limitation that a law imposes on the freedom of those it controls, which is not necessary for the objectives which it seeks to promote, cannot be said to be rationally connected to these objectives. Similarly, ruling laws unconstitutional which have no purpose other than the limitation of human freedom is simply another way of saying the costs and benefits of such a law are way out of wack. See generally my "The End of Law . . . . At Least As We Have Known It", in R. Devlin (ed), *Canadian Perspectives on Legal Theory* (Toronto: Emond Montgomery, 1990).

91 The phrases "inner morality" and "neutral principles" are well-known in constitutional law and are most closely associated with the work of two American legal academics: Lon Fuller, *The Morality of Law* (New Haven: Yale U. Press, 1975), and Herbert Wechsler, "Toward Neutral Principles of Constitutional Law" (1959), 73 Harv. L. Rev. 1.

92 See A. Petter and P. Monahan, "Developments in Constitutional Law: The 1985-86 Term" (1987), 9 S. Ct. L. Rev. 69, 105-112; Bertha Wilson, "The Making of A Constitution: Approaches to Judicial Interpretation", 1988 Public Law 370, 371. See Chapter 3, *supra*, note 60.

Indeed, if the Court continued to apply the model as it did when it was able to resist the conservative approach, the reviewer could be confident that it would be the principle of alternate means, rather than the balancing principle, which would organize most 'constitutional conversations' in the future. As we have noticed, in virtually every judgment in which the Court, or one of its members, proposed to strike down some aspect of a law as being unconstitutional, it was based on a finding that the law impinged upon the rights and freedoms of those it affected more than was necessary to accomplish the legislators' or executive's objectives.[93] Alternate policies, which were more consistent with Charter values, were known to exist and be readily available, and Governments were found not to have offered good enough reasons for why they had not been tried. Because, when it invalidated a law, the Court always applied the proportionality principles in the order in which they were described,[94] the Court invoked the second principle òf alternative means much more frequently than the third.[95] In a large part because of the deference everyone on the Court showed the other two branches of government when they undertook the balancing function, more often than not the Court did not disturb the balance of interests struck by the law they had been asked to review.[96]

Described in this way, a reviewer could present the model in *Oakes* in very attractive terms. On the theory of review set out in *Oakes*, it is apparent that the real significance of entrenching a written bill of rights in a constitution lies in the general infusion of principles of justice, and in particular the principle of alternative means, into the system of government rather than in the distillation and identification of a series

---

93 See, e.g., *R. v. Smith, R. v. Vaillancourt, R. v. Morgentaler, Andrews v. Law Society of B.C.*, Chapter 3, *supra*, note 2; *Ford v. Quebec, R. v. Thibault*, Chapter 3, *supra*, note 3, *Black v. Law Society of Alberta, supra*, note 46. See also *R. v. Stevens* (1989), 51 D.L.R. (4th) 395; and *R. v. Schwartz* (1989), 55 D.L.R. (4th) 1. The major exceptions would be the judgments of Wilson and Beetz in *R. v. Morgentaler* (1988), 44 D.L.R. (4th) 385; of Beetz and McIntyre in *Irwin Toy v. Quebec, supra*, note 18; and of Beetz by himself in *Slaight Communications v. Davidson* (1989), 59 D.L.R. (4th) 416.

94 Thereby implicitly, if not consciously, following the Rawlsian idea of lexical ordering. See Chapter 3, *supra*, note 67.

95 Even when the Court declared a law to be constitutional, its analysis generally centered more on the question of alternate means than on evaluating whether the public interest it promoted outweighed the restrictions it imposed on constitutional guarantees — see, e.g., *R. v. Whyte, R. v. Hufsky*, Chapter 3, *supra* note 2; *Irwin Toy v. Quebec, supra*, note 18.

96 *Edwards Books, Slaight Communications v. Davidson*, Chapter 3, *supra*, note 2; *Canadian Newspapers v. R., R. v. Hufsky, R. v. Thomsen, R. v. Whyte*, Chapter 3, *supra*, note 3; *Irwin Toy v. Quebec, supra*, note 18. In two other cases, not involving a direct challenge to an Act of the legislature, the balance struck by the Court seems especially open to criticism — *R. v. Milne* and *B.C.G.E.U. v. A.G. B.C., supra*, note 86.

of very precisely defined individual rights and freedoms which alone enjoy the protection of the Charter. Judicial review is mostly about justification not interpretation.[97] In the jargon of economists and policy analysts, all law must be evaluated against two standard measures of social well-being. The principle the Court has called alternate means is known to economists as a standard formulation of Paretian welfare. The balancing principle in turn evaluates laws against a conventional utilitarian or cost/benefit criterion.[98] Certainly on the performance of the judges who applied the model most consistently, constitutional review can be held out as an effective way of enhancing the progressive quality of the substantive policies that Governments choose to transform into law. Laws that were drafted too broadly, that interfered with or threatened human freedom too much, would be struck down in the same way the liberals ruled unconstitutional the collective bargaining, extradition, and dangerous offender laws they had been asked to review. No law that did not respect, as much as it could, the personal dignity and autonomy of those whose lives it controlled would be expected to survive.

As well as pointing to its generally progressive tendencies, the reviewer could also highlight the fact that the model in *Oakes* is quite consistent with our tradition of democracy and the sovereignty of the popular (legislative) will. It is not a theory of the Charter and written bills of rights which is afflicted with the tension that makes judicial review so problematic for populists and conservatives alike. The two principles of justice that are at the centre of the review process are highly supportive of the democratic values and aims that underlie the system of government that distinguishes free and democratic societies. The principle of alternative means certainly does not challenge the sovereignty of the legislature or executive in any way. It allows the elected branches of Government virtually unfettered freedom in deciding what their agendas will be.[99] The principle merely asks whether there are any other policies a Government might

---

97 This orientation and focus is exactly contrary to the conventional wisdom in the United States where constitutional scholars of all stripes have turned to theories of interpretation to ground their understanding of constitutional law. See, e.g., O. Fiss, "Objectivity & Interpretation", 34 Stan. L. Rev. 739; P. Brest, "Interpretation & Interest", 34 Stan. L. Rev. 765.

98 Formally, one policy is said to be Pareto superior to another if it can make some individual or group better off without making anyone worse off. On a utilitarian formulation a law would be said to enhance social well-being if the benefits gained by those affected by it outweigh the costs it imposes. See generally J. Coleman "Economics and The Law: A Critical Review of the Economic Approach to Law" (1984), 94 Ethics 649; D. Winch, *Analytical Welfare Economics* (New York: Penguin, 1971).

99 *Supra*, Chapter 3, note 60. It might be noted that the attitude the Court has adopted in evaluating legislative purposes is not exceptional. The European Court of Human Rights, for example, has adopted a similar approach. See B. Hovius, "The Limitation

have adopted, which would have been just as effective in realizing its objectives as the one it used, but which would interfere less with the freedom of people to control their own lives. Indeed, in many of the most important cases in which the Court ruled that a law could not pass this most basic principle of review, the Court made it very clear how the Government's objectives might be formulated in a way which would meet the principle of alternative means.[100]

In theory, the balancing principle involves a more serious threat to our democratic tradition and the principle of popular sovereignty. Balancing, as we have seen, unambiguously involves the Court in second guessing the other two branches of government no matter where it is done. In this function the Court comes closest to performing what is recognized to be the essence of political judgment.[101] But, it is precisely at this stage of the review process that the model in *Oakes* insists that the Court be cognizant of and deferential to the sovereignty of the legislative will, as befits its subordinate position. A 'margin of appreciation', to use the terminology of the European Court of Human Rights, is extended to the legislative and executive branches when the Court enters this final phase of its inquiry.[102] The Court's evaluation of the balance struck by laws aimed at prohibiting Sunday shopping,[103] impaired driving[104] and advertising aimed at young children[105] showed that when it was applied sensitively, the balancing principle was not likely to result in the wholesale frustration or rejection of the legislative will. Indeed, the very small number of instances in which a law was struck down because it violated either of the proportionality principles suggests that if there is a danger in how the

---

Clauses of the European Convention on Human Rights: A Guide for the Application of Section 1 of the Charter" (1985), 17 Ottawa L. Rev 213. As Hovius points out, the critical criterion of evaluation for the European Court, like our own, is the principle of alternative means.

100 See, e.g., *R. v. Smith, R. v. Vaillancourt, R. v. Morgentaler, Andrews v. Law Society of B.C.*, Chapter 3, *supra*, note 2; *Black v. Law Society of Alberta*, *supra*, note 46. See also the judgments issued by the liberals in *R. v. Stevens* (1989), 51 D.L.R. (4th) 394; the *Extradition and Labour trilogies, R. v. Holmes, R. v. Schwartz*, Chapter 3, *supra*, note 2.

101 R. Beiner, *Political Judgment* (Chicago: U. of Chicago Press, 1983).

102 For an analysis of the margin of appreciation, see J.G. Merrill's *The Development of International Law by the European Court of Human Rights* (Manchester University Press, 1988), pp. 136-160.

103 *Edwards Books and Art Ltd. v. R., supra*, note 84.

104 *R. v. Hufsky, R. v. Thomsen, R. v. Whyte*, Chapter 3, *supra*, note 2. For two assessments that the Court was too deferential in these cases see E. Colvin and T. Quigley, "Developments in Criminal Law and Procedure: 1987-88 Term", 11 S. Ct. L. Rev. 165, and M. MacCrimmon, "Developments in the Law of Evidence: The 1987-88 Term", 11 S. Ct. L. Rev 275.

105 *Irwin Toy Ltd. v. Quebec* (1989), 58 D.L.R. (4th) 577.

Court will apply the model in the future it is that it will act more diffidently than it should.

If a reviewer were so inclined, she could be even bolder in her claims about how compatible a process of constitutional review is with our democratic traditions of government. Certainly, as it was applied by the more liberal members, the model in *Oakes* can fairly be portrayed as a new means by which individuals and groups, who traditionally have not had much influence in the process of politics, can now make their voices heard. Far from distracting or distancing people from involvement in the political process,[106] groups like workers, refugees, religious and linguistic minorities are given an avenue through which they can participate directly in the administrative and legislative processes of government. It provides a new opportunity for individuals to be involved in the political process through interest groups other than the more traditional, party organizations. With the opportunity to ask the Court to review the constitutionality of virtually any law or action taken by Government, or one of its agents, interest groups like these acquire a new credibility in demanding that the laws which impinge most directly on their lives be made to conform to the principles outlined in *Oakes*. Governments would know that they would likely be taken to Court if they chose summarily to reject the complaints of those adversely affected by a policy they had decided to enact into law. Few Governments would relish the prospect of being publicly censured for having acted in an extreme and arbitrary way, and so it would be expected that, in the majority of cases, they would take this new kind of political talk seriously.

Even if politicians proved to be more arrogant and/or indifferent to public criticism of this kind, and it was necessary to challenge the constitutionality of a law all the way to the Supreme Court, judicial review would still promote involvement in our system of government overall. Judicial review itself would become a new way of addressing and having an influence in the political arena. As well, simply going through the exercise of having the constitutionality of a law evaluated by the Court is likely to have an energizing effect on the political community at large. That certainly was the impact of the Court's decisions in cases like *Big M Drug Mart, Edwards Books,* (Sunday shopping); *Morgentaler* (abortion); and *Ford* (language signs) where vigorous debates and legislative activity followed as much when a

---

106 A concern raised by, amongst others, Peter Russell, "The Effect of the Charter of Rights on the Policy-Making Role of Canadian Courts" (1982), 25 Can. Pub. Admin. 1, 32; Russell, "The Political Purposes of the Canadian Charter of Rights and Freedoms", 61 Can. Bar Rev. 30, 52; but see Russell, "The First Three Years in Charterland", 28 Can. Pub. Admin. 367. See also Douglas Schmeizer, "The Case Against Entrenchment of a Canadian Bill of Rights", 1 Dal. L.J. 15; Michael Mandel, *The Charter of Rights and the Legalization of Politics in Canada* (Toronto: Wall & Thompson, 1989).

challenged law was held to be constitutional as when it was not.[107]

With the model in *Oakes* as the centerpiece of her review, it would be entirely legitimate for a reviewer to end on an up-beat and positive note. Even if the Court's record over the first five years warranted only mixed reviews, a reviewer could forecast a long run of much stronger performances. Future presentations, reviewing laws which touched some of the most basic aspects of human existence, had already been scheduled by the Court. Challenges to laws regulating religious exercises and instruction in the schools; different kinds of political and electioneering activities; how one establishes one's refugee status; and the compulsory payment of union dues, to name only a few, have already passed through one or more levels of review in the lower courts and sooner or later will be referred to the Supremes. In good conscience a reviewer could encourage these groups, and others, to press on with their claims in the expectation that they would find the Court's performance stimulating and ultimately quite gratifying. The boldest reviewers might dare to close by venturing the prediction that even though no one cheered when the Charter was entrenched into Canada's Constitution, there is good reason to hope that the applause will begin shortly and continue for a long time to come. Indeed, perhaps the only reason a reviewer might decide not to end on such a strong note would be a concern that the five new judges who joined the Court over the last year of the performance might repeat the mistakes of those they replaced, instead of following the leadership and method of review practised by the three more liberal members who remained on the Court.[108]

---

107 For a very critical and generally pessimistic evaluation of how politicians have responded to the decisions of the Court in these and several other cases decided in the lower courts, see M. Mandel, *The Legalization of Politics, supra*, note 106.

108 At the time the manuscript was sent to press, the new judges had written too few opinions to indicate clearly which approach they will favour. Of the judgments handed down since the curtain fell on year five, the most worrisome, in terms of compromising the integrity of the model in *Oakes* would be *U.S.A. v. Cotroni, supra*, note 55, where, led by Gerard La Forest, the Court imposed a further restraint on the principle of alternative means. See also *Moysa v. Labour Relations Board* (1989), 60 D.L.R. (4th) 1, and *Mackay v. Manitoba* (1989), 61 D.L.R. (4th) 385, in which, led by two of the newest members John Sopinka and Peter Cory, the Court repeated the mistakes of denial and avoidance that had plagued its performance in the years immediately following *Oakes*. For a brief glimpse into Sopinka's view of the Charter prior to his joining the Court, see J. Sopinka, "The Charter: A View from the Bar" in G. Beaudoin, *Charter Cases*, L. Rev. 13, 1987, p. 403. For an extra-judicial statement by the newest member of the Court, Beverley McLachlin, see "The Charter of Rights and Freedoms: A Judicial Perspective" (1989), 23 U.B.C. L. Rev 579. For an evaluation of the performances of the new judges on the Court, see my essay "A Conservative's Court: The Politicization of Law", forthcoming U.T.L.J.

PART II

Talking Heads:
The Practice of Constitutional Review

5

Freedom of Religion:
Of Students in Our Schools

All of the first Part of this book has been written from the perspective of a person reviewing the performance of the Supreme Court of Canada as it tried to understand and work out a theory about what the Charter and judicial review really mean. Not without difficulty we have come to the conclusion that even though the performance of the judges, as a group, was disappointing, and even constitutionally defective at certain points, there is still reason to see the entrenchment of a written bill of rights in the Canadian Constitution in a positive light. Paradoxical as it may seem, by analyzing the weakest points of the performance very carefully, a reviewer can identify a very powerful theme in the performance overall. Reviewers should see that there is good reason at the end of the performance to applaud, and even to cheer, for some of the individual performances they have seen.

Although it is reasonable to expect that there are many who would read such a review and find it persuasive, it seems equally certain that the most serious of the sceptics will remain unconvinced. For them, the way in which we have come to praise the Court will likely seem highly contrived. For many sceptics substantial doubts would remain about the model itself. There would be a nagging suspicion that even if everyone on the Court embraced the theory of review set out in *Oakes*, that would be no guarantee that the results would be as positive as a believer might hope. People will say that in the review of the Court's performance that we have followed so far, too little attention has been paid to how the principles and doctrines outlined in *Oakes* were actually applied. Rather than a mechanical, automatic model which the believer presents, sceptics will say that, in fact, there is a good deal of flexibility and ambiguity in the liberal method which allows for a wide range of possible results.[1]

Even from our cursory examination of how the various members of the Court applied the model in *Oakes*, we know that the sceptic would be able to point to a good deal of evidence to support such a claim. As we saw in the first Part, the rough division between the conservative and liberal members of the Court applied as much in their views as to how they should exercise their powers of review, as in their ideas about whether they should be used at all.[2] On almost every aspect of the model, we have seen instances in which, even among those who favoured the more liberal approach, there was substantial variation in the judgments that were "handed down". The principle of purposeful interpretation certainly did not always lead to the same conclusions as to what interests a right or freedom might guarantee. The Court's decisions in *Morgentaler*, the *Labour trilogy* and other less well known cases attests to that.[3] Neither did the

---

1 See, e.g., J. Bakan, "Constitutional Arguments: Interpretation and Legitimacy in Canadian Constitutional Thought" (1989), 27 Osgoode Hall L.J. 123; P. Monahan and A. Petter, "Developments in Constitutional Law: The 1985-86 Term" (1987), 9 S. Ct. L. Rev. 61; M. Mandel, *The Charter of Rights and The Legalization of Politics In Canada* (Toronto: Wall & Thompson, 1989); P. Russell, "Canada's Charter of Rights and Freedoms: A Political Report" (1988), Public Law 388.

2 See generally the discussion in Part One, Chapter 3, p. 57 & ff. The divergence of views that developed within the Court on the application of the principles established in *Oakes* was picked up and made the focus of an essay by Robin Elliott within a year of its decision in that case. See "The Supreme Court of Canada and Section One — The Erosion of the Common Front", 12 Queens L.J. 277. See also P. Monahan and A. Petter, "Developments in Constitutional Law", *supra*, note 1.

The division in the Court, essentially along liberal/conversative lines can be seen in many of the most important cases in which the Court applied the model in *Oakes*, including *R. v. Vaillancourt* (1988), 47 D.L.R. (4th) 400; *R. v. Morgentaler* (1988), 44 D.L.R. (4th) 386; *Andrews v. Law Society of B.C.* (1989), 56 D.L.R. (4th) 1; *Black v. Law Society of Alberta* (1989), 58 D.L.R. (4th) 319; *Irwin Toy Ltd. v. Quebec* (1989), 58 D.L.R. (4th) 577; *Slaight Communications v. Davidson* (1989), 59 D.L.R. (4th) 416.

3 See, e.g., *R. v. Smith* (1988), 40 D.L.R. (4th) 435; *R. v. Lyons* (1988), 44 D.L.R. (4th) 193; *R. v. Mills* (1986), 29 D.L.R. (4th) 161; *R. v. Vaillancourt* (1988), 47 D.L.R. (4th) 400; *R. v. Rahey* (1987), 39 D.L.R. (4th) 481; *Mellino v. Argentina* (1987), 40 D.L.R. (4th) 74.

For an essay arguing that the failure of the Court to agree on what purposes were served by s. 2(d) (Freedom of Association) demonstrates the indeterminacy and illegitimacy of the purposeful approach, see J. Bakan "Constitutional Arguments . . . ." *supra*, note 1. Bakan's argument, in my view, is flawed in a number of ways. In the first place, the case law he relies on to support his position is too thin to sustain his thesis. He never considers, let alone accounts for, the majority of cases when everyone on the Court was agreed on the purposeful approach. More seriously, he misreads the major case he cites — the *Ref. re Alberta Public Service Employee Relations Act*. In that case, as we saw in Part One, it was not how Le Dain applied the purposive approach, but the fact that he completely ignored it which makes his opinion so wanting. By contrast, the judgments of McIntyre and Dickson on this aspect of the case is much closer than

principle of alternative means always lead the judges to the same conclusion, as the separate opinions of Wilson and Dickson in the *Labour trilogy* so clearly illustrate.[4] As well, we have noticed that deference was a principle which meant very different things to Bertha Wilson than it did to Brian Dickson and Antonio Lamer and especially to Gerard La Forest.[5] And, balancing was a function which was notoriously unprincipled and on which all members of the Court struggled on their own. Not only did the judges differ as to when the balancing function should be performed, they also frequently disagreed about what interests and activities could be weighed in the scales[6] and, in the final analysis, what an appropriate balance was.[7] Moreover, on occasion, even when the members of the Court were generally agreed on how the balance of competing interests should be weighed, many would say their judgment was patently wrong.[8]

The concern of those who are very sceptical, then, would be that the model in *Oakes* is not as objective and determinative as some reviewers might be inclined to suggest. In their minds, the Court's own record shows

---

Bakan suggests (see S. Kennett and D. Beatty, "Striking Back: Fighting Words, Social Protest and Political Participation in Free and Democratic Societies" (1988), 67 Can. Bar Rev. 573). Throughout his analysis of the purposeful method, Bakan never considers the possibility that there are right, or at least better, answers about the meaning of the various rights and freedoms which the Charter guarantees.

4 See also *Edwards Books* (1987), 35 D.L.R. (4th) 1; *R. v. Lyons*, *supra*, note 3; *Andrews v. Law Society of B.C.*, *supra*, note 2; *Irwin Toy v. Quebec*, *supra*, note 2; *Black v. Law Society of Alberta*, *supra*, note 2.

For an argument that the principle of alternative means is as indeterminate as the method of purposeful interpretation, see J. Bakan, "Constitutional Arguments . . . .", *supra*, note 1. For a critical assessment of the Court's application of the principle in evaluating different parts of our criminal code, see E. Colvin and T. Quigley, "Developments in Criminal Law and Procedure: The 1987-88 Term", 11 S. Ct. L. Rev 165; M. MacCrimmon, "Developments in the Law of Evidence: The 1987-88 Term", 11 S. Ct. L. Rev. 275, 333; Don Stuart, "Holmes and Whyte: ZigZags on Reversing the Onus, Section One, and Care and Control" (1988), 64 C.R. 143.

5 See Chapter 3, *supra*, pp. 59-60

6 See, e.g., *R. v. Mills*, *R. v. Rahey*, *supra*, note 3; *R. v. Holmes* (1988), 50 D.L.R.(4th) 680; *R. v. Schwartz* (1989), 55 D.L.R. (4th) 1. See also, at the beginning of year six, *R. v. Kalanj*, [1989] 1 S.C.R. 1594.

7 *R. v. Smith*, *supra*, note 3; *Andrews v. Law Society of B.C.*; *Black v. Law Society of Alberta*; *Irwin Toy v. Quebec*; *Slaight Communications v. Davidson*, *supra*, note 2. There were also disagreements in several s. 24 cases in which the action of some Government official, rather than Act of some legislature was at stake — see e.g. *R. v. Simmons* (1989), 55 D.L.R. (4th) 673.

8 See e.g., *R. v. Milne* (1988), 46 D.L.R. (4th) 487. For a review of the Court's decision in *Milne*, see E. Colvin and T. Quigley, "Developments in Criminal Law and Procedure: The 1987-88 Term", 11 S. Ct. L. Rev. 165, 227. See also *B.C.G.E.U. v. A.G. B.C.* (1989), 53 D.L.R. (4th) 1. For a critique of the Court's judgment in this case, see P. Macklem, "Developments in Employment Law: The 1988-89 Term", forthcoming, 12 S. Ct. L. Rev.

that even this theory of constitutional review allows each judge a good deal of discretion to decide whether a law is constitutional or not. Even if the Court were to abandon those approaches and methods of analysis which are constitutionally flawed, the strong sceptic would still challenge the democratic legitimacy of judges having this power and question whether it would make any difference in the result. If, as it does, the model in *Oakes* leaves considerable freedom for each judge to rule in each case, how can it reasonably be expected, the sceptic will ask, that the choices will be any different from those the Court has given over the course of its first five years?

Any reviewer bent on ending her review on a positive note must, I think, be bothered by the sceptic's last question. Even though there were many cases, especially in year five, when the Court was able to return to the consensus it had shown in the first two years,[9] the fact remains, as we saw in the first Part, that there were also repeated instances in the three years following *Oakes* of significant differences of opinion among the members of the Court in how the model of review developed in that case should be applied. Before submitting her review for publication, it would be incumbent on the reviewer to consider the possibility that such a pattern of decision making was endemic to the model in *Oakes*. After all, it would be quite wrong for someone to encourage people to take in a performance which, as likely as not, was destined to disappoint.

A simple way for a reviewer to be responsive to the sceptics' concern would be to try and imagine how various cases now at, or on their way to, the Court would be decided if all of the judges stuck to the model in *Oakes*. She could cast herself in the role of one of the judges on the Court and endeavour to determine whether, in the cases which, sooner or later, the Court will be asked to resolve, the principles and doctrines laid out in that case generally lead to determinative and progressive results. There are already an enormous number of challenges, working their way through the different levels of review in the lower courts, from which the reviewer might choose. She could easily select particular cases which involved individuals who traditionally have not been well represented, or had much influence, in the political process and which, collectively, touched on all of the major rights and freedoms entrenched in the Charter.

Religious minorities, for example, have challenged the constitutionality of school boards incorporating religious instruction and religious exercises in the curricula and the daily life of the public schools. Fundamental issues about freedom of expression in the political and electoral processes have been raised in a series of challenges by prisoners'

---

9 A list of the cases decided in year five, in which all members of the Court were agreed on how a challenge should be resolved, is set out in Chapter 3, *supra*, note 3.

groups, public servants and public interest organizations of all stripes. Dissident workers have initiated challenges claiming compulsory union laws violate their freedom of association, while refugee groups and their supporters have asked the courts to strike down a new refugee determination law which is seen as threatening the lives, liberty, and the security of countless persons. If the reviewer discovered that in each of these cases the principles and doctrines set out in *Oakes* generally led to results which were both determinative and progressive, she could safely conclude that any lingering scepticism was not really justified. She could be confident in the integrity of a review which concluded on a positive note and could reasonably assume that after these cases had been finally resolved even the most sceptical critic would concede some progressive and democratic tendencies of constitutional review.

It would be natural for a reviewer, reflecting in this way, to begin by considering the question of whether and/or to what extent religion can be made part of daily life in our schools. Religion, after all, appears first, along with freedom of conscience, in the fundamental freedoms which are entrenched in section 2. It is also a subject about which the courts have shown some sensitivity even before the Charter was entrenched.[10] Indeed for some, religious freedom lies at the very core of the values which the Charter is meant to protect.[11]

The issue would be of interest to the sceptics as well. So far, as we shall see, the judges in the lower courts who have tackled the legitimacy of Government policy mixing religion and schools have been all over the map. The treatment this issue has received in the lower courts would offer some confirmation of the sceptics' doubts as to the objectivity of the model in *Oakes*. On the other hand, many sceptics, most of whom are on the political left, would likely be intrigued by these particular challenges because at least one of them was spearheaded by a "talking head" whose passion and commitment to social justice is as deep and vigorous as their own.[12]

As a practical matter, beginning with freedom of religion would allow

---

10 For a pre-Charter case in which the Supreme Court protected the freedom of religious minorities against the power of the State, see *Saumur v. Quebec*, [1953] 4 D.L.R. 641. See also *Chabot v. School Commissioners of Lamorandiere and A.G. Quebec* (1957), 12 D.L.R. (2d) 796; *Walter v. A.G. Alberta*, [1969] S.C.R. 383.

11 See L. Weinrib, "The Religion Clause: Reading the Lesson" (1986), 8 S. Ct. L. Rev. 507.

12 See *Zylberberg v. Sudbury Board of Education* (1986), 29 D.L.R. (4th) 709, reversed (1989), 52 D.L.R. (4th) 577. It might be noted that not only has Philip Zylberberg claimed the benefit of the Charter to demand respect for his own religious freedom, he is also counsel to Gary Grondin who is claiming that the Ontario Government violated his constitutional rights by not allowing him to vote when he was imprisoned in a federal penitentiary. See *Re Grondin and A.G. Ontario* (1988), 65 O.R. (2d) 427, discussed in Chapter 6, *infra*.

the reviewer to move into her new role in a fairly gradual way. This is a subject on which we have considerable experience with the Court's approach. Religion, it will be recalled, was the constitutional freedom asserted in at least four major cases heard by the Court in its first five years.[13] Moreover, the cases in which religious instruction and religious exercises in the public schools have been challenged are themselves very focused and present a relatively simple context in which the model in *Oakes* can be tested.

Two types of challenges have been initiated so far.[14] The first group of cases has contested the constitutionality of beginning and/or ending the school day by saying prayers and reading from religious scriptures. The second has challenged the requirement that all schools include some period of religious instruction as part of the regular school curriculum during the normal hours of the week. The first complaints were filed against the opening exercises that were held in some Ontario schools and soon after parallel challenges in British Columbia, Manitoba, and Alberta followed suit.[15] Although there were some variations in the details of the different provincial programmes that were attacked, for the most part, the general contours were the same. In every case, the challengers' objection was based on the claim that students were being compelled to take part either in religious exercises or in religious instruction against their will.

For the reviewer's purposes it will be sufficient to focus on the situation in Ontario where both parts of the religious studies programme were challenged and where the cases have gone furthest in the courts. Ontario's scheme is governed by section 50 of the *Education Act* which is divided into two parts. The first section operates as a kind of grant of legal authority from the legislature to the local school boards. It says that every student

---

13 *R. v. Big M Drug Mart* (1985), 18 D.L.R. (4th) 321 (the *Lord's Day Act*); *Jones v. R.* (1986), 31 D.L.R. (4th) 569 (Alberta *School Act*); *Edwards Books, supra*, note 4 (Ontario *Retail Business Holidays Act*), and *Re Education Act* (1988), 40 D.L.R. (4th) 18 (financing of Roman Catholic schools in Ontario).

14 If American experience repeats itself in Canada, sooner or later challenges can be expected by Christian fundamentalist groups to the teaching of evolutionary theories of science in the schools. For an introduction to the American experience see N. Strossen, " 'Secular Humanism' and 'Scientific Creationism': Proposed Standards for Reviewing Curricular Decisions Affecting Students' Religious Freedom" (1986), 47 Ohio State L.J. 333; "The Lessons of Creation-Science: Public School Curriculum and the Religion Clauses", 50 Fordham L. Rev. 1113.

15 At the time of writing, two of these cases had been argued and decided by Ontario's Court of Appeal. See *Zylberberg v. Sudbury Board of Education* and *Canadian Civil Liberties Association v. Ontario, infra*, notes 18 and 19. Other cases, involving challenges by teachers to their participation in religious programmes have been initiated but not yet heard in Court. In British Columbia, one judgment has been rendered in *Russow and Lambert v. A.G. B.C.* (1990), 62 D.L.R. (4th) 98, while in Manitoba and Alberta the cases were still in the process leading up to argument in their courts.

shall be *allowed* to receive religious instruction if the parents, (and in some cases the students) consent.[16] The second part of the section is an exemption from or limitation on the first. It provides that no student can be *required* to study a religious book or participate in a religious class or religious exercise, if his or her parents object.

Pursuant to powers the Act granted to the Government, Regulations were drawn up which contained more detailed rules on when the courses of instruction should be offered and what the content of the opening and closing exercises should be. As well, and to conform to the second part of section 50, the Regulations contained an explicit exemption for students who objected to participating either in the religious exercises or the religious instruction or both. Subject to the broad caveat that all students who asked to be excused would be exempted, the Regulations provided that each day every school must be opened with a lesson from the Scriptures, or other suitable reading, and the repeating of the Lord's Prayer or other suitable prayers. In addition the Regulations called for two, one-half hour periods of religious education each week.[17]

In a case called *Zylberberg v. Sudbury Board of Education*,[18] a group of parents challenged the constitutionality of the opening exercises. In *Canadian Civil Liberties Assoc. v. Ontario*[19] (*Elgin County Board of Education*), the periods of religious instruction were attacked. In both, the claim was that the Regulations passed by the Government of Ontario, as well as the curricula and prayers designed by the particular school boards, violated section 2(a) of the Charter even though the law and curricula provided that any student who objected to participating in the exercises or instruction would be automatically excused.

In both cases, the challengers argued that the policy of "compulsory provision" and "automatic exemption" was constitutionally flawed because it failed to offer students, who did not want to participate, a meaningful choice. The claim was that the compulsion-exemption policy forced students to choose between two alternatives both of which impinged on their religious freedom. Some students, it was argued, would choose not

---

16 An interesting issue, not canvassed in the text, will arise when a student and his or her parents disagree. See E. Hurlbert and M. Hurlbert, *School Law Under the Charter of Rights and Freedoms* (Calgary: University of Calgary Press, 1990), and D.A. Schmeiser and R.J. Wood, "Student Rights Under the Charter", 49 Sask. L. Rev. 49; A.W. MacKay, "The Canadian Charter of Rights and Freedoms: A Springboard to Students' Rights" (1984), 4 Windsor Yearbook of Access to Justice 174.

17 It might be noted that the Regulations also provided an opportunity for a School Board to apply to the Ministry for an exemption from having to provided any religious instruction in its schools. See Ontario Regulation 262, R.R.O. 1980, as amended, s. 28(15).

18 (1986), 29 D.L.R. (4th) 709, reversed (1989), 52 D.L.R. (4th) 577.

19 (1988), 50 D.L.R. (4th) 193, reversed (1990), 65 D.L.R. (4th) 1 (Ont. C.A.).

to take advantage of the exemption policy and would remain in the class. As a factual matter the exemption would not provide any real choice because, either out of embarrassment, peer pressure and/or disapproval of their teachers, they would be deterred from using it. For these students, the exemption policy was simply not perceived as providing a realistic means to preserve their religious freedom. For these students, it was said, the psychological impact of the law would coerce them into witnessing religious exercises and taking instruction in religious ideas which were antithetical to their own.[20]

Even for students who were not affected by the law in this way, and who could overcome the pressure and embarrassment others might feel, the law was said to be defective because it forced them to make a public statement about their differences with the religious views held by the majority. It forced them to make a public profession of their religious faith in circumstances which, psychologically at least, could be equally burdensome. In the result, the challengers said, however a student reacted to the exemption opportunity which the law provided, his religious freedom would have been compromised. Parallelling the dilemma which Ontario's Sunday closing law presented to retailers whose religious holy day did not fall on Sunday, the exemption provision was said to present students and their parents with a Hobson's choice. Whichever way they chose, the law would have compelled them to participate in a religious activity or make a religious statement which they would otherwise not have made.

As the reviewer begins to reflect on how these challenges should be resolved, she should sense very quickly that they provide an excellent introduction to the judicial role she has assumed. For someone intent on testing the theory of review set out in *Oakes*, these cases, it turns out, present a very simple and straightforward opening act. In neither case is there any reason to expect the analysis will deviate from the model in *Oakes* or that it will have a regressive effect. There should be no surprises or distractions in the reviewer's debut on the judicial stage. As the model predicts, the reviewer should find that the challengers will have no difficulty establishing the legal and factual bases of their claims. As she would expect, the first phase of the review process will not take very long to complete. Rather most of her attention will be focused on deciding whether religious exercises and courses of religious instruction can be justified on the means/ends analysis on which the model in *Oakes* is based. Indeed, she should discover that she will be able to move almost immediately to the principle of alternative means and to concentrate on identifying whether other exercises and programmes of instruction could be devised which would

---

20 Similar evidence was adduced in the challenge to the parallel provisions in B.C.'s *School Act*. See *Russow v. A.G. B.C.*, *supra*, note 15.

interfere less with the freedom of religious minorities.

In contrast with some of the cases the Supreme Court considered in its first five years, the reviewer can be reasonably certain that in these cases there will be no question whether this is the kind of law and policy which is subject to review. Based on the record of the cases in the lower courts, she would not expect that anyone on the Supreme Court would have any doubts that religious exercises and courses of instruction, of the kind that were involved in these cases, are a part of Canadian law which falls within the scope of the Charter and the principle of constitutional supremacy. Even though none of the challengers attacked the constitutionality of section 50 of the *Education Act* itself, both the Regulations, which provided for the religious exercises and instruction, and the actual curricula developed by the school boards, are unquestionably the kinds of laws that the Charter and the principle of constitutional supremacy govern. All of the judges who heard the *Elgin County* case were quite explicit that the Charter applied to laws of this kind and neither the trial court nor the Court of Appeal in *Zylberberg* raised any question that either the Regulations or the content of the religious exercises lay beyond the Charter's reach.[21]

Moreover, the reviewer will know that, from a constitutional point of view, it makes no difference whether the Legislature formulated the content of the courses and the religious exercises explicitly in the statute or whether, as it did, it delegated this power to the local school boards.[22] The fact that the Act, and parts of the Regulation, are written in permissive rather than compulsory language should not affect the scope of the Court's powers of review. In either case it is evident that it is the Government of Ontario, and ultimately the Legislative Assembly of that province, which

---

21 In the *Elgin County* case, the Ontario Court of Appeal treated the Board's curriculum as Government conduct rather than law *per se*. See generally P. Hogg, *Constitutional Law of Canada*, 2nd ed. (Toronto: Carswell, 1985), p. 671.

   It should also be acknowledged that even though on the record of the lower courts the reach of the Charter was not in issue, it is still possible the Supreme Court might raise the issue on its own motion. That, in fact, was what happened in *Dolphin Delivery*, where the Court raised the question of the applicability of the Charter to private litigation in the middle of oral argument, on its own, and without the prompting of either party. See A. Petter and P. Monahan, "Developments in Constitutional Law: The 1986-87 Term", *supra*, note 1, at 123. Some argue it was the resulting lack of adequate preparation by counsel in advising the Court whether the Charter applied to law involved in private litigation which best explains the Court's much criticized decision in that case. For reviews of the Court's decision in *Dolphin Delivery* see Chapter 4, *supra*, note 60.

22 In a case decided just as the curtain fell on year five, the Court acted on this principle in ruling that the Charter applied to the decisions of arbitrators whose powers were derived from an Act of the legislature. See *Slaight Communications v. Davidson* (1989), 59 D.L.R. (4th) 416.

is responsible for the inclusion of religious exercises and instruction in the regular programme of the schools. Without the grant of permission which section 50 contains, no school board would have any authority to introduce these kinds of exercises and subjects of instruction into the schools. In effect, the scheme of the Act and the Regulations drafted by the Government is to delegate to each local school board the legal authority to develop the specific kinds of religious exercises and courses of instruction that are most appropriate for their communities' needs. However they are formulated, the reviewer will know that the rules and policies — the law — in force in each school would have to defer to the principle of constitutional supremacy. From the analysis she followed in Part One she will know that whether a law threatens personal freedom directly or indirectly does not affect the Charter's reach.[23] To hold otherwise would mean that a Government could achieve indirectly what the Constitution prohibits it from doing itself.

Nor would the fact that the coercion effected by the Government's policy involves psychological pressure rather than a physical threat alter the reviewer's analysis in any way. Certainly as a legal matter the reviewer can be confident that, after its decisions in cases like *Morgentaler* and *Edwards Books*,[24] the Court will find nothing novel in extending the reach of the Charter to protect against laws which impinge on personal freedom in this way. Mental well-being, including freedom from anxiety and stress caused by the State, is as much a part of the personal autonomy protected by the Charter as invasions of a more physical kind.

As well, and even though some of the judges in the lower courts struggled with this question,[25] the reviewer would have no reason to think that anyone on the Supreme Court would have any difficulty with the factual basis of these claims. In all of these cases, the evidence was essentially uncontested that individual students did feel coerced into attending religious exercises and courses of instruction, which were antagonistic to their own beliefs, even though the law explicitly said that they would be automatically exempted if they didn't want to be involved. In the cases in both Ontario and British Columbia, evidence was given by the challengers and members of their families, under oath, that they personally felt considerable pressure not to take advantage of the exemption because they were worried that if they did their children would be subjected

---

23 See Chapter 4, *supra*, notes 45 and 49.
24 *R. v. Morgentaler* (1988), 44 D.L.R. (4th) 386; *Edwards Books and Art Ltd. v. R.* (1986), 35 D.L.R. (4th) 1. See also *R. v. Rahey* (1987), 39 D.L.R. (4th) 481.
25 See, e.g., William Anderson's, Dennis O'Leary's and Maurice Lacourcière's judgments in *Zylberberg v. Sudbury Board of Education* (1986), 29 D.L.R. (4th) 709, reversed (1989), 52 D.L.R. (4th) 577, and the judgments of David Watt and William McKeown in the *Elgin County* case (1988), 50 D.L.R. (4th) 193.

to embarrassment and ridicule. Indeed, in the *Elgin County* case the trial court heard one family describe how this pressure was so strong that they did not use the exemption even when their child was suffering nightmares from the religious instruction she had received. In none of the material before the Courts, in either case, was there a shred of evidence to challenge the veracity or sincerity of these claims.

There was some conflicting testimony from psychologists, who were hired by both sides in these cases, about how widespread and how harmful the pressure described by the challengers really was. Psychologists for those attacking the laws told the judges that students from minority groups would be "under great pressure" to conform and to remain in the classroom for religious exercises and instruction that was not their own. In their opinion, the position of the challengers was not unique.[26] Psychologists retained by those supporting the religious programmes disagreed. Indeed they said not only that any pressure a student might feel would be relatively insignificant, if not trivial, but also that, in many cases, it would actually be beneficial for the students affected. In their view it was common practice in today's schools for students to be channelled into specialized, alternative activities of all kinds and whatever pressure a student felt in being singled out would likely strengthen his or her personal convictions and ultimately the learning process itself.

Whatever other conclusions the Court might fairly draw from this evidence, it is clear that, on its own terms, it could not be used to deny the factual basis of the challengers' claims. None of it alters — indeed even addresses — the particulars of the challengers' cases. At no point did the psychological evidence elicited by the Government and the school boards discredit or dispute the claims of the individual challengers that they did feel considerable pressure to participate in or at least witness religious exercises and courses of instruction which were antithetical to their beliefs. To the contrary, the primary expert retained by those supporting the Government's policy expressly conceded that individual students could feel the kind of pressure and coercion the challengers described.[27] What he did say was that, for the kinds of reasons noted above, whatever pressure the challengers felt was "not a normal or usual result" of an exemption policy, would not be substantial, and in the end would likely be beneficial rather than harmful to the students' development and educational experiences.

Not only did none of the psychologists' testimony try to refute the factual basis of the challengers' claim, but we know from our analysis

---

26 For reference to a parallel body of opinion in the United States, see *Abington School District v. Schempp*, 374 U.S. 203.

27 *Canadian Civil Liberties Assn. v. Ontario, supra*, note 19, at 237-238.

of the Supreme Court's own performance that it would be wrong for the reviewer to consider the testimony they did give, in the first stage of the review process. On the model in *Oakes*, evidence of the kind they gave should not be considered until the very end of the review process when the balancing principle is applied. The fact that whatever pressure the challengers felt was exceptional, or insignificant, or even beneficial in the end, is only relevant when the advantages and disadvantages, the purposes and effects, of the law are being balanced under the last measure of proportionality. To weigh the pros and cons of these exercises and courses of instruction prematurely would be to repeat the mistakes the various members of the Court made in cases like *Jones* and *Edwards Books*.

From our review of the two sets of judgments written in *Jones*, we know that it violates the principles embedded in the Charter, and in particular the principle of alternative means, to apply the *de minimis* principle in the first stage of the review process.[28] As happened in that case, failing to keep the two phases of the review process analytically distinct can lead to the validation of laws which needlessly restrict constitutional guarantees. Similarly, if the reviewer ruled that the challengers had failed to establish that their freedom had been limited because in her view the law would ultimately help not harm their personal development and ability to learn, she would fall into precisely the same errors of avoidance and denial which Messrs. McIntyre and Beetz made in *Edwards Books*. In effect, she would be relying on a fact which was relevant to the strength or weight of the challengers' claims, to conclude that there was no coercion or interference with their freedom at all.

In the absence of any evidence which contradicted the factual basis of the challengers' claims, it seems certain then that the first phase of each of these cases will conform to the pattern of decision-making which distinguishes the model in *Oakes*. Neither the fact that the coercion exerted by the Government's policy on religious practices and instruction in the schools works indirectly rather than directly, nor the fact that it involves psychological pressure rather than a physical threat, would affect the Court's analysis in any way. In the result the reviewer will find, as the model predicts, that her analysis of these challenges will pass relatively quickly to the second stage of the review process. On the evidence adduced in the lower courts there is no reason to think that the challengers would have to spend much time on their feet to persuade the Court that the laws which authorize these exercises and courses of instruction do burden their religious freedoms in the ways they claim. The fact that almost half the judges who heard the cases in the trial courts and Ontario Court of Appeal relied on the Government's psychological evidence to dismiss the chal-

---

28 See Chapter 4, *supra*, p. 106.

lenges in the first phase of the review process would cause her no concern.[29] She would know that in ruling as they did these judges were themselves acting unconstitutionally and in a way that was not authorized by the model in *Oakes.*

In passing from the first to the second stage of the review process the reviewer's first job would be to evaluate the objectives which lay behind the Government's decision to integrate religious exercises and courses of instruction into the life of its schools. In embarking on this line of inquiry, the reviewer would find herself almost immediately in the same situation she was in when she considered the legal and factual bases of the challengers' claims. On the one hand, on the basis of the way in which the Supreme Court had applied the object test over the course of the first five years, the reviewer would expect that the Government would have no more difficulty surmounting this first hurdle of review than the challengers did in establishing the legal and factual bases of their claims. On the other hand, the reviewer would be faced with two decisions of a lower court — in this case the Ontario Court of Appeal — in which the policy was struck down precisely because its purpose was said to be constitutionally flawed. Fortunately, for the reviewer, the parallel between the two situations holds all the way through, and in the end there is no reason for her to worry that her expectations, about how the model should work, would not be confirmed once again.

Certainly if the Court of Appeal had not struck down the compulsory religious exercises as it did, the reviewer could have been completely confident that Ontario's law would have passed the object test with ease. Identifying the purpose which the Government intended to accomplish with its policy would have been a simple and straightforward matter. Two separate objects stand out clearly in the structure and text of the Act and the Regulations and are reflected, as well, in all of the supplementary material that was filed in the lower courts describing how the Government's policy was first initiated and has subsequently evolved over time.

Broadly speaking, the purposes of the law could be said to be to recognize, and to be supportive of, the interests and ideas of the two major groups which the policy most directly affects. In the first part of the law the Government can be seen trying to be attentive to the interests of those individuals and groups in the community who feel strongly about incorporating religious exercises and instruction in the schools. For these people

---

29 In the *Elgin County* case, two of the three judges in the trial court, David Watt and William McKeown, were prepared to dismiss the challengers' claims on this basis. In *Zylberberg v. Board of Education of Sudbury,* both William Anderson and Dennis O'Leary in the trial court and Maurice Lacourière in the Court of Appeal ruled that the challengers' constitutional guarantees had either been limited in only marginal and trivial ways or, indeed, not at all.

it is important that their children be made familiar with and be taught a deeper appreciation of the role religion has and continues to play in the life of their particular communities. As well, they want their children to be aware of the connection between the most basic principles and ideas of their religious traditions, their personal value systems and their own powers of moral reasoning. Requiring schools to be opened with a religious and/or spiritual exercise and allowing religious instruction for an hour a week, was the Government's way of showing respect for the people who think that religion has an important role to play in the education of their children.

In the second part of the law the Government switched its focus and tried to accommodate the wishes of the other group of people whose ideas on the integration of religion and education are in direct conflict with the first. By providing an automatic exemption from any religious activity which takes place in a school, this aspect of the Government's policy endeavoured to show respect for the views of those people who think that there should be a very sharp line drawn between church and state. Excusing any student who did not want to take the courses and exercises which others were required to attend, represents a clear attempt by the Government to strike a balance between the freedom of those who want a religious component in the life of their schools and the freedom of those who do not. The two-pronged, compulsory provision-automatic exemption approach reflects a deliberate effort by the lawmakers to reconcile the competing visions and conflicting freedoms (positive and negative) of the two groups.[30]

Described in this way, no reviewer would have any reason to think that the Supreme Court would rule the Government's policy was unconstitutional because of the goals it was trying to achieve. From our review of the Supreme Court's performance, the reviewer would be aware that the only objective which it had ever identified as being unconstitutional was a *deliberate* attempt to interfere with and limit the rights of those affected by a law.[31] Whatever else one may say about the Government's policy of religious exercises and instruction in the schools, it is just not credible to claim that it was passed *for the purpose* of infringing the rights of those who objected to religion having any place in the schools. There was not a shred of evidence to support a finding that this was a law which

---

30 Amy Gutmann describes these two approaches as "the family as state" and "the state of families" in *Democratic Education* (Princeton, 1987). For a discussion of how all rights and freedoms have both a positive (freedom to) and negative (freedom from) aspect, see Peter Westen, " 'Freedom' and 'Coercion' — Virtue Words and Vice Words" (1985), Duke L.J. 541.

31 Chapter 2, *supra*, notes 59 and 60; Chapter 3, *supra*, note 60; and Chapter 4, *supra*, note 92.

was covertly aimed at the indoctrination of unwilling and recalcitrant students. There was nothing to suggest that the Government did not sincerely believe that the exemption opportunity would protect the religious freedom of those who were opposed to the introduction of sectarian exercises and courses of religious instruction in the schools. In fact it would have been completely irrational, if not counter-productive, for the Government to have enacted such a sweeping and comprehensive exemption if its purpose had been to indoctrinate students in religious traditions and ideas in which they did not believe. Even though some students were inhibited from taking advantage of the exemption, many others just as certainly were not. If the Government's objective was to indoctrinate its students, this was a policy which, for the most part, would be self defeating.

What the exemption makes clear is that this part of the school curriculum has a religious as well as a secular dimension; not that the Government tried to *impose* spiritual and ethical values and ideas on schoolchildren against their will.[32] The fact that the policy may not have been effective in every case and that some students still felt coerced into attending religious exercises and instruction only shows it was an imperfect policy choice. It does not and indeed cannot establish that it was a colourable one.

On the assumption that the Supreme Court will continue to apply the object test as it has in the past, and adhere to the model in *Oakes*, the reviewer would have no reason to doubt that Ontario's law and the school boards' curricula would survive the first hurdle of review. This is simply not a law which can fairly be described as a *deliberate* attempt to restrict the constitutional rights of those it affects by indoctrinating them in a religion which is not their own. Although, it is true that, in the *Elgin County* case, the Ontario Court of Appeal did rule that the programme of religious instruction authorized by Ontario's law was unconstitutional precisely on this ground, on closer examination reviewers will see that the Court virtually ignored the exemption half of the Government's policy. Except for a passing reference to the exemption provision, the Court focused all of its attention on what the course of instruction was trying to achieve. In the terminology used in the first Part of this book, the Court of Appeal simply "avoided" the argument that, seen as a whole, Ontario's law could never be characterized as designed to indoctrinate students against their will for as long as the automatic exemption provision remained in place. In sharper terms, by dissolving the link between the instruction

---

32 The failure to keep the ideas of religion and indoctrination separate can be seen especially clearly in Allan Austin's and the Court of Appeal's judgment in *Civil Liberties Association v. Ontario* (1988), 50 D.L.R. (4th) 193, 304, reversed (1990), 65 D.L.R. (4th) 1, 19-25 (Ont. C.A.).

and exemption features of the law, the Court effectively rewrote the purposes of the Act.

Significantly, in *Zylberberg*, the Court of Appeal did not follow this approach of ascribing to Ontario's education law a purpose it could not have. In this case, in holding that compulsory religious exercises at the beginning of the school day were unconstitutional, even though they contained an automatic exemption, at no point did any of the judges actually declare that the purpose of the legislature was one of indoctrination. Rather than ruling the opening exercises were unconstitutional on the ground they were covertly trying to indoctrinate students against their will, in *Zylberberg* the Court of Appeal said the Government's policy was defective simply because the law's primary purpose was religious. According to the members of the Court who sat on this case, the fact that the basic objective of the law was religious in nature was sufficient to render it unconstitutional under the Charter.

Although, in *Zylberberg*, the Court of Appeal did not ascribe to the law a purpose (of indoctrination) which it could not have, the judges made an equally fatal mistake in saying it was unconstitutional because of the religious objectives it promoted. While the Court's characterization of the purpose which the Ontario Government was trying to achieve was much closer to the mark in this case, still there is nothing in any of the Supreme Court's earlier decisions, or in the larger theory of *Oakes*, which would justify the ruling it made. Although, at the time they wrote their decision there may have been some basis for the judges' belief that the Supreme Court's judgment in *Big M Drug Mart* supported their decision, it is clear it does nothing of the sort.[33] The *Lord's Day Act* which was challenged in that case, was compulsory in its terms and was designed to ensure that everyone would observe a common religious practice/holiday even if it was not their own. There was no universal, automatic exemption of the

---

33 In its judgment, the majority in the Court of Appeal made reference to a passage in Brian Dickson's judgment in *Big M Drug Mart* which seemed to give credence to a distinction between laws which limited and laws which denied people's constitutional rights. See (1989), 52 D.L.R. (4th) 577, 597-598. According to this idea, first articulated in the *Quebec Protestant School Board* case, laws that denied and were in direct conflict with a right or freedom which the Charter guaranteed could be declared unconstitutional by the Court without it ever having to resort to s. 1. After the Court of Appeal rendered its judgment in *Zylberberg*, the Supreme Court expressly repudiated the distinction in its decision in *Ford v. Quebec* (1989), 54 D.L.R. (4th) 577. For a discussion of the distinction between limits and denials written before the Court's repudiation in *Ford*, see L. Weinrib, "The Supreme Court of Canada and Section One of the Charter" (1988), 10 S. Ct. L. Rev. 469, 479. See also T. Christian, "The Limited Operation Of The Limits Clause" (1987), 35 Alberta L. Rev. 264. For a critique of the Court's reasoning in the *Quebec Protestant School Board* case, see P. Hogg, *Constitutional Law of Canada*, 2nd ed. (Toronto: Carswell, 1985), pp. 682-683.

kind the *Education Act* and the Regulations contain. Read carefully, the Supreme Court's decision in *Big M* provides no support for the idea that laws whose primary objectives are religious in nature are unconstitutional for that reason alone.[34]

Not only has the Supreme Court never said that the Charter prohibits Governments from introducing laws which have religious objectives, it is unimaginable that it ever would. Such a ruling would be completely at odds with one of the most basic ideals on which the Charter and the model in *Oakes* is built.[35] To rule that Government cannot pass laws for the purpose of enhancing the understanding of students of the religious ideas and practices in the societies in which they live would constitute a massive derogation from our tradition of democracy and popular rule. It would mean communities, like Elgin County, could not teach its children about the spiritual aspect of the environment in which they were growing up. They would not be able to use — or make extensive reference to — the dominant religious ideas and practices in teaching students how to develop their powers of moral reasoning and a system of personal values. No

---

34 It should be noted that, strictly speaking, provincial Governments cannot pass laws whose primary objectives are religious in nature. However, this is because of the way the Constitution divides legislative powers between the provincial and federal levels of government, and has nothing to do with the Charter of Rights. According to the way the Courts have interpreted the distribution of powers in the original British North America Act, only the federal Government has the power to enact laws regulating religious activities *per se* and it would be a violation of those clauses of the Constitution if a province tried to legislate on these matters directly.

   However, once it is conceded that these exercises and courses of instruction also advance (however imperfectly) important secular and educational goals, it is equally certain it would be found to be within the competence of the provincial legislature to include them in the curriculum of the public schools. Even though they unavoidably affect matters of religion, the provinces' power over matters of education would permit them to develop programmes of this kind. It is a settled principle in the rules of constitutional law which control the division of powers between the two levels of government that either one of them can enact laws which affect interests and activities of the other where it is acting to further interests and objectives over which it does have authority and there is no way the spillover can be avoided. See Peter Hogg, *Constitutional Law of Canada*, 2nd ed. (Toronto: Carswell, 1985), Chapter 15.

   It might be noted that this principle, known as the "necessarily incidental" rule or "ancillary" power, serves exactly the same function in deciding division of powers questions in the Constitution as the principle of alternative means serves under the Charter. In the language of economists and policy makers, both reflect the Paretian ideal of looking for solutions which make some people better off without worsening the situation of anyone else.

35 It would also be at odds with our constitutional tradition of State support of religious communities. See L. Weinrib, "The Religion Clauses: Reading the Lesson" (1986), 8 Sup. Ct. L. Rev. 507. In its decision in *Elgin County*, the Court of Appeal explicitly recognized the legitimacy of requiring students to take courses in religion for purposes of education rather than indoctrination.

community could explain or explore with its children the ways in which and the extent to which its religious ideas and practices are played out in and help shape almost every domain (work, leisure, family, art, literature, music, etc.) of their relations with others. Strictly applied, even a course on comparative religion would run afoul of the test the Court of Appeal propounded in *Zylberberg*.

In the absence of any legal precedent to support either approach followed by the Ontario Court of Appeal in *Zylberberg* and *Elgin County*, and in the face of its obvious tension with the model in *Oakes* , no reviewer would have any reason to think that these decisions would find favour with any of the Supremes. She would expect the members of that Court to apply the object test in the usual way, in the context of section 1, and then to move on to evaluate the means by which the Governments and school boards have set out to accomplish their purposes against the last two proportionality principles in *Oakes*. In theory, there is a possibility that the Court might be distracted from this path by several decisions of the American Supreme Court which have repeatedly held that educational programmes with religious purposes violate the guarantee of religious freedom in the U.S. Bill of Rights.[36] More likely, however, the U.S. Supreme Court's decisions on school prayers and religious instruction will be seen as further evidence of how little assistance American jurisprudence is in the determination of the constitutionality of Canadian law.

In the first place, the American rule, which creates a very thick wall between the realms of church and state, is built on a very different constitutional tradition and text.[37] The American Bill of Rights explicitly provides that Congress[38] cannot make "any law respecting an establishment of religion or prohibiting the free exercise thereof", a choice of words which was intended by at least some of its framers as building an impenetrable "wall of separation" between church and state. The language protecting religious freedom in the Charter suggests that no similar constraint circumscribes the powers of Canadian legislators. Indeed as others have been quick to point out, our constitutional heritage explicitly contemplates governmental support to assist religious minorities in the exercise of their spiritual beliefs.[39]

---

36 See, e.g., *McCollum v. Board of Education*, 333 U.S. 203 (1948); *Engel v. Vitale*, 370 U.S. 421 (1962); *Abington Township v. Schemp*, 374 U.S. 203 (1963); and *Wallace v. Jaffrey*, 472 U.S. 38 (1985).

37 L. Weinrib, "The Religion Clauses: Reading the Lesson", *supra*, note 35.

38 Subsequently interpreted to extend to State legislatures, see *Cantwell v. Connecticut*, 310 U.S. 296 (1939).

39 See L. Weinrib, "The Religion Clauses: Reading the Lesson", *supra*, note 35. See also Wayne MacKay, "The Canadian Charter of Rights and Freedoms: A Springboard to Students' Rights", *supra*, note 16.

Moreover, not only would the American rule be entirely out of keeping with the Canadian model of constitutional review, even on its own terms there is nothing to recommend it to a Canadian court. As even the most cursory review of the American literature quickly reveals, the U.S. Supreme Court's rulings on the legitimacy of integrating religion in the schools consist for the most part of arid, *a priori*, conceptual discussions of what religion means and are heavily influenced by what each of the judges on that Court understood the intention of the framers of the American Constitution to be.[40] Not only is this approach quite inconsistent with the liberal, purposeful method the Canadian Supreme Court endorsed in *Oakes*, it is, it turns out, also a very controversial reading of what the framers of the American Bill of Rights were trying to protect.[41] In the end, the American approach has given rise to a jurisprudence which is so hopelessly inconsistent and confused, there is little reason to think our Court would turn to it for any guidance or assistance.

In the same way then, in which these challenges should pass easily through the first stage of the review process, the Court's treatment of the object test should conform to the reviewer's expectations as well. The resolution of these cases should stick to the pattern which is characteristic of the analytical method of *Oakes*. In the end, neither those challenging nor those defending the Government's policy are likely to have much difficulty in surmounting the first hurdles they face. As we have seen the legal and factual bases of the challengers' claims are essentially undisputed and it seems undeniable that trying to design a policy to accommodate conflicting religious ideas and competing freedoms of different individuals and groups is one of the most basic functions performed by any Government in a liberal democratic state.

In the result, in relatively short order, the reviewer should find herself focusing her attention on the means the Government of Ontario chose to accomplish its goals. Once again it will be the proportionality principles where the reviewer's, and eventually the Court's, scrutiny will be most rigorous and searching. Indeed, consistent with the decisions we reviewed in the first Part of this book, it seems virtually certain that it will be the principle of alternative means which will do most of the work.

When the reviewer turns to the principle of alternate means, she will find the pattern of the model in *Oakes* continues to hold. Indeed these

---

40 See, e.g., "The Unconstitutionality of State Statutes Authorizing Moments of Silence in the Public Schools", 96 Harv. L.R. 1874; D. Richards, *Toleration and the Constitution* (Oxford U. Press, 1986); M. Galanter, "Religious Freedoms in the United States: A Turning Point", 1966 Wisc. L. Rev. 217.

41 L. Weinrib, "The Religion Clauses", *supra*, note 35, at 507; P. Kurland, "The Irrelevance of the Constitution: The Religion Clauses of the First Amendment and the Supreme Court", 24 Vill. L. Rev. 3.

cases seem to present particularly simple and straightforward applications of this measure of Paretian well-being.[42] As soon as she begins to sift through the material that was filed in the lower Courts she will discover that there is at least one improvement which could easily be made to attenuate some of the coercion generated by the challenged programmes. Even at the most critical stage of the review process the reviewer will find that these cases should not take up much, if any,[43] of the Court's valuable time.

If the defect of the existing policy could be broadly described as its generally segregationist orientation, the obvious antidote would be to develop alternatives which encourage the integration of individuals with different values and ideas. Rather than separating people with different religious faiths and trying to keep them apart, an integrative approach would try to create common structures and programmes in which a multiplicity of attitudes and understandings about religion could be explored and examined simultaneously. The basic method would be to design exercises and courses so that they would be acceptable to all reasonable people, whatever their religious affiliation and beliefs.[44] Rather than any part of the programme being a vehicle to proselytize a particular faith, an integrative approach would expand horizons by being both more secular and more pluralistic. The differences and similarities in the religious ideas that people hold would be compared and celebrated within common exercises and courses of instruction. In terms of the latter, for example, different religious faiths and practices could be studied in a comparative way. The relationship between religious ideas and traditions and the ethical, artistic, cultural, social, etc. life of a community could be presented in a way to encourage better understanding and respect for different points of view. In terms of religious exercises, readings from a wide variety of spiritual and religious sources would replace reference to a single book or set of ideas.

The idea of creating more pluralistic and secular programmes of

---

42 See Chapter 4, *supra*, note 98.

43 As we shall see (p. 147, *infra*), neither the Governments of Ontario nor British Columbia chose to appeal the decisions of their provincial Courts which held their opening and closing religious exercises were unconstitutional. Instead both Governments amended the relevant statutes and regulations. The Government of Ontario altered the nature of its religious exercises by making them voluntary for each school and making them more secular and pluralistic in their orientation. See *Education Act*, O.Reg. 6/89. In British Columbia, the Government took a more extreme response and brought all opening and closing exercises of a religious nature to an end. See *Schools Act*, S.B.C. 1989, c. 61, s. 95.

44 For a more theoretical invocation of reasonableness standards of this kind see T. Scanlon, "Contractualism and Utilitarianism" in A. Sen and B. Williams (eds.), *Utilitarianism and Beyond* (New York: Cambridge U. Press, 1982), pp. 103, 116.

religious studies is not new. In fact, it is one which has been around for a long time. The approach was central to the recommendations of the MacKay Committee which studied the question of religion in the public schools of Ontario in 1969. As well, it is reflected in an important amendment the Ontario Government made to its Regulations in 1978. At that time, almost ten years after the MacKay Committee had submitted its Report, the Government finally adopted the recommendation that the opening exercises should be inspirational and dedicational rather than confessional and stopped insisting that the readings should only be taken from the Bible and the students should always repeat the Lord's Prayer. Reflecting a more integrative approach, the amendments provided that "other suitable" prayers and readings could be used in the opening exercises as well.

Integrationist policies enjoy one clear advantage over the programmes that were attacked in the cases under review. All of them tend to minimize the psychological pressure to which individuals, like the challengers, have been exposed. Integration means that the pressure felt by members of minority groups in having to single themselves out can be reduced if not eliminated completely. In theory, if the exercises and courses were designed carefully enough, it should be possible to introduce students to the most basic issues of moral reasoning and spiritual beliefs within a common curriculum without the necessity of anyone seeking an exemption and being separated from their fellow students. Although it is virtually certain that some students would find parts of even these courses and exercises objectionable to their moral and/or religious beliefs, the reviewer could reasonably assume that the coercive effect of these courses would be less than what the challengers had endured. The challengers, it will be recalled, had been pressured into attending exercises and courses of study which made little or no attempt to present a balanced curriculum or to show any respect for their religious traditions and beliefs.

Moreover, the Government could continue to provide an automatic exemption for students who objected to any religious component in the school curriculum if it decided that it was not possible to design a religious studies programme with sufficient sensitivity and care or that no inter-ference with a student's religious freedom, no matter how small, could be justified any more. If the religious studies programme was primarily intergrationist in its approach, the segregationist impact of permitting each student to seek an exemption would lose most of its sting. Rather than being a statement about one's religious views, opting out of a religious studies programme of this kind would be no different than any other course selection which all students must make.[45]

---

45 Whether a Government retained the exemption would depend on whether it thought

It is true that in some communities, pluralistic, secular, and comparative programmes of this kind would not achieve all of the objectives a school board might want to accomplish. Some school boards might prefer to offer courses which had a more focused or sectarian orientation. It is quite conceivable, for example, that a community or a school board which was very homogeneous and whose members were, by and large, all adherents of one particular religion (Christian, Judaic, Muslim, Hindu) or faith (Catholic, Mormon, Mennonite) might want to design a programme which focused primarily, if not exclusively, on the values and practices most central to their own lives. This seems, in fact, to have been the case in Elgin County where, at least initially, the programme had a very strong, fundamentalist, Christian orientation to it.

Even in these circumstances, however, an integrationist approach can effect an improvement on the challenged regimes. Even though a single, comprehensive course or set of religious exercises may not always be feasible, an integrative approach can still alleviate some of the alienation and separation which the exemption policy entails. In communities like these, an integrative policy would call for students to be given a choice in the options or courses they could take to meet the requirements of whatever programme in religious studies a school board chose to offer. They could take either a pluralistic and more secular course designed by the Government for the province as a whole, or the narrower programme put together by the local board to sensitize their students to the religious life of the communities in which they live.

Although not as integrative as a single, all-encompassing common curriculum, offering optional courses would go part way to alleviate some of the alienation and pressure entailed in the current approach. Options integrate each student in a broader curriculum in a way exemptions, at least by themselves, cannot. Even if no exemptions were permitted, just having the option of choosing a course which was more sensitive to their own religious or ethical values and beliefs should make it easier for members of religious and ethical minorities to resist the psychological pressure to attend more sectarian courses of instruction when they are favoured by the local authorities. Although it is true that a policy of requiring students to choose between alternative courses would still impinge on the students' freedom by requiring them to publicly proclaim which course in religious studies they wanted to take, again it would be less burdensome than the pressure involved in the challenged policy and

religious studies should be put on the compulsory side of the curriculum, along with courses like physical education, arts and math, or whether it should made optional like the courses in economics, urban geography or German. On the model in *Oakes*, either objective would be within a Government's constitutional powers to pursue.

in all events more equally shared. Being able to choose a course which was more sensitive to their religious and ethical values would be better for most members of minority groups than having to sit through courses which were completely antagonistic to their own ideas or having no instruction in these subjects at all.

In the result, adopting an integrative approach to the presentation of religion in public schools would seem to constitute an unambiguous improvement over the way it has been traditionally offered. Without limiting the freedom of any community to instruct its children in accordance with its own religious traditions and beliefs, integration can provide some relief from the psychological pressure which at least some students now feel. Moreover, implementing an integrative approach would not be a difficult task. In effect it would parallel and allow the Government to complete the changes it made in 1978. It would ensure that the integrationist ideal was taken as far as it could rather than being applied in a partial and half-hearted way.

In practical terms it would mean making clear that secular readings and alternate modes of reflection were just as suitable for the opening exercises as those with a more sectarian orientation.[46] As well it would argue in favour of beginning (or ending) the school day with the opportunity for a moment's quiet contemplation rather than with the public recitation of prayers. Moments of silence offer everyone the option of praying or reflecting in a way that is consistent with their own beliefs. They allow those who want to say the Lord's Prayer to do so, while simultaneously permitting others the freedom to engage in other forms of spiritual or ethical contemplation. Moments of silence make everyone better off.[47]

In terms of courses of instruction, the integrative approach would continue to allow each individual school board to decide what it wanted to include in its programme of religious studies. The policy, also adopted in 1978, of allowing local communities to design programmes which are most compatible with their community needs, would not be affected in any way. The only change would be that the Government would have to guarantee that the secular, pluralistic programme designed for use throughout the province would be available for any student to select. The only

---

46 This would respond to the concerns expressed by Robert Reid and the majority in the Court of Appeal in *Zylberberg* that the challenged regulations did not seem to permit the inclusion of purely secular material. See (1986), 29 D.L.R. (4th) 709, 781, reversed (1989), 52 D.L.R. (4th) 577, 587.

47 Contrast the position in American constitutional law that even moments of silence are unconstitutional because of their inherently religious purpose. See *Wallace v. Jaffrey*, 472 U.S. 38 (1985); "The Unconstitutionality of State Statutes Authorizing Moments of Silence in the Public Schools", 96 Harv. L. Rev. 1874; "Daily Moments of Silence in Public Schools: A Constitutional Analysis" (1985), 58 N.Y.U. L. Rev. 364.

practical consequence would be that the provincial Government would once again be responsible for designing a course of instruction that would be suitable for province-wide use.[48]

Governments and their supporters would have a very difficult task countering the conclusion that the method of integration and the policy of offering different course options is a more reasonable approach than the regimes which the challengers attacked. To succeed it would be necessary for the Government and the school boards to show that this alternative approach was not as effective in realizing the objectives they wanted to achieve. From the evidence that was filed in the lower courts, it is not easy to imagine how a policy of integration might be impugned in this way. The fact that the options approach is used in other free and democratic societies both in Canada and abroad makes it unlikely that it is not administratively viable.[49] Moreover, whatever additional financial cost was entailed in staffing the alternative courses would be substantially, if not completely, offset by the reduced number of teachers who would be required to give lessons in the course preferred by the majority.[50] Except for the development of materials and courses of instruction, replacing exemptions with options would seem more a matter of reallocating rather than augmenting personnel requirements.

Unless supporters of the impugned policies were able to identify some substantial advantage that they could accomplish which the options approach could not, our reviewer, and then the Court, would be expected to bring their analyses to a close. There would be no reason to go any further and, for example, analyse the objectives promoted by these programmes against the balancing principle. Even if, as many of the judges of the lower courts were inclined to believe, the restriction imposed by the challenged policies on the challenger's freedom was relatively small,

---

48 From 1944-1978, the Ministry did authorize a particular course of study that all school boards were obliged to use. Described as "dogmatic", "emotional", "bland", and "elementary" by the MacKay Committee, it was scrapped by the Government at the same time as it made amendments to the Regulations in 1978.

49 In Quebec, students are given a choice between Protestant, Catholic and secular moral values programmes of instruction. See *An Act Respecting Public Elementary and Secondary Education*, R.S.Q. 1984, c. 39. In Spain, students can choose between courses with a Catholic and those with a more secular and pluralist orientation.

50 In addition to being quantitatively relatively insignificant, as we saw in Part One, on more than one occasion, the Court has indicated that qualitatively it weights considerations of administrative cost and convenience very lightly as well. See, e.g., *Singh v. M.E.I.* (1985), 17 D.L.R. (4th) 422; *Ref. re s. 94(2) Motor Vehicle Act* (1986), 24 D.L.R. (4th) 536. See also Dickson's judgment in *R. v. Schwartz* (1989), 55 D.L.R. (4th) 1, 23; cf. Gerard La Forest's judgment in *R. v. Jones* (1986), 31 D.L.R. (4th) 569. For a strong endorsement of this position see L. Weinrib, "The Supreme Court of Canada and Section One of the Charter" (1988), 10 S. Ct. L. Rev. 469, 483-492.

it would still be declared unconstitutional because, with the possibility of following an integrative approach, it is a limitation or burden which is completely unnecessary.

For the reviewer, analysing the constitutionality of religious programmes in public schools in this way would conform completely with her expectations as to how the model in *Oakes* should work. Her reasoning would track exactly the pattern the Supreme Court followed every time it applied the model in *Oakes* over the course of the first five years. These cases would offer clear examples of how the proportionality principles, and in particular the principle of alternative means, can work in a way which ensures that Governments, and those to whom they delegate legal authority, will begin to listen to individuals and interest groups they have traditionally ignored or paid very little attention to in the past.

Resolved in this way, the reviewer could point to them as offering clear support for her belief in the objectivity and progressivity of the model in *Oakes*. At least for the individuals and groups involved in these cases there would be good reason to be positive about the practice of constitutional review. These cases would be a start in the right direction. They provide the reviewer with some evidence to respond to the concerns of those whose instincts are inclined to be more sceptical and conservative. They show how the model in *Oakes* can enhance the democratic character of our system of government by providing an effective means for those who traditionally have not had much influence on the processes of politics to participate in the formulation of social policies which impact directly on their lives.

Indeed, these cases do even more than that. In addition to showing how the Courts and the process of constitutional review can be an effective forum for organizations and groups without much political influence to make their voices heard, these cases also illustrate how the Charter can have an energizing effect on the processes of politics as well. In the same pattern that followed the Supreme Court's resolution of the challenges to the Sunday closing, abortion, and French language sign laws, litigating the constitutionality of religious studies programmes prompted at least two of the provincial Governments whose laws have been challenged to rethink their policies even before the cases reached the Supreme Court. In British Columbia, the Government brought all religious exercises and instruction to an end as part of a major overhaul of their *Schools Act*. In Ontario, following the decision of its Court of Appeal, the Government of the day adopted a more moderate response by making the religious exercises much more integrative in their orientation and approach.[51] Now the Regulations in Ontario explicitly direct that the opening and closing exercises may

---

51 See note 43, *supra*.

make use of a wide range of secular and comparative readings and call for a period of silence instead of the recitation of prayers.[52] Indeed and even before the Ontario Court of Appeal ruled that the two, half-hour periods of religious instruction were also unconstitutional, the Government commissioned an independent inquiry to re-evaluate this part of its religious studies programme as well. Collectively, the way in which the Governments involved in these cases responded to the direction and judgment of their own provincial courts offers some encouragement that relations between the politicians and the judges can be more supportive and less conflictual than sceptics have been inclined to believe.[53] They also offer some support for the view that the Charter should provide a new vehicle for single-issue, interest groups to play a much more effective role in the processes of politics and policy formulation.[54]

---

52 In addition to making the opening exercises voluntary and more comparative in their orientation, the Ontario Regulations maintain the automatic exemption for any student who objects to attending even courses and exercises of this kind. See *Education Act*, O.Reg. 6/89.

53 For a theoretical treatment of the reciprocal responsibilities of the legislative and executive branches of Government and how they dovetail with those of the Court, see Brian Slattery, "A Theory of the Charter", 25 Osgoode Hall L.J. 701.

54 See Peter Russell, "The Effect of The Charter of Rights on the Policy Making Role of Canadian Courts", 25 Can. Pub. Admin. 1.

6

Freedom of Expression:
Of Ordinary Canadians in the Political
Life of the Community

Satisfied that the Charter will promote the interests of religious minorities, at least in the context of public education, the reviewer could shift
her attention to how other challenges, which are on their way to the Court,
would fare under the model in *Oakes*. One group of cases, of particular
interest to both believers and sceptics, involves a series of challenges to a
variety of different laws which impose constraints on the freedom of people
to engage in political discussion and debate and even to participate in the
electoral process itself. There are a lot of these cases and they range widely
both in the different laws whose constitutionality they question and in the
interests and activities for which protection is sought.

Perhaps the most basic and certainly the most numerous of these
challenges involves attacks against provincial and federal election laws which
disqualify people who are incarcerated in jail and/or on probation from voting.
A second group of cases has been initiated by public servants and their unions
against restrictions, set out in the legislation which governs their employment,
on the extent to which they can engage in partisan political activity. Other
challenges have been launched by interest groups against laws which limit
their freedom to disseminate their views in public places like airports and
in the course of election campaigns. Indeed, several people in Manitoba
attacked the whole system of public, financial support for candidates and
parties in general elections as violating their constitutional guarantee of
freedom of expression by forcing them to contribute (a part of their taxes)
to help disseminate ideas which are antithetical to their own.[1]

---

1 After the manuscript had been completed in draft, the Supreme Court handed down

Both sceptics and believers would be especially interested in how cases of this kind would be resolved by the Court. All of them deal directly with the question of what impact the process of constitutional review will have on the democratic quality of the rules that organize our system of government. Collectively they involve some of the most basic and long-standing rights and freedoms in our legal and political tradition. Almost all are grounded, in one way or another, in the Charter's guarantee of freedom of expression which, in both text and tradition, has a pedigree as rich and significant as the constitutional guarantee of religion and conscience which we have just reviewed. Freedom of expression, like freedom of religion, goes back very far in the development of free and democratic societies and received recognition and protection from the law even before the Charter was entrenched.[2] As well, as we saw in our review of the Supreme Court's performance in the first Part of this book, it is a constitutional entitlement which has already attracted a lot of recognition and support from everyone on the Court, conservatives and liberals alike.[3]

These cases would also be of interest to believers and sceptics because, at first blush, they seem to offer some support for the positions each of them would instinctively be inclined to take. Certainly the sceptics would welcome the choice. The way in which lower courts have addressed the question of what limits and restrictions on political activity are demonstrably justified in a free and democratic society seems to offer strong support for both their indeterminacy and regressivity theses. In some of these cases, the reasoning of the lower courts runs in all directions and in a substantial number of them the results could only be described as regressive or neutral at best. The challenges to election laws, which disqualify prisoners incarcerated in jails from voting, provide a simple but clear example. In at least one province the members of the same court have gone different ways on this issue and the results across the country

---

its judgment in this case. See *Mackay v. Manitoba* (1989), 61 D.L.R. (4th) 385. Even though this makes this case different from all the others analysed in this Part, which have yet to be decided by the Supreme Court, I decided not to remove it from the text. Because the issue of public funding of election campaigns is such an important one and, (as we shall see), because the basis of the Court's decision was so narrow, it seems likely the issue will eventually be relitigated and, at some point, a decision on the merits will be required. For a brief analysis of the Court's decision in *Mackay*, see notes 23 and 26, *infra*.

2 See, e.g., *Switzman v. Elbling* (1957), 7 D.L.R. (2d) 337; *Ref. re Alberta Legislation*, [1938] 2 D.L.R. 81.

3 See *Irwin Toy v. Quebec* (1989), 58 D.L.R. (4th) 577; *Ford v. Quebec* (1989), 54 D.L.R. (4th) 577; *Slaight Communications v. Davidson* (1989), 59 D.L.R. (4th) 416. See also *Dolphin Delivery v. R.W.D.S.U.* (1987), 33 D.L.R. (4th) 174.

are equally mixed.[4] While some judges have ruled that laws which disenfranchise these people violate the rights that are guaranteed by the Charter in section 3,[5] just as many others have come to the opposite conclusion and the prisoners' claims have been rejected.[6]

The record of challenges brought by the public servants against employment laws, which limit their right to be actively involved in elections and the political affairs of the community, follows a similar pattern. Here too the reasoning of the lower courts across the country varies dramatically and, in Ontario at least, has resulted in at least two decisions that the Charter does not provide these persons any relief.[7] Sceptics could also point to a successful challenge brought by the National Citizens' Coalition against a provision of the Canada Elections Act which prohibited individuals and interest groups not registered as political parties from making any election expenditures during the course of a campaign.[8] Sceptics would say this case underscores their contention that the Charter and judicial review represents an inherently regressive and anti-democratic turn in the development of our system of government. Here, sceptics will claim, is clear evidence of the Charter being used by individuals and groups, which are endowed with substantial institutional and financial resources, to frustrate an effort by the elected representatives of the people to make participation in the political life of the community more egalitarian and fair.[9]

While there is much in the record of the lower courts' treatment of issues like these to encourage sceptics that their reservations are well founded, the evidence is not completely one-sided. There is also a good deal in how the lower courts have evaluated laws which limit involvement in the political process from which a believer could take optimism as well. While recognizing that the lower courts have been far from uniform in their application of the model in Oakes, believers could point to the fact that frequently they did strike down the most draconian laws which

---

4 Compare Re Grondin and A.G. Ontario (1988), 65 O.R. (2d) 427 with Sauvé v. A.G. Canada (1989), 53 D.L.R. (4th) 595. In B.C., compare Re Reynolds and A.G. B.C. (1985), 11 D.L.R. (4th) 380 with Re Jolivet and Barker and R. (1983), 1 D.L.R. (4th) 604.

5 Re Grondin, Re Reynolds, ibid.; Levesque v. A.G. Canada (1986), 25 D.L.R. (4th) 184; Badger v. A.G. Manitoba (1986), 30 D.L.R. (4th) 108. See also Maltby v. A.G. Sask. (1982), 143 D.L.R. (3d) 649.

6 Re Jolivet, Sauvé, supra, note 4; Badger v. A.G. Manitoba (1989), 55 D.L.R. (4th) 177 (Man. C.A.). See also Gould v. A.G. Canada (1985), 13 D.L.R. (4th) 485, affirmed (1985), 13 D.L.R. (4th) 491.

7 Ontario Public Service Employees Union v. A.G. Ontario (1989), 52 D.L.R. (4th) 701; Rheaume v. A.G. Ontario (1990), 63 D.L.R. (4th) 241. See also Re Jones and A.G. Ontario (1989), 53 D.L.R. (4th) 273.

8 National Citizens' Coalition v. A.G. Canada (1984), 11 D.L.R. (4th) 481 (Alta. Q.B.).

9 See, e.g., M. Mandel, The Charter of Rights and the Legalization of Politics in Canada (Toronto: Wall & Thompson, 1989), p. 207.

restricted the democratic freedoms of prisoners and public servants.[10] As well, believers will not fail to notice that at the same time as the National Citizens' Coalition's success, other courts were upholding the constitutionality of the reimbursement provisions of our election financing laws[11] and were insisting that Governments must provide access to public places (like airports) to groups which wanted to communicate their views to their fellow citizens.[12]

In addition to promoting the democratic quality of our system of government by rulings of this kind, believers could also point out that simply asking a court to rule on the constitutionality of these laws frequently had the effect of energizing the political process and stimulating public discussion and debate. Here again Charter challenges have provided an opportunity for relatively powerless individuals to participate in the political process as an effective lobby or interest group. Thus, long before several of these cases reached the Supreme Court of Canada, various Legislatures took a cue from the decisions of their provincial courts and began a process of dialogue and debate with the persons affected by these laws, exploring how they might be re-drafted in ways which would make them more compatible with the Charter. In the same way the challenges to religious studies programmes in the schools spawned new initiatives from the Governments involved in those cases, new proposals regulating the rights of prisoners to. vote, expenditures in and the financing of election campaigns, and the opportunity of public servants to be more politically active have already been designed, discussed, and in some cases even drafted into law.[13]

So it would seem that this group of cases, involving challenges to laws which limit the freedom of various individuals and groups to

---

10 *Osborne v. Canada (Treasury Board)* (1989), 52 D.L.R. (4th) 241 (Fed. C.A.); *Re Fraser and A.G. Nova Scotia* (1986), 30 D.L.R. (4th) 340, and see the cases in note 5, *supra*.

11 *Re Mackay and Manitoba* (1985), 19 D.L.R. (4th) 185, affirmed (1986), 24 D.L.R. (4th) 587; and see note 1, *supra*.

12 *Comité pour la Republique du Canada v. R.* (1986), 25 D.L.R. (4th) 460, affirmed (1987), 36 D.L.R. (4th) 501.

13 See, e.g., *1984 Statutory Report of the Chief Electoral Officer*, recommending extending the franchise to prisoners and allowing lobby groups more freedom to be active in political campaigns. In the case of challenges initiated by public servants, considerable political activity was stimulated at the federal level with a private member's bill proposing substantial revisions to the *Public Service Employment Act*, R.S.C. 1985, c. P-33, and in the case of Nova Scotia it resulted in the enactment of a new law. See *Nova Scotia Civil Service Act*, S.N.S. 1978, c. 3, as amended by S.N.S. 1987, c. 44.

It might also be noted that in a related case involving a challenge to B.C.'s electoral boundary laws, the Government of the day responded positively to a ruling of that province's Supreme Court and introduced new rules and regulations defining election districts which were more faithful to the principle of equal representation. See *Dixon v. A.G. B.C.* (1989), 59 D.L.R. (4th) 297.

participate fully in the political life of the community, provides another good test for the competing theories of believers and sceptics. The issues they raise are among the most important for societies which claim to adhere to liberal democratic theories of government and the record of the cases in the lower courts seems fairly evenly balanced. Both viewpoints about the legitimacy of judicial review seem to gain some support from the treatment these cases have received so far.

To see which side of the debate these cases really favour the reviewer would proceed in the usual way. Each step of the analysis in *Oakes* would be taken in turn. First, she would satisfy herself that each of the laws in question really did limit an interest or activity protected by the Charter. If the model in *Oakes* held true to form, her expectation would be that this would not be a difficult task in any of the cases under consideration. As with the religion cases we have just examined, the reviewer would anticipate that so long as the Court stuck to the model in *Oakes*, none of the challengers should have any difficulty in passing this first hurdle of review.

When the reviewer begins to examine the record of these cases in the courts below she will find, for the most part, her expectations confirmed. By and large, the judges in the provincial trial courts and courts of appeal readily accepted the legal and factual integrity of all of these claims. In none of these cases, for example, was there any question about whether the laws which were being attacked fell within the Charter's reach. Except for the challenge brought by the Comité pour la Republique du Canada, against the manager of Mirabel Airport and the Minister of Transport, all of these challenges were aimed at statutes or regulations enacted or authorized by Parliament or one of the provincial legislatures.[14] In each of the challenges pressed by the prisoners, the public servants, and the various individuals and groups attacking the constitutionality of Canada's system of election financing laws, the involvement of one or other of the branches of a Canadian Government was clear. Even in the *Comité pour la Republique du Canada* (CFC) case, there was never any suggestion that the action of the airport manager and the legal basis on which it was grounded, was beyond the Charter's reach. The only question about the manager's legal authority was whether it could be said that he and/or the Government had acted in a manner which had been "prescribed by law".[15]

---

14 *Comité pour la Republique du Canada v. R.*, *supra*, note 12. *Levesque v. A.G. Canada* (1986), 25 D.L.R. (4th) 184, is also an exception. The challenge in that case was really aimed at the *failure* of the federal Government to take the necessary administrative action which would have allowed him to vote.

15 For members of the Supreme Court, it seems certain that this case will be seen to fall squarely within its reasoning in *Slaight Communications v. Davidson* (1989), 59 D.L.R. (4th) 416.

Nor did most of the judges in the lower courts have any difficulty recognizing that each of the challenged laws did in fact limit the freedom of those affected to pursue interests and activities which were protected by the Charter. The overwhelming majority of the judges who sat on these cases in the lower courts agreed with the challengers that these laws did limit important constitutional guarantees in the ways they described. In not one of the half-dozen challenges to federal and provincial election laws initiated by people who had been imprisoned or were on probation, did any one even question that, as a factual matter, these persons had been denied the right to vote in various federal and provincial elections as they claimed. In two cases, the Attorneys-General who defended these laws actually conceded that the disqualification denied prisoners the very entitlement which section 3 guarantees.[16] Similarly, the statements of the public servants and members of political organizations like the National Citizens' Coalition and the Comité pour la Republique du Canada, who claimed that they had been prevented or deterred from engaging in the various electoral and political activities which the law proscribed, went essentially uncontested. In these cases as well, the factual bases of the challengers' claims was not in issue before the lower courts.

In addition to accepting the factual integrity of these claims, most of the judges in the lower courts also accepted that the interests and activities for which protection was being sought were ones which fell squarely within at least one of the Charter's guarantees. The right to vote, to participate in all of the normal activities of an election campaign, and to express one's political views to others in the community, were recognized as being among the most fundamental an individual can possess, and were said to be guaranteed either by the explicit reference in section 3 to a right to vote and/or by the Charter's more general protection of a person's freedom of expression and association. All of the conventional forms of political activity at stake in these cases were seen as among the most basic forms of expression which all constitutional bills of rights invariably protect. Full and unfettered liberty in the processes of politics, liberally understood, was seen as a condition on which all of the other constitutional guarantees were based.[17]

It is true that not all of the judges who sat on these cases in the lower courts agreed that the laws did limit the challengers' constitutional rights and freedoms in the ways that they claimed. For example, in the *Mackay*

16 See, e.g., *Re Grondin, Re Reynolds, supra,* note 4; see also *Re Badger, supra,* note 5.
17 In the view of some writers the importance of political rights and freedoms transcends and indeed gives meaning to all of the other rights and freedoms which the Charter guarantees. See P. Monahan, *Politics and the Constitution* (Toronto: Carswell, 1987), Chapter 6.

case, which involved a challenge to the reimbursement provisions of Manitoba's *Elections Finances Act*, two of the three judges in Manitoba's Court of Appeal dismissed the complaint on the basis that the law did not actually limit the individuals' freedom in the way they claimed. In reasoning very reminiscent of the Supreme Court's earlier ruling in *Jones*, these two judges said that by providing financial support to all but the most marginal candidates, the law actually enhanced, rather than inhibited, political expression in Manitoba.[18]

Judges in some of the other cases also ruled that the interests for which the challengers sought protection did not fall within any of the Charter's guarantees. For example, in rejecting a challenge brought by the Ontario Public Service Employees Union (OPSEU) against the constraints which Ontario's *Public Service Act* imposed on the political activities of public servants, the trial court judge ruled that, in the final analysis, these provisions were not open to challenge because political expression by public servants was not an interest or activity which the Charter reached.[19] Similar reasoning found favour with at least one of the judges in the Federal Court of Appeal in the *CFC* case who dismissed the challengers' complaint on the ground that section 2(b) did not guarantee anyone the right to express themselves on public property — such as airports — which were not intended to be used in that way.[20] Finally, in *Re Jolivet*, one of the challenges brought against the disqualification of prisoners from voting, the trial judge ruled that the guarantee of the right to vote in section 3 of the Charter did not entrench the simple activity of casting a ballot. In his view, that guarantee only offered protection to the much narrower entitlement to an "informed electoral choice reached . . . . with complete freedom of access to the process of 'discussion and the interplay of ideas' by which public opinion is informed".[21] Because he thought that administrative and security considerations prevented prisoners from being allowed to enjoy the full freedom which is required before an informed and independent choice could be made, the judge ruled that the constitutional rights of prisoners had not been infringed.

It would be natural for a reviewer to wonder whether any or all of these judgments threw into question their expectations about how the model should work. All seem to suggest that there are some parts of our legal

---

18 *Mackay v. Manitoba* (1986), 24 D.L.R. (4th) 586. Very similar comments were made by the Supreme Court in its ruling in this case. For a brief discussion of its judgment see notes 23 and 26, *infra*.

19 *Re O.P.S.E.U.*, *supra*, note 7. In a parallel ruling in *Rheaume v. Ontario*, *supra*, note 7, William McKeown ruled that membership in a municipal council was not the kind of interest or activity protected by s. 2(d).

20 *Comité pour la Republique du Canada*, *supra*, note 12, *per* Louis Pratte.

21 *Re Jolivet*, *supra*, note 4, at 607.

order which are immune from constitutional review and the principle of constitutional supremacy. On closer examination however, she will realize that none of these decisions should be accepted as persuasive authority for refusing to exercise her powers of review. In the first place, as noted, they represent a distinct minority of the judgments written in these cases and in some instances, the reasoning employed was explicitly rejected or discredited by other judges hearing the case. More importantly, when they are read carefully, the reviewer will see that they are based on precisely the kind of faulty analysis which, from her review of the Supreme Court's own performance, she will know the Constitution forbids.

Take the judgment of the majority of the Manitoba Court of Appeal in *Mackay*. Read carefully, it can be seen to be a classic example of the strategies we earlier described as avoidance and denial.[22] For the most part the emphasis of the Court is taken up with explaining how laws, like Manitoba's, which reimburse parties and candidates who achieve a minimum percentage of votes with money from the public purse, enhance rather than constrict freedom of speech. The major thrust of the judgment is in underscoring how laws of this kind promote the ability of groups without substantial resources to participate more effectively in political campaigns. Again and again the Court stresses that laws like these neither force anyone to agree with the views which receive financial support from the State, nor do they prevent anyone from expressing their own ideas and/or incurring whatever expenditure they think appropriate for that purpose.

No reviewer who had studied the performance of the Supreme Court over the first five years would be persuaded by reasoning of this kind. The flaw would be easy to spot. By focusing on the public interest which the law promotes, the Manitoba Court of Appeal ignored the constitutional infringements which it also effects. When the two judges who formed the majority of the Court were talking about how laws promote the freedom of minority groups, including the challengers, to express themselves in any way they wish, they completely avoided the substance of the challengers' complaint. Their claim was that regardless of how they and others might

---

22 A second judgment in which the Court dismissed a challenger's claim by a process of avoidance and denial is William McKeown's in *Rheaume v. Ontario, supra*, note 7. In this case, the Court ruled that sections of Ontario's *Municipal Act* which required municipal employees to take a leave of absence if they ran for municipal office and to resign their employment if they were elected, did not limit their freedom of expression or association because they were still free to join or work for any political party, to run as a candidate, to be elected, and to express any views they wanted to convey to the public. By concentrating on the freedoms municipal employees still retained, McKeown simply ignored the restrictions — being required to take a leave without pay and ultimately to resign — that the law imposed.

benefit from laws of this kind, they still have a constitutional right to be *free from*, and unconnected with, views and programmes of individuals and groups with which they fundamentally disagree.

Logically, of course, there is no connection between the two sides of the law. The fact that legislation of this kind positively enhances freedom of expression in the community at large does not mean it does not simultaneously impose limits on particular individuals like Murdoch Mackay and his friends. However supportive of expression a law of this kind may be, does not alter the fact that it simultaneously imposes a symbolic, if not financially onerous, limit on the freedom of individuals like Mackay by compelling them to "put their money where their mouths are not", and to support the expression of views and ideas which are antithetical to their own. It was a mistake for the Court of Appeal to think that the challengers' freedom was not limited at all simply because, on balance, the law encouraged freedom of expression in Manitoba more than it interfered with it.

A reviewer would expect the members of the Supreme Court to see that however much Manitoba's election financing law facilitates free expression and vigorous elections, the fact remains that, in accomplishing these goals, it also forces people like Mackay to contribute to the formulation and dissemination of ideas to which they are opposed.[23] Everyone should recognize the error of the Manitoba Court of Appeal is exactly the same one the Supreme Court itself made in *Jones*. In that case, it will be recalled, a majority of the Court denied that Alberta's *School Act* impacted negatively on Jones' freedom of religion on the ground that by allowing for alternative schools it actually enhanced religious freedom in the community at large.

Certainly no one would doubt that Mackay's freedom of expression and conscience would have been flagrantly infringed if the law had explicitly provided that a percentage of everyone's taxes would be used to defray the election expenses of the Progressive Conservative party. Forcing people to contribute to a particular party or specific set of ideas with which they fundamentally disagreed would be a clear violation of those persons' constitutional rights. It would offend the constitutional guarantee of freedom of expression in exactly the same way that forcing Philip Zylberberg's children to attend religious exercises which were antithetical to their own violated their entitlement to be free from such coercion by the State. In both, it is the entitlement to be *free from* ideas

---

23 In a worrisome concluding paragraph in the judgment he wrote for the Supreme Court in *Mackay, supra,* note 1, Peter Cory (one of the new judges who joined the Court at the end of year five), showed he could be distracted by arguments of this kind as well. For a brief discussion of this case, see note 26, *infra.*

which they believe to be fundamentally ill-conceived and not their *freedom to* express their own views that is at stake.[24]

A reviewer would have every reason to think the members of the Court would be entirely sensitive to the two kinds of entitlements that this freedom provides. In many of its own decisions, as we saw in Part One, the Court explicitly made reference to the positive and negative protection which all rights and freedoms guarantee. In *Big M, Edwards Books, Ford, Turpin* and *Slaight Communications*,[25] the Court repeated its understanding that the Charter is infringed as much when Governments force people to do something against their will as when it prohibits them from engaging in an activity they want to pursue. On its record over the first five years, the Court should have no difficulty with the idea that just because a law may have nothing to say about or is even supportive of one dimension of a right or freedom does not mean it may not compromise or violate the other. Described accurately, the Court should say that laws like Manitoba's *Elections Finances Act* strike a balance between the two sides of freedom of expression in exactly the same way that Ontario's law governing religious exercises and instruction in the schools tried to reconcile the competing freedoms of different religious groups.

Some reviewers might question whether the analogy between the *Mackay* and *Zylberberg* cases is really accurate because in the former, unlike the latter, it seems impossible to prove, as a matter of fact, that anyone is forced to support views that are antithetical to his own. It seems that whereas Philip Zylberberg could categorically claim that his children were pressured into remaining in the classroom, Murdoch Mackay and his friends cannot prove that portions of their personal tax payments were actually used to support one particular party or set of ideas to which they were opposed. Indeed it was just such an argument which the majority of the Manitoba Court of Appeal relied on to support its decision that Mackay's challenge was completely unfounded. They held that it was both impossible and inappropriate to say which item of expenditure was supported by which unit of tax revenue or receipts. In their view, the financial support given to a particular candidate or party could not be linked to the personal tax payment of a specific individual or group.[26]

---

24 On the relationship between the negative and positive aspects of all rights and freedoms see P. Westen, " 'Freedom' and 'Coercion': Virtue Words and Vice Words" (1985), Duke L.J. 541.

25 *R. v. Big M Drug Mart* (1985), 18 D.L.R. (4th) 321; *Edwards Books and Art Ltd. v. R.* (1987), 35 D.L.R. (4th) 1; *Ford v. Quebec* (1989), 54 D.L.R. (4th) 577; *Singer v. Quebec* (1989), 55 D.L.R. (4th) 641; *R. v. Turpin*, [1989] 1 S.C.R. 1296; *Slaight Communications v. Davidson, supra*, note 3.

26 When the case was argued at the Supreme Court of Canada, the challengers themselves apparently succumbed to the force of this argument and conceded that in order to prevail

What is a reviewer to make of such an argument? Empirically it is no doubt true that a person like Mackay cannot identify the actual party or candidate who was the beneficiary of his personal tax dollars. Does that mean that neither he nor indeed any taxpayer can ever complain about how their tax payments are spent? I think not. Indeed, neither legally nor logically would there be any basis for a reviewer dismissing a challenge like Mackay's on this ground.

As a legal matter, taxpayers can argue that even though they are unable to link their personal payments with a party or candidate whose ideas they oppose, there is a *risk* their money will be used in this way. They can say that even though they cannot prove with certainty that the taxes they paid actually ended up in the pockets of candidates they opposed, neither can the province guarantee that they didn't. For the reviewer, and the Court, that should be sufficient. She will, and they should, know from the Court's own rulings in the first five years that it has never required an actual infringement to be proved; that the mere threat of a violation is enough.[27]

More importantly, the reviewer should resist an argument of this kind as being quite out of keeping with the general understanding of how public revenues are collected and spent. Even the judges on Manitoba's Court of Appeal recognized that it is not only impossible, it is inappropriate to try and account for an individual's tax contributions in this way. It would

they were under an obligation to trace their tax dollars to payments made to candidates to whom they were opposed. By failing to take issue with this linkage argument, the challengers allowed the members of the Supreme Court to make exactly the same mistake as the Manitoba Court of Appeal. The fact that the Supreme Court was never required to address the argument (set out in the text which follows) that the challengers should not have been required to trace a specific connection between their tax dollars and the particular expenditures to which they objected, makes it likely that the campaign contribution provisions of the election financing laws in force across the country will be challenged again at some point in the future.

It might also be noted that the challengers also apparently abandoned their argument that Manitoba's election financing laws discriminated against smaller, minority parties in violation of s. 15. On this issue as well, the Court took the position that in the absence of any evidence submitted to substantiate the claim, it must be dismissed. Given the ease with which evidence could be secured to establish how small, fringe parties almost never receive any financial assistance from such reimbursement schemes and the exacting standards that have been demanded by other constitutional courts, it seems Canadian legislation (which generally requires candidates and parties to secure at least 10% of the vote before they can take advantage of the Act) is especially vulnerable to being attacked on s. 15 grounds. In West Germany, the constitutional court insisted that analagous laws must make provision for parties and candidates who receive .5% of the vote. For a discussion of the West German case see D. Kommers, "Politics and Jurisprudence in West Germany: State Financing of Political Parties" (1971), Am. J. of Juris. 215.

27 See the cases collected in Part One, Chapter 4, *supra*, note 45.

conflict with the idea that in a free and democratic society when Government "acts" it rules in the name of the State, and the people as a whole, and not as an accountant doing the bidding and directing those financial projects which each individual taxpayer chooses to support. In the absence of provisions which explicitly allow the taxpayer to earmark how his contributions will be spent, conventional analysis would require the reviewer to assume that a *pro rata* share of each person's taxes (however small) is included in every expenditure that is made on behalf and in the name of the State.

On closer inspection, then, there is nothing in the reasoning of the Manitoba Court of Appeal which should persuade the reviewer to abandon her expectation that this case is the same as all of the others she has considered so far and should be decided on a simple and straightforward application of the model in *Oakes*. Nor is there anything in any of the other judgments written in the lower courts, in which it was held that the interests and activities for which protection was being sought did not fall within one of the rights or freedoms that the Charter guaranteed, that would likely cause the reviewer to change her approach. In fact, in every case in which a court refused to exercise its powers of review according to the principles and tests in *Oakes*, it turns out that it committed the same mistakes as the Supreme Court did whenever it ruled that an interest or activity fell beyond the protection that the Charter guaranteed.

In the first place, in none of these cases did any of the judges make even the slightest effort to justify their rulings by reading the relevant sections of the Charter in a purposeful and liberal way. No reference is made to the accepted sources of meaning that we reviewed in Part One. Rather, in defining which interests or activities were or were not protected by the Charter's guarantee of freedom of expression or the right to vote, these judges relied exclusively on arguments or justifications which they should have considered in the second phase of the review process. Contrary to the requirement that the two stages of the review process be kept separate and analytically distinct, in defining what interests and activities are protected by the Charter, these judgments do all of the balancing of the competing interests affected by the laws under review in the first phase rather than under section 1.

In *O.P.S.E.U.*, for example, the whole thrust of John Eberlee's decision that partisan political activities by public servants do not fall within the scope of the Charter's guarantee of freedom of expression, was balancing pure and simple. Explicitly, what Eberlee said was that such activities would be inconsistent with another (unwritten)[28] part of the Constitution which

---

28 At one point, Eberle seems to infuse statutory rules with the status of constitutional law. See *O.P.S.E.U.*, *supra*, note 7, at 727.

requires the public service to be impartial and politically neutral. Implicitly, Eberlee was telling public servants that the interests and activities for which they were seeking protection did not fall within any of the Charter's guarantees because there was a "constitutional convention" of an impartial public service which was more important than — viz outweighed — their freedom to engage in the kinds of activities which the Act proscribed.

In the other two cases in which a judge ruled that an interest or activity was not protected by the Charter the analysis was essentially the same. In *Re Jolivet*, for example, Martin Taylor of the British Columbia Supreme Court ruled that disqualifying prisoners from exercising their right to vote was not a violation of section three because that section only protected the right to make an informed electoral choice rather than the more basic entitlement of casting a ballot. Again, in support of this position Taylor made no attempt to undertake the kind of liberal, purposive interpretation which the Supreme Court endorsed in *Oakes*. To the contrary, the only reason given favouring the narrower interpretation was an administrative one. The argument was that for practical reasons of maintaining security, order and discipline in the prisons, it was impossible to allow the inmates the freedom of access to the "process of discussion and the interplay of ideas" without which, informed electoral choice was impossible. In effect, Martin Taylor ruled that the State was justified in denying prisoners the right to vote because, for reasons of security and administration of the penitentiary, they would not be able to make the kind of informed choice that casting a ballot implies.[29]

The challenge by the Comité pour la Republique du Canada to the federal Government's rule prohibiting political propagandizing in airports was another case in which a judge inverted the two phases of the review process and failed to keep the analysis in each separate and distinct. According to Louis Pratte, a member of the Federal Court of Appeal, the challengers' freedom of expression had not been infringed because the owner of any property — whether public or private — has a right to refuse entry to those who want to make use of it for purposes which are inconsistent with those for which the owner intended it to be put. Here again the reviewer will recognize that what the judge has done is to mix the two phases of the review process together and to balance the public interest promoted by the regulation in defining what interests and activities the Charter guarantees. Holding that the Charter's guarantee of freedom of expression did not protect the challenger's interest in using the airport facilities for a purpose other than flying, is simply another way of saying that such forms of expression were less important — less weighty — than

---

29 For a rejection of this position, see *Sauvé v. A.G. Canada, supra,* note 4, at 600; and *Levesque v. A.G. Canada, supra,* note 5.

the interests of the property owner to determine the uses to which property which is under his or her control can be put. The only difference between Louis Pratte's judgment and the others which rejected the legal and/or factual basis of a challenger's claim was that it did not prove persuasive to the two other judges who sat on the case and it was, as a result, written only as a dissent.

Once the reviewer recognizes the common error that undermines the reasoning in each of these decisions, she will put them to one side and examine them later, in the second stage of the review process. Although the ideas and considerations which led these judges to dismiss the challengers' claims are not relevant in the first phase of the Court's inquiry, they could be very pertinent in the second. Indeed in some instances, as we shall see, the arguments on which these judges relied may even carry the day. It is not difficult to imagine, for example, that there will come a point at which everyone would say that the interests in having an impartial and neutral public service does outweigh and must override the interests of public servants to engage in every conceivable form of political activity which is open to everyone else. Similarly, it seems likely there will come a point at which the interests of the Government in managing public property would outweigh the interest of individuals to engage in the kinds of political activites which were restricted by the airport manager in the *CFC* case.

In the result, from her preliminary review of the record of these cases in the lower courts, it seems reasonable for the reviewer to assume that as long as it sticks to the model in *Oakes*, the Court should follow the example set by the majority of the judges who sat on these cases in the provincial trial courts and courts of appeal, accept the legal and factual bases of the challengers' claims, and move on to the second phase of the review process. However, as she passes to the second stage, the reviewer will discover that the analysis which she will be obliged to follow in resolving these cases will not always be as simple and straightforward as her ruling on the constitutionality of incorporating religious exercises and courses of instruction in the schools. In some cases it will, and overall there will be no doubt that the principle of alternative means will remain at the core of the review function. In the challenges brought by the National Citizens' Coalition and the Comité pour la Republique du Canada, for example, the reviewer will find that this principle will be able to do most, if not all, of the work in determining the outcome of these cases. As well, the principle of alternative means should play a decisive role with respect to the most extreme restrictions that various Governments have placed on the freedom of their public servants to be politically active. However, in the other cases, initiated by prisoners against the laws disqualifying them from being able to vote, and by members of smaller and more principled, issue-oriented public interest groups against

Canada's election financing laws, this principle will not be so controlling. Here the reviewer will see that even though the principle of alternative means will figure prominently in the Court's analysis, the object test and the balancing principle have very important roles to play as well. As a result, at the end of the day the reviewer should be able to draw from these cases a much richer appreciation of how all of the principles and tests in *Oakes* can figure in the Court's analysis and how the model works as a whole.

Before she turns her attention to these more complicated cases, the reviewer might be inclined to continue her approach of easing her way into her new role by first examining those challenges that conform most closely to the pattern of analysis with which she is most familiar. To be cautious, she could begin her review with either of the challenges initiated by the National Citizens' Coalition or the Comité pour la Republique du Canada. At first blush, both seem to provide textbook examples of how the reviewer expects the model in *Oakes* to be applied, and in particular of the critical importance of the principle of alternative means.

The challenge initiated by the NCC, it will be recalled, was directed at that part of the *Canada Elections Act* which prohibited all expenditures made in the course of an election campaign except those made by and to registered political parties and their candidates. All other forms of political expenditures, made by ordinary Canadians and interest groups, to support or oppose particular candidates and parties, were proscribed during the official campaign period. For example, no individual or group which was not registered as a political party could take out advertisements advising the public of the positions of different candidates and parties on various issues of public policy and encouraging the election of those whose views they endorsed.

The prohibition against this kind of "interest group" participation in election campaigning was built into the *Canada Elections Act* in 1983.[30] Prior to that time, the law had permitted individuals and groups to incur expenditures for the purpose of expressing their views where they were made in good faith (meaning they were not made surreptitiously, to circumvent the spending limits on registered parties and candidates) and were related to promoting issues of public policy and/or advancing the aims of the group. By an amendment to the Act this limited exemption was repealed in 1983 and the prohibition against non-party expenditures was made absolute. The amendment was introduced on the recommen-dation of the Chief Electoral Officer who believed that a complete prohibition on interest group expenditures was necessary to safeguard the

---

30 Note that a parallel law prohibits all third party expenditures in Quebec: *Loi régissant le financement des partis politiques*, R.S.Q. 1977, c. F-2, ss. 62, 66.

basic objectives which underlay the overall scheme of the Act.

In its most general terms the object or purpose of the *Canada Elections Act*, like all election financing laws, was to secure a rough equality in the conduct of election campaigns. To accomplish this, in addition to various rules of financial disclosure and reporting, the main provisions of the Act imposed ceilings on the amounts that could be spent by parties and their candidates and, simultaneously, guaranteed that varying percentages of the costs incurred in the course of a campaign would be reimbursed by the State.[31] The prohibition against non-party expenditures was added in order to ensure these larger objectives could not be overwhelmed and/or evaded by expenditures made by individuals and groups which lay completely outside the control of the Act. The concern was that, at least as it was originally worded, an exception which allowed for "bona fide" expenditures might become a loophole through which the rough equality of participation which the Act intended to guarantee could be compromised or even deliberately circumvented. There was some evidence that a number of individuals and groups had used the exception in the past to spend large sums supporting or opposing particular parties and candidates.[32] There was also an awareness that, in the absence of effective limits on non-party expenditures, there was a real possibility that groups like "political action committees" could be organized to avoid the spending limits stipulated in the Act as had happened in the United States.[33]

Justified on these grounds it is not difficult to see how the model in *Oakes* would be applied in the standard way and with its usual effect. There can be little doubt that the purpose which motivated the restriction on non-party expenditures during the course of an election campaign would meet the requirements of the object test. After the corporate campaign in favour of freer trade with the United States that was launched on the eve of the federal election in the fall of 1988, it would be impossible to deny the legitimacy of a concern that the overriding objective of the whole legislative regime required some restriction on the expenditures made by individual Canadians and unregistered interest groups. Ensuring that the rough equality of opportunity which the Act guaranteed was not undermined by individuals and groups bent on circumventing its terms unques-

---

31 It was the parallel reimbursement provisions in Manitoba's Elections Finances law which Mackay attacked.

32 The history of this provision is set out by the Court in *N.C.C. v. A.G. Canada, supra*, note 8, at 489-491. See generally K. Ewing, "The Legal Regulation of Campaign Financing in Canadian Federal Elections" (1988), Public Law 577, 596-606.

33 See K. Ewing, "The Legal Regulation of Campaign Financing", *ibid.*; R. Atkey, "Corporate Political Activity" (1985), 23 U. of Western Ontario L. Rev. 129; P. Boyer, *Political Rights: The Legal Framework of Elections in Canada* (Toronto: Butterworths, 1981).

tionably is a purpose which is "pressing and substantial" within the meaning of the first test in *Oakes*.

Consistent with the pattern she has come to expect, the reviewer will see that the defect in a rule prohibiting all public interest groups like Pollution Probe, CARAL, CLC, CMA, NCC, etc., from making election expenditures on their own behalf and to propagate their own ideas is not in the purpose it is meant to serve. Once again the object of a challenged law can easily satisfy the requirements of *Oakes*. The injustice of the restrictions imposed on the campaign activities of individual Canadians and interest groups lies in the way in which the law goes about its objectives. An absolute prohibition of the kind attacked by the NCC is just too heavy-handed a tool.[34] It is overkill in the extreme. In terms of the model in *Oakes*, it seems unimaginable that a law which prohibits all expenditures to promote the propagation of political ideas during the course of an election, except those made to and by registered political parties, can be justified on the principle of alternate means.

To protect the rough degree of equality which the overall scheme of the Act seeks to establish, it is simply not necessary to prohibit everyone, except registered political parties, from expressing themselves during the course of an election campaign. Much more focused and sensitively drawn constraints would do the trick. If Parliament was worried that an exception might be abused by individuals and groups whose object was to circumvent the spending limits in the Act, the law could be re-written to ensure that only bona-fide communications, on issues which these groups were organized to address, would be permitted. If, on the other hand, the concern was that even groups and individuals who are acting bona-fide, and in furtherance of issues and ideas with which they are legitimately concerned, may frustrate the objectives of the Act, by spending large sums of money to support or oppose particular parties and/or their candidates, the obvious alternative is to subject these groups to spending limits and disclosure requirements as well. Restrictions of this kind would be constitutionally superior to absolute prohibitions because they ensure the maximum protection of constitutional guarantees without compromising the objectives which Parliament seeks to achieve.

It is true that if the objective of Parliament had been to establish an absolute equality in the resources that were available to every party and candidate for public office, then such a moderated alternative would not have been available. In that case, any expenditure by an individual or group in support of, or in opposition to, a candidate or party would

---

34 In the words of one commentator "Parliament was trying to 'kill a gnat within a sledge hammer'". See W.H. McConnell, "Recent Developments in Constitutional Law" (1986), 18 Ottawa L.R. 721, 765.

unavoidably compromise the purposes of the Act. But that, quite clearly, was not the intention which lay behind the *Canada Elections Act*, or indeed any of the provincial campaign financing schemes. All of these laws explicitly anticipate that candidates and parties will receive different amounts of contributions, will spend different amounts, will be reimbursed varying sums, and will have substantially divergent access to the electronic media.

From these provisions it is clear the purpose of the Act was only to achieve a very rough degree of equality between parties and candidates. Except in the overall limits imposed on all candidates and parties, there was no attempt to equalize the involvement between individuals and groups in the time and money they might commit to an election campaign. The idea of the Act was to build in a floor of minimum public support for all the major parties and their candidates and to impose a ceiling on the maximum amount that they could spend, leaving open a wide range of opportunity and inequality in between.

Limited, bona-fide, expenditures by ordinary individuals or public interest groups are clearly consistent with the spirit and overall objectives of the Act. Even the Chief Electoral Officer eventually recognized that limited expenditures by individuals and unregistered groups would not interfere with Parliament's ambition of securing a basic measure of equality in the resources available to and expendable by political parties and their candidates. In fact, after Donald Medhurst of the Alberta Court of Queen's Bench struck down the absolute prohibition, that was one of the solutions he proposed that Parliament should adopt.[35]

At the end of the day the federal Government came to the conclusion, that there wasn't any need to act on the Chief Electoral Officer's report and it allowed Medhurst's decision to stand. In fact the leaders of the two major national parties were of one mind that there was really no need for any limits at all.[36] From the reviewer's perspective, nothing turns on how the challenge initiated by the NCC actually turned out. Whatever the outcome, the case would remain an important one for any reviewer intent on testing the democratic and progressive quality of the model in *Oakes*. The way in which the case was finally resolved certainly provides further support for the view that Charter litigation can have an energizing effect on the political process. Here again we find Government responding

---

35 In his 1983 report, the Chief Electoral Officer considered, but in the end recommended against, a scheme in which non-political organizations could be registered and subjected to the same rules and regulations governing political parties. In his 1984 Report, however, following Medhurst's decision in the *NCC* case, he recommended that the proper solution was imposing "certain restrictions" rather than a "total prohibition" on expenditures by individuals and groups. See 1984, *Statutory Report of the Chief Electoral Officer*, p. 24.

36 See R. Atkey, "Corporate Political Activity", *supra*, note 33, at 131.

positively to a decision of a lower Court without the need for testing the issue through two or three levels of appeal. Moreover, even if at some future date the federal Government felt the need to impose limits on what individuals and interest groups can spend in the course of an election campaign, from her analysis of the NCC case the reviewer could be confident that such an initiative would meet the constitutional standards of *Oakes*. Conversely the reviewer would also know that laws which parallel the provisions which were struck out of the *Canada Elections Act* (such as those still in force in the province of Quebec[37]) would not survive a similar review by the Court.

In the result and whichever political scenario the future may hold, the progressive and democratic influence of the Charter will have been demonstrated once again. With the pattern of the analytical method still on track the reviewer could move on to consider how the Court is likely to respond to the other challenges that have been made to laws which limit the expression of political views. The next case to which a reviewer would naturally be inclined to turn, would likely be the challenge launched by the Comité pour la Republique du Canada against the Government's decision to prevent its members from using the public concourses in Mirabel Airport in order to communicate their political ideas. Here again the reviewer should find the same scenario unfold although there is a slight possibility, depending on how the lawyers for the federal Government decide to present their case, that this challenge could be decided on the object test instead.

There are two ways the federal Government might try to justify the action taken by the airport authorities. The most obvious justification is that rules and regulations restricting the use of places, like airports, are necessary in order to guarantee the safety and convenience of the travelling public. Alternatively, the lawyers might argue that the motivation of the airport authorities was to prevent the members of the Comité or indeed anyone else from disseminating political views. Although it might be thought that it would be unlikely for the federal Government to adopt the latter position, the reviewer will want to consider it, if only briefly, because that was the way at least one of the judges, James Hugessen, of the Federal Court of Appeal, thought he heard the Government present its case.[38] Moreover, if he was right in how he understood the Government's lawyers, there would also be no doubt that he was correct in his ruling that, in its treatment of the members of the Comité, the Government was acting unconstitutionally.

As a matter of constitutional law, property rights are no different from

---

37 *Supra*, note 30.
38 *La Comité pour la Republique du Canada*, *supra*, note 12, *per* James Hugessen.

any other legal rule or regulation. They cannot be created or enforced just for the purpose of denying other people their constitutional guarantees. Muzzling the challengers, because the views they wanted to disseminate were political, is the one purpose which the model in *Oakes* will not allow Governments, or indeed anyone with legal authority, to pursue. To be validated constitutionally, the Government would have to do more than rely on a bare assertion of its property rights. It would have to identify the benefits which these rights secured for the community in order to justify the limitations on constitutional freedoms which they imposed.

That, of course, is precisely what the Government would be expected to do. It would explain how political activities can cause disturbances and may interfere with the convenience and/or the safety of the travelling public. It is unimaginable that, in justifying the expulsion of the CFC, the Government will not emphasize the public good it was expected to promote.

Nor can there be any doubt about how the Court would respond if the Government argued its case this way. On the model in *Oakes* there can be nothing wrong with a Government putting restrictions on the uses to which public places like community parks or theatres or airports can be put. In terms of the objectives these institutions are meant to serve, it would be perfectly proper for a Government to enact laws which, for example, outlawed rock concerts and unleashed dogs in all three. Equally, in terms of controlling access to airports, it is perfectly proper, in terms of the objectives being sought, for the Government to draw up rules and regulations to ensure that the primary purpose of moving people from one place to another as efficiently and pleasantly as possible, is achieved. Custody of public property carries with it the right, indeed the responsibility, to ensure it is used to promote the purposes for which it was created.

Assuming that the federal Government does not argue its case in the manner Hugessen understood, the reviewer would expect it would be decided in exactly the same way as she thinks the challenge by the NCC should be resolved. Once again the principle of alternative means should do all of the work and it should lead the Court to results which are equally progressive and supportive of the democratic character of the Canadian State. Once it is committed to justifying the exercise of its legal authority on the basis of the interests of the travelling public, it is highly improbable that the reviewer or anyone on the Court would regard the Government's absolute and all-encompassing prohibition of all political (or religious) expression as the most reasonable way for it to have proceeded. Much more likely, the challenged rule and regulation would be characterized as another example of legislative — or in this case executive — overkill.

To satisfy the principle of alternative means, the regulations would have to be drafted in a way which would permit peaceful forms of political expression at times and in places which do not cause disturbances or interfere with the safety or convenience of the travelling public. If the interests of the travelling public are the only legitimate concerns which the Government can point to in justifying the expulsion, specific and well-defined limitations of this kind are more reasonable than the broad, all pervasive prohibitions which the airport manager tried to enforce. By definition "time, place and manner" restrictions offer greater protection to the rights and freedoms protected by the Charter without compromising the Government's aims and ambitions in any way.

In addition to doing most, if not all, of the work in vindicating the challenges initiated by the NCC and CFC, the principle of alternative means will also be of critical importance in deciding how the attacks by public servants, against laws which limit their freedom to engage in a wide range of political activities, will turn out. Although it is unlikely to be able to provide answers on each and every rule and regulation which the challengers have questioned, it is certain to be decisive with respect to the most extreme prohibitions and limitations which these laws contain. Indeed, evaluating the constitutionality of the most restrictive aspects of Canada's public sector employment laws may be the simplest and most straightforward application of the principle of alternative means that the reviewer will have considered so far.

Consider three examples taken from the relevant legislation of Ontario, Nova Scotia, and the federal Government. In the first, the law provides that no public servant in Ontario, no matter how anonymous her position or simple his task, can "speak in public or express views . . . . on *any* matter that forms part of the platform of a political party".[39] In Nova Scotia, the *Civil Service Act*[40] provided that anyone who wanted to run for political office had to give up their job before they could do so. Federal public servants, for their part, were prohibited, on pain of dismissal, from "engaging in work for and/or against the election of a candidate or . . . . political party".[41]

When the Court comes to review the constitutionality of each of these laws it should have no use for any other principle than alternative means. The object test should not be a factor and the reviewer would expect it would be applied automatically. In none of these cases was a question even raised in the lower courts about the purposes which these laws were intended to serve. In two of them, in fact, counsel for the challengers

---

39 *Public Service Act*, R.S.O. 1980, c. 418, s. 14.

40 S.N.S. 1980, c. 3, s. 34(2),(3). A slightly different provision in Ontario's *Municipal Act* calls on municipal employees to take an unpaid leave if they choose to run for municipal office and to resign if they are elected. See *Rheaume v. Ontario, supra*, note 7.

41 *Public Service Employment Act*, R.S.C. 1970, c. P-32, s. 32.

explicitly acknowledged that it was entirely legitimate for a legislature to take whatever steps were necessary to create an impartial, neutral and effective public service, one which enjoyed the trust and confidence of both the public and the politicians whom they served. Given that, in a pre-Charter decision,[42] the Court has already made clear its own endorsement of these objectives, it would not be expected that the challengers would change their position in this regard. Their sole argument in the lower Courts was that these laws were constitutionally defective because of the means that were used to accomplish the objectives. Their complaint was that while it was legitimate for a legislature to impose some restrictions on the political activities of public servants, the laws they were challenging had gone too far. They said there were more reasonable alternatives available to the legislature to accomplish its objectives in ways which interfered with their political freedom less.

Framed in this way, once again the only question the reviewer, and ultimately the Court, would have to address is whether each of the Governments involved in these cases had been able to prove that the particular prohibition or restriction they had adopted in their law was necessary to ensure the impartiality and integrity of their public service. On the evidence that was filed with the lower courts neither the reviewer nor any member of the Court should have any doubt as to what answers such questions deserve. In each of these cases the challengers provided the judges with a broad range of alternative policies which all of these Governments could have used to guarantee the neutrality and effectiveness of their public service, without imposing such sweeping restrictions on the political freedoms of those they employ.

For many, the most reasonable way of ensuring the integrity of the public service is through rules and regulations which require strict adherence to the merit principle and establish codes of appropriate personal behaviour. The merit principle consists of rules and personnel practices which stipulate that appointments to and promotions within the public service must be based on personal merit and professional qualifications for a job rather than on any extraneous factors such as a person's political allegiances or family connections.[43] Codes of conduct usually proscribe a range of personal behaviour, such as engaging in acts which give rise to conflicts of interest, apprehension of bias, breach of confidentiality etc., which would apply to political and non political activities alike. Alternatively, these codes can be written in less general terms and refer only

---

42 *Re Ontario Public Service Employees Union and A.G. Ontario* (1988), 41 D.L.R. (4th) 1. See also *Fraser and Public Service Staff Relations Board*, [1985] 2 S.C.R. 455.
43 For a brief discussion of the merit principle see W.D. Kernaghan, "Public Administration in Canada: Selected Readings" (Toronto: Methuen, 1968), p. 367.

to very specific kinds of political activities in which public servants are not permitted to engage.

In a wide range of communities and States including British Columbia, Australia, New Zealand, Switzerland and Sweden some combination of policies establishing the merit principle and codes of behaviour is relied on to ensure the neutrality and effectiveness of the public service.[44] With the merit principle and personnel codes firmly in place, none of these societies feel the need to impose *any* further restrictions on the political activity of any public servant except for those in the most senior and sensitive positions. Unless the Governments defending the kinds of restrictions the reviewer is considering could show that the political activities of public servants in these other societies have compromised their effectiveness or neutrality in some way, the kinds of sweeping prohibitions they have adopted could not be justified. If the merit principle and codes of personal behaviour can do the trick, they would be the only policy which could satisfy the principle of alternative means.

Indeed, even if it could be shown that the fairness and effectiveness of the public service had suffered in societies where all or most restrictions on political activities by public servants had been lifted, that would not be enough. To justify the kind of extreme restrictions in force in Ontario, Nova Scotia and the federal arena, each of these Governments would have to show that it was impossible to draft their laws more narrowly, both in terms of the number of the employees to whom they applied and in the range of activities they prohibited.[45] Unless it could be shown that rules and regulations which proscribed only the most problematic activities, like politicking during working hours, or soliciting funds for a political party, and which focused on those public servants who held sensitive positions of policy or high visibility, would not preserve the requisite degree of neutrality in the public service, the monolithic, all-encompassing prohibitions that have been challenged in these cases could not pass the principle of alternate means. In the absence of such proof, these more finely tuned rules and regulations would show that the challenged restrictions were broader than were required to achieve the

---

44 A review of the strengths and weaknesses of this approach and where it is used is contained in the *Report on Political Activity, Public Comments and Disclosure by Crown Employees*, Ontario Law Reform Commission, Ministry of Attorney General, Toronto, 1986. See also W.D. Kernaghan, "The Political Rights and Activities of Public Servants", in *Bureaucracy in Canadian Government* (Toronto: Methuen, 1969).

45 Laws like these, which are vague and uncertain, are analogous to laws that are overly broad. In the absence of any certainty as to what such terms will eventually be interpreted to mean, it is recognized that they will have a chilling or deterring effect on the political activity of public servants. See *Osborne v. Canada (Treasury Board)*, *supra*, note 10, at 247-250. On the relationship of vagueness and overbreadth generally, see C. Rogerson, "The Judicial Search for Appropriate Remedies Under The Charter: The Examples of Overbreadth and Vagueness", in R. Sharpe (ed.), *Charter Litigation* (Toronto: Butterworths, 1987).

objectives of the legislation and were completely gratuitous abridgments of constitutional guarantees.[46]

Once again it seems most unlikely any of the Governments involved would be able to adduce the necessary evidence to support such a claim. No other Governments, except those which enacted them, have felt it necessary to pass such sweeping and far reaching restrictions on the political freedom of their public servants. Compared to the more focused, individualized proscriptions which other provinces and countries have found sufficient to maintain the impartiality and effectiveness of their public service, all of these laws are further examples of legislatures succumbing to the temptation of overkill.

So far, in each of the three cases concerning the freedom of people to engage in various forms of political activity that the reviewer has considered, everything seems quite regular and routine. The pattern of the analysis in *Oakes* continues to hold. Both the conclusions that all of the restrictions imposed by these laws are unconstitutional, as well as the reasoning used to arrive at these results, is consistent with everything that the reviewer has observed so far. With the principle of alternative means the Court should be able to pick out and strike down laws which impose unnecessary limits on some of the most basic interests and activities people pursue. The analysis should reveal to Governments more moderate ways to accomplish their objectives. Collectively, the challenges by the NCC, CFC and the different groups of public servants across the country provide three more examples supporting the believers' claim that the Court can play an effective role in promoting more progressive policies regulating political activities and do so in a way which is compatible with and indeed very supportive of the sovereignty of the popular will.

This unbroken repetition of the same refrain may cause some reviewers to wonder whether this is the only song she and the members of the Court will ever have to perform. As soon as she turns to the other two cases we have been considering in this chapter, she will realize this is not the case. In one, in which Murdoch Mackay and his friends challenged the constitutionality of Manitoba's *Elections Finances Act*, she will find that the principle of alternative means has no role to play at all. In the other, in which various prisoners have contested the legality of Governments denying them their right to vote, although the principle should figure prominently in the Court's analysis, it is doubtful that it will be able to give a definitive answer as to what the final outcome should be.

---

46 In the legislative debates surrounding the introduction of the *Public Service Act* it is clear that the Government's intention was to draft a law which would apply uniformly to all employees and would not "stratify the service" in any way. See *Debates of Legislature of Ontario*, Feb. 14/63, p. 717.

Because these cases cannot be resolved in the usual way, they will take on a special significance. Both of these challenges provide the reviewer with an opportunity to see how the other principles included in the model will be applied by the Court. They will give the reviewer a chance to see whether, when the principle of alternative means is not capable of providing the final answer to a case, the model retains its objective and progressive character. In the end, these cases will give the reviewer a fresh perspective from which the debate between believers and sceptics can be assessed.

Of the two cases left to analyse, the reviewer will find it easier if she begins with the challenge to the reimbursement provisions of Manitoba's *Elections Finances Act* initiated by Murdoch Mackay. His complaint, it will be recalled, was that paying a portion of the election expenses of the major parties and their candidates from the public purse violated the entitlement of taxpayers to be free from and unconnected with views and ideas which are antithetical to their own. Even though it turns out that the principle of alternative means should have no role to play in deciding the resolution of such a case, it is much the simpler of the two legal regimes she has left to review. In the final analysis, challenges to the reimbursement provisions of election finances laws can be settled on a very straightforward application of the balancing, or third proportionality principle in *Oakes*.

Neither the object test nor the principle of alternative means should have any bearing on whether the reimbursement provisions of election financing laws are constitutional or not. As the reviewer would know from her analysis of the challenge initiated by the NCC, by promoting equality of participation and plurality of expression during the course of election campaigns, these laws unambiguously affirm the very purposes and objectives on which "free and democratic societies" are based. However imperfectly they may have been designed, it is inconceivable that any member of the Court would dispute the legitimacy of the goals the legislature was trying to accomplish.

Nor does it seem possible that the principle of alternative means will work in the usual way. Quite simply, there does not appear to be any other policy that will allow the State to *guarantee* that most, if not all candidates and parties, will have a fixed percentage of their expenses reimbursed except by taxing each citizen for his or her proportional share. Alternative schemes like tax credits and matching grants from Government, which are voluntary, can not ensure the same level of support that a compulsory system can provide.

Unlike any other case she has considered so far, the reviewer should find herself very quickly in the situation in which the constitutionality of a law will depend on the last proportionality principle (balancing) in *Oakes*. Whether the reimbursement provisions of election financing laws are valid or not will depend on whether their benefits can be shown to outweigh the restrictions on constitutional guarantees which they impose. Instinctively the reviewer should be cautious in applying this final criterion of constitutionality. To remain faithful to the model in *Oakes*, she should only apply the balancing principle with deference and care. As we saw in the first Part, at this stage of the process the reviewer unavoidably is cast in the role of second-guessing the legislature's judgment as to how the balance of competing interests affected by the law should be struck.

In a case such as Mackay's, however, the tension that usually exists when the Court exercises its powers of review under the third proportionality principle shouldn't arise. Here there is virtually no risk that anyone on the Court would be tempted to question the legislature's judgment as to how the competing interests affected by these laws should be reconciled. In principle the balance is clear and clean cut.[47] All of the interests affected by election financing laws can be measured in a common currency (freedom of expression) and their weights should not be controversial or uncertain in any way. On any scale, paying a part of the costs of those who participate in political campaigns and elections from the public purse promotes freedom (of expression, association) in the community much more than it restricts it.

On the one hand, making available substantial resources to cover a major part of the costs of contesting an election enormously enhances both the quality and quantity of political expression in the community. It permits many people to engage in one of the most basic forms of political activity which otherwise would be beyond their means. Laws of this kind offer significant material support for the (positive) freedom of the less powerful and well-off in the community to communicate their political ideas.

Against such a direct and immediate expansion of personal freedom and political expression, the restriction entailed on the (negative) freedom of people like Mackay, not to be associated in any way with ideas to which they are opposed, seems relatively trivial; not non-existent as the majority of the Court of Appeal tried to say, but hardly substantial nonetheless. In the end, as the majority in the Manitoba Court of Appeal also pointed out, the reimbursement rules do not interfere with anyone's freedom to form their own thoughts, or to incur any expense to express their views; nor do they cause others to attribute ideas or opinions to people that in fact they do not hold. The infringement involved in requiring people to

---

47 But see note 26, *supra*, where it is argued that although the public reimbursement of a portion of the election expenses of candidates and parties can be justified on the principles in *Oakes*, the particular limit imposed to qualify for state support in most Canadian jurisdictions may be open to attack under s. 15.

contribute (their proportional share) to candidates and parties whose ideas are hostile to their own is mostly of a symbolic kind. Relative to the enhancement of expression and the improvement in the opportunities for participation in the political process, it is unimaginable that the reviewer or anyone on the Court[48] would regard the constitutional cost of securing these objectives to be anything but a very small price to pay. Measured against the actual increase in the expression of political ideas, the largely symbolic restriction the law imposes on people like Mackay does not weigh very much.

The conclusion that, in principle, the reimbursement provisions of election financing laws are constitutionally sound makes *Mackay* an important case. It confirms that the balancing principle can also be applied objectively to achieve progressive results.[49] With her analysis of *Mackay*, the reviewer will have a better appreciation of the fullness of the model which has not been visible before. Still, *Mackay* remains a relatively simple case and it won't be until she turns her mind to the prisoners' challenges that she will really get a sense of how all of the principles set out in *Oakes* work together and how rich and sophisticated the model really is.

What makes the prisoners' cases so different from all of the others that the reviewer has considered so far is the way in which Governments have gone about justifying their decision to deny inmates and people on parole the right to vote. The prisoners' cases are not like the others where Governments have relied on one or at the most two objects or goals to explain what they were trying to do. Here, over half a dozen different purposes might be said to be promoted by rules of this kind.

Denying prisoners and/or people on parole the right to vote is commonly defended as a legitimate part of the country's or a province's election laws. The justification is pitched at both a practical and theoretical level. Practically, it is said, voting by prisoners gives rise to a host of problems. In the first place, it is argued that some of the most basic rules and practices governing the conduct of elections cannot be adapted easily to the prison context without substantial revisions and adjustments being

---

48 In the concluding paragraph of its own judgment, *supra*, note 1, the Supreme Court sent a strong signal that it too saw the balance in this way.

49 In confirming the constitutionality of the subsidy provisions of election financing laws, this case would fall in line with *Edwards Books* (1987), 35 D.L.R. (4th) 1; *Irwin Toy v. Quebec, supra*, note 3; *R. v. Whyte* (1989), 51 D.L.R. (4th) 481; *R. v. Thomsen*, [1988] 1 S.C.R. 640; and *R. v. Hufsky*, [1988] 1 S.C.R. 621. In each of these cases as well, the Court found the laws in issue satisfied each of the tests in *Oakes*. It bears repeating, however, that to be confirmed constitutionally, current reimbursement rules may have to be amended to ensure smaller fringe parties in addition to the major national and provincial parties are eligible for assistance. See note 26, *supra*.

made. It is pointed out, for example, that special rules and procedures would have to be designed for everything from canvassing and electioneering within the prison to more mundane and detailed matters like the publication of voters lists or how ballots will actually be cast.[50] More fundamentally, it is often said that giving prisoners the right to vote raises a real danger of widespread corruption and electoral fraud. In the view of some, prisoners are especially vulnerable to being coerced — or bribed — by fellow inmates and/or prison officials in deciding how they should cast their vote. For still others the major disadvantage of enfranchising prisoners is that it carries with it the possibility of distorting local politics by placing the area in which the penitentary is located in the shadow of the prison walls. A large inmate population in a relatively small community could radically alter the priorities and agenda of local politicians and could conceivably determine what the outcome in any election would be.

At other times, the disqualification policy is justified in more general and theoretical terms. Prisoners are described as people who, by their criminal behaviour, have shown themselves to be incapable of looking after their own lives responsibly and so should not be permitted to participate in organizing the affairs of others. Excluding those who have breached society's rules from the election process is portrayed as protecting the "currency" of the vote. It promotes the idea of a decent and responsible citizenry on which the very foundation of free and democratic societies is based.[51] As a matter of political theory, disqualifying people who violate society's laws is presented as the logical corollary of the idea that the State is organized around a social contract, consisting of the terms and conditions on which society is based, to which everyone has given their consent.

When it is not being defended as a perfectly reasonable piece of election policy, disqualifying prisoners and/or those on parole from being able to vote is often justified as sound criminal law.[52] Disqualifying those who commit crimes and are sentenced to jail from being able to vote may be put forward as a natural way of trying to rehabilitate people to conform to society's rules. In addition, it can and has been said that denying prisoners

---

50 It was arguments of this kind which persuaded Martin Taylor to uphold the disqualification in the *Canada Elections Act* in *Re Jolivet and R.*, *supra*, note 4.

51 This was the kind of argument which appealed to Mabel Van Camp in *Sauvé v. A.G. Canada* (1989), 53 D.L.R. (4th) 595.

52 Because under the division of powers sections (91 and 92) of the old B.N.A. Act, criminal law matters are assigned to the federal Government, it may be difficult for a province to rely on such an argument in defending the disqualification of prisoners in provincial elections. For an example of a similar constraint imposed on the range of argument that could (constitutionally) be advanced by the federal Government see *R. v. Big M Drug Mart* (1985), 18 D.L.R. (4th) 321.

the right to vote will act as a deterrent to others not to break society's laws in the future. More broadly still, it is often claimed that disqualification from voting is an entirely appropriate way to stigmatize those who violate society's rules. It is said to be fitting to punish those who break laws by denying them the right to participate in the selection of those who make the law. In a word, disqualification is presented as a legitimate way for society to retaliate against those who refuse to play by the rules.

As well as being justified as a legitimate component of a society's electoral and/or penal policy, disenfranchising prisoners is occasionally defended simply as a matter of prison administration and security. It is argued that to guarantee the safety and security of the institution and the inmates, steps would have to be taken and procedures put in place which would be both costly and inconvenient to effect. To avoid the administrative hassles and expenses entailed in permitting inmates to vote in elections, the argument is that it is both safer and more efficient simply to suspend people's right to vote during the periods they are confined to jail.

This long list of public benefits which the disenfranchisement of prisoners and people on parole is meant to achieve makes this case different, and in the end more complex, than any the reviewer has considered so far. It should not, however, change her analytical approach. To determine whether any or all of these reasons justify disqualifying people in prison and on parole from casting ballots, she should proceed in the normal way. First, each of the objects which Governments put forward in defense of such laws would have to be screened against the object test to ensure it was "pressing and substantial". Even though the reviewer will know that ordinarily this is not a difficult criterion for Governments to meet, she might anticipate that it would play a more decisive role in these cases. Given the number of objectives which can be put forward in defense of this policy, if the object test was likely to have a bite in any case, this would be a logical place where it would take hold.

When the reviewer sits down to examine each of the purposes which Governments claim to be pursuing when they disenfranchise people in jail, it is unlikely, however, that she will be prepared for just how central the role is which the object test will play. Although, as she would expect, in the end Governments should be able to satisfy the object test, it turns out that many of the goals which are put forward to justify the disqualification will, in one way or another, have considerable difficulty meeting the "pressing and substantial" criterion the Court established in *Oakes*.

One purpose which is clearly suspect constitutionally is a society's desire to seek retribution against persons who have violated some part of its criminal code. Denying prisoners the right to vote, in retaliation for what they have done, runs directly counter to the one limitation which the object test contains. Whatever philosophers, psychologists, and criminologists may say about retribution as a way of treating others, the Charter no longer permits Canadian society to deny constitutional rights as a form of sanction or punishment.[53] The one goal we know lawmakers cannot pursue is the deliberate denial of peoples' rights for no other purpose than inflicting such a deprivation on them. On the model in *Oakes* some other purpose, some other public good — such as deterring criminal activity or protecting the integrity of the electoral process or protecting the administrative and security arrangements of our prisons — must be put forward if such laws are to be validated constitutionally.

Ruling out retribution as a valid justification for denying prisoners the right to vote is a conclusion a reviewer might have anticipated. She has, after all, seen the object test rule out deliberate attempts to restrict constitutional freedoms before.[54] So far, however, that is the only role the reviewer will have seen the first test in *Oakes* play. It is less likely therefore she will have foreseen that, in addition to invalidating intentional infringements of constitutional guarantees, the object test will also screen out purposes which, although theoretically consistent with the standard in *Oakes*, in fact are very difficult, if not impossible, to prove. So far, the question of the Government producing sufficient evidence to establish the motives that underlie a law has not arisen. In all of the cases we have analysed in this Part it was taken for granted that the Government would have no difficulty in proving the purposes it sought to accomplish. In the prisoners' challenges, however, it seems less certain that this will be the case. In fact, it seems highly unlikely that any Government would be able to adduce the necessary evidence to support many of the goals which it says justifies treating prisoners in this way.

As a matter of criminal law, for example, the federal Government would be hard pressed to make its claims about deterrence and rehabilitation stick. Intuitively, as several of the judges in the lower courts have observed,[55] it seems highly implausible that being disqualified from voting will deter people from engaging in most types of criminal activity and/ or contribute to their rehabilitation and reformation. As for the matter of rehabilitation, there is evidence to suggest that the involvement of prisoners in the election process actually enhances the prospects for their successful

---

53 For an argument that the disqualification of prisoners from voting is at best an historical anachronism with punitive overtones, see Gordon Kaiser, "The Inmate as Citizen" (1971), 2 Queen's L.J. 208. For a discussion of the rights of prisoners generally under the Charter, see Wayne Mackay, "Inmates Rights: Lost in the Maze of Prison Bureaucracy", 11 Dal. L.J. 698. For an argument that the Court has already rejected retribution as a valid goal of sentencing policy, see K. Roach "Smith and the Supreme Court: Implications for Sentencing Law and Reform", 11 S. Ct. L. Rev. 433.

54 See Part One, Chapter 2, p. 27.

55 See, e.g., *Re Jolivet, Re Sauvé, supra*, note 4.

reintegration in the community.[56] Although it may be possible to establish a link between deterrence and disqualification in the case of people convicted of electoral offences, it is very doubtful Governments would be able to establish any wider connection than that.

Other justifications, advanced to support the disenfranchisement rule, for example that it enhances the quality of the election process, seem to be based on equally shaky factual foundations. To say, for example, that prisoners cannot be given the vote because they are unable to participate in the full range of electoral activities (like campaigning or canvassing) and so will not have access to all the information and the full range of freedoms on which a rational voting choice depends, runs contrary to the reality of life inside a modern penitentiary. In fact, all of the important means of mass communication are available to prisoners who, compared to most people on the "outside", have an abundance of "free time" on their hands. In these circumstances it is arguable that prisoners will be more informed, and in a better position to make more considered choices, than large numbers of Canadians who seem to have little inclination, and less time, to invest in elections beyond what it takes to cast a ballot.

Even more farfetched is the argument that persons who engage in *any* form of criminal activity, no matter how trivial or spontaneous, and who end up in jail, have demonstrated their incapacity to manage their own lives and, *a fortiori*, the affairs of others. Like the deterrent argument, while the claim might have some credibility if the disqualification were aimed specifically at individuals who had engaged in criminal activity of a kind and to a degree that showed their capacity for rational thought was indeed impaired,[57] it seems wildly implausible in the cases of the vast majority of persons who are incarcerated in our jails. The mere fact a person is sentenced to jail says nothing about whether he will exercise his franchise responsibly or not. In the absence of any direct evidence linking the two,[58] the characterization of all people locked in our jails as being incapable of voting responsibly constitutes stereotyping of the crudest kind.

In the case of the deterrence and rational voter arguments, it is true that Governments would likely be able to substantiate their claims if their objectives were drawn more narrowly. Intuitively there does seem to be something in the idea that disenfranchising people who are convicted and/

---

56 G. Kaiser, "The Inmate as Citizen", *supra*, note 53; *Re Grondin, supra*, note 4; *Re Badger, supra*, note 5.

57 E.g., persons found not guilty by reason of insanity or perhaps individuals found to be dangerous offenders and sentenced to indefinite detention.

58 In her judgment in *Sauvé v. A.G. Canada, supra*, note 4, Mabel van Camp, who relied on this argument, did not point to a single piece of evidence that would establish the connection.

or incarcerated for acts of electoral fraud and related criminal activity may assist their rehabilitation and deter others from engaging in similar behaviour in the future. Equally, it might be expected that Governments would be able to identify extreme forms of anti-social behaviour which would, in fact, certify an incapacity for rational reflection and responsible choice. However, once a Government restated its objectives to concentrate on this narrower class of persons, the existing, universal disqualification of everyone in jail would not be able to satisfy the principle of alternative means. If, as a matter of proving its case, the Government was restricted to saying that it wanted to deter fraud and corruption in the electoral process or prevent people who are incapable of rational behaviour from voting, the principle of alternative means would take hold and would require that the disqualification be limited to those groups. At most, the goals of deterrence and protecting the integrity of the electoral process would justify disqualifying those whose criminal activity was of a kind that (i) might reasonably be expected to be deterred by the imposition of such a sanction, and/or (ii) reasonably supported the inference that they were incapable of making rational choices.[59]

In whichever way a Government decided to justify its position, the reviewer will come to see the object test as being much more important than she might initially have suspected. These cases show that the first test in *Oakes* does more than just screen out laws which are passed with the sole purpose of restricting peoples' freedom and rights. It also blocks any attempt to justify a law with reference to objects and goals which cannot be proven. Perhaps most important of all, the prisoners' cases show how the object test anchors everything that follows. Aims and ambitions which satisfy the first stage of the Court's evaluation of a challenged law provide the focus for the rest of the review process. They orient and provide the framework against which the two proportionality principles will be applied. In the end, the object test ensures the process will have that degree of objectivity which is essential for the integrity of constitutional review.[60] Purposes which pass the object test provide a fixed reference point against

---

59 For examples of legislation which is drawn in this more narrow and focused way see *Election Act*, R.S.B.C. 1979, c. 103, s. 3(1)(b); *Disenfranching Act*, R.S.C. 1985, c. D-3. This more focused approach is also employed in Australia, Iceland and the Netherlands. See *Badger v. A.G. Manitoba, supra*, note 5.

60 It has been argued by some that the object test is not capable of objective application because the judges can manipulate the purposes which a law is said to serve. Examples are cited which are said to show how various members of the Supreme Court engaged in such conduct over the course of the first five years. See, e.g., J. Bakan, "Constitutional Arguments: Interpretation and Legitimacy in Canadian Constitutional Thought", 27 Osgoode Hall L.J. 123, 166-168; M. Mandel, *The Charter of Rights and the Legalization of Politics in Canada* (Toronto: Wall & Thompson, 1989), pp. 278ff. For a description of how the test could be misapplied in the future in cases considering the constitutionality

which the reasonableness of alternate means can be measured and the weight of the restrictions on constitutional guarantees can be balanced and compared.

The objectivity of the means/ends analysis can be seen regardless of whether a Government defends the disqualification of prisoners as a matter of criminal or electoral law. If a Government justified the disqualification as a way of deterring certain kinds of criminal actions and/or of screening out people who are incapable of rational choice, the principle of alternate means would require the law to be aimed specifically at these groups. In identifying policies which are more precisely tailored to suit the purposes of the Government, the prisoners' cases follow exactly the pattern the reviewer has seen in just about every case she has considered so far. Here again the principle of alternative means would figure crucially in the resolution of the case. Similarly, when it comes to deciding whether disenfranchising prisoners or people on parole can be justified as a matter of sound electoral policy, the reviewer will discover that alternatives abound. A review of the comparative laws in force elsewhere in Canada and around the world shows that many of the concerns about prison administration, inmate safety, and the integrity of the electoral process can be met by alternative policies which respect and accommodate the prisoners' interests and entitlement to vote. Even the Chief Electoral Officer of Canada has acknowledged there is no basis to continue with the current approach.[61]

There is a very long list of "free and democratic" societies around the world and even within Canada's own borders that have shown that public concerns about prison administration and security can be accommodated without the need of denying prisoners their constitutional rights.

---

of abortion laws, see R. Dworkin, "The Future of Abortion", 36 New York Review 47 (28/9/89). For a glaring example of a lower court manipulating the purposes of a challenged law, see the decision of the Ontario Court of Appeal in the *Elgin County* case (1990), 65 D.L.R. (4th) 1; Chapter 5, pp. 137-138, *supra.*

It is unlikely our reviewer would be persuaded by arguments of this kind. From her review of the Court's performance in the first Part, she would know that while there may have been instances of judges manipulating the objects a law was said to serve, certainly in the vast majority of cases the Supreme Court heard, establishing a law's purposes was a decidedly uncontroversial task. Her reaction to whatever isolated exceptions could be identified would be to condemn them as unconstitutional and an abuse of the Court's own powers of review. She would be fortified in this view, no doubt, by her own experience with the cases she had considered in this Part, including the prisoners' challenges. As we have seen in every case, it has been an easy task for her to identify the actual objectives of a law, and in every case these objectives have provided a fixed point of reference on which the objectivity of her analysis has been secured.

61 See *1984 Statutory Report*, Chief Electoral Officer of Canada, p. 18.

If Governments in Quebec and Newfoundland[62], and in a large number of western European countries[63], can attend to whatever security problems are raised by the publication of voters' lists or make whatever administrative arrangements are necessary to register prisoners in the most appropriate constituency and to ensure the integrity of the voting process,[64] it seems very unlikely any Government in Canada can credibly claim that these problems are not soluble in a similar way.[65] If administrative and security concerns are driving the voting disqualification, the example set by these societies shows there are ways of solving them without encroaching on the constitutional guarantees of prisoners in such a fundamental and all-encompassing way.

Now at this point a sceptic might object that the policies adopted in these other provinces and countries are not really possibilities that fit within the principle of alternative means. All of them, it might be said, involve the creation of a costly and complex administrative process. By contrast, a single virtue of the disqualification approach is that it can ensure prison security, electoral integrity and inmate safety without having to add elaborate and costly administrative structures and procedures. No other approach is really an alternative to a disqualification rule because none of them are able to match its administrative simplicity and economic efficiency. The sceptic would remind the reviewer that under the second proportionality principle in *Oakes*, to be a true alternative, policies must be identical in the purposes they promote.

In addition to its administrative advantages, a sceptic might also point to the symbolic value the public gains in disenfranchising those who breach society's rules. Disqualification is said to protect the "currency" of the vote and it preserves the idea of a responsible and decent citizenry in a way none of the alternatives can. The sceptic can say that these are also benefits which can only be achieved by an absolute and universal disqualification rule and for which there are no true alternatives.

A reviewer would have to take an argument of this kind very seriously. If these were objectives which a Government sought to achieve, the

---

62 It might be noted that the Attorney General of Ontario and the Chief Electoral Officer of Manitoba have also conceded there is no administrative rationale which supports a blanket disqualification. See *Re Grondin and A.G. Ontario, supra*, note 4; *Re Badger and A.G. Manitoba, supra*, note 5, at 115, and note 6, at 184.

63 For a reference to the practice in Europe, see G. Beaudoin, "Les Droits Democratiques", 61 Can. Bar Rev. 151.

64 Proxies and mail-in ballots are the most obvious alternatives. See *Re Grondin and A.G. Ontario, supra*, note 4; *Re Badger and A.G. Manitoba, supra*, note 6; *Maltby v. A.G. Sask.* (1983), 143 D.L.R. (3d) 649.

65 Lynn Smith makes the same point in her "Charter Equality Rights: Some General Issues and Specific Applications in British Columbia to Elections, Juries and Illegitimacy" (1984), 18 U.B.C. L. Rev. 351, 382.

reviewer would not be able to decide these cases by focusing just on the question of means. The objections of the sceptic would mean that, as with *Mackay*, the reviewer would be forced to turn to the balancing principle to decide if the disenfranchisement of prisoners and people on parole is constitutional or not. The principle of alternative means could take the reviewer through a large part of her analysis, but it couldn't do all of the work. Once again, the reviewer would have to weigh the costs and the benefits of competing interests and ideas. She would have to compare purposes with effects. In the final analysis, whether denying prisoners the right to vote is constitutional or not would depend on whether the reviewer and the members of the Court think that the symbolic and economic advantages that such a rule uniquely provides outweigh and therefore justify the disqualification.

In evaluating the balance struck by laws that prevent prisoners from voting, the reviewer should see some similarity with her analysis in *Mackay*. There, it will be recalled, the competing interests which were put on the scales could be expressed in a common currency. The positive freedom of people with limited resources to run for political office and to express their views was balanced against the negative freedom of people like Mackay not to have to have anything to do with ideas which gave them offence. In a similar way, in the prisoners' cases, one can see how both sides are trying to defend competing interests in the electoral process. On the one hand prisoners argue for what is widely regarded as one of the most basic forms political activity characteristic of all democratic societies. On the other there is the symbolic statement of a society underscoring its commitment to the idea of a decent and responsible citizenry.

If the reviewer applies the same weighting in this case as she did in *Mackay*, it is not difficult to predict what her decision will be. Although the method of analysis would remain exactly the same, it seems almost certain that the results would be reversed. Here it seems certain that the reviewer's judgment would be that the challenged law could not satisfy the last measure of proportionality established in *Oakes*; the benefits just don't weigh as much as the costs. Here it is the public interest, not the limitation on personal freedom, that is largely symbolic and weighs lightly in the balance. In addition this law, unlike Manitoba's *Elections Finances Act*, imposes a very real and very fundamental restriction on the right of people to govern themselves.

It is true that in the prisoners' cases Government could and indeed did argue that the disqualification rule also achieves a measure of administrative efficiency and saving. It is not likely, however, that such additional benefits will be perceived by most reviewers as sufficient to tip the scales in favour of the community's objectives. Given the very elaborate administrative bureaucracies already established to oversee both our penitentiaries and the conduct of elections, any administrative savings and convenience enjoyed by a disqualification rule are certain to be very small. In these circumstances the Supreme Court has already been clear that it does not consider administrative considerations to be weighty enough to justify laws which limit the most basic aspects of personal freedom in very fundamental ways.[66]

In the result, the reviewer's analysis of the challenge by prisoners to laws disqualifying them from the right to vote should be on all fours with her evaluation of *Mackay*. Even though in the latter case the analysis leads to affirming the constitutionality of financing election campaigns through the public purse, while here it results in striking down laws disenfranchising prisoners, both show that the balancing principle in *Oakes*, like alternative means, is capable of being applied objectively and generating progressive results. Indeed, as she reflects on how the full model has played itself out in determining the validity of the prisoners' claims, the reviewer will not fail to have noticed how in all of the cases touching on the freedoms of various individuals and groups to participate in different forms of political activity, there is a real consistency and coherence in the analytical method.

In every case, the purposes and objectives which underlie a challenged law provide the framework for the Court's review. It is the purposes specified by those defending a challenged law, in order to meet the object test, that grounds the analysis and gives it its objectivity and determinacy. Within the parameters of stated purposes the same pattern repeats itself in case after case. Paralleling the Supreme Court's own experience, when it adhered to the model in *Oakes*, for the most part it is the second proportionality principle, of alternative means, which does most of the work. These cases offer additional confirmation that, in reviewing the constitutionality of any law, the primary focus in the Court's evaluation is measuring how well the means of any given policy are adapted to its ends. In the vast majority of cases in which the Court can reasonably be expected to rule that a law is unconstitutional it is because the Government will have been unable to explain why it didn't use means that limited rather than completely prohibited the challengers from participating in the kinds of political activities in which they wanted to engage. Even when purposes are balanced against constitutional costs in the third proportionality principle these cases provide further evidence that judicial review can be objective and progressive, at least as it is practised in *Oakes*.

In each of these cases the steps in the analysis are always the same and at each stage these challenges confirm that the model is capable of generating objective and progressive results. Indeed, although we have not

---

66 See *supra*, Chapter 5, note 50.

taken time to dwell on it, even the Court's sources of reasoning should conform to the practices we observed in Part One. In particular, American constitutional law is likely to have little relevance in any of these challenges. Although parallel challenges have been initiated in the United States against laws that are substantially similar to those we have been reviewing, for the most part the Court will find American authorities to be of little assistance. American jurisprudence on the laws which regulate financing and expenditures in elections is not relevant because the U.S. Supreme Court proceeds from the premise that it is an unlawful objective for Congress to try and equalize participation in the political process,[67] a purpose which, as we have seen, is manifestly constitutional under *Oakes*. Equally, the Court will find American case law on the rights of public servants to engage in normal political activities not very helpful because a close reading of these cases shows the U.S. Supreme Court has consistently ignored and/or refused to apply the principle of alternative means.[68] Similarly, although the American Supreme Court has heard and dismissed challenges to the disqualification of prisoners from voting, the basis for the American position is a section in their Bill of Rights that explicitly contemplates the possibility of disenfranchising those who have been convicted of criminal activity, which has no parallel in our Charter of Rights.[69] Indeed, except for the question of providing access to public property for the purpose of communicating political ideas,[70] the American experience is not likely to play a particularly significant role in any of these cases even as a source of alternative policies that the Court might consider in its application of the second proportionality principle. Here, just as with the challenges by prisoners and public servants, it is likely the experience of the free and democratic societies of western Europe will prove to be more relevant to the Court's resolution of these cases.

---

67 *Buckley v. Valeo*, 424 U.S. 1 (1976); L. Tribe, *American Constitutional Law*, 2nd ed. (Foundation Press, 1988), 1141; see also *National Citizens' Coalition v. A.G. Canada, supra*, note 8, at 494. As a result of its ruling on what constitutes a legitimate purpose for election financing laws, the American jurisprudence has drawn a distinction between contributions to candidates and independent expenditures. There seems general agreement that this distinction has robbed this body of American constitutional law of all of its coherence and integrity.

68 See, e.g., *United Public Workers of America v. Mitchell*, 330 U.S. 75 (1947); *United States Civil Service Commission v. National Association of Letter Carriers*, 413 U.S. 548 (1973).

69 See, e.g., *O'Brien v. Skinner*, 414 U.S. 524 (1974); *Richardson v. Ramirez*, 418 U.S. 24 (1974).

70 Although the American cases on access to public property may be of some assistance in delineating alternative policies which may be open to our legislatures, it is unlikely they will be found appropriate or useful in the method of analysis they employ. See Richard Moon, "Access To Public and Private Property Under Freedom of Expression" (1988), 20 Ottawa L. Rev. 339.

Collectively all of these cases, touching the opportunity of ordinary Canadians to be politically active, provide very strong support for the reviewer's belief that, if the Court remains faithful to the model in *Oakes*, judicial review and the Charter can exert both a progressive and a democratic influence on our system of government. On the assumption that the Court will stick to the analyical method of *Oakes*, the outcome of these challenges should result in the modification of numerous laws and rules governing elections and politics which will allow for fuller and fairer opportunities for participation and in turn for a more democratic system of government. Most, if not all, prisoners would acquire the right to vote, and the vast majority of public servants the right to engage in virtually all forms of conventional political activity. In turn, laws that limited the opportunities of groups to disseminate their ideas as widely and powerfully as possible would be narrowed considerably. Conversely, rules and regulations which were sympathetic to the values and purposes on which the Charter itself is based, like those providing public support for candidates and parties with a following of any size[71] would be validated as being constitutional. Indeed, as we have earlier observed, these cases provide further evidence of how Charter litigation can also stimulate and energize the legislative process. Finally, in addition to providing a new forum in which their voices may be heard, these cases show how the Charter can empower ordinary Canadians in the processes of politics as well.[72]

---

71 See note 26, *supra*.
72 *Supra*, note 13.

7

Freedom of Association: Of Workers Outside Their Places of Employment

Many sceptics might be willing to concede everything in the last two chapters and still be reluctant to embrace the model in *Oakes* without reservation. Even those who would acknowledge that, at least in the cases we have reviewed so far, the model can be applied objectively and yield modestly progressive results, still might harbour gnawing doubts whether they had heard the full story. Amongst other concerns most sceptics would worry about two well-publicized decisions touching the political freedoms of workers and their unions about which nothing, so far, had been said. Both cases arose in Ontario[1] and both involved the Ontario Public Service Employees Union — OPSEU. In the first the union initiated the challenge; in the second it was cast in the role of defender. In each, different judges of that province's Supreme Court wrote judgments which limited the opportunity of unions and their members to participate fully and freely in the political process.[2]

One of the cases in fact we have already encountered. This was the

---

1 Although they might have arisen in any province in Canada with similar laws. On the freedom of unions to participate in the political process, see P. Boyer, *Political Rights: The Legal Framework of Elections in Canada* (Toronto: Butterworths, 1981).

   On the status of compulsory dues across Canada, see G.W. Adams, *Canadian Labour Law* (Toronto: Canada Law Book, 1985), pp. 780-781. Note that in British Columbia parallel cases have been initiated in *Bhindi v. A.G. B.C.* (1986), 29 D.L.R. (4th) 47; *Baldwin v. B.C. Government Employees Union* (1986), 28 D.L.R. (4th) 301. See also B. Etherington, "Freedom of Association and Compulsory Dues: Towards a Purposive Conception of a Freedom Not to Associate" (1987), 19 Ottawa L. Rev. 1.

2 The two cases are *OPSEU v. A.G. Ontario* (1989), 52 D.L.R. (4th) 701, and *Lavigne v. OPSEU* (1986), 29 D.L.R. (4th) 86. As we shall see in the second case, the Court of Appeal subsequently overruled the trial court's decision: (1989), 56 D.L.R. (4th) 477.

first OPSEU case in which, at the same time as it attacked the restrictions on the political activity of individual public servants in Ontario, the union also challenged related sections of Ontario's *Crown Employees Collective Bargaining Act*, which severely limited its own ability to be active politically. According to the provisions of the latter Act, any union which contributed money to or expressed support for any political party would lose all their rights to bargain on behalf of public sector employees. The union said these sanctions constituted substantial and unjustifiable invasions of its own and their members freedoms of expression and association. The trial judge disagreed however and he ruled that even if the law did limit the union's rights it could be justified under section 1.

In the second case, various sections of the *Colleges Collective Bargaining Act*, which allowed unions, such as OPSEU, to insist that everyone on whose behalf they bargained pay compulsory union dues whether they belonged to the union or not, were in issue. This case arose when a community college teacher, named Merv Lavigne, challenged the constitutionality of a rule (known as the Rand formula or agency shop), which allowed unions to spend any dues collected at the workplace on political and ideological purposes even if they were unrelated to collective bargaining and even if they were objectionable to the person who was compelled to pay. As a sometime candidate for the Liberal party, Lavigne was strongly opposed, amongst other things, to OPSEU contributing funds and expressing its support for the New Democratic party. He also objected to the union using any part of the dues he had been compelled to pay for various charitable purposes, (including giving aid to workers in Nicaragua and striking miners in Great Britain) and social causes (including campaigns supporting free abortions, disarmament, public housing and social assistance).[3] Lavigne claimed that the legal system which permitted OPSEU to dip its hand into his pocket and spend his money on causes like these was an unjustified and unconstitutional invasion of his entitlement to be free from — unconnected to — all ideas, activities and organizations to which he was unalterably opposed. In this case the trial judge, John White, sided with the challenger and struck down the provisions of Ontario's law to the extent that it permitted unions to make expenditures of this kind.

Many sceptics, understandably, would see both of these judgments as strong evidence against the position which the reviewer wants to maintain. Before they would accept her claims of objectivity and progressivity, they would want the reviewer to address these decisions and explain

---

3 The union endorsed the latter, *inter alia*, by opposing provincial expenditures for a domed stadium in Toronto. In the view of the union, this money could better have been spent on improving the stock of public housing and the quality of social assistance in Ontario.

how they can be reconciled with the cases, such as *Mackay*, which we have just considered. On their face, the sceptics will say, these cases strongly suggest that the model in *Oakes* is susceptible to considerable manipulation and that when they have an opportunity to do so, by and large, judges can be expected to rule against interests and organizations (like trade unions) which are foreign, if not inimical, to the ideas and classes with which they have most affinity.

Now the sceptics' demand for an explanation and reconciliation of these cases is hardly an unreasonable one. Something certainly does seem amiss when, as we saw in the last chapter, the model is generally quite supportive of the rights of interest groups and fringe parties to be more active in the political affairs of the community but then produces outcomes which essentially deny unions and their members the same opportunities. Such differential treatment seems blatantly discriminatory and, in the context of the other cases we have considered in which organized labour was involved, suggests the model is at best insensitive to the interests of the working class.[4] Indeed, read in the context of the Supreme Court's own refusal in *Dolphin Delivery* and the *Labour trilogy*, to envelop workers' most basic forms of collective action and expression (striking and picketing) with the protection of the Charter, the two OPSEU cases seem to reveal a pattern of decision making which is both subjective and highly regressive.

A reviewer will want, therefore, to consider the two OPSEU cases raised by the sceptics very carefully. On the believer's theory, workers and organized labour should be exactly the kind of persons and groups who would be expected to do better and treated more seriously in the process of constitutional review than they normally do in the hurly-burly of political life.[5] An explanation is required. The choices, however, are not very great. In fact, in reflecting on these cases there are only two ways the reviewer can respond. Either she can show that the decisions raised by the sceptics were wrongly decided or, alternatively, that the sceptics themselves are mistaken in some way. Her response must either be that when these cases reach the Supreme Court they will be corrected to the sceptics' satisfaction, or that they can in fact be reconciled with the cases in the last chapter and that in both reasoning and result they are essentially correct.

No doubt the reviewer's instinct will be to take the first route and to say that it was the trial judges who were mistaken and that the sceptics'

---

4 P. Weiler, "The Charter at Work: Reflections on the Constitutionalizing of Labour and Employment Law", 40 U.T.L.J. 117; B. Etherington, "Freedom of Association and Compulsory Union Dues: Towards a Purposive Conception of a Freedom Not to Associate", 19 Ottawa U. L. Rev. 1; K. Ewing, "Freedom of Association in Canada", 35 Alta. L. Rev. 437; A Borovoy, *When Freedoms Collide* (Toronto: Lester & Orpen Dennys, 1988), pp. 252ff.

5 See my *Putting the Charter to Work* (Montreal: McGill-Queen's Press, 1987).

objections to them are indeed well-founded. In addition to being more congenial with her own expectations that constitutional review will have a progressive influence on the content of our law, it would also be considerably easier for the reviewer simply to agree with the sceptics than try to persuade them that it is they, rather than the judges, who are wrong. As well, given the very uneven record of the lower courts in the cases we have considered so far, it would be natural for the reviewer to think she will find mistakes in these judgments of first instance as well.

Certainly in the case in which OPSEU launched its challenge against the sections in the *Crown Employees Collective Bargaining Act*, which effectively prohibited all public sector unions from actively supporting any political party, the reviewer is likely to approach the decision of John Eberle with a good deal of scepticism. Instinctively, it seems quite unfair, if the Charter is able to ensure that interest groups generally have the right to participate and be involved in election campaigns, to rule that unions are not guaranteed the same protection as well. Moreover if, as the model in *Oakes* seems to require, public servants have the right to support political parties actively as individuals, then it seems to follow that they should be allowed to do so through their unions — or indeed through any organization they may choose.

When the reviewer actually sits down to read the Court's decision in the first OPSEU case, it should not take very long before her instincts will be confirmed. When John Eberle's twenty-five page judgment is read through in its entirety, there are, in the end, only two reasons offered to support his ruling that a law which prohibits OPSEU — or indeed any other union operating in the public service — from contributing to or endorsing any political party, is constitutional. First and foremost is the matter of a neutral and impartial public service. Repeating the concern he had expressed with regard to the involvement of individual public servants, Eberle characterized the union's support of political parties as the kind of "partisan politicalization of the public service" that would compromise its integrity. Beyond that, the judge said, it was important to remember that unions, like OPSEU, were not entirely voluntary organizations. Laws of this kind ensured that unions would not be able to use the dues that are paid to them, under the compulsion of law, in order to advance political parties and causes to which some of those who were forced to contribute were opposed. For John Eberle, either or both of these reasons justified prohibiting public sector unions from providing any support, financial or otherwise, to political parties.

For the reviewer, however, neither of these reasons will suffice. She will know, from her analysis of the other part of this case which we considered in the last chapter, that the first purpose will not carry those seeking to defend this legislation very far. Once it is accepted that the

Constitution requires that all but the most senior public servants be permitted to engage in all normal political activity,[6] then logically it follows that they must be allowed to pursue their political interests through their union organizations as well. What people have the constitutional right to do as individuals they must, of necessity, have the right to do in association with others. Certainly it would be expected that the logic of this position would be apparent to everyone on the Supreme Court. Even the most conservative of their number, it will be recalled, recognized that the constitutional guarantee of freedom of association must provide protection for people to do collectively those things which they have the right, as individuals, to do on their own.[7]

Nor will the second reason offered by John Eberle fare much better. Not that it isn't a valid reason. It is. No one can doubt Government's right to try and protect people from being forced to contribute to or be associated with causes to which they are opposed. In pursuing objectives of this kind Governments would be pursuing values and principles on which the Charter itself is based.[8] In terms of the model in *Oakes*, protecting people when they are subject to the (coercive) authority of others would easily satisfy the object test.

The problem is it couldn't satisfy the proportionality principles and in particular the principle of alternative means. Although the protection of peoples' "negative freedom", is a perfectly valid objective for Government to pursue, it just doesn't justify the kind of extreme response the legislature of Ontario took in this case. If the purpose of the Government was to minimize the circumstances in which one group of persons could coerce a second group, to support causes that the latter opposed, the means chosen were absurdly heavy-handed. Once again, overkill in the extreme.

To accomplish its purpose, of course, all the Government needed to do was enact a law which *limited* spending by public sector unions rather than one which *prohibited* the union from making any expenditures at all. The more reasonable alternative would have been to insist that when unions participate in the political process by providing financial support for a particular party, they may only do so with the funds of those who endorse the use of their dues in this way. By drafting the law more narrowly, the Government could not only realize its objectives (of limiting the coercive powers that some people can exercise over others) but it could do so in

---

6 See Part Two, Chapter 6, *supra.*

7 See *Ref. re Alberta Public Service Employee Relations Act* (1987), 38 D.L.R. (4th) 161.

8 In the language of "rights talk", the Government would be said to be protecting (or balancing) the negative freedom of one group of individuals from (against) the positive freedom of others. For parallel issues in the cases involving religious programmes in the schools and the freedom to engage in political expression, see Chapter 5, *supra*, at note 30; and Chapter 6, *supra*, at notes 24 and 25.

a way that showed greater respect for the (positive) freedom of those members who do want to participate actively in politics through their union associations. Practically, all that was necessary was a law which would allow those who objected to having their dues spent supporting political parties to which they were opposed to be able to opt out and receive a rebate from the union. In the result, and to the extent that the union would only be spending money which had been voluntarily subscribed, it would be free to endorse and support financially political parties and candidates of their choice in precisely the same way as every other third party or interest group is allowed to do.

So, in responding to the sceptics' concern about the first OPSEU case, the reviewer would be able to be short and to the point. She can tell them that she shares their evaluation of John Eberle's rejection of OPSEU's challenge, but she can go on to reassure them that his mistake will not be repeated by the Supreme Court if it sticks to the model in *Oakes*. From the reviewer's perspective, this first OPSEU case should provide additional support for her thesis that, for the most part, constitutional review is a process in which judges evaluate the means by which Governments have chosen to "act" against the objectives they seek to achieve. Once again, once the Court is clear as to the objectives a Government wants to accomplish, it will not be uncommon for it to be able to identify alternative means which will be superior to those it has been asked to review. In the first OPSEU case, the model points to a policy which protects the (negative) freedom of those who do not want to support particular causes or ideas without limiting in any way the (positive) freedom of those who do. In the end, the reviewer can say to the sceptics that if the model is applied in its proper way, OPSEU's challenge will be sustained and the apparent inconsistency with the other cases she reviewed in the last chapter will have been resolved.

Having been able to respond so supportively to the sceptics' complaints about the first OPSEU case, the reviewer can turn her attention to the second. Here the reviewer's instincts will unquestionably be to approach this case with the same expectation and understanding. Certainly, the easiest way to react to the sceptics' concerns would be to endorse them by showing that, like John Eberle's judgment, John White's decision in *Lavigne* is also mistaken in very basic and critical ways. Moreover here, the reviewer will be aware that there is a lot of judicial authority which would support her adopting this point of view. In British Columbia, for example, several judges on that province's Supreme Court and Court of Appeal have rejected the approach adopted by White.[9] Even more significantly, the reviewer will know that her decision was subsequently

---

9 See *Bhindi v. A.G. B.C., Baldwin v. B.C.G.E.U., supra*, note 1.

overturned by three judges in the Ontario Court of Appeal.[10]

When the reviewer actually sits down with this second OPSEU file, however, she will sense, almost immediately, that there is something very different about this case than the one she just closed. Indeed, the longer she reads the judgments and material filed in the courts below, the more she will realize that it is certain that she and the sceptics will take radically different positions on the merits of this case. For the reviewer, White's judgment is almost certainly going to stand out as one of, if not the strongest judgment in the lower courts she has read so far. Tightly reasoned, it conforms almost exactly to the ends/means analysis that the reviewer expects to be the central inquiry of the model in *Oakes*. Following the procedure established in *Oakes*, White first satisfied himself that Lavigne's constitutional entitlements had, in both fact and law, been compromised by being forced to contribute and support political and social causes to which he was opposed. Surprisingly, this was the part of the case that gave John White his greatest difficulty and for a while he was clearly distracted by the question whether the Government of Ontario really had interfered with Lavigne's constitutional guarantees in any way. In the end, however, he recognized that Lavigne's constitutional guarantees had indeed been infringed.

With the first phase of his review complete, White turned his mind to whether the purposes of the Rand formula and agency shop rule could meet the object test in *Oakes*. Unlike the initial phase of his review, this second step did not take him very long. White had no difficulty ascertaining that the purpose of the law which the compulsory payment of union dues was designed to achieve was to prevent some people freeloading or "free riding" on the efforts and resources of others. Nor did he have any doubt that such a purpose was "pressing and substantial" and completely within the legal authority of any Government to pursue.

In fact, White indicated that he had a good deal of sympathy with it. He recognized the essential unfairness in allowing people to enjoy the benefits of collective bargaining without bearing their fair share of their cost. It was not the objective the Government was trying to achieve that was troublesome for White. It was the way in which the law went about its objective. Conforming to the pattern we have seen repeated in almost every case we have reviewed in this Part, his judgment was that the law failed the principle of alternative means essentially because it was too broad. If the purpose of the law was to prevent freeloading, White said, the law must be redrafted so as to restrict the use to which dues could be put to those which were reasonably related to collective bargaining and the administration of the collective agreement. That, in his view, was

---

10 (1989), 56 D.L.R. (4th) 474.

all that was required to meet the purposes of the rule. The freeloading or "free rider" problem could be solved by a law that made each person represented by a union pay his or her fair share of the expenses that were reasonably related to securing the employment benefits that all of them ultimately enjoyed.

In practical terms, the principle of alternative means led John White to the conclusion that laws that compelled the payment of dues to a union had to include a mechanism by which those who objected to expenditures, which were not reasonably related to collective bargaining, could opt out of the portion of their dues which was spent on such purposes. Although White recognized that laws which distinguished between collective bargaining and other expenses would put the union to some administrative inconvenience and expense, he did not think they would be so burdensome as to outweigh the constitutional freedoms involved. Paralleling the attitude we saw the Supreme Court adopt in the first five years, White rejected the idea that considerations of administrative convenience warranted overriding the constitutional guarantees that were at stake in this case.[11]

For the reviewer, White's reasoning would have a strong appeal if for no other reason than it conforms so closely to the way in which she has come to expect the model in *Oakes* to be applied.[12] It is a very clear and coherent rendition of the ends/means analysis. But form is not the only characteristic of White's judgment which the reviewer would find attractive. She almost certainly would regard the substantive results of the decision very positively as well.

It is true, as John White recognized, that the alternative he favoured would force the union to the inconvenience and expense of setting up systems to allow individual members to opt out of expenditures that could not reasonably be related to collective bargaining. As well, it would be expected that, on balance, the union would have less money available for such causes than they had under the challenged law. Some people, it is certain, would take advantage of the opportunity to opt out. Lavigne is one of them. However, the reviewer would also know that studies show that the size of the expenditures and the amounts of money that unions

---

11 Chapter 5, *supra*, note 50; Chapter 6, *supra*, note 66.

12 Although the reviewer would certainly rate White's judgment as highly as any she has read so far, she is not likely to give it a perfect score. For one thing, the reviewer is likely to find White's treatment of the scope of the Charter and in particular its application to collective agreements (p. 353-354) highly problematic in light of her evaluation of the Supreme Court's decision in *Dolphin Delivery*, see Part One, Chapter 4, *supra*, pp. 95-97. See also *Putting the Charter to Work*, *supra*, note 5, at 95-100. In addition, his rejection of Lavigne's claim that his freedom of expression had also been infringed seems to fall prey to the mistakes of denial and avoidance she identified in the first Part.

are likely to lose will be minuscule.[13] For all practical purposes the ability of the unions to support political and other social causes would be the same under either alternative.

More interesting to the reviewer than the marginal impact, if any, that John White's judgment would have on the union's financial strength and capacity to support various humanitarian and social causes, would be how the outcome in this case meshes so perfectly with the result to which the model has led in OPSEU #1. In a sense, these cases are mirror images of each other. At the time of their enactment the two laws that were involved in these cases were really quite contradictory. In *Lavigne*, the *Colleges Collective Bargaining Act* allowed unions to spend their dues in ways in which the *Crown Employees Collective Bargaining Act* seemed intent on preventing. This inconsistent and discriminatory behaviour by Government seems quite untenable. As a result of applying the model in *Oakes*, however, the two laws could be reconciled and brought into line. Public servants and community college teachers would both be able to participate politically through their unions if they wished but they could not be compelled to do so if that was not what they wanted to do.

In the first OPSEU case, the model shows that the *Crown Employees Collective Bargaining Act* is *too restrictive* of the (positive) freedom of thousands of public servants to participate politically through their unions. In *Lavigne*, application of the same principles reveals that the *Colleges Collective Bargaining Act* is *too permissive* of the same freedom of a parallel group of workers in the public sector to the extent it allows some people to spend the money of their colleagues on causes and political parties to which the latter are opposed. In effect White's ruling, and the process of constitutional review, can be seen as a direction to the Ontario Government to ensure that the law regulating the ways in which unions operating in the community colleges participate in politics is consistent with the law which applied to public sector unions generally. Coming at the issue from two completely different cases the model would insist that Government recognize the right of all trade union groups to participate actively in the political life of the community with the only proviso being that when they spend money on causes not reasonably related to collective

---

13 See B. Etherington, "Freedom of Association and Compulsory Union Dues: Towards a Purposive Conception of a Freedom Not to Associate", 19 Ottawa L. Rev. 1, 33; J. Henkel and N. Wood, "Limitations on the Uses of Union Shop Funds After Ellis: What Activities are Germane to Collective Bargaining" (1984), 35 Lab. L.J. 736, 744-746.

In spite of acknowledging the very limited financial impact the ruling will have, at least one critic persists in the belief that the real significance of *Lavigne* will be its impact on the ability and willingness of unions to engage in political activity. See M. Mandel, *The Charter of Rights and the Legalization of Politics in Canada* (Toronto: Wall & Thompson, 1989), pp. 209-217.

bargaining, they do so only with funds which have been specially ear-marked for such purposes. For the reviewer, the coincidence in the outcomes of these two quite discrete cases would provide very powerful evidence in support of her belief in the objectivity and determinacy of the model in *Oakes*.

As enthusiastic as the reviewer is certain to be about John White's judgment in *Lavigne*, there can be no doubt that the reaction of most sceptics will be exactly the reverse. For sceptics, White's decision will be regarded as nothing short of a disaster. Substantively, sceptics would describe it as a serious blow to workers and their unions and very clear evidence of the regressive influence of judicial review. They would say it is simply another example of how judges are generally quite unsympathetic to the interests of workers and others who are not part of the ruling elite.[14]

Analytically, White's judgment would be open to challenge on at least two fronts. On the one hand some people, although not likely many sceptics, will argue that White's decision is defective because it tries to stretch the Charter beyond its natural reach.[15] These people will say the decision of the Ontario Court of Appeal, which overturned White's judgment, was right on the mark in ruling that this really was a dispute between two private parties to which the Charter simply had no application. Other people, including most sceptics, will argue that even if White was correct in reviewing the constitutionality of the *Colleges Collective Bargaining Act*, the way he exercised his powers should dispel any myth that the model in *Oakes* is as objective as the reviewer would like everyone to believe. Sceptics will think that White's reasoning shows how easily the model can be manipulated to secure whatever result a judge may want to achieve.

Anyone who argues that White was fundamentally wrong even applying the Charter to the circumstances of Lavigne's case is certain to rely heavily on the judgment of the three judges of the Ontario Court of Appeal who overruled White on this point and who held that the Charter

---

14 See Michael Mandel, *The Charter of Rights and the Legalization of Politics in Canada*, *ibid.*, Chapter 5; H. Glasbeek, "Workers Avoid the Charter", 21 Canadian Dimension (April 1987). See also Paul Weiler, "The Charter at Work", *supra*, note 4.

15 The argument is discussed in P. Cavalluzzo, "Freedom of Association — Its Effect on Collective Bargaining and Trade Unions", *Labour Law Under the Charter* (Kingston: Queen's University, 1988); and in B. Etherington, "Freedom of Association and Compulsory Union Dues", *supra*, note 13.

Most sceptics will be quite ambivalent over this part of White's judgment. Although they are not likely to find his reasoning on this question to be very persuasive, they are generally quite committed to the idea that the Charter should apply to all forms of coercive legal authority whether it is "public" or "private" in nature. See, e.g., M. Mandel, *The Charter of Rights and the Legalization of Politics in Canada, ibid.*, pp. 209ff., and A. Hutchinson and A. Petter, "Private Rights/Public Wrongs: The Liberal Lie of the Charter" (1988), 38 U.T.L.J. 279.

had no application to a case such as *Lavigne*. Sydney Robbins, Charles Dubin and Lloyd Houlden were the three judges of Ontario's Court of Appeal who heard the appeal of White's decision and on the basis of the Supreme Court's earlier decision in *Dolphin Delivery*, and one of the decisions of the British Columbia Supreme Court on the question of union dues, they ruled that the Government of Ontario wasn't really involved in this case. They accepted the argument that this was nothing more than a dispute between two private parties. In their view, Lavigne's sole complaint was with OPSEU and how it spent his money. The Government really had no responsibility for Lavigne's plight. They said the Government had neither compelled Lavigne to pay dues to the union nor, obviously, had it been involved in any way in deciding how those dues would actually be spent. The Government's only involvement was the enactment of a section of the *Colleges Collective Bargaining Act* which allowed unions and the colleges to provide for compulsory dues in their collective agreements if they chose to do so. In the view of these three judges, that was not sufficient action by the Government to attract review by the Court. They remained fixed in their opinion that the essence of Lavigne's complaint was in how his dues were spent by a union which represented him at his work place and that was essentially a private matter about which Government, and therefore the Charter, had nothing to say.

Indeed, in addition to their belief that the Government of Ontario was not really involved in limiting Lavigne's freedom to support only causes he personally endorsed, Robbins, Dubin, and Houlden also doubted whether his freedom had actually been limited at all. As they were at pains to stress, compelling Lavigne to pay dues to OPSEU left all the important aspects of his freedom to associate completely unimpaired. The agency shop, or Rand formula, they said, did not limit or interfere with any aspect of Lavigne's "positive" right to associate with others for the purposes of protecting common interests and pursuing common goals. Lavigne was still free to join with others to achieve any purpose he wished including opposing the union and any cause it might support. Equally in their view, compelling him to pay union dues was consistent with his "negative" freedom not to have to associate with others whose causes and ideas were different than his own. His right not to associate, in their view, also remained unimpaired. They said that not only was Lavigne not forced to join the union or participate in its activities, the compelled payment did not identify him personally with any of the political, social or ideological objectives which OPSEU supported, nor did it require him to change his views to bring them in line with the union's. Because the compulsory payment of union dues did not restrict Lavigne's freedom in any of these ways Robbins, Dubin and Houlden ruled that there was no threat to a constitutional interest protected by the Charter involved in this case. In their opinion, the interest in not having any part of his payment to the union directed to purposes to which he was opposed, regardless of how much money was involved, was not an interest which was of sufficient status to warrant protection under the Charter.

Although few sceptics will want to side with Sydney Robbins, Charles Dubin and Lloyd Houlden in their dispute with John White, as to whether the Charter should apply to disputes of this kind, most of them can be expected to find fault with virtually every other step in White's analysis. Their most basic criticism will almost certainly focus on White's handling of the object test. Two objections can be anticipated. First, strong exception will be taken to the way in which White described the purposes which the Rand formula was designed to accomplish. Sceptics will insist that there was no basis in theory or in fact to support White's ruling that the "agency shop" rule was only intended to prevent employees from "free riding" with respect to expenditures made by the union on collective bargaining and related activities. They would argue that such a description of the purposes and objectives which are promoted by compelling everyone to pay union dues is too narrow and shows how, even at a factual level, the object test can easily be manipulated to serve whatever outcome a judge wants to achieve.

Beyond the narrow purposes White described, sceptics would list a whole host of other benefits which the compulsory payment of union dues can secure. They would say that leaving unions free to spend compulsory dues in any way they see fit would, for example, allow workers to speak with a more authoritative and powerful voice in advising Governments on all matters of social policy which are relevant to their interests, a state of affairs which is as much a benefit to Government organizations as to the unions themselves. It would also promote the principle of majority rule and encourage unions not to be afraid to speak out on social and political issues which affect employee interests. Indeed, even if it were limited to the freeloading rationale, sceptics would respond that individuals like Lavigne benefit just as much by gains unions are able to achieve in the political process as those that are won at the bargaining table.[16]

In addition to challenging the factual basis of White's characterization of the purposes which the Rand formula is expected to promote, sceptics are almost certain to be equally suspicious about the objectivity of the standard itself. They would see the requirement of drawing lines between collective bargaining and other purposes as allowing judges virtually unfettered freedom to come to any conclusion they wanted. Those aware

---

16 See B. Etherington, "Freedom of Association and Compulsory Union Dues", *supra*, note 13; M. Mandel, *The Charter of Rights and the Legalization of Politics in Canada*, *supra*, note 13.

of the American Supreme Court's experience with the identical test would regard such a distinction as being highly ambiguous and likely to generate very arbitrary and artificial results.[17] They would be quick to point out that the American Supreme Court has just recently ruled, for example, that organizing and litigation expenses, designed to protect the interests of workers in a particular industry, were not reasonably related to the union's collective bargaining activities and therefore could not be demanded as part of the union's dues.[18]

With such radically different reactions to John White's judgment in *Lavigne*, it is not likely that the reviewers and sceptics will see eye to eye as quickly on this case as they did on OPSEU #1. To bring sceptics and believers to a common understanding of Lavigne's complaint will be a much more difficult task than it was in the first OPSEU case. Rather than endorsing the legitimacy of the sceptics' concern, and showing that the judgment is wrong, here the reviewer will have to persuade the sceptics that the mistake is theirs and that it is they, not the judge, who must rethink their position. Given the intensity with which views are held on this issue by all sides, the reviewer cannot reasonably expect that sceptics will find such an exercise a very easy thing to do.

Of the two criticisms which the reviewer can anticipate will be made of White's decision in *Lavigne*, she should be most dubious of the first. Not only is this an argument which few sceptics would care to advance, the reviewer will be cognizant of the fact that as yet she has discovered no ordinary law which lies beyond the reach of the Charter. Moreover, no one who had analysed the Supreme Court's performance with the Charter in the way the reviewer has could regard the reasoning of the Ontario Court of Appeal as persuasive. To the contrary, the reviewer will immediately see it as being riddled with exactly the same kind of mistakes which the Supreme Court itself committed in the first five years.

In the first place, to say that the Government is not involved in imposing a legal obligation on a person like Lavigne to pay compulsory dues is to repeat the same mistake the Supreme Court made in cases like *Spencer* and *Dolphin Delivery*. It fails to keep clearly in mind that the focus of constitutional review is the law which governs some aspect of social activity, not the actions of the persons who are affected by it. The Ontario Government's involvement in the coercion of Lavigne is exactly the same

---

17 See B. Etherington, "Freedom of Association and Compulsory Union Dues", *supra*, note 13. See also C. Rehmus and B. Kerner, "The Agency Shop After Abood: No Free Ride, But What's the Fare?", 33 I. & L.R.R. 90; M. Mandel, "Courts and Liberal Ideology: An Analysis of the Application of the Charter to Some Labour Law Issues" (1989), 34 McGill L.J. 87, 116.

18 *Communication Workers v. Beck* (1988), 108 S. Ct. 2641.

as the federal Government's treatment of refugee claimants which the Supreme Court reviewed in *Singh*. In both cases, Governments passed a law which allowed some people to threaten and abuse the freedom of others. Although it could not be said, in either case, that the Government was directly responsible for the violation of the individual's rights, indirectly they were, and that, as the Supreme Court recognized on several occasions, is sufficient to attract judicial review.[19]

Indeed the error made by Charles Dubin, Sydney Robbins and Lloyd Houlden is even more glaring than the mistake the Supreme Court made in *Spencer* and *Dolphin Delivery* because in this case the involvement of Government was even more open and direct. In fact, it took two separate initiatives by the Ontario Government before OPSEU could legally insist that Lavigne be compelled to pay union dues. In the first place, it was necessary for the Government to add a section to the *Colleges Collective Bargaining Act* which provided that collective agreements would be binding not only on the unions and employers who signed them but on the employees to whom they applied as well. This it did in section 51 of the Act which was one of the sections attacked by Lavigne.[20] Although it might seem to be a relatively innocuous section, anyone who has studied contract law will see it as a provision of great importance. Without it, OPSEU could not have claimed *any* dues from Lavigne. Essentially, by this section of the Act, the Government brought to an end one of the oldest and most basic rules in all of the common law. The rule, known as the third party beneficiary rule, stipulates that it is not legally possible for two parties to a contract to bind a third person to its terms. By enacting section 51 of the *Colleges Act*, the Government put an end to that principle and by doing so made it possible, for the first time, for OPSEU and the community colleges to conclude agreements in which employees who were not party to them were compelled to abide by their terms.

By itself, the enactment of this law, overturning the common rule law on third party beneficiaries, should be sufficient to attract the Court's power of review. An important lesson of the analysis of the Supreme Court's performance over its first five years with the Charter is that all laws must conform to the principle of constitutional supremacy and this law can be no exception. When it enacted section 51, Government policy unambiguously shifted to permit some individuals to exercise a coercive, "mini taxing" power over the lives of their colleagues at work. It changed the rules of employment to allow for the enforcement of compulsory union

---

19 See Part One, Chapter 4, *supra*, note 49.
20 See *Lavigne v. O.P.S.E.U.*, *supra*, note 2, at 479. It might be noted that inexplicably (and inexcusably) the Court of Appeal avoided this part of Lavigne's challenge by denying, contrary to his pleadings, that he had sought such a declaration (p. 494).

dues where such arrangements were not possible before. It bears repeating that even though the Government did not, as it might, directly compel the payment of union dues in the *Colleges Collective Bargaining Act*, we know from our analysis of the Supreme Court's performance that indirect action on the part of Government is sufficient to attract constitutional review.[21]

Enacting a law which overruled the third party beneficiary rule was a necessary condition before Lavigne could be compelled to pay union dues to OPSEU. But it was not a sufficient condition. At the time the *Colleges Collective Bargaining Act* was enacted, a Regulation was in force which specifically provided that all of the dues which the employees were compelled to pay to OPSEU could only be used for collective bargaining purposes and could not be used for activities in support of or on behalf of any political party. Although the enactment of the *Colleges Collective Bargaining Act* brought an end to the third party beneficiary rule and made it possible for unions to compel the payment of dues, at the time it came into force public sector unions, like OPSEU, were still prohibited from using such monies to support political causes. In the case of unions representing employees in the community college sector, it took a second Government initiative, repealing this Regulation, two years after the enactment of the *Colleges Collective Bargaining Act*, before OPSEU was legally in a position to spend Lavigne's dues supporting political parties and social causes to which he was opposed.[22]

Conscious of the principle of constitutional supremacy and what that principle unavoidably implies, no reviewer should fail to see how deeply the Government really was involved in forcing individuals like Lavigne to contribute to causes to which they were opposed. She will see, quite clearly, that the Government of Ontario "acted" on two separate occasions: the first time to reverse a long standing rule of common law; the second to repeal a law (regulation) of its own making. Nor is it likely that any reviewer will be distracted very long by the other line of argument used by Charles Dubin, Sydney Robbins and Lloyd Houlden to support their decision that this was not a case in which the Court should exercise its powers of review. In this part of their judgment the reviewer will recognize very quickly a series of mistakes that parallel exactly the other errors she saw the Supreme Court commit in its first five years with the Charter.

---

21 *Supra*, note 19.

22 It warrants emphasizing, as the Court of Appeal did, that the fact that Merv Lavigne was opposed to the NDP, and other political causes OPSEU chose to support, should not be interpreted as implying that he was anti-social in any way. To the contrary, he was a supporter and sometime candidate for the Liberal party and played an active role supporting voluntary services in his community.

For the most part, when Dubin, Robbins and Houlden argue that Lavigne's freedom of association remained unimpaired, they engage in the methods of "denial and avoidance" that we identified and found so wanting in Part One. Listing the various liberties and freedoms that compulsory dues leave unimpaired, avoids rather than responds to Lavigne's complaint that whatever interests and activities compulsory dues leave him free to pursue, he is still being compelled, by law, to contribute a part of his resources, and therefore a part of himself,[23] to causes and ideas to which he is opposed. Moreover, when they are not avoiding dealing directly with Lavigne's complaint, Robbins, Dubin and Houlden are guilty of either ruling by assertion or of impermissibly failing to keep the two phases of the review process analytically distinct. In several passages the judges invoke the method of denial and, without reasons or authority, simply declare that the interest for which Lavigne seeks protection is not one worthy of protection by the Charter. On other occasions, referring to how trivial and insubstantial the extent of the coercion is, and/or what a significant role the Rand formula plays in Canada's systems of labour relations, the judges make reference to reasons and factors which, as matters of justification, the reviewer will know should only be considered in the second, not the first, phase of the review process.[24] The fact that the constraint on Lavigne's freedom is small, or that union dues play a very important role in our system of collective bargaining, may provide reasons why the Government is justified in delegating coercive authority to individuals in this way. It cannot, in any sense, establish that Lavigne's freedom has not been limited in fact.

Showing where the judgment of the Ontario Court of Appeal parallels the mistakes the Supreme Court made in its first five years should suffice to persuade most people that White was correct in ruling that Lavigne's challenge did fall within the Charter's reach. Convincing them that he also applied the model correctly, however, may prove to be a more difficult task. Certainly, in reflecting on the first criticism which sceptics are likely to make about the way White applied the object test, the reviewer would have to concede that there was no explicit statement by the author of the agency shop rule, Ivan Rand, that he actually intended that unions be limited in the uses to which compulsory dues could be put. Nowhere in the award in which he introduced compulsory union dues to modern Canadian labour law did Rand explicitly say unions should be prohibited from spending any of the money they receive on projects unrelated to collective bargaining. Indeed, it is also true, as sceptics will point out, that the only limit that

---

23 For a discussion of the parallels between taxation and forced labour, see R. Nozick, *Anarchy, State and Utopia* (New York: Basic Books, 1974), p. 169.

24 See *Lavigne v. O.P.S.E.U.*, *supra*, note 2, at 500-506.

Rand did impose was that no part of the compulsory dues could be used for purposes — like insurance benefits — from which some employees (e.g., those who were not members of the union) would be excluded.

However, Rand's silence on the question of whether a union could use part of the dues it collected for purposes unrelated to collective bargaining, could hardly be interpreted as his endorsement that unions could spend money in this way. To the contrary, everything in his award makes it clear that Rand said nothing explicit about the union spending part of the dues on objects and activities unrelated to collective bargaining because collective bargaining was the *only* activity he was considering. The whole orientation of his award is focused on, and limited to, the union's role in collective bargaining and related activities. The context, after all, in which Rand made compulsory union dues part of Canadian labour law, was the settlement of a particular and particularly high profile labour dispute between the Ford Motor Company and its union, the United Automobile Workers.

Everything in the text of his award supports the conclusion that, in ordering all of the employees represented by the UAW at Ford to pay compulsory union dues, Rand was only thinking about collective bargaining and the union's role as the exclusive bargaining agent for Ford's employees. In the critical part of his decision, when he was explaining the reasons why he was ruling in favour of making the payment of dues compulsory, all of his references were to the "law of employment" or the "plant law" which the union had negotiated and administered on the employees' behalf. It was "entirely equitable", he wrote, that "all employees be required to shoulder their portion of the burden of the expense for administrating the law of their employment, the union contract".[25] It was "this sharing of the fruits of unionist work by the non member" which Rand recognized as provoking deep resentment and conflict within a plant and which provided further justification for obliging all employees to contribute to the costs associated with the benefits which the union negotiated and administered on their behalf.

In addition to these direct references to collective bargaining and relations within the workplace, in other passages Rand wrote in a way which makes it highly implausible to assume he intended unions to be free to spend any part of the dues he had ordered employees to pay on causes which were not related to collective bargaining. From even the most cursory reading of his decision, it is apparent that Rand did not have an unconstrained faith in the integrity of unions and how they would use the power which they had just acquired with the enactment of our modern

---

25 The terms of Rand's award are set out in 1946 Canadian Labour Law Reports (CCH Canada Ltd.), Topic 2000 Union Security: 75 Rand Formula, p. 17.

collective bargaining laws. Early in his award he expressed a concern about leaving individual workers exposed to the "dangers of arbitrary action . . . and . . . the threat of . . . power in an uncontrolled and unmatured group". In fact, because of this concern, Rand refused to award the union the stronger form of union security — the union shop — which it had originally requested.[26] With such basic reservations about how unions would exercise their legal authority over the working lives of the employees they represented, it would have been quite incongruous for Rand to have intended that the unions be able to use the dues they obtained from employees on interests and activities that were unrelated to collective bargaining even when some employees objected to having their money spent in this way.

White's characterization of the purposes which underlie our laws authorizing the agency shop rule has considerable support, then, in the words of Rand's own award. Both the text and the context of the document which made compulsory union dues a fixture in Canada's labour laws strongly suggest that Rand intended that union dues were only to be used to defray expenses which were related to the union's collective bargaining functions. Moreover, White's description also accords with how compulsory dues, or solidarity contributions, as they are sometimes called in other free and democratic societies, are expected to fit into our whole system of union-management relations. Regardless of what other uses Rand personally thought union dues might validly be put, it is clear that compulsory payments of this kind were, and continue to be, designed to ensure that collective bargaining systems are not plagued by freeloaders and the attendant problems of unfairness and conflict which they cause.

Against this, it is sometimes said that compulsory dues also serve the purpose of strengthening the power of unions so they can best serve the interests and welfare of all employees.[27] It is clear, however, that union dues only enhance the strength of unions by ensuring their financial solvency and by avoiding the conflict and dissension among the workers which the presence of "free riders" would cause. Except insofar as it deals with the free rider problem, the agency shop clause does not affect the power of unions in any additional way. That is why it is recognized as one of the weaker forms of union security. Stronger forms, like the union shop or closed shop, give unions much more strength by ensuring that they can control the activities of all employees during the course of a

---

26 See Rand Formula, *ibid.*, at 13-14. For an analysis of the different forms (and degrees) of union security in operation in Canada and around the world, see M. Mitchnick, *Union Security and the Charter* (Toronto: Butterworths, 1987).

27 This was the position advanced by counsel for the Canadian Labour Congress in *Lavigne* at para. 111 of the Factum which they filed with the Court of Appeal.

strike.[28] Where, as in a number of free and democratic societies, systems of collective bargaining have been designed in ways to avoid the problem of free riders, the law generally does not require persons who are not members of unions to pay dues to organizations to which they do not belong.[29]

In most free and democratic societies, however, free riders do pose a problem for their systems of collective bargaining. In Canada (and the United States), a potentially serious free rider problem exists because of a principle, characteristic of the North American approach to collective bargaining, which designates a union as the exclusive bargaining agent for all the employees in a unit which is found to be appropriate for collective bargaining whether the employees are members of the union or not. As a practical matter, the principle of "exclusivity" means that all employees are entitled to enjoy all of the benefits negotiated by the union and, as a result, there is little, if any, financial incentive for anyone to join the union or pay their fair share of the union's costs. Compulsory union dues flow directly from the designation of the union as the exclusive bargaining agent and are designed to remedy the free rider problem which that designation creates.

Within this logic of compulsory dues, it is perfectly rational to rule, as John White did, that the dues paid to the union be spent in ways, and on projects, which are reasonably related to the collective bargaining system. If the dues are designed to ensure that everyone pays their pro-rata share of the benefits which the union is able to provide, White can not fairly be accused of being arbitrary in holding that the union must use the dues to defray the costs and expenses that are reasonably related to collective bargaining. To the contrary, both logic and justice insist that the dues should be spent on projects which are directly related to the union's status as exclusive bargaining representative and which give rise to the problem of freeloading. If that is the basis on which the payment of dues is justified, it follows that, unless the union secures the consent of the employee, those are the only kinds of projects on which the money can validly be spent.

Showing the sceptics the factual and logical basis on which White's characterization of the purposes which underlie the compulsory payment of union dues can be defended, should go some way in responding to their doubts about how objective he was in the applying the model in *Oakes* to the facts of Lavigne's case. But it will not likely allay all of their fears in this regard.

---

28 For a discussion of the constitutionality of these stronger forms of union security, see *Putting the Charter to Work, supra*, note 5, at 130-131.

29 This is true, for example, in West Germany and Sweden. See M. Mitchnick, *Union Security and the Charter, supra*, note 26.

In addition to questioning the basis on which White's characterization of the Rand formula was grounded, it will be recalled that many sceptics are also likely to have serious reservations about whether the purposes he identified would create a standard that could be objectively applied. In view of the experience of the American Supreme Court, many will instinctively be quite dubious about the integrity of a principle which attempts to distinguish between collective bargaining and other purposes. They will say trying to draw a line in this way is entirely arbitrary and open to manipulation by the Courts. They will point to the American Court's rulings in cases like *Ellis* and *Beck*[30], that expenditures made by a union in support of organizing drives and litigation designed to improve working conditions in an industry could not be reasonably related to the union's status as exclusive bargaining agent and the free rider rationale, to show how amorphous, and ultimately very subjective, such a standard really is.[31]

In responding to the sceptics' doubts about the objectivity of drawing a distinction between collective bargaining and other purposes, most reviewers will almost certainly share their wonderment at the U.S. Supreme Court's decisions in cases like *Ellis* and *Beck*. These are judgments which seem impossible to justify and have been the subject of widespread criticism by American and Canadian commentators alike. For experts in matters of labour relations, expenditures made to extend the number of plants a union has organized or to support litigation designed to protect benefits enjoyed by workers in a particular industry are directly related to the union's function as exclusive bargaining agent and do fit comfortably within the free rider rationale.[32] Expenditures of this kind are critical in ensuring that the "plant law" negotiated and administered by the union continues to exist.

Where the reviewer will take issue with the sceptics, however, is the lesson to be drawn from American decisions like *Ellis* and *Beck* which stand so widely condemned. For the reviewer, the American jurisprudence does not justify such an extreme reaction of gloom and despair. For him, the important lesson is the much more moderate, but now to be expected, one of advising caution whenever a Canadian court is referred to American authorities to solve a problem of Canadian constitutional law. Even in a case of this kind, when the legal rule being challenged is the same in

---

30 See *Communication Workers v. Beck, supra,* note 18; *Ellis v. Brotherhood of Railway Workers,* 104 S. Ct. 1883 (1984).

31 See, e.g., B. Etherington, "Freedom of Association and Compulsory Union Dues", *supra,* note 13; M. Mandel, *The Charter of Rights and the Legalization of Politics in Canada, supra,* note 13, at 209-217.

32 B. Etherington, "Freedom of Association and Compulsory Union Dues", *ibid.,* at 28.

both countries and when the analytical framework used by the American Supreme Court is so similar to the model in *Oakes*, our Court must be careful to distinguish those decisions which are cogently reasoned from those which are not. For the reviewer, the fact that the American Supreme Court has written judgments which seem so mistaken and poorly reasoned doesn't mean that the distinction the Court drew between collective bargaining and other activities to support its decision, is itself inherently defective or arbitrary. Just the opposite in fact. It is precisely because one can say so confidently that the kinds of expenses the Court considered in *Ellis* and *Beck* were directly related to the union's role of exclusive bargaining agent and the free rider rationale that the reviewer can be so certain that the distinction is in fact quite objective and can produce highly determinate (and socially progressive) results. To say, as sceptics do, that the American Supreme Court's decision is wrong, must mean that there was a better answer which it missed.

To avoid the kinds of mistakes the American Supreme Court made in cases like *Ellis* and *Beck* should not be a difficult task. We know from our analysis of the other cases we have reviewed in this Part that the key to the Court exercising its powers of constitutional review properly lies in its keeping the *actual* purpose or purposes which underlie a challenged law squarely in the forefront of its mind.[33] In a case like *Lavigne*, this means the Court must concentrate its inquiry on whether the failure of employees represented by the union to contribute to the cost of different activities will give rise to complaints about freeloading and in turn create dissonance and dissension in the workplace.

Freeloading is the mischief that compulsory dues are meant to solve and it provides the standard against which every expenditure made by the union must be evaluated. If the union can show that the costs it incurred were aimed at promoting interests and activities which (i) were designed to have a beneficial effect on the working environment of those it represents, and (ii) give rise to a problem of freeloading, such expenditures can reasonably be attributed to the union's function of exclusive bargaining agent and can be included in the dues the union is entitled to demand from everyone it represents. However, expenditures which do not give rise to free rider problems, even if they can be related to collective bargaining and the union's role of bargaining agent, do not fall within the *purpose of the rule* and so must not be included in that portion of dues which each employee can be compelled to pay. What is determinative is not whether it can be shown that the union's expenditure will likely have an impact

---

33 See *R. v. Big M Drug Mart* (1985), 18 D.L.R. (4th) 321, and see the discussion in Chapter 6, *supra*, note 60. See also *Irwin Toy v. Quebec* (1988), 58 D.L.R. (4th) 577; and *Ref. re Alberta Public Service Employee Relations Act* (1987), 38 D.L.R. (4th) 161, *per* Dickson J.

on the working lives of the employees it represents. Virtually all causes and activities supported by unions can be related back to and found to have some connection with the workplace. What is critical is whether the union's actions will result in the employees enjoying a benefit which has a serious free rider dimension to it.

If the reviewer and the members of the Supreme Court keep the purpose which the agency shop rule is meant to serve clearly in mind, it is highly unlikely they will experience the same difficulties that have plagued their American counterparts. Though the Court will be engaged in a line drawing exercise every time it considers whether a particular expenditure gives rise to a free rider problem, that does not mean that the standard is purely subjective and completely malleable in the hands of each judge. To the contrary, if the expenditures which were at issue in *Lavigne* are typical, in most cases it should be quite clear on which side of the line an activity falls.

At one end of the spectrum will be a group of interests and activities which unambiguously give rise to freeloader problems because they are undertaken with a view of benefitting *only* the workers the union represents. Costs incurred in the negotiation and administration of a collective agreement are the clearest example of this type of expenditure. But they are not the only one. A union might incur expenses in the political arena, for example, which are also focused primarily on some aspect of the "law of the plant" and the employees it represents. The line separating expenditures which may be included in compulsory dues, from those which cannot, is not drawn between those incurred at the bargaining table and those which arise in the processes of politics. Drawing the line in that way, in fact, was how the American jurisprudence got so badly off track.[34] Certainly lobbying legislators to support the bail-out of enterprises facing financial difficulties[35] or to oppose a law which is aimed at preventing collective bargaining at a particular plant,[36] to cite two well-known case studies in Canadian law, are examples of expenditures which, though not

---

34 For reference to the American literature criticizing the U.S. rule which is based on this dichotomy, see B. Etherington, "Freedom of Association and Compulsory Union Dues", *supra*, note 13. Of the articles referred to by Etherington, I found the most helpful to be Norman Cantor, "Forced Payments to Service Institutions and Constitutional Interests in Ideological Non-Association", 36 Rutgers L.R. 3; and R. Raggi, "An Independent Right to Freedom of Association", 12 Harv. Civ. Rights — Civ. Liberties L. Rev. 1. See also A. Cox, "The Role of Law in Preserving Union Democracy", 72 Harv. L. Rev. 609 (1959), and H. Wellington, "The Constitution, The Labour Union and Governmental Action", 70 Yale L.J. 345.

35 See, e.g., M.J. Trebilcock, M. Chandler, P. Halpern and J. Quinn, *Business Bailouts in Canada*, Ontario Economic Council, 1985, vol. 2.

36 See B. Langille, "The Michelin Amendment in Context" (1981) 6 Dal. L.J. 523.

incurred at the bargaining table, would be focused primarily, if not exclusively, on the employees the union represents. With expenditures of this kind, wherever they arise, the problem of free riding is, as Ivan Rand clearly foresaw, most acute. Without a rule compelling each employee to pay his or her pro rata share, everyone would have a strong financial incentive not to contribute to these costs and to enjoy the benefits from which, by law, they could not be excluded.

While expenditures which are made exclusively for the benefit of the employees the union represents fall unambiguously within the free rider rationale, it is also easy to identify other expenses which just as obviously do not. Donations made for charitable and humanitarian causes are perhaps the clearest examples of expenditures which do not give rise to free rider problems of any kind. By definition, gifts and charitable donations of the kind OPSEU made, for example, for the relief of workers in Nicaragua, are given for altruistic, selfless purposes, and the employees represented by the union are not expected to benefit in any way. In these cases the union is simply conferring a voluntary benefit on a group of persons from whom it neither seeks nor expects any contribution in return.

Because the employees represented by the union do not benefit from expenditures which are *truly* charitable and humanitarian, no free riding can possibly occur.[37] Although one may say that those who do not want to make charitable donations of this kind lack a particular sense of moral character, it is not an instinct to freeload on the efforts of others. Nor is it one which can, or likely will, be changed by forcing them to give to causes which they do not believe.[38]

In analyzing which expenditures fall within the free rider rationale, and so are properly included in the compulsory assessment made on each employee, it is easy to identify cases at either end of the spectrum. In some cases the only beneficiaries of the union's expenditures will be the employees it represents and here the free rider problem is presented in its sharpest relief. In others, the employees represented by the union are not expected to benefit in any way and here, by definition, there can be no free rider problem at all. In the vast majority of cases, however, the expenditures can be expected to fall between these two extremes. They will share characteristics of both types of expenditures. They will be expected to benefit not only those whom the union represents but others, whom it does not, as well. Even in these cases, however, the Court should be able to distinguish expenditures which can be included in the agency

---

37 In some cases donations, like those sent to the U.K. miners, may be given with more self-interested purposes and where that is true a free rider problem may arise.

38 In terms of the object test, of course, it would be unconstitutional to argue that dues were made compulsory to force people to give. See Part One, Chapter 2, p. 27.

fee from those which cannot. If the reviewer continues to make the free rider problem the focus of her analysis, these cases should be as easy to resolve as the others we have just considered. Certainly if the expenditures at issue in *Lavigne* are typical, the lines will not be difficult to draw.

Whether, and/or the extent to which, this kind of hybrid expenditure creates a problem of freeloading depends on whether the employees whom the union represents can be said to benefit in ways and to degrees which distinguish them from the others who will profit from the union's activities and from the general public at large. In some cases the employees will benefit basically in the same way as everyone else. Here it will be difficult, if not impossible, to say that a free rider problem exists. Expenditures made by OPSEU promoting social causes like disarmament, public housing, income assistance, abortion clinics or political parties in general are of this kind. In these cases, the presence of very large numbers of people who will benefit basically in the same way as the employees whom the union represents, but who clearly are not required to help defray the costs of these activities, makes any claim that all employees must contribute their fair share of these expenditures, so as to avoid the problem of freeloading, highly implausible if not quite disingenuous. The very fact that the union is prepared to participate in these kinds of projects, even though it will benefit many more people than those it represents, makes a mockery of the claim that it would be inequitable and divisive if a few additional employees were also able to enjoy the same benefits without paying their proportionate share of the cost. The large number of people who will benefit gratuitously and in exactly the same way as the members of the union makes expenditures of these kinds very much like the charitable donations we just considered.

In other cases, however, free rider problems will arise even though the expenditures made by the union will benefit others in addition to those it represents. This will generally be true when the expenditures can be related directly to the terms and conditions which are contained in the union's contract and where, accordingly, it can be said that the employees represented by the union will profit in ways and to degrees which differentiate them from the others who benefit from the union's activities and from the general public at large. The organizing and litigation costs considered by the American Supreme Court in *Ellis* and *Beck*, are expenditures of this kind. Unlike the money spent supporting the broad social programmes considered in *Lavigne*, here the employees would not benefit simply as members of the general public or some broad interest group. Although other workers throughout an industry or sector of the economy may also benefit from expenditures of this kind, it remains the case that these activities are undertaken principally to protect the terms and conditions the union has negotiated in the "law of the plant" and because of that it is "entirely equitable", to use Ivan Rand's turn of phrase, that each employee represented by the union should bear his or her personal share of the cost.

Expenses incurred to cover the costs of lobbying legislators and Governments for more favourable employment laws share the same characteristics as organizing and litigation costs. Even though many people, beyond those represented by the union, will benefit from improvements in the minimum wage or in health and safety laws, for example, the major significance of these changes for the employees represented by the union will again be on the impact they will have in the shape and substance of their own specific "plant law".[39] Changes in the general law of employment provides the framework from which all future negotiations between the union and the employer will proceed and so will have special importance for the employees the union represents. As with the organizing and litigation costs, the direct connection between the union's lobbying efforts and the specific terms and conditions of employment under which the employees work, unavoidably gives rise to questions of equity and fairness as to how such expenses should be defrayed. Employees who do not want to pay for expenditures of this kind cannot describe themselves as just a few individuals in a very much larger pool of beneficiaries. Freeloading makes the likelihood of dissension and conflict within the plant very real once again.

In all these cases then, concentrating on the free rider problem which the agency shop rule was designed to resolve, produces clear lines between what can properly be included in a compulsory levy and what can not. In practical terms, virtually all of the major expenditures made by unions would fall within the free rider rationale and be immune from a constitutional challenge like Lavigne's. The major exceptions, which would fall outside the scope of the rule, would be (i) partisan contributions to political parties and their candidates, (ii) lobbying and/or associated activities on issues and causes not reasonably related to the law of employment, (iii) charitable donations and (as Rand explicitly proscribed), (iv) expenditures undertaken to secure benefits which are not available to all the employees represented by the union.

With such very clear divisions which the free rider rationale is able to draw between so many different kinds of union expenditures, it would not be unreasonable for the reviewer to think that the objectivity of the model in *Oakes* had now been established beyond all reasonable doubt.

---

39 Lobbying for liberalization of abortion laws might also be justified in this way to the extent that it could be shown that the negotiation of a medical benefits plan covering abortion related services is part of the bargaining agenda the union desires to include in the law of the plant.

The analysis of White's decision in *Lavigne* has shown again that the purposes which underlie a challenged law, like those that compel the payment of union dues, can and do provide an objective standard from which very determinative results can repeatedly and consistently be achieved. On top of all that, as we have already noted, the model produces a result in this case which is on all fours with the results it can be expected to generate in OPSEU #1.

Lavigne is an important case then because it should mean that a reviewer should be able to finally placate the doubts of reasonable sceptics about the objectivity of the model in *Oakes*. It is not likely, however, that the reviewer's analysis of *Lavigne* will persuade sceptics that their other suspicions, that judicial review is really a very regressive change to our system of our government, are similarly misplaced. In a case like *Lavigne* there is really not much a reviewer can say about the progressive effect of the model except repeating what she said in reporting on her first impressions about White's judgment. She can point out that, practically speaking, the limit which the model imposes on how unions can spend their dues is hardly a limit at all. From past experience the reviewer can say, the effect of White's judgment on the union's ability to participate effectively in the political process will be minuscule.[40] She can stress that, as our analysis has shown, the union will still be able to claim contributions from the employees it represents to help defray those expenses which are related to their "law of employment" and for which a free rider problem exists. She can also remind the sceptics that studies show that the number of persons who are likely to opt out of the voluntary contributions for other political causes is likely to be very small. As well, she might add that when *Lavigne* is considered alongside the first *OPSEU* case, it is possible to say that, as a result of the adoption of the Charter, the opportunity for unions to participate in the political process should now be the same as every other interest group and, on balance, would have been enhanced.

Against this, some have argued that, however White's judgment in *Lavigne* is rationalized and defended, the fact remains it really does discriminate against unions because other non-voluntary organizations to which people are forced to contribute dues and fees, like professional (law, medicine) societies, student organizations, or public utilities etc., are allowed to spend money on political causes even though those who are forced to pay or belong may disagree.[41] Merv Lavigne's situation, some

---

40 See note 13, *supra.*
41 See, e.g., B. Etherington, "Freedom of Association and Union Dues, *supra*, note 13; P. Weiler, "The Charter at Work", *supra*, note 4. See also K.D. Ewing, "Freedom of Association in Canada", 35 Alta. L. Rev. 437; A. Borovoy, *When Freedoms Collide, supra*, note 4.

might be tempted to say, was no different than Murdoch Mackay's and should be resolved in a similar way. On the analysis the reviewer has been following, the strength of such a claim depends on knowing very precisely the purpose or purposes for which such fees or monies or taxes were paid. In each case, the purpose for which the payment is made must be determined and then the expenditure examined in light of that purpose. As the purposes of the forced payments in all of these cases differ, so will the conclusions that follow.[42] In some cases, for example the payments each of us makes to a public utility like Hydro, do not give rise to problems of free riding because everyone is, in fact and in law, forced to pay for the amount of service he or she uses. However, even in a case of this kind, if it can be established that an agency or institution receives monies under compulsion of law and uses them for purposes beyond those to which its authority extends, challenges paralleling the one initiated by Lavigne would certainly be expected to meet with similar results.[43]

But even with such an explanation of how the results in *Lavigne* really are not as regressive as the sceptics are inclined to make out, the fact remains that Lavigne's challenge is not one which can fairly be advertised as advancing the cause of the politically disadvantaged and economically exploited. It is simply not that kind of case. As a person, Merv Lavigne is not of that class. Realistically, if the reviewer is going to be able to

---

42 See *Putting the Charter to Work, supra*, note 5, at 127-130.

43 For an argument that dues paid to student organizations and professional societies ought to be subject to a similar limitation on the purposes to which these monies can be put, see N. Cantor, "Forced Payments to Service Institutions", *supra*, note 34. See also V. Brudney, "Business Corporations and Stockholders Rights Under the First Amendment" (1981), 91 Yale L.J. 285.

Beyond these direct parallels, it seems unlikely unions will be able to establish that they are being discriminated against by a ruling of the kind authored by John White. There is, however, another legal regime restricting the political activities of employees generally which, subject to the Court's ruling in *Andrews*, does seem vulnerable to such a claim. The suspect law is contained in those provisions of the *Income Tax Act* which permit people who are self-employed (called businesspeople) but not those who are employed by others (called workers), to deduct from their reported income monies contributed to lobby groups whose primary function relates to the advocacy of political and ideological views.

But for the Supreme Court's discrediting of the "similarly situated" test in *Andrews*, drawing a distinction as to the ways by which and the ease with which people can support political lobby groups, between those who work for themselves and those who work for others, seems impossible to sustain. Certainly there is nothing in the judgment of Patrick Galligan, who dismissed a challenge by OPSEU to the relevant sections of the *Income Tax Act*, which a reviewer would expect would prevail at the end of the day. His three-page, oral judgment (reported at (1987), 39 D.L.R. (4th) 449) makes no effort to follow the analytical method of *Oakes* and trips over the *de minimis* fallacy she will have encountered in Part One. For a critical analysis of the Supreme Court's handling of the similarly situated test in *Andrews*, see Part One, Chapter 4 at note 6, *supra*.

convince sceptics that the model really is as distributively just as she believes, then she will have to look for another case on its way to the Court which is as clear and decisive about the progressive character of judicial review as *Lavigne* was in establishing its objectivity. Even though we have considered some examples of how the Charter can promote the interests of groups like prisoners and religious minorities, it is unlikely that the sceptics will be satisfied that these cases are sufficient to prove that the Charter really will have a progressive influence on the way our Government works. Given the importance of this feature of the Charter and judicial review to both sides of the debate, it would be neither surprising nor unreasonable for the sceptics to ask that the reviewer point to a different case where the outcome of a constitutional challenge unambiguously improves the lot of people who are at the bottom of the heap.

8

Life, Liberty and Security: Of Those Who Seek Refuge in Our Country

Most reviewers would have no quarrel with such a request. Most also would have little difficulty in deciding which case would shed most light on the question of whether the Charter, and the process of constitutional review, will have a progressive or regressive influence on the way in which our system of government works. One case, involving a challenge initiated by the Canadian Council of Churches, against the most recent amendments to Canada's refugee laws, seems ideally suited to the task.

The laws challenged in this case affect a group of people who are unquestionably among the most unfortunate in the world. On virtually every relevant criterion of disadvantage and powerlessness, refugees are among the most disadvantaged people on the face of the earth. No one disputes their suffering. The vast majority of today's refugees have fled from developing countries where social conflict, personal persecution and economic hardship are most acute. Like all aliens, the predicament of refugees is compounded by the fact that their interests are especially vulnerable to being compromised or completely ignored in the countries to which they flee because they lack all of the essential attributes of citizenship and political power.[1] Facing conditions of extreme privation and without any political influence to persuade Governments to be sensitive to their needs, refugees present a litmus test for whether, with the Charter in their hands, judges will exert a progressive or regressive influence in the way social policy is developed and transformed into law. The outcome of this case should provide clear evidence as to whether refugees, and others who suffer similar disadvantages, should look to the third branch

---

1 A fact the Supreme Court has already recognized in much less extreme circumstances in *Andrews v. Law Society of B.C.* (1988), 56 D.L.R. (4th) 1.

of government to attend to their needs when the legislative and/or executive branches have failed to listen to their pleas.

The challenge to Canada's new refugee laws is also a good vehicle through which the reviewer can explore the progressive potential of constitutional review because a tension already exists between the judiciary and the other two branches of government on the question of what constitutes a constitutionally valid refugee law. This will not, like the other cases the reviewer has analysed, be a case of first impression for the Court. As she will have seen in Part One, refugee claimants and church groups have already launched one successful challenge to an earlier version of Canada's refugee law.[2] In the context of the Court's earlier ruling in *Singh*, the possibility that the Court may decide to strike down the Government's refugee determination procedure for a second time takes on added significance. On the one hand, some sceptics might say that if the Court interferes with Parliament's choice again this will show the Court is being obstructionist and completely insensitive to our most basic notions of popular rule.[3] Alternatively, such a decision could be cited by believers as conclusive evidence that the first two branches of government can, and will, "act" in a very regressive, mean spirited and abusive way if they think that, politically, it is in their best interest to do so. Such extreme possibilities makes analysis of the challenge to Canada's new refugee laws of special significance to both sides of the debate. Depending on which characterization is closer to the mark, judicial review could either be dismissed as an atavistic return to Government by ruling elites or hailed as the ultimate assurance that the power of the State cannot be used in arbitrary and regressive ways.

The contours of this second review of Canada's refugee laws must be seen within the context of the first. Under the refugee determination procedure which existed prior to *Singh*, refugee claims could pass through as many as half-a-dozen separate stages before a final decision was made.[4] When this scheme was put in place, however, the Government didn't anticipate either the large number of refugee claims that would be filed

---

2 *Singh v. Minister of Employment and Immigration* (1985), 17 D.L.R. (4th) 422.

3 Cf. M. Mandel, *The Charter of Rights and the Legalization of Politics in Canada* (Toronto: Wall & Thompson, 1989), pp. 172-185, who launches a strong attack on Bertha Wilson's decision in *Singh* on the ground that by adding what is a purely formalistic entitlement of a hearing to the refugee determination process, the Court has only served to give legitimacy to a policy which otherwise remains "the furthest thing from humanitarianism" (p. 182).

4 For a description of the Canadian system of refugee determination at the time of the Court's decision in *Singh* and how it compared to ten other countries around the world, see C. Avery, "Refugee Status Decision-Making: The Systems of Ten Countries" (1983), Stanford Journal of International Law 255, 258ff.

or the additional resources that would be needed to process their applications. The result was that very quickly a large backlog of undecided cases had begun to build up. In turn, the emergence of a backlog encouraged a substantial number of unfounded claims to be filed since anyone who applied for refugee status, and used every opportunity of appeal, could remain and work in Canada for as long as two or three years before they could be removed from the country.[5] Many people knew that, with a long list of cases waiting to be decided, they would have had several years of remunerative employment before they would face the possibility of being sent back to their homes.

Following the Court's decision in *Singh*, the backlog got even worse. In *Singh*, it will be recalled, the Supreme Court held that the refugee determination procedure contained in the 1976 *Immigration Act* was unconstitutional because it permitted the rejection of a refugee claim solely on the basis of a written record. The Court ruled that because a serious issue of credibility was involved in making a determination of whether someone is a genuine refugee, and because the stakes — often involving physical liberty and human life — can be exceedingly high, an oral hearing was required at some stage in the refugee determination process. The claimant had to be given an opportunity to state his or her case before the decision maker, and to know and respond to the case he or she had to meet.

To comply with the Court's decision in *Singh*, the Government adopted a procedure in which an oral hearing was provided by the *Immigration Appeal Board* (I.A.B.) to anyone whose claim for refugee status had been dismissed at an earlier stage in the proceedings. Not only were all new claimants afforded this right, but all those who had made an application between the time Singh filed his challenge and April 4, 1985, when the Court issued its ruling, were extended this opportunity as well. The increased workload faced by the I.A.B. added to the length of the delays which in turn attracted even more unfounded claims. While the Government studied how the refugee determination process should be redesigned, the number of undecided claims continued to grow exponentially. From an average of 3000-5000 in the years immediately prior to *Singh*, the number of refugee claims rose to 8,400 in 1985, 18,000 in 1986 and over 25,000 in 1987. In 1986 alone, frivolous claims from Portugal and Turkey accounted for approximately 6000 of the total number of claims made in that year.[6]

---

5 See the *Report on Delays in the Refugee Status Determination Process*, prepared by Program Policy Development Division, Enforcement Branch, Department of Immigration, Ottawa, April 20, 1983.

6 See Interchurch Committee for Refugees, Brief to Senate Standing Committee on Legal and Constitutional Affairs Concerning Bill C-55, January 1988. See also J. Hathaway,

It was in these deteriorating circumstances that Canada's new refugee process was born in the summer of 1987. After having commissioned two independent reports, and submitting the question of refugee policy to one of its own standing committees, the Government finally decided to Act.[7] Two separate bills known as C-55 and C-84 were introduced in Parliament. These bills proposed sweeping amendments to the 1976 *Immigration Act* changing numerous aspects of Canada's refugee laws including: the process for determining whether a person meets the definition of a Convention refugee;[8] the detention of those claiming refugee status; the removal and deportation of those whose claims were dismissed; the creation of new administrative agencies to oversee the whole process, as well as the provision for criminal sanctions against people assisting undocumented persons to enter Canada. Broadly speaking, all of the amendments were directed at two separate but related goals. Collectively the two pieces of legislation were intended to respond to the failures and inequities that plagued the system since the Court's decision in *Singh* by putting a process of refugee determination in place which would not be vulnerable to abuse but which would ensure protection for those claimants who, in the Government's mind, genuinely merited it.[9]

Although the new legislation touched many aspects of refugee policy,

---

"Selective Concern: An Overview of Refugee Law in Canada" (1988), McGill L.J. 677; and "Postscript" (1989), 34 McGill L.J. 354. It should be noted that, although many claimants from Turkey turned out to be fraudulent, not all claims from that country could be characterized in that way.

7 See E. Ratushny, *A New Refugee Determination Process For Canada* (Ottawa: Department of Employment & Immigration, 1984); G. Plaut, *Refugee Determination in Canada* (Ottawa: Department of Employment & Immigration, 1985); The Standing Committee on Labour, Employment & Immigration (House of Commons), prepared a study on the recommendations made in the Plaut Report. See House of Commons, Minutes of Proceedings and Evidence of the Standing Committee on Labour & Immigration, No. 46 (1984-85).

8 A Convention refugee as defined by the 1951 *International Convention Relating to the Status of Refugees* and 1967 *Protocol* included someone who "owing to a well-founded fear of being persecuted for reason of race, religion, nationality, membership of a particular social group or political opinion, is outside the country of his nationality and is unable, or owing to such a fear, is unwilling to avail himself of the protection of that country". For a complete definition as adopted by Canada, see *Immigration Act, 1976*, S.C, 1976-77, c. 52 s. 2(1); R.S.C. 1985, c. I-2.

9 Linking the protection of genuine refugees to the deterrence of abusers, which would allow the Government to focus all of its resources on those most in need of protection, was emphasized throughout the legislative process by Government officials. See, e.g., the testimony of G. Weiner, Minister of State (Immigration), before the Standing Committee of the House of Commons on Employment and Immigration 26/08/87 (afternoon sitting), and the testimony of Benoit Bouchard before the Standing Senate Committee on Legal and Constitutional Affairs 8/12/87, pp. 46:7-8. These and similar statements were eventually incorporated into the stated objectives of the *Immigration Act*. See *An Act to Amend the Immigration Act 1976*, S.C. 1988, c. 36, ss. 2.1(a) and (b).

the centrepiece was the new procedure by which a person's refugee status would be determined. Basically the Government's objective was to design a system which would immediately identify abusers and others who, for one reason or another, were not regarded as deserving of Canada's protection and to remove them from the country as quickly as possible. The theory of the new system was that the best way to deter and counteract abuse was to signal people who might consider coming to Canada and claiming refugee status, as a way of circumventing regular immigration procedures, that this was an ineffectual and possibly quite a costly decision to make. In the Government's mind, the most effective way to avoid the kind of abuse which had undermined the system both before and after *Singh*, was to create a series of screening devices which would limit access to the refugee determination process.

In designing a system to meet its objectives, the Government scrapped two of the central pillars of the old system which had existed even before the Court's decision in *Singh*. First, the Government removed the right of every refugee claimant to have his or her case decided on the merits. Secondly, it eliminated the entitlement of unsuccessful claimants to have a negative determination reconsidered on appeal. With the amendments, access to the refugee determination procedure would no longer be automatic and the opportunity for review would be restricted so that the system would no longer be bogged down by dubious claims.

In more detailed terms, the new refugee determination process was broken down into three quite distinct stages. In the first phase, an Immigration adjudicator, who is an employee in the Minister's Department, and a member of a new, independent, Refugee Board would decide whether a person making a claim was even *eligible* to have his or her case put in front of the new Refugee Board. This "eligibility screen" was designed to weed out half-a-dozen different groups, including individuals who had been recognized as Convention refugees in another country; who had previously been in a "third country" which Canada considered safe; who had already received a negative response to their claim; or who had committed offences which were regarded as so serious as to exclude them from being considered as Convention refugees.[10] It was expected that persons deemed ineligible to have their claims evaluated by the Refugee Board would be removed from Canada within a matter of days. According to the projections of senior officials in the Department, it was anticipated that "in its ideal form", the safe 'third country' screen alone would remove 30% of all individuals making refugee claims at our borders.[11] Although

---

10 *An Act to Amend the Immigration Act, 1976*, S.C. 1988, c. 35, s. 48.01(1).
11 Department of Immigration, Ottawa, "Program Delivery Strategy — 1989", Operations Memorandum IE 249 (December 22, 1988), p. 14.

these persons would be entitled to ask a Court to review a decision denying their eligibility to make a refugee claim, the new law provided that removal from Canada could take place after 72 hours and before their case had even been heard, let alone decided, by the Court.[12]

By the terms of the new Act, refugee claimants who passed through the eligibility screen would be allowed to proceed to the second phase of the inquiry. At this stage the Immigration adjudicator and the Refugee Board member would determine whether the claimant had a "credible basis" for the claim. Here the idea was to screen out those claims that were manifestly unfounded and stood no chance of success. According to the new procedure if, after considering all of the evidence, including the human rights record of the country from which the claimant was fleeing, and how other claims from that country had been handled in the past, either the adjudicator or Refugee Board member were of the opinion that there was a credible basis upon which a person might be found to be a Convention refugee, then the claimant would be entitled to pass on to the third and final stage of the process and to have a full oral hearing of their case before the Refugee Board.[13] By contrast, those who were found not to have a "credible basis" for their claim were to be removed summarily from the country. Like those caught by the eligibility screen, these people might not even be permitted to remain in Canada pending review of a negative decision. The first and second phase of the process were expected to take one or two weeks to complete.[14] It was estimated that, in total, 40% of border refugee claims would be screened out by these procedures.[15]

It was only claimants who passed the first two screens, relating to eligibility and credibility, who would enjoy all of the protection that a full hearing, before an independent decision maker, guarantees. All of the financial and personal resources required to establish a fair refugee determination process would be focused on those who were considered to be in genuine need of protection and whose presence in Canada would not be threatening or prejudicial to the public interest in any way. Spared the expense of listening to cases which, in the Government's mind, were either not pressing or transparently fraudulent, the third stage of the review process could be designed with the most rigorous principles of procedural fairness, including the right to counsel, time to prepare, two independent decision makers and a full hearing of each individual's claim on its merits.

---

12 *An Act to Amend the Immigration Act, 1976*, S.C. 1988, c. 35, s. 83.1, s.51(1)(b).

13 *An Act to Amend the Immigration Act, 1976*, S.C. 1988, c. 35, s. 48.01(6).

14 Canada, Department of Immigration, "Program Delivery Strategy — 1989", Operations Memorandum IE 249 (December 22, 1988).

15 *Ibid.*, p. 14. Note that it was also estimated that one third of all claimants who received a full hearing before the Refugee Board would be rejected and subject to removal.

Although the Canadian Council of Churches directed its challenge at almost every aspect of the new refugee law, it will be sufficient for the reviewer's purposes to focus her attention on the procedural changes that were made to the refugee determination process.[16] They were the key feature of the Government's new refugee policy and they have been the focus of most of the criticism of those who argued against its enactment into law. Moreover, limiting her analysis to this part of the case will allow the reviewer to concentrate her attention on section 7, (and to a lesser extent section 15) of the Charter which, so far, she has not had occasion to address. From our discussion of the Court's performance in Part One, the reviewer will know that sections like 7 (and 15) are different from the other Charter guarantees that we have considered in this Part because the protections they provide are written in qualified terms. Unlike the guarantees of expression, religion or association, section 7 does not protect the "life, liberty, and security of a person" absolutely. Rather, it only guarantees that these most basic and long-standing entitlements will not be infringed in ways which offend "principles of fundamental justice".

---

16 It should be noted that the federal Government has challenged the right of the Canadian Council of Churches to launch an integrated, "public-interest" attack of this all-encompassing kind. Although it was unsuccessful at the trial level (see *Canadian Council of Churches v. R.*, [1989] 3 F.C. 3), the Government's argument was substantially sustained in the Federal Court of Appeal (A-223-89, March 12, 1990). In denying the Canadian Council of Churches status to launch this suit, Mark MacGuigan applied the public interest test, set out in the standing trilogy (see *infra*, Chapter 11, note 2), in a very narrow and conservative way. Essentially MacGuigan rejected the argument that the churches' public interest challenge was the most reasonable way of testing the constitutionality of the new law because of the costs it would save, and he simply denied that there were any additional risks to the lives, liberty etc., of refugee claimants in waiting for individual challenges to be made against each of the disputed sections of the new law by people who were directly affected by them.

If the Supreme Court follows the liberal approach in designing its own rules of procedure (see Chapter 11, *infra*), there is not much in Mark MacGuigan's judgment which it should find appealing, and it would be expected that it would restore the judgment of the trial court judge, Paul Rouleau, in due course. In the first place, the cost advantages in time and resources of broad, public-interest challenges are simply impossible to deny. More importantly, as we shall see, there is in fact considerable evidence showing that waiting for individual challenges to be mounted against each of the sections the churches have attacked is not only uneconomical, it would put the lives, liberty, etc., of numerous persons at serious risk (see *infra*, pp. 222-232). Because they are commonly burdened by serious economic and psychological pressures, as well as very stringent time constaints, it is unavoidable that numerous, genuine refugee claimants have been and will continue to be threatened by the new procedures without even knowing, let alone being able to assert, that their constitutional rights have been violated.

The Canadian Council of Churches has sought leave to appeal and, at the time of publication, the Court's decision is still pending. Regardless of how the Supreme Court rules on their request, there can be little doubt that sooner or later all of the provisions attacked in the Churches' suit will be tested in the courts.

Similarly, rather then guaranteeing everyone the equal protection and benefit of all law, section 15 only protects people from unequal treatment which is "discriminatory". An examination of the challenges directed at the new refugee determination process will allow the reviewer to see whether these textual differences have an effect on how the model in *Oakes* will be applied.

With respect to those parts of the challengers' claims which are based on section 7, the Court has already given a good deal of guidance on how it expects to exercise its powers of review. In contrast with its much more limited involvement with section 15, section 7 was directly involved in numerous cases which the Court heard in its first five years. It is true that three of the most important judgments — *Operation Dismantle, Singh,* and the *B.C. Motor Vehicle Act Reference* — were decided before the Court's decision in *Oakes.*[17] As well, in others,[18] the Court was often quite divided in its views. Still, there is much in these decisions which is the subject of widespread agreement among all the judges and which will unquestionably control how the Court will address the merits of the present case.

In determining whether the new, three stage, refugee determination procedure interferes with the constitutional entitlements guaranteed in section 7, the reviewer can be confident about how the Court will begin. As in every other case she has considered in this Part, the Court's first order of business will be to determine whether the new procedure threatens a refugee claimant's life, liberty and/or security of the person. The way in which a right or freedom is worded in the Charter has no bearing on how constitutional dialogue will begin. The Canadian Council of Churches will still have to prove that the new process actually does impinge on those aspects of personal freedom which are protected in section 7.

In all of the cases the reviewer has considered so far she has seen that the first stage of the review process invariably is simple and straightforward. In every case she has found that those initiating the challenge should have little difficulty in showing how the disputed law impinges on some aspect of their personal freedom which the Charter protects. It is unlikely that, in this respect at least, the challenge to Canada's new refugee determination process will be any different. When they are considered carefully, the first two stages of the refugee determination process can be seen to expose large numbers of people to serious risks

---

17 *Operation Dismantle v. R.* (1985), 18 D.L.R. (4th) 481; *Singh v. M.E.I., supra*, note 2; *Ref. re s. 94(2) B.C. Motor Vehicle Act* (1986), 24 D.L.R. (4th) 536.

18 *R. v. Jones* (1986), 31 D.L.R. (4th) 569; *R. v. Morgentaler* (1988), 44 D.L.R. (4th) 385; *R. v. Lyons* (1988), 44 D.L.R. (4th) 193; *R. v. Vaillancourt* (1988), 47 D.L.R. (4th) 400. See also *R. v. Stevens* (1989), 51 D.L.R. (4th) 394; *R. v. Beare/Higgins* (1988), 55 D.L.R. (4th) 481; *B.C.G.E.U. v. A.G. B.C.* (1989), 53 D.L.R. (4th) 1; *R. v. Gamble*, [1988] 2 S.C.R. 595.

to their physical liberty, their personal security, and even their lives. Both of the screening devices designed to weed out abusers and others who have no valid claim to our protection turn out to be very crudely designed. Separately, and together, the eligibility and credibility screens threaten[19] the security[20] of large numbers of people, who are in genuine need of protection, to the risk of being removed from Canada without ever having a full hearing on the merits of their cases, and being sent to situations where they may face detention, imprisonment, physical abuse and even death. To make matters worse, the risk of error is compounded by the fact that the legislation fails to provide claimants with an effective opportunity either to respond to the Government's case or to appeal a decision which dismisses their claims.[21]

The possibility of error and the risk of sending persons with genuine refugee claims into situations where their personal safety and even their lives may be endangered, is most acute at the first stage of the review process. The eligibility screen is, without question, the crudest and most threatening part of the new procedure. As noted above, half a dozen different categories of individuals and groups have been deemed to be ineligible to have their refugee claims determined on the merits and, as a result, are liable to deportation virtually overnight. The most important ineligible group, certainly in terms of the numbers affected, are people who come to Canada from what are commonly, but often incorrectly, called "safe third countries". "Safe" countries are those designated by the Cabinet which, based on their policies and practices with respect to refugee claims and human rights, can be taken to honour the internationally recognized rule, known as "non-refoulment", which protects against the involuntary

---

19 As we saw in Part One, on more than one occasion the Court recognized that a claimant need only prove that his or her constitutional entitlements were threatened and not that they had actually been impaired. See *supra*, Part One, Chapter 4, note 45. See especially *Singh v. M.E.I.*, *supra*, note 2; *R. v. Morgentaler* (1988), 44 D.L.R. (4th) 385.

20 The Court explored the meaning of security of the person in *Singh v. M.E.I.*, *supra*, note 2; *Ref. re s. 94(2) Motor Vehicle Act (B.C.)*, *supra*, note 17; *R. v. Morgentaler*, *supra*, note 19.

21 Canada, House of Commons, *Minutes of Proceedings and Evidence of the Standing Committee on Labour, Employment and Immigration*, (August 27, 1987).

The seriousness of the risk created by the failure to create an appeal mechanism was emphasized in the testimony given by Joe Stern, Chairman of the former Refugee Status Advisory Committee (RSAC). Stern notes that between January 1987 and August 1987, 127 negative determinations made by RSAC in the first instance were overturned upon an appeal on the merits. Despite the care and attention that his staff gave all cases, Stern acknowledged that members of RSAC were not infallible and it was inevitable that mistakes would be made. "For these 127 people, if there had been no provision for review, these people could have been, and certainly under the new system, will be sent to a country where it is very likely that they will face persecution". See also J. Hathaway, "Postscript", *supra*, note 6, at 356.

return of persons to countries where their lives or security will be at risk.[22] By the terms of the Act, refugee claimants are automatically excluded from the system if they come to Canada through one of these safe countries and if (i) they would be allowed to return to that country or (ii) they would be allowed to have their refugee claims determined on the merits there.[23]

The basic defect of the safe third country concept is that the criteria set out in the Act to define which countries are safe, are radically incomplete and underinclusive and cannot guarantee that a country so designated will really be safe in fact. Countries which may be considered safe on the criteria set out in the Act may actually be very dangerous places to be. This is especially true in the case of developing countries which collectively house over 80% of the world's refugees. Even though a developing country may have a good record in terms of not expelling refugees, and although it may permit a claimant to return, it may simply be unable to adequately protect refugees within its borders. In Malawi, for example, Mozambican refugee settlements are frequently invaded by Renamo rebels who steal food, rape women, and kidnap refugees forcing them to work as their porters and field hands inside Mozambique. Similarly, Salvadoran refugees living in camps in Honduras, Palestinian refugees in Lebanon, and Cambodian refugees confined to border camps in Thailand have been subjected both to military and rebel raids. Mob violence, such as that experienced by Ethiopian refugees in Sudan, is also not an uncommon occurrence. Other more subtle, yet just as egregious threats to personal security are also experienced by many refugees, especially women and children, who are particularly vulnerable to abuse. Iranian boy refugees in Pakistan, for example, are often enticed into drugs and prostitution as a means of survival, as are many Ethiopian women refugees in Sudan.

But it is not just developing countries in the third world which pose a threat to the lives, liberty and security of genuine refugees. Liberal and otherwise very enlightened countries in the developed world can sometimes be very threatening places as well. The way the Act is worded, virtually all of the free and democratic countries of western Europe would qualify as "safe third countries", even though they may not guarantee either that refugee claimants would be allowed to remain in their country *permanently* or that their refugee claims would be evaluated in a *fair manner* and in accordance with international standards and conventions.

The risks inherent in the criteria contained in the Act are not purely speculative. Actual case histories of genuine refugees, who have been returned from "safe countries" in western Europe to places in which

---

22 *An Act to Amend the Immigration Act, 1976,* S.C. 1988, c. 35, s. 114(1)(s).
23 *An Act to Amend the Immigration Act, 1976,* S.C. 1988, c. 35, s. 46.01(1)(b).

persecution is feared, are now well documented.[24] In some cases refugee claimants have been shuttled from one State to another, literally put in "orbit" for months until some country permits their admission.[25] Much worse, some refugees have been put into an orbit which returns them to the countries from which they have fled. In one case an Iranian refugee claimant, fleeing the Ayatollah Khomeini's fundamentalist regime, was refused admission into Denmark on the application of a safe country screen similar to our own, returned to the country from which he had embarked, and eventually sent back to Iran where he was imprisoned.[26]

The threat that may be posed to genuine refugees is no different under Canada's new law. The fate of this Iranian refugee would have been exactly the same even if somehow he had been able to reach Canada after passing through Denmark. Based on the criteria set out in the Act, there is no doubt Denmark would qualify as a safe country. In the result, even if this Iranian refugee had made it to Canada, if the safe country provisions were in effect, he would have been liable to being returned to Denmark and eventually back to Iran. According to the procedures contemplated by the Act, at no point would he have been able to explain why it would not be safe for him to return to Denmark. The Immigration officer and the member of the Refugee Board assigned to his case would have had no authority to consider the claimant's individual circumstances. They would have been required to find him ineligible to have his claim determined

---

24 See Lawyers Committee for Human Rights, "The Growing Problem of Refugees in Orbit: A Report and Proposal for Corrective Legislation" (New York, 1986); Dansk Flygtningehjaelp (Danish Refugee Council), "Current Asylum Policies and Humanitarian Principles, In Light of the Amendments to the Aliens Act of October 17, 1986" (Copenhagen, 1987), pp. 4.1-4.33.

25 The case of William Ahmed, an Eritrean from northern Ethiopia, is a well publicized example. In 1984 he was arrested by the Ethiopian government for allegedly assisting guerrillas from the Eritrean Liberation Front. He spent four years in a prison in Addis Ababa where he was subjected to severe torture. He was later moved to a hospital where he escaped to Djibouti. In Djibouti he purchased a Somalian passport and an air ticket to Canada, via Cyprus, Cairo and Geneva. Upon landing in Geneva, immigration authorities noticed that his passport was about to expire and so they sent him back to Cairo. He was refused entry into Egypt and sent by the Egyptian authorities to Cyprus where he languished in the airport holding lounge for four months. Finally, after receiving assurances by the United Nations High Commissioner for Refugees that he would receive assistance in Egypt, he flew back to Cairo. When Egyptian authorities tried to send him to Somalia he physically tried to resist and it was only when the Somalian Ambassador confirmed that he would be imprisoned in Somalia that the Egyptian authorities agreed to return him to Cyprus. Six weeks later the British Government agreed to grant him admission and subsequently he received refugee status there. See "A Man in Orbit" *Time International*, July 3, 1989, p. 28.

26 Dansk Flygtningehjaelp (Danish Refugee Council), "Current Asylum Policies and Humanitarian Principles, In Light of the Amendments to the Aliens Act of October 17, 1986", *supra*, note 24, at 4.14.

by the Refugee Board and to order him to be returned to Denmark.[27]

In each of the examples the reviewer has considered so far, the risk to refugee claimants is caused by the fact that the criteria set out in the Act cannot guarantee that their lives, liberty and the security of their persons will be free from all danger and threats. A quite separate risk in the use of a safe country screen is that, even if the criteria used by the Government were completely failsafe, there remains a danger that when the Minister and other members of the Cabinet are drawing up the list, they will be subjected to strong diplomatic pressures to include countries which do not really meet the criteria.[28] Even if the definition of what constitutes a safe country were unobjectionable in theory, in practice it is susceptible to manipulation and abuse. Certainly no foreign Government with which we have close ties could be expected to stand idly by while the Canadian Government made a decision to leave that country completely or partially off the list. Such a decision unavoidably carries with it a negative evaluation and condemnation of that country's treatment of refugees. One can imagine the reaction of the American Government if, as all the evidence suggests it should, the United States were left off the list for Salvadoran and Guatemalan refugees.[29] It is unlikely any Canadian politician will welcome having to make a decision of this kind, and very few will feel comfortable at having to offend the Americans in this way.[30] If in this, or parallel situations,[31] the Canadian Government did succumb to such diplomatic

---

27   It should be noted the Minister has a discretion to allow people who are subject to removal from Canada to remain on humanitarian and compassionate grounds by granting them a "Minister's permit". See *Immigration Act, supra*, note 8, ss. 37, 114.

28   This concern was raised in the Standing Senate Committee on Legal and Constitutional Affairs' *Report on Bill C-55*, 33rd Parl., 2nd Sess., 1987-88, pp. 5-7.

29   That the U.S. is not a safe country for people fleeing from these countries is evident in the statistics. The U.S. accepts less than 3% of the refugee claims of Guatemalans and Salvadorans as compared to Canada's acceptance rate of 50% of the claims originating in these countries. See Canadian Bar Association, "Critique of Bill C-55: A Proposed Refugee Determination Process" submitted to Senate Standing Committee on Legal and Constitutional Affairs (Sept. 28, 1987), p. 27.

30   It is a common belief among those who practise refugee law that it is precisely this example which explains why the Government still had not drawn up a safe country list a year after the passing of the amendments to the Act. Certainly the Government was aware that the United States might not be regarded as a safe third country for people fleeing from Central America. See the testimony of G. Weiner, Minister of State (Immigration), before the House of Commons Standing Committee on Employment and Immigration 26/08/87, afternoon session, p. 34.

31   Another concrete example, involving Tamils fleeing Sri Lanka, of how political pressure can bear on the determination of whether a person has fled from a safe third country, was discussed by J. Stern, the former Chairperson of the Refugee Status Advisory Committee, in his testimony on Bill C-55 to the House of Commons Standing Committee on Employment and Immigration 27/08/87, afternoon sitting, p. 43.

pressures, the life, liberty and security of refugee claimants sent back to these countries would be seriously threatened. As we have observed, there is no possibility for errors to be either detected or corrected. Under the scheme of the Act, at the first stage of the determination process the claimants do not have any opportunity to challenge the Government's decision to put a country on the list. Again, neither the Immigration officer nor the member of the Refugee Board has any jurisdiction to correct any error in the designation of a country as being safe no matter its magnitude or cause.

Unquestionably, persons fleeing persecution who pass through safe third countries, where it was possible to make a refugee claim and/or seek asylum, are the largest group threatened by the eligibility screen. They are not, however, the only group so exposed. In addition to those coming from "safe countries", the screen also applies to anyone who has been convicted of a serious criminal offence and who, in the Minister's opinion, may be a danger to the Canadian public. As well, it excludes persons who are considered security threats when the Minister believes that it is not in the public interest to let them make a refugee claim in Canada.[32] Like anyone who is deemed ineligible to make a refugee claim, people excluded on either of these grounds are liable to be removed from Canada and sent directly back to the country from which they fear persecution. Worse, the Act provides no opportunity for these individuals to challenge the Minister's determination that they are a danger to the public in Canada or that it would be contrary to the public interest to have their claims heard and determined on the merits. Indeed the Act does not even permit a person to remain in Canada a reasonable time in order to gain admission to another State. Removal takes place without consideration of the consequences to the person involved.

As several commentators pointed out during debate on the bills, people who are characterized as security risks are especially vulnerable under the new procedure.[33] Although the new system allows these people to ask a Court to review the security certificates that have been issued against them, it also provides that the Government can request that the evidence on which it has based its decision not be disclosed to the refugee claimant

---

32 *An Act to Amend the Immigration Act, 1976*, S.C. 1988, c. 35, s. 48.01(e).
33 See the testimony given before the Senate Standing Committee on Legal and Constitutional Affairs concerning Bill C-84, "An Act to amend the Immigration Act, 1976 and the Criminal Code in consequence thereof". In particular note the testimony of George Cram, Secretary, Primates' Fund for World Relief and Development, Anglican Church of Canada, Issue No. 42 (November 5, 1987), p. 29:12; and of Barbara Jackman from the Canadian Bar Association, Immigration Law Section, in Issue No. 28 (September 29, 1987), pp. 28:19-28:39.

on the ground that it raises national security concerns.[34]

For genuine refugees it would be hard to exaggerate the risk entailed in not knowing and being able to counter the Government's case. Not infrequently, for example, evidence that a person is a security risk comes from the person's country of origin. If the person is a genuine refugee, the security information upon which the Minister has relied may be tainted. From experience, it is known that when it suits their purposes to do so, persecuting countries will not hesitate to provide unfounded or misleading information to prevent the person from receiving refuge in another State. Under the scheme of the Act, not only will claimants be unable to dispute the factual basis upon which a security certificate is issued, but they will also be unable to dispute the inferences that are drawn from facts that may not be in dispute. In either case, a security certificate could be upheld without the person having a meaningful opportunity to know and counter the Government's case.[35] Exclusion from the refugee determination process on these grounds alone denies the person the opportunity of establishing that he or she is a Convention refugee in need of protection. Removal from Canada can take place without the consequences to the individual ever having to be balanced against the extent to which it would be contrary to the public interest to determine the individual's refugee claim.

Similar problems arise for persons who have been convicted, inside or outside Canada, of serious criminal offences and whom the Minister has certified are a danger to the Canadian public. Once again, there is no opportunity for these persons to challenge the Minister's certificate that they are dangerous. A conviction and a certificate are all that is necessary to refuse claimants admission to the refugee determination procedure and to return them to the country where persecution is feared. Many examples have been cited to demonstrate how this provision can expose genuine refugees to serious risks. A person coming from China, for example, may have spent years in prison on a conviction of treason simply by speaking out against the Communist Government. Although it could be said his conviction was for a serious offence, his exclusion from Canada and possible removal to China would be out of all proportion to the crime he actually committed.

Even where the actual offence is less benign, there are compelling reasons why genuine refugees should not be exposed to the risks inherent in denying them the opportunity of seeking protection in Canada. Take the case of another Iranian who flees his country because he faces

---

34 *An Act to Amend the Immigration Act, 1976*, S.C. 1988, c. 36, s. 41.04(1)(e).

35 See J. Hathaway, "Postscript", *supra*, note 6. See also testimony of Barbara Jackman, Ontario Branch Immigration Law Section, Canadian Bar Association before the Senate Standing Committee on Legal and Constitutional Affairs 29/9/87, p. 28:37.

persecution for being a member of the Mojahedin, and who subsequently comes to Canada where he commits robbery. Clearly he would be guilty of committing a serious crime and the Minister may have a perfectly valid concern that the person is a danger to the public. Yet it would be difficult to justify returning him to Iran where he would likely face imprisonment or execution simply because he committed a robbery in Canada. However, by the terms of the Act, because he will be denied the opportunity to establish his refugee claim, there would be no possibility that the gravity of the consequences of removal from Canada would ever be weighed against the seriousness of his crime and conviction.

Because it admits of no exceptions, and allows for no meaningful appeals, and because it affects so many people, the eligibility screen unquestionably poses a greater threat to lives, liberty and the security of people who claim Canada should recognize their status as Convention refugees than any other part of the new procedure. It is not, however, the only section of the new Act which puts human lives and safety at risk. Even persons not included in one of the classes caught by the eligibility screen, may lose their opportunity to have a full and fair hearing of their case if they fail to assert their claims the first chance they have. According to the Act, at the beginning of each inquiry, and before evidence is taken, the adjudicator must ask the person if he or she intends to claim refugee status. If the person fails to respond to the adjudicator's question positively, the opportunity to make a refugee claim will be lost.[36] Even if the person had very understandable reasons for failing to make a refugee claim on the first occasion when a Canadian Government official offered him the chance to do so, the Act once again allows for no discretion and no consideration of the individual's personal circumstances. Like the eligibility screen, this section of the Act raises another irrebuttable assumption that all genuine refugees will identify themselves at the first opportunity they have.

If the experience of those working with refugees is to be believed, the assumption which underlies this "time of request" screen also poses a very real threat to the lives, liberty, and security of many persons who are genuine refugee claimants. On their evidence, the idea that only abusers will fail to avail themselves of the first opportunity to claim refugee status is completely unfounded. As described by them, it is not uncommon for people who have genuine claims, to arrive in Canada without any understanding of legal proceedings, with an instinctive fear of anyone clothed with governmental powers, who are unfamiliar with our language, who are traumatized, tired, and who do not have the faintest idea of what will befall them if they fail to make a refugee claim the first chance they

---

36 *An Act to Amend the Immigration Act*, S.C. 1988, c. 35, s. 45(2).

have. Particularly in the case of refugee women, who often have suffered sexual abuse, the reluctance to describe their personal ordeals may be especially acute.[37]

It is easy to see the conceptual link between the time of request and the safe country screens and the defect that is common to both. Each is aimed at a group of individuals who did not claim asylum the first chance they had even though, in the opinion of the Government, it would have been easy for them to have done so. Essentially, by irrebuttable presumptions, these different provisions of the Act treat all such persons as abusers and/or not in need of Canada's protection. The defect with both presumptions is that they are much too broad and guilty of stereotyping of the crudest kind. Legislative overkill once again. As we have seen, there are many legitimate reasons why a person may be reluctant to claim asylum in Canada, or any other country, on the first occasion when the opportunity presents itself.

People who fail to make a refugee claim the first chance they have are one of the major groups the Government thinks of as abusers and on that basis has denied them the opportunity even to make a refugee claim. In addition to these people, the Government has also singled out for special treatment individuals from countries with good records of human rights and from which Canada has recognized very few claims in the past. Under the terms of the new Act these people face the risk of being screened out at the second stage of the review process on the grounds that there is no "credible basis" for their claims. Although the credibility screen does not create an irrebuttable presumption that every claim which comes from such countries is abusive and manifestly unfounded, it does put individuals in this class at a serious disadvantage. Even though, in contrast with individuals who are unable to get past the first phase of the inquiry, this is not the only evidence the adjudicator and Board member can consider, there remains a real danger that a claimant's personal circumstances will be discounted on account of the historical record of the countries they are fleeing, and that they will be sent back to situations where they will face persecution and abuse. The screen operates like a reverse burden of proof. The suspicion shown to the Sikhs fleeing India, a democratic country

---

37 See the testimony of Ninette Kelley before the Senate Standing Committee on Legal and Constitutional Affairs 22/3/88, pp. 69-8, and of Michelle Falardeau-Ramsay, Immigration Appeal Board before the House of Commons Standing Committee on Employment and Immigration 27/8/87, afternoon sitting, pp. 46, 55. For an illustration of a case of this kind, see *Kaur v. M.E.I.*, Federal Court of Appeal #A1161-88, December 1989, in which it was held that parallel provisions limiting a person's right to introduce new evidence after an inquiry had been closed, violated s. 7 of the Charter. See generally *Handbook on Procedures and Criteria for Determining Refugee Status*, United Nations High Commissioner for Refugees, Geneva, 1988.

with generally a good record of human rights, shows how strong a bias these factors can exert. More generally it can be said that the credibility screen represents a particularly serious threat to those persons who are among the first to flee a new source of persecution and oppression.

The other danger posed by the credibility screen is that even if the adjudicator and the member of the Refugee Board do consider each person's individual circumstances, they could base their decision on whether the individual claimant's story struck them as credible rather than whether there was *any* credible basis for the claim. There is a risk, in other words, that this second phase could become a summary hearing on the merits of the case rather than a threshold test to determine whether the claimants have presented any evidence upon which they might be found to be Convention refugees. The second stage could become a credibility hearing, pure and simple. A person who has established a *prima facie* claim to be a refugee might be denied a full hearing before the Refugee Board simply because there was something in the person's demeanour or other evidence that led the decision makers to doubt the person's credibility. Even those from known refugee producing countries, and from which Canada has recognized claims in the past, could be screened out in this way.[38] Unlike the third stage of the process, however, the credibility of the claimant would be settled without all of the procedural safeguards, which are normally part of a full oral hearing, being in place. At this point in the process the claimants will not have the same opportunities to select their own counsel and prepare their cases that are available when a full oral hearing is scheduled. Nor are the decision makers as independent and impartial as those who preside over the third and substantive stage

---

38 It is interesting to note that there appeared to be some confusion as to how the screen should be applied even before it was made operational. For example, a directive from one senior Department official suggested that the test was primarily a subjective one. See Canada, Department of Immigration, "Program Delivery Strategy — 1989", Operations Memorandum IE 249 (December 22, 1988), p. 18.

More recently, in his testimony before the House of Commons Standing Committee on Labour, Employment and Immigration, the Director General, Refugee Affairs and Settlement Branch, suggested that there was a difference of opinion between the Immigration Department and the Refugee Division on how the test should be applied. In particular, he referred to a memo by the legal advisor to the Chair of the Refugee Board, advising that a person who may not appear credible in terms of his own testimony, could still have a credible basis for a claim. According to the Department of Immigration, however, a person who is not credible can rarely have a credible basis for a claim. For this reason the Department refused to circulate the memo to adjudicators and members of the Refugee Division as part of their training package. Canada, House of Commons, *Minutes of Proceedings and Evidence of the Standing Committee on Labour, Employment and Immigration*, No. 8 (May 25, 1989), p. 8:40.

of review.[39] Compounding all of this, like those who are caught by the "eligibility" and "time of request" screens, the danger to people found not to have a credible basis for their claims will be exacerbated by the fact that they will have no opportunity to appeal an adverse decision on the merits and will be subject to deportation almost overnight. For claimants who are rejected at this stage, it would be virtually impossible, owing to the very limited right of appeal, to prove that the credibility screen was being applied as something more than a minimum threshold test even if that in fact was how it was being used.

The ease with which the reviewer can identify ways in which Canada's new refugee determination procedure threatens the lives, liberty and security of the person of different groups of refugee claimants suggests this case will also conform to the pattern of analysis she has seen in every case she has considered in this Part. On the evidence available, the Canadian Council of Churches should have little difficulty in establishing that Canada's newest refugee law continues to represent a serious and substantial threat to human freedom and liberty. The imposition of two threshold inquiries, which cannot be appealed on their merits, puts the lives, liberty and security of untold numbers of genuine refugees at substantial risk. Indeed, in justifying this policy, prior to its enactment into law, no one even tried to deny that some individual claimants might be threatened. Rather than argue that the new procedure would work perfectly, the Government said that, with the limited resources available to it, and the possibility of error in all human institutions, it was simply impossible to design a system which would not involve some risk or threat to individuals who had genuine claims.

Now in all of the other cases which the reviewer has considered so far, it would be at this stage of the review process when the "onus" would shift. Having shown that the new refugee determination process threatens the lives, liberty and security of many persons it would be the Government's

---

39 Canada, House of Commons, *Minutes of Proceedings and Evidence of the Standing Committee on Labour, Employment and Immigration*, (August 27, 1987), note the testimony of Joseph Stern, Chairman, Refugee Status Advisory Committee, where he states that because adjudicators are Immigration Department officials, whose duties and careers are lodged firmly in the administration of the immigration programme, they are likely to bring immigration concerns into the adjudication of refugee claims which would be entirely inappropriate. See also Parliamentary Standing Committee on Labour, Employment and Immigration, *Fourth Report* (June 1985), where the Committee notes that in theory Immigration adjudicators should be non-affiliated with the Immigration Department and render independent judgments. However, according to many witnesses (including adjudicators themselves), adjudicators are often located in the same premises, even share the same support staff, and are often selected from within the Department. As a result a concern has been expressed that adjudicators possess an inherent enforcement bias which affects their decision in significant ways.

turn to start talking and show how a law, which threatens human rights and freedoms in such menacing ways, is consistent with the principles and tests set out in *Oakes*. In the refugee case, however, it will not be enough for the challengers to show that the new law threatens the lives and liberty of genuine refugee claimants before insisting that the Government and those defending the law begin to speak. Because the claim is based on section 7 of the Charter, which has a built-in qualifier, something else is required. A challenger's burden is heavier when it is based on one of the very broad and sweeping sections like section 7. In addition to proving that the law threatens the lives and liberty of refugee claimants, the complainants will be obliged to show that it does so in ways which offend the most basic principles of fairness and justice known in our legal system. Showing that a challenged law fails to respect "principles of fundamental justice" is a second hurdle anyone claiming the protection of section 7 must clear before they can expect the Court to allow them to sit and ask the Government to get to its feet and justify the policy choices it made.

In the present case, the challengers are not likely to have any more difficulty clearing this second hurdle than they did the first. Although the reviewer will know that the Court did not always follow its own advice,[40] it was quite explicit, on more than one occasion, that the principles of fundamental justice should be interpreted generously and in a way which would further the values and objects on which the Charter is based. All of the members of the Court recognized that to give these words a narrow meaning would be quite inconsistent with the purposive approach because it would increase the chances that individuals might be denied the rights and freedoms which section 7 protects. Indeed, the Court has already identified a number of principles of fundamental justice which seem to have direct application to the refugee case. Rather than having to persuade the Court to recognize some new principle of justice, the challengers will only need to ask the Court to apply principles it has already found imbedded in our legal and constitutional order.

At least four different principles of fundamental justice have already been identified by the Court which the new refugee determination procedure seems to transgress. Unquestionably the most relevant of these is the principle that where, as in the determination of whether a person is a genuine refugee, a serious issue of credibility is involved, and where the threat to a person's freedom is as basic as it is in cases of this kind, an oral hearing must be provided in which the person will be permitted not only to fully state his or her case but also to be fully informed of

---

40 The major exceptions, when the Court mistakenly adopted the conservative approach in its interpretation of s. 7, would include *R. v. Jones*, *R. v. Lyons*, and *B.C.G.E.U. v. A.G. B.C.*, *supra*, note 18.

the case he or she has to meet. It was this principle which was dispositive of Singh's complaint under the Charter and it should be controlling in this case as well. Although not all of the judges made reference to the Charter in upholding Singh's claim, it is clear that this was a point on which all of the members of the Court were agreed.[41]

That the new refugee determination process still does not respect what is one of the most basic principles of procedural justice known to our law, seems beyond dispute. All refugee claimants caught in the net of one of the preliminary screens either have no chance to state their case, and challenge the Minister's characterization of their claims, or they only have an opportunity for an abbreviated and expedited inquiry without the possibility of a full scale review. In the first phase of the review process, it is simply not possible to challenge either of the Minister's determinations that they have come from a country which is safe for them or that they represent a threat to the general welfare of Canada. At the second phase, if evidence pertaining to the claimant's individual circumstances is received, it will be considered in a setting which does not provide the procedures and safeguards normally applied when issues of credibility are at stake. In the truncated and expedited proceeding that is contemplated in the second phase, claimants will have only a very restricted opportunity to counter the Government's evidence that they are fleeing countries which generally have a good record on human rights and which, in Canada's experience, have not caused people to flee in fear of persecution in the past. In effect the Government has paid lip service to the Court's judgment in *Singh* by allowing refugee claimants to appear in person at the first two stages of the review process without giving them the substantial protections which a full hearing guarantees.

In addition to violating the right of refugee claimants to have a full oral hearing on the merits of their cases, and to be given an opportunity to know and meet the case against them, the new refugee determination process also offends several basic principles of justice embedded in international law. In the *B.C. Motor Vehicle Reference*, Antonio Lamer singled out international conventions as a rich source of principles of fundamental justice.[42] In terms of the challenge to Canada's new refugee law, this would refer the Court to the 1951 *Convention Relating to the Status of Refugees* and to the *Protocol* which was added sixteen years later.[43] As interpreted by the agency charged with overseeing the *Convention* and

---

41 See the concurring judgment of Jean Beetz, *supra*, note 2, at 433-435.

42 *Ref. re s. 94(2) Motor Vehicle Act (B.C.)*, *supra*, note 17.

43 *Convention Relating to the Status of Refugees*, July 28, 1951, United Nations Treaty Series, Vol. 189, p. 137; *Protocol Relating to the Status of Refugees*, January 31, 1967, United Nations Treaty Series, Vol. 606, p. 267.

Protocol, the norms of international law contained in these treaties require, among other things, that refugee laws will not be designed in a way which will: (i) expose persons to the risk of being "refouled", that is of being returned to countries where their lives or freedom will be endangered;[44] (ii) refuse asylum solely on the ground that it could have been sought from another State;[45] (iii) exclude from consideration refugee claims made by individuals who failed to meet one of the formal requirements concerning the timing or making of a refugee claim;[46] (iv) authorize an official, other than the authority competent to determine refugee status, to screen out claims as manifestly unfounded or abusive without enabling the claimant to have the negative decision reviewed before rejection or forceable removal from the country;[47] and (v) prohibit a person who is not recognized as a refugee, a reasonable time to appeal for a formal reconsideration of the decision.[48]

From the description of how the new refugee determination procedure is designed, it should be clear to the reviewer that, in one way or another, it offends all of these requirements. In particular, the screening mechanisms expose refugees to the risk of being returned, either directly or indirectly, to countries where their freedom and even their lives may be threatened. The safe country screen explicitly denies individuals the opportunity of having their refugee claims adjudicated on the ground that they could have made their claims in other countries they passed through on their way

---

44 Article 33 of the *Convention* obligates signatory States to protect a refugee from expulsion or return, in any manner whatsoever, to a country where the person's life or freedom may be endangered, except a refugee who is a danger to the security of the country which the refugee is in, or who having been convicted of a particular serious crime, is a danger to the community of that country. *Convention, ibid.,* Article 33. Moreover, signatory States have reaffirmed the fundamental importance of the observance of this principle of *non-refoulement* " — both at the border and within the territory of a State — of persons who may be subjected to persecution if returned to their country of origin irrespective of whether or not they have been formally recognized as refugees". *Conclusions on the International Protection of Refugees,* Adopted by the Executive Committee of the United Nations High Commissioner for Refugees Programme [hereinafter *Ex. Comm. Conclusion*], No. 6 (XXVIII), 1977, Non-Refoulement, para. c. A refugee who is not entitled to remain in a signatory State, must be given a "reasonable period and all necessary facilities to obtain admission into another country". *Convention, supra,* note 43, Article 31.

45 *Ex. Comm., Conclusion, ibid.,* No. 15 (XXX), Refugees Without an Asylum Country, para. (h)(iv).

46 *Ex. Comm., Conclusion, ibid.,* No. 15 (XXX) Refugees Without an Asylum Country, para. (i).

47 *Ex. Comm. Conclusion, ibid.,* No. 30 (XXXIV), The Problem of Manifestly Unfounded Or Abusive Application for Refugee Status or Asylum, para. (e).

48 *Ex. Comm. Conclusion, ibid.,* No. 8 (XXVIII), Determination of Refugee Status, para. (e)(vi).

to Canada. As well, as we have just seen, the new Act is quite categorical in denying persons who, for whatever reason, fail to make a claim for refugee status at the beginning of the inquiry, the opportunity to do so at a later date. In addition, the determination of whether there is a credible basis for a claim will be made by a tribunal not wholly competent to determine refugee status, and persons screened out at this stage will have no opportunity to have the decision reviewed before being removed from Canada. Finally, as the reviewer will have seen, no one whose claim is rejected is *guaranteed* the chance to appeal for a formal reconsideration of their case.

As well as violating the principles of fundamental justice which the Court identified in *Singh* and the *B.C. Motor Vehicle Reference*, Canada's new refugee determination procedure also seems deficient against two other principles recognized by different members of the Court in the *Morgentaler* case.[49] The first of these might be characterized as the illusory principle. As described by Brian Dickson and Antonio Lamer another tenet of fundamental justice is that if a law provides a defence or an exception to a prohibition or a rule, it should not be designed in such a way as to make it practically impossible to use. It was on this principle that these two judges ruled that Canada's abortion law was unconstitutional. They said that the hospital abortion committees, which controlled access to therapeutic abortions, contained so many barriers to their own operation that in many instances the possibility of therapeutic abortions was quite illusory.

A similar aura of unreality pervades the Government's new refugee determination process. Illusory is precisely the word critics of the new law used to describe the review mechanisms available to claimants who fail to pass either the first or the second preliminary stages of the determination process. Although entitled to ask the Federal Court to review any adverse decision of the Immigration officer and the member of the Refugee Board, this review is entirely discretionary and is available only with the permission of the Court; is limited to questions of law and jurisdictional error; and, most egregiously, may take place long after the claimant has been expelled from the country. Once returned to the country in which the protection was inadequate, if it existed at all, any opportunity to appeal, even on the merits, would be completely illusory and of no value whatever to the claimant. The threat posed to the life, liberty and security of genuine refugee claimants by such review procedures is certainly no less, and in some cases manifestly greater, than the danger hospital abortion committees posed to women.

A second principle of fundamental justice that figured in the *Mor-*

---

49   *R. v. Morgentaler, supra*, note 18.

gentaler case was the principle of alternative means. Although they did not refer to the principle by name, it effectively formed the basis of Jean Beetz's and Willard Estey's decision that the procedure by which women had to procure an abortion violated their rights in section 7. They said Canada's abortion law violated the principles of fundamental justice, not so much because it made its own provisions illusory, than because it imposed risks to the physical and emotional security of women that were completely unnecessary. In their words, "An administrative structure made up of *unnecessary* rules, which result in an additional risk to the health of pregnant women is manifestly unfair and does not conform to the principles of fundamental justice." (Emphasis added).

That the principle of alternative means should also qualify as a principle of fundamental justice should not be surprising.[50] It is derived directly from the purposive method of interpretation and from the recognition that the Charter itself is an essential source of principles of fundamental justice. Nor can there be much doubt about its relevance to the instant case. Indeed virtually every change effected by the new legislation has been challenged on this ground.[51] Certainly in terms of the procedure by which a person's status as a convention refugee will be determined, there is little likelihood that any of the screening devices used in the Act can meet this principle of fundamental justice. As the reviewer has seen, all of them are drawn in ways which are unnecessarily broad and which, because of that, put the lives, liberty and security of many refugees at risk. All the abusers they are aimed at catching could be identified and dealt with by methods which were not nearly so threatening to human rights. As proposed by virtually every religious, civil libertarian and legal group with an interest in the treatment of refugees, a simple, one-step, oral hearing on the merits, with the opportunity for a centralized, paper appeal, could accomplish all of the Government's aims of clearing the system of people who are not genuine claimants as, if not more,

---

50 It seems, implicitly, to have been used by the Court in *R. v. Vaillancourt, supra,* note 18, and by Bertha Wilson in the judgments she wrote in *Ref. re s. 94(2) Motor Vehicle Act (B.C.), supra,* note 17, and *R. v. Lyons, supra,* note 18. Cf. the Court's failure to be sensitive to the question of alternative means in *B.C.G.E.U. v. A.G. B.C., supra,* note 18.

51 Among the other amendments to the *Immigration Act* that have been challenged on the basis that they do not meet the second proportionality principle of alternative means are: the automatic and indefinite detention of persons, other than Canadian citizens or permanent residents, where a security certificate has been issued; the detention of those suspected of being members of an inadmissible class without providing them an absolute right to know the case against them; the imposition of serious criminal sanctions for acts taken in accordance with conscience or religious beliefs and/or in accordance with the duty of a barrister and solicitor; and the extensive search and seizure powers in the investigation of possible contraventions of the Act.

effectively and expeditiously as the three-tiered system the Government designed.[52]

In the end, then, the reviewer should find that the fact the challenge to Canada's new refugee determination process is based on a section, like section 7, which requires challengers to show that their rights have been limited in a particular way, is not likely to change the conduct of the proceedings very much. As with every other case the reviewer has considered so far, it is unlikely that counsel for the churches will be on their feet very long. Even though they will have to prove not only that the challenged law threatens the lives, liberty and security of large numbers of people, but also that it does so in ways which offend our most fundamental sense of fairness and justice, it seems certain that the first stage of the Court's evaluation of the new refugee law will be completed as quickly as in any of the other cases the reviewer has considered. In practice, the obligation of having had to meet a second criterion, to establish that a law impinges on the constitutional entitlements which section 7 guarantees, will not have proven to be much of an additional burden at all.

Indeed, paradoxical as it may seem, not only will the presence of the second hurdle not have extended the first stage of judicial review very much, it seems likely that it will have the effect of shortening the length of the hearing overall. Having established that Canada's new refugee policy is flawed on both of these dimensions, counsel for the churches will have made it practically impossible for the Government and its supporters to justify it under section 1. Even though it has not taken much effort on their part, by surmounting the second hurdle which section 7 requires challengers to clear, counsel for the churches will have effectively ensured that the second stage of the process of constitutional review will be as short as the first.

The Court's performance with section 7 over the course of the first

---

52 See for example, Canadian Bar Association, Immigration Law Section, testimony and supporting brief to the Senate Standing Committee on Legal and Constitutional Affairs, *Proceedings of the Senate Standing Committee on Legal and Constitutional Affairs*, Issue No. 28 (September 29, 1987), and the testimony and supporting brief of the Inter-Church Committee for Refugees, *Proceedings of the Senate Standing Committee on Legal and Constitutional Affairs*, Issue No. 42 (November 5, 1987). According to these commentators, this alternative is likely to be faster and cheaper because it avoids the duplication that unavoidably takes place in the Government's system for people who make it all the way through.

Standing alone against the view that oral hearings reduce the risk of the "refoulement" of genuine refugees is Michael Mandel who argues that oral hearings have not substantially improved the justice of our criminal law and should not be expected to help refugee claimants either. See Michael Mandel, *The Charter of Rights and the Legalization of Politics in Canada, supra*, note 3, at 181-182.

five years shows very clearly that where a challenger is able to meet both of the criteria which section 7 contains, it is extremely difficult for the Government to offer adequate reasons to justify the law under section 1. In fact, the record shows that in every case in which the Court accepted the challenger's claim, that a law did impinge on the constitutional guarantees protected in section 7, all of the judges were agreed that the Government could not justify its behaviour under section 1.[53] Although, over the course of the first five years everyone on the Court eventually accepted the theoretical possibility of a Government being able to justify the enactment of laws of this kind, the Court was very clear that the circumstances in which it would be able to do so would be rare indeed.[54] If the Court is true to its past decisions, it is not likely it will be very tolerant of arguments that the Government was justified in passing a law which threatens some of the most basic freedoms of people who are among the most disadvantaged in ways which are so fundamentally unfair.

This would seem to be especially true given the basis on which the Government defended its new refugee policy. Ultimately, it will be recalled, the Government justified its choice based on arguments of administrative cost and convenience. Government and its officials said it was impossible to design a refugee determination procedure which would be as expeditious and inexpensive as their three-tiered choice if a full hearing and an opportunity for a substantive review were made available in every case.[55] Administrative cost and convenience, it was said, were the reasons why all of the alternative policies, which provided a full oral hearing to all refugee claimants, were inferior to the three-tiered process the Government ultimately chose.

Neither legally nor factually would the reviewer expect anyone on the Court to be impressed by claims of this kind. As a factual matter, as those with experience in refugee determination procedures have already pointed out,[56] whatever savings will be gained by denying a full hearing

---

53 See, e.g., *Ref. re s. 94(2) Motor Vehicle Act; Singh v. M.E.I.*, *supra*, note 17; *R. v. Morgentaler, R. v. Vaillancourt; R. v. Gamble, supra*, note 18; see also *R. v. Stevens, supra*, note 18, *per* Wilson.

54 Although Bertha Wilson questioned whether a law which offended the principles of fundamental justice could ever be justified under s. 1 in *Ref. re s. 94(2) Motor Vehicle Act, supra*, note 17, she eventually deferred to her colleagues on this point in *R. v. Morgentaler, supra*, note 18. John Whyte made the same observation even before these cases had been decided. See his "Fundamental Justice: The Scope and Application of Section 7 of the Charter", in the *Canadian Charter of Rights and Freedoms*, Canadian Institute for the Administration of Justice (Yvon Blais, 1983), p. 31.

55 See testimony of Raphael Girard, Coordinator, Refugee Task Force, before House of Commons Standing Committee on Employment and Immigration, 27/8/87, *Minutes of Proceedings and Evidence*.

56 See note 52, *supra*.

to those declared to be ineligible and to those without a credible basis for their claims will be largely, if not completely, offset by the duplication and repetition that is involved in processing the cases that make it all the way through. For these cases, the first and second stages of the review process will have only served to delay and increase the cost of determining whether a person has a genuine refugee claim or not.

It seems equally certain that, as a matter of constitutional law, arguments about administrative cost and convenience will not impress the Court. That the judges will not listen long to arguments of this kind, at least where substantial freedoms are at stake, could hardly be clearer.[57] Indeed in *Singh*, and again in the *B.C. Motor Vehicle Reference*, the Court was very explicit that considerations of administrative cost and convenience could not justify the enactment of laws which threatened the most basic aspects of human freedom. Although the rule may be otherwise when less pressing freedoms are at stake, where lives are endangered and physical liberty is threatened the Court has been quite clear that "only in cases arising out of exceptional conditions, such as natural disasters, the outbreak of war, epidemics and the like will arguments of administrative cost and convenience prevail". Absent such extreme circumstances, considerations of human life and personal security will always weigh more heavily in the balance.

The clarity of the Court's position on what it understands section 7 to guarantee means that the Government's new refugee determination procedure should be invalidated on this basis alone. It also means, as a practical matter, that there would be no need for the Court to consider how it would evaluate the refugee determination procedure against the equality guarantees in section 15. Once the new law is found to offend one section of the Charter, the Court will declare it to be null and void and it will have no further force or effect. If considerations of cost and convenience cannot justify threatening the lives, liberty, and security of people under one section of the Charter, they cannot logically justify allowing them to be put at risk under another. If lives, liberty and security of the person weigh more heavily than concerns about administrative efficiency it cannot matter whether the Canadian Council of Churches bases its claim on section 7 or 15. In either case the relative weights of the competing interests would remain unaffected and the scales of the balance would look the same.

However, and even though it is not strictly necessary to do so, the

---

57 See the cases cited in Chapter 5 at note 50, *supra*. It might be noted that in the only case in which considerations of administrative convenience carried the day, the infringement imposed by the law was regarded as being of a relatively trivial or marginal kind. See *R. v. Jones, supra*, note 18.

reviewer may find it worthwhile to briefly consider how, if it did turn its mind to the question, the Court would evaluate the refugee determination process against the equality guarantees of section 15. This is so even though the Court had much less to say about section 15 than section 7 over the first five years and even though, at times, in the one judgment in which it considered this section at any length, the judges seem confused in their understanding of what equality means.[58] Even on the very restricted interpretation the Court gave to section 15, it seems certain that refugee claimants would be seen to fall within its protection and that the Government's new refugee determination procedure will be judged to be deficient against the Charter's equality guarantees as well.

The churches, in fact, have attacked more than one section of the new refugee law as offending section 15.[59] Of these, the review mechanisms, which are a central part of the determination process, seem particularly flawed. As noted earlier, those who are screened out at the initial phases, and those who receive a negative decision on the merits of their claim, have exceedingly limited opportunities for review. Aside

---

58 As we noted in our analysis of the Court's performance in Part One, even though the judges purported to adopt a purposeful and liberal approach in their interpretation to s. 15, in rejecting the 'similarly situated' test, the Court really abandoned that method and in so doing imposed a very substantial constraint on its reach. For a discussion of the mistakes made by the Court in its analysis and rejection of the "similarly situated test", see Part One, Chapter 4, *supra* at note 6. As a result of failing to apply the similarly situated test in a purposeful way, the Court was eventually led to the conclusion that while lawyers who are citizens of other countries are members of a disadvantaged class, unorganized workers and their dependents as well as persons charged with murder outside of Alberta are not. Compare *Andrews v. Law Society of B.C.*, *supra*, note 1, with *Ref. re Workers' Compensation Act* (1989), 56 D.L.R. (4th) 766 and *R. v. Turpin*, [1989] 1 S.C.R. 1296.

In the instant case the similarly situated test would have no application because refugee claimants will almost certainly be found to be members of the kind of discrete and insular minorities which s. 15 has been interpreted to protect. If, as in *Andrews*, non-citizens who are lawyers qualify for admission to this group, refugee claimants must be included as well.

59 Among the other provisions of the Act that have been challenged as offending s. 15 are: (i) the safe country screen which treats refugee claimants coming from countries on the safe country list differently from those who are already in Canada or who have come to Canada without having been in, or passed through, a country on the prescribed list; (ii) the provisions which permit Convention refugees recognized elsewhere to establish that they have a credible basis to fear persecution in that country but which denies a non-recognized refugee coming from a prescribed safe country the same opportunity; (iii) the sections of the Act which deny refugee claimants for whom a security certificate has been issued and against whom a deportation or conditional deportation order has been made, the same appeal rights as those who are under the same orders but who are not the subject of a security certificate; (iv) the provisions which permit the Minister to seek a determination that a person ceases to be a Convention refugee without providing refugee claimants a corresponding right to seek a rehearing of a negative decision

from the time constraints that make review illusory for those who have been screened out, the law also imposes a requirement that all claimants who want to challenge a decision denying their refugee status must secure the permission of a judge of the Federal Court. In contrast with other individuals affected by rulings of federal Government agencies and officials, and who have unrestricted access to this Court, refugee claimants do not have an automatic entitlement to have an unfavourable decision reviewed. Indeed, in breaking with all precedent, refugee claimants are even denied the opportunity to appeal a refusal by the Court to give its permission to have the rejection of the refugee application reviewed.

Requiring refugee claimants to obtain the permission of the Court before a negative decision can be reviewed is only one feature of the new procedure which discriminates against refugee claimants.[60] Even if the Court agrees to listen to a disappointed claimant's story, it will not bother with the merits of the case. Even if a claimant is successful in persuading a Court to take a second look at the case, the review will be restricted to technical points of law. In contrast with criminal offences, no matter how trivial and small, refugee claimants are not allowed to ask for a second judgment of a decision that may well threaten their lives.

The failure to provide a meaningful opportunity for someone to have a second look at every case violates section 15 by treating refugee claimants differently from other people who are affected — often much less seriously — by decisions of the federal Government's agents and tribunals. As well, failure to incorporate an independent, centralized reviewing agency treats each refugee claimant in a way which violates section 15 because it allows for the possibility of inconsistent decision-making across the country.[61] Without somebody having the responsibility of overseeing the operation

---

that a person is a Convention refugee on the grounds of new or additional evidence such as changed conditions in the country from which the person claims fear of persecution; and (v) the sections of the Act which permit the Minister to apply to have a decision that a person is a Convention refugee reconsidered on the grounds that it was obtained by fraudulent means, misrepresentation or suppression of material fact yet which do not provide refugee claimants a corresponding right to have a negative determination reconsidered on the same grounds.

60 Actually, the *Immigration Act* discriminates in this way against everyone who is affected by its terms. People whose applications to immigrate are denied, as well as refugee claimants, must receive the "leave" of the Court before it will act positively on their request.

61 Canada, House of Commons, *Minutes of Proceedings and Evidence of the Standing Committee on Labour, Employment and Immigration*, testimony of Michelle Falardeau-Ramsay, Chairperson Immigration Appeal Board, (August 27, 1987). She stressed that, in her experience as Chairperson of the Immigration Appeal Board, with a regionalized setup, there could be no guarantee that refugee claimants would receive equal treatment in the absence of a centralized reviewing mechanism.

of the new procedure, there is a real danger that Immigration adjudicators and members of the Refugee Board will apply different standards in deciding whether a person is eligible to make, and has a credible basis for, a refugee claim. Certainly at the second phase of the procedure, these decision-makers exercise some discretion in deciding who is entitled to a full hearing on the merits, and in the absence of a centralized reviewing agency, there can be no certainty either that the same standards will be used across the country or that, even if they are, they will be applied in the same way.

To the extent that the Government's new refugee policy fails to provide any control against the possibility that different standards are being used across the country to determine if a person has a credible basis to make a refugee claim, it clearly offends the core entitlement which section 15 guarantees. It means that individuals, who in all relevant respects are situated in exactly the same circumstances, will enjoy unequal measures of benefit and protection from the new law. Some individuals may find it relatively easy to pass the second screen and obtain a full hearing on the merits of their case, while others, whose circumstances are exactly the same, will be denied that opportunity. Only by ensuring everyone can appeal an adverse decision to a body which has overall responsibility for the system as a whole, can the law ensure that all claimants enjoy the equal benefit and protection of its terms. Without such a central reviewing agency the reviewer would expect the Court to say that the Government's new refugee determination procedure fails to measure up to the constitutional norms guaranteed in section 15 as well as those entrenched in section 7.

In the result, the Court's earlier pronouncements on both section 7 and section 15 make it very unlikely that the lawyers for the Government will be on their feet much longer than were counsel for the churches. Reflecting the fact that the refugee law seems to be the most seriously flawed piece of legislation the reviewer has considered so far, it is likely that the second phase of the review process will be over even more quickly than the first. In the event, the Government will be faced with the same choice it confronted following the Court's earlier ruling in *Singh*. On the one hand, it could insist on the sovereignty of the popular will and rely on its powers under section 33 to re-enact, for a third time, a law which is otherwise constitutionally deficient. It clearly has the right to do so.[62]

---

62 On the importance of s. 33, see P. Weiler, "Rights and Judges in a Democracy: A New Canadian Version" (1984), 18 J.L. Reform 51. For a critical comment, see L. Weinrib, "Learning to Live with the Override" (1990), 35 McGill L.J. 542. For a description of its historical roots, see A. Bayefsky, "The Judicial Function Under the Canadian Charter of Rights and Freedoms", in Bayefsky (ed.), *Legal Theory Meets Legal Practice* (Edmonton: Academic Printing & Publishing, 1988).

Alternatively, it could finally accept the judgment of nine, relatively independent "social critics" and, as many expected it would after the decision in *Singh*, design a refugee determination procedure that is consistent with our highest ideals of social justice and procedural fairness.[63] To follow the latter course would mean reformulating the process to ensure universal access, with an oral hearing and at least a paper review on the merits, for everyone who makes a refugee claim in our country. From the Court's earlier decisions in *Singh* and the *B.C. Motor Vehicle* reference that, at a minimum, is the kind of procedural justice our Constitution requires.[64]

Whichever route the Government chooses to follow, the believer's point to the sceptics will have been made. If the Government chooses the first option, and insists on its right to design its refugee law without regard to the most basic principles and values upon which our whole constitutional system of social relations is based, the sceptics' claim that the branches of Government which are directly elected by the people are most responsive to the needs of the disadvantaged will sound hollow indeed. It will show very clearly that the politicians are more likely than the judges to use their law making powers in heavy handed ways when they are dealing with individuals, like refugee claimants, who have little or no influence in the processes and institutions of politics. Alternatively, if the Government follows the Court's advice, and provides a full and fair oral hearing and review for everyone who claims the need of our protection, the progressive character of judicial review will have been established beyond doubt. In the context of how refugee policy has evolved over the years, the Court would have established itself as the most dependable forum in which the most desperate people could insist that our society pay attention to their needs.

In either event, with this analysis of how the challenge initiated by the Canadian Council of Churches should turn out, the reviewer can assume that she has done all that can reasonably be required to demonstrate to the sceptics that judicial review can have both an objective and progressive influence on our system of government, at least as it is practised on the model in *Oakes*. It is neither practical nor necessary for the reviewer to continue indefinitely reviewing cases now being litigated in the lower courts. At some point the reviewer is entitled to insist that the sample of cases she has chosen for review, fairly and effectively responds to the doubts sceptics are inclined to harbour about giving courts the power to

---

63 See, e.g., J.H. Grey, "Comment on *Singh v. M.E.I.*" (1986), 31 McGill L.J. 496; C. Wydrzynski, "Immigration Law — Determination of Refugee Status" (1986), 64 Can. Bar Rev. 172.

64 Grey, *ibid.*, at 500.

evaluate laws against a written bill of rights.

In bringing the conversation with the sceptics to a close, the reviewer can claim to have touched upon all of the major rights and freedoms which the Charter guarantees. All of the fundamental rights and freedoms enumerated in section 2, the democratic rights in section 3, the rights to life, liberty and security of the person guaranteed in section 7 and to the equal benefit and protection of the law in section 15 have been canvassed and the results have always been the same. From all of the cases reviewed in this Part, adding a process of constitutional review to the way we govern ourselves emerges as a very fair and a very effective way for those who are least advantaged in our society to make their influence felt. Having taken the sceptics' most basic doubts about the very legitimacy of law as seriously as she can, the reviewer can in good faith sit down and compose the positive review she wanted to write at the end of Part One. The reviewer can, in good conscience, tell her readership that the Supremes should give a performance that can be appreciated by anyone who really does have the good sense of a talking head.

PART III

Stage Production:
The Procedure of Constitutional Review

9

The Real World of Constitutional Review

Any reviewer who had been able to identify a series of cases showing radical sceptics how the model in *Oakes* could actually enhance the democratic and progressive character of our system of government might be forgiven if she thought that the actual writing of a positive, up-beat review would be a relatively easy and straightforward task. Certain of the objectivity and integrity of the model, the most obvious, and certainly the simplest, approach would be just to summarize the analysis she had followed in Part One. The review could be broken down into three distinct parts. The beginning would describe the two different styles of judging displayed by the Court over the course of the first five years it worked with the Charter. It would recount how, in years one and two, and frequently in year five as well, the judges spoke in unison and with a single voice, while in the period in between each of them seemed intent on developing his or her own ideas about what the Charter meant, and a much more pluralistic style of judging held sway. The reviewer could advise her readers that by the end of year five, there were almost as many views about the Charter as there were judges in the Court. To dramatize the extent of the schism, the reviewer might highlight the performances of Bertha Wilson on the one hand and William McIntyre and Jean Beetz on the other by contrasting their radically different understandings of their role in reviewing the constitutionality of Canadian law.

The second part of the review would be given over to an evaluation of the two broad approaches that developed on the Court. Here the reviewer could explain why, on the one hand, the more liberal method embraced most consistently by Bertha Wilson, Antonio Lamer, and to a lesser extent Brian Dickson, was the correct approach and how, on the other, the ideas and doctrines favoured by William McIntyre, Jean Beetz, and their more conservative brethren were defective and flawed constitutionally. By finding fault with the Court's performance when the conservative view prevailed, and the Court refused to exercise its powers of review, the reviewer could finish off her piece by showing how the liberal approach fits comfortably within and indeed strengthens the most basic values on which our tradition of democratic and progressive government is based.

The progressive influence that the preferred model of constitutional review can exert could be summarized in a single paragraph. The protection the Court extended to people caught in the criminal justice system, refugees, and women, together with the relief which Wilson and her liberal colleagues were willing to provide in cases like the extradition and labour trilogies, or in the challenge brought by the Acadiens in New Brunswick, shows quite clearly how constitutional review can enrich the progressive quality of those social policies which are eventually enacted into law.

Similarly, the ways in which constitutional review can enhance the democratic quality of our system of government would be easy to describe. As we have seen, democratic values and the prerogatives of Parliament are not seriously threatened by the liberal approach. On the model in *Oakes*, constitutional review and the role of the Court is mostly about means. Almost never did the judges question the motives or reasons which caused the law makers to act. On this theory of constitutional review, the primary role of the third branch of government is to guarantee a measure of moderation is always applied in the exercise of all legal authority, whatever its source. In all of the cases in which the liberal method prevailed, the Court's role in the policy-making process was, essentially, to ensure there were no alternative policies available to a Government which would have allowed it to accomplish its objectives in a way which interfered with human freedom less. In non-legal terms, a reviewer could liken the role of the Supremes to that of a social critic, checking to see that legal authority is used in a way which respects a very basic and very conventional principle of distributive justice and social welfare.[1] To underscore, and close off, on the democratic character of constitutional review, the reviewer might point to some of the cases she considered in the second Part to show her readers that, when it is working most effectively, it can even stimulate activity in the political arena and cause politicians to correct earlier excesses on their own.

Easy to describe, in terms familiar to policy makers at large, the

---

1 In economist's terms, the principle is known as the Pareto criterion. In the jargon of distributive justice it has been called the maximization principle and it lies at the root of John Rawl's difference principle as well. See J. Rawls, *A Theory of Justice* (Harvard, 1971). As we noted in Part One, the third proportionality principle can also be described as a utilitarian principle of economic efficiency or justice. See Part One, Chapter 4, *supra*, note 98.

reviewer would not anticipate that the actual writing would take her very long. A short, snappy, up-beat review seems not only the right kind of piece to write, it seems very "do-able" as well. Nor would the reviewer anticipate that there would be any difficulty in getting her review published. Certainly if she submitted it to one of the law reviews, where essays of this kind are conventionally put, it would be grabbed up right away. Even if it were slightly unorthodox, in personalizing the ideas and decisions of individual judges, a review exploring the development of such an important new body of law would meet all of the standard criteria to which essays in law journals are expected to conform.

On reflection, however, it is not likely that a reviewer who was intent on writing a positive review about the Charter, and the performance of the Court, would want to submit it to a journal of that kind. There would be a rather jarring inconsistency in writing about the way in which judges and the Court can enhance the democratic quality of our system of government and then burying it in a journal where it would, for the most part, be lost to everyone not trained in the law. If the reviewer intended to hail the democratic and progressive influence which the Charter can be expected to have on our system of government, she would want to consider vehicles which would reach a wider readership than those who subscribe to law reviews.

Once a reviewer began to consider alternative places where she might publish her comments and ideas, however, it is unlikely her initial optimism, in being able to dash off a review simply by repackaging and summarizing the kind of analysis she followed in Part One, would be sustained very long. A moment's reflection would lead to the realization that publishing outside traditional law journals would require that something be added to the review. While it might be adequate for an academic law journal, a purely theoretical piece would not likely hold as much attraction for a review which tried to reach a wider and more general audience.[2] For the latter group, such a review would probably be seen as too abstract and not nearly practical enough. In addition to a theoretical discussion of how the Court's new function could be integrated with the most basic precepts and traditions of our system of government, lay readers would want to know something more about the detailed, day-to-day, nitty gritty practice and procedure by which the Court's new role was being performed.

---

2 I should say that in suggesting a lay audience would be less attracted to a purely theoretical review than lawyers, I do not mean to imply the latter group would not have any interest in the practical questions of process and cost. My only point is that lawyers would be more likely to accept a purely theoretical piece on its own terms and not insist that the practical and institutional questions which would bother lay readers be addressed in the same review.

They would also, almost certainly, be curious about the personalities of the judges and the backgrounds from which they came. They would want to know very basic things, like how a constitutional challenge is actually initiated and how long, on average, the whole show is likely to take. As well, they would likely want a direct answer to the question of how much a performance like this was going to cost. Only if they were satisfied about the institutional integrity of the Court could a reviewer reasonably expect a non-legal readership to put its trust in the Charter and the process of constitutional review.

Before a reviewer could submit a review which would be of interest to a non-legal audience, she would have to turn her mind to, and write something about, the institutional and procedural setting in which the Court's performance had taken place. However, as soon as she begins to reflect on these matters it is likely that, very quickly, she will despair of there being any possibility of writing a positive review. The moment she begins to think about the practical and procedural aspects of the Court's performance, it is certain she will be struck by a glaring inconsistency between the theory of judicial review that underlies the model in *Oakes* and the practical reality of how constitutional complaints are actually resolved.[3] From the perspective of anyone actually contemplating challenging the constitutionality of some law, the process of judicial review will appear in a very different and indeed in a very negative light. To their eyes, rather than the democratic and progressive institution the theory describes, judicial review will likely appear as the very regressive and anti-democratic institution which the sceptics have always claimed it to be.

Democratically, the hard reality is that there is almost no public participation in the appointment of the nine people who are entrusted with these powers of review. To make matters worse, once appointed they remain essentially unaccountable and unknown to the public for the rest of their lives. Notwithstanding the widespread condemnation of the existing

---

3 One part of this inquiry that a reviewer will find reassuring is that when the members of the Court addressed these procedural issues themselves, the basic liberal-conservative division reappears. See, e.g., *R. v. Mills* (1986), 29 D.L.R. (4th) 161; *R. v. Rahey* (1987), 39 D.L.R. (4th) 481; *R. v. Smith* (1988), 40 D.L.R. (4th) 435. In *Mills* and *Rahey*, the Court was faced with the question of when a person charged with an offence could raise a constitutional question and how quickly he could process an appeal. Characteristically, the Court divided on this question with Lamer, Wilson and Dickson taking the more liberal position and McIntyre, Beetz, and La Forest favouring a slower and less direct route. Note also in *R. v. Smith* how, standing alone, William McIntyre would have denied standing to persons challenging a mandatory, minimum sentence rule who themselves had not been incarcerated under it. Shortly after the curtain fell on the performance we reviewed in Part One, the Court unanimously endorsed McIntyre's approach on the question of how constitutional appeals would be processed. See *R. v. Meltzer*, [1989] 1 S.C.R. 1764.

procedure, appointment to the Supreme Court of Canada continues to be done in secret and behind closed doors. There is, practically speaking, no involvement by members of the public, or by their elected representatives, except for a small group who belong, or are close, to the Government and in particular to the Prime Minister and the Minister of Justice. Traditionally, most appointments are considered to be within the sole discretion of the Minister of Justice who acts in consultation with the Prime Minister, as well as with selected members of the provincial Governments and Canada's legal elite. Once appointed, members of the Court are essentially immune from any official review and, unless they choose to retire voluntarily, are guaranteed their positions until age 75.[4]

In addition to its very anti-democratic underpinnings, it will appear to those starting a challenge that judicial review is very expensive and regressive as well. As others have observed,[5] and a review of the cases heard by the Court in its first five years confirms,[6] judicial review is a game which plays to those who are already powerful and well-to-do. Access to the Court is really only available to people who are themselves very wealthy or who have the support of interest groups with sufficient resources to fund a constitutional challenge. Notwithstanding the concern expressed by various members of the Court that judicial review not become another

---

4 For a brief review and criticism of the existing system of appointment, see J. Ziegel, "Federal Judicial Appointments in Canada: The Time is Ripe for Change" (1987), 37 U.T.L.J. 1. See also P. Russell, "Constitutional Reform of the Judicial Branch: Symbolic vs. Operational Considerations", 1984 C.J.P.S. 227. For a more general and wide-ranging critique of the undemocratic role played by the Court in the "legalization of politics", see M. Mandel, *The Charter of Rights and the Legalization of Politics in Canada* (Toronto: Wall & Thompson, 1989). For arguments that criticisms about the democratic character of judicial review are essentially misconceived or at least exaggerated, see B. Langille, "The Jurisprudence of Despair, Again" (1989), 23 U.B.C. L. Rev. 3; and P. Weiler, "Rights and Judges in a Democracy: A New Canadian Version" (1984), 18 Jnl. L. Reform 51, 65.

5 See, e.g., M. Mandel, *The Charter of Rights and the Legalization of Politics in Canada*, *ibid.*, p. 43; Roy Romanow, "And Justice for Whom?" (1986), 16 Man. L.J. 102. See also E. McWhinney, *Supreme Courts and Judicial Law Making: Constitutional Tribunals and Constitutional Review* (Martinus Nijhoff Publishers, 1986), p. 101.

6 It is impossible not to notice how those who already do very well and enjoy considerable influence in our country's affairs, such as business interests (see *R. v. Big M Drug Mart* (1985), 18 D.L.R. (4th) 321; *R.W.D.S.U. v. Dolphin Delivery* (1987), 33 D.L.R. (4th) 174; *R.W.D.S.U. v. Saskatchewan* (1987), 38 D.L.R. (4th) 277), lawyers (see, e.g., *Skapinker v. Law Society of Upper Canada* (1984), 9 D.L.R. (4th) 161; *Andrews v. Law Society of B.C.* (1989), 56 D.L.R. (4th) 1; *Black v. Law Society of Alberta* (1989), 58 D.L.R. (4th) 319), doctors (see *R. v. Thibault*, [1988] 1 S.C.R. 1033), as well as powerful and well-financed minority groups, such as women (*R. v. Morgentaler* (1988), 44 D.L.R. (4th) 385), and the Anglophones of Quebec (*Ford v. Quebec* (1989), 54 D.L.R. (4th) 577) were quick to take advantage of the Charter. See also Part One, Chapter 3, *supra*, note 13.

tool for those who are already influential and well-off,[7] the fact remains that it can cost well in excess of a million dollars a case. At prices like that, constitutional challenges are not a game which many poor people can afford to play.

Very quickly then, it is likely that a reviewer who had expected to be able to write a very positive review would come to think she had been thrown back to the very beginning of the whole enterprise. By deciding to write the review in a way which would be of interest and accessible to people outside the legal profession, the reviewer is suddenly forced to confront facets of the Court, and the process of review, which seem to contradict everything positive which she had intended to write. To many reviewers it may seem that, in the end, the repeated warnings of the sceptics turned out to be well grounded. Whatever its theoretical promises, as a practical matter the process of review and the organization of the Court is highly regressive and quite out of keeping with our tradition of democratic and responsible government.

Indeed, the more she thinks about the financial and institutional realities of how judicial review has been practised before the Court over the first five years, the more difficult the dilemma is likely to appear. Unlike the approach she followed in Part Two, it is not possible to show the sceptics that their objections and concerns are mistaken and misplaced. Here the reviewer is confronted with factual claims, the truth of which can neither be avoided nor denied. It simply is a fact that the cost of challenging the constitutionality of a law is well beyond the means of ordinary Canadians. Equally, it is indisputable that those given the power to rule on the constitutionality of Canadian law are drawn from an economic and professional elite and are never made accountable to public scrutiny or review. For students of Canadian political history, the role of the Court might seem like the re-emergence of the family compact.

Faced with such a sharp discrepancy between theory and fact, the only way a reviewer could salvage a positive review would be to acknowledge the deficiencies in the current practice and hope she will be able to think of relatively simple ways in which the system could be changed to remedy them. For reviewers who were new to the field of constitutional review this might seem like a daunting task. For the uninitiated, it would be reasonable to assume that if there were easy solutions to the access and accountability problems they would already have been identified and tried in Canada long before. Fortuitously, the reality is just the opposite. As those familiar with comparative systems

---

7 A call it made on more than one occasion in the first five years: see e.g., *R. v. Edwards Books* (1987), 35 D.L.R. (4th) 1; *Slaight Communications v. Davidson* (1989), 59 D.L.R. (4th) 416.

of constitutional review would know, there are in fact relatively simple adjustments that can be made to ensure that the practice of judicial review is as democratic and progressive as its underlying theory holds it out to be.

10

The Democratic Integrity of the Court

1. APPOINTMENT

Unquestionably, the most basic lesson of comparative constitutional law is how easy it is to guarantee that the power of the judges and the process of review has a legitimate democratic grounding.[1] Except for states like Canada whose legal heritage is British (e.g., India, Ireland), most countries with a system of constitutional review have solved the problem of democratic legitimacy by ensuring that the legislative branch has a meaningful role to play in the appointment of those who are given the final say in whether their laws are constitutional.[2] In one way or another, almost every country which includes a process of judicial review in their system of government uses the consent of the elected representatives of the legislative branch of government to ensure that the Court is accountable to the people and subject to the sovereignty of the popular will.

The way in which the legislative branch is involved in the appointment process varies from country to country. At one extreme is a country like West Germany, where the power of appointing the judges to its Consti-

---

1 There are several very useful texts on comparative constitutional law. See E. McWhinney, *Supreme Courts and Judicial Law Making*, (Martinus Nijhoff Publishers, 1986); M. Cappelletti, *Judicial Review in the Contemporary World* (Indianapolis: Bobbs-Merill, 1971); W. Murphy and J. Tanenhaus (eds.), *Comparative Constitutional Law* (N.Y.: St. Martins Press, 1974); J. Grossman and J. Tanenhaus (eds.), *Frontiers of Judicial Research* (N.Y.: John Wiley, 1969).

2 An exception would be Japan, which also uses a system of unfettered executive appointment, although the Japanese electorate has an opportunity to approve or disapprove of the continued tenure of Supreme Court judges appointed since the last election. See E. McWhinney, *Supreme Courts, supra*, note 1, at 47. See also D. Danelski, "The People and the Court in Japan" in Grossman and Tanenhaus, *Frontiers, supra*, note 1.

tutional Court is given over exclusively to the legislative branch.[3] Each of the two houses which make up the West German Parliament — the Bundestag and the Bundesrat — is given the power of appointing half of the 16 judges who sit on that country's highest court. The Bundestag, or lower house, is like our House of Commons. It is made up of representatives chosen in national elections and it exercises its power of appointment through a parliamentary committee whose membership reflects the pattern of party representation in the house. It requires the agreement of two thirds of this committee for an appointment to be approved. In the Bundesrat (or upper house) which is made up of the heads from the Länder (provincial) Governments in the federal German state, there is a similar requirement that appointments be approved by a two-thirds majority but in this case, because of its small size, voting is conducted by the Bundesrat as a whole.

In other countries, the power of the legislative branch to participate in the selection of persons to sit on the nation's highest court is similar to that in West Germany, but it is shared with one or both of the other branches of government. In Austria, for example, collectively the two chambers of the legislative branch appoint six of the fourteen judges who sit on its Constitutional Court.[4] The executive — in this case the President of the country — appoints the other eight. In Italy, the legislature controls the appointment of one third of the members of the Corte Costituzionale,[5] while in Spain the percentage is two thirds.[6] Interestingly, in the latter two countries, the power of appointment is also shared with the judicial

---

3 In addition to the comparative texts, *supra*, note 1, there are several essays and texts written in English describing the practice and procedures of the West German Court. See D. Kommers, *Judicial Politics in West Germany* (Sage, 1976); H. Rupp, "Judicial Review in the Federal Republic of Germany", 9 A.J.C.L. 29; G. Brinkmann, "The West German Federal Constitutional Court" (1981), Public Law 83; M. Singer, "The Constitutional Court of the German Federal Republic", 1982 International and Comp. L.Q. 331; J. Ipsen, "Constitutional Review of Laws", in *Main Principles of the German Basic Law* (Baden Baden: Nomos Verlagsgesellschaft, 1983). See also *The Constitution of the Federal Republic of Germany*, Karpen (ed.), (Nomos Verlagsgesellschaft, 1988). Switzerland is another western European country whose highest court — The Tribunal Federal — is chosen exclusively by the legislative branch. See J.F. Aubert, *Traité de Droit Suisse* (Neuchatel, 1982).

    For an overview of the various approaches to the appointment of judges to a country's highest court, see C. Baar, "Comparative Perspectives on Judicial Selection Processes", paper prepared for the Ontario Law Reform Commission, September 14, 1989, Kingston, Ontario.

4 K. Heller, *Outline of Austrian Constitutional Law* (Kluwer, 1989).

5 A. Pizzorusso, V. Vigoriti and G. Certoma, "The Constitutional Review of Legislation in Italy" (1984), 3 Civil Justice Q. 311.

6 M. Eibert, "The Spanish Constitutional Tribunal in Theory and Practice" (1982), 18 Stanford J. of Int'l Law 435.

branch as well as the executive. In Italy, the country's senior judges make a third of the appointments to that country's highest court, while in Spain the judiciary has been given the power to appoint two of the twelve persons who sit on that country's constitutional tribunal.

Although the extent to which the legislative branch controls the appointment of judges differs in these countries, the way it is involved is the same in each. Whatever number of appointments are within its control, in all of these countries the legislative branch is involved from the beginning. In Germany, Switzerland, Austria, Italy and Spain the legislators participate in the search, screening and selection of candidates as well in their appointment and confirmation. This stands in contrast with a second model, in which the legislative branch only comes in at the end of the appointment process. This is the system used, for example, to appoint the members of the United States Supreme Court[7] and the European Court of Human Rights in Strasbourg.[8] It is also a system which has attracted a good deal of interest in Canada in the past.[9] Under this system, the role of the legislative branch is limited to ratifying a selection made by the executive. It plays no part in the initial screening and nomination of candidates. In the ratification model the executive retains control of the search and nomination process and the legislature is only asked to give its consent to whatever choice the executive has made.

For the reviewer, the important lesson of comparative constitutional law is not in all of the different ways which the legislative branch can be involved in the appointment of judges to a country's highest court. It is conventional wisdom among those expert in comparative law that the details of any country's legal system are very much the product of local legal traditions, governmental institutions, political forces, etc. For the reviewer, much more striking will be the similarity in how all of these countries have gone about establishing the democratic legitimacy of constitutional review. In the general method, there is a real convergence in approach.[10] In one way or another all of these countries ensure that

---

7 For a very accessible, non-legalistic treatment of the American appointment process, see L. Tribe, *God Save This Honorable Court* (New York: Random House, 1985). For an historical overview of the American system see P. Freund, "Appointment of Justices, Some Historical Perspectives", 101 Harv. Law Rev. 1146.

8 A brief description of the system of appointment to the European Court of Human Rights is described in J.G. Merrills, *The Development of International Law By the European Court of Human Rights* (Manchester University Press, 1988), p. 6.

9 For a review of the various groups and commissions, including the most recent MacDonald Commission, which have endorsed a ratification model of this kind, see Peter Russell, "Constitutional Reform of the Judicial Branch", 1984 C.J.P.S. 227.

10 This convergence is noted in E. McWhinney, *Supreme Courts, supra*, note 1, Introduction; and M. Cappelletti, "Judicial Review in Comparative Perspective" (1970), 58 Calif. L. Rev. 1017.

the people, through their elected representatives, are directly involved in the appointment of those who sit on their highest courts.

The logic which explains this common approach to securing the democratic legitimacy, for whatever particular institution is entrusted with the final power of review, is not difficult to understand. No one, today, denies that judges do have a real discretion in applying the rules that govern whether a law will be declared constitutional or not. Everyone is agreed that judges do more than mechanically apply self-executing rules to the facts of each case.[11] There remains an important element of judicial control and choice in how every challenge will be resolved. Even on the understanding of constitutional review that is implicit in the model of *Oakes*, it can matter a great deal who gets appointed to the Court. Although the "means-ends" framework of analysis will be the same in each case, the judge retains a discretion in how the two governing principles will be applied.

The differences that developed within the Canadian Supreme Court over the first five years that it worked with the Charter show very clearly that even though the principles in *Oakes* are objective and generally lead to quite determinate results, an element of creativity remains at the core of the judicial role. Bertha Wilson and William McIntyre, it will be recalled, differed not only in their theories about *when* the Charter should be applied, but also *in the way* each of them thought it should work. For one thing, as we saw in Part One, each of the judges tended to adopt quite distinctive postures with respect to the evidentiary burdens that each of the parties would bear in a case. On the one hand, judges like William McIntyre and Jean Beetz tended to be more demanding in requiring challengers to show that the laws they attacked really did limit their freedom in some way, while Bertha Wilson was inclined to be more rigorous in evaluating the evidence adduced by Government in support of the constitutionality of its laws.[12]

In addition to the different attitudes they displayed on questions about burdens of proof, the judges also disagreed as to how principles like

---

11 This idea seems now to be conventional wisdom in all systems of constitutional review. In Canada the point has been made most powerfully by Paul Weiler, *In the Last Resort* (Toronto: Carswell, 1974). For more recent treatments of the same theme, see Patrick Monahan, *Politics and the Constitution* (Toronto: Carswell, 1987), and Marc Gold, "The Mask of Objectivity", 35 U.T.L.J. 454. For comparative analyses of the law-making powers inherent in judicial review, see McWhinney, *Supreme Courts, supra*, note 1; Cappelletti, "The 'Mighty Problem' of Judicial Review", 53 So. Cal. L. Rev. 437. For L. Tribe's treatment, see *God Save This Honorable Court, supra*, note 7, Chapters 1 and 3.

12 See Part One, Chapter 3, *supra*, pp. 66-67. Cf. McIntyre's judgment in cases such as *R. v. Smith* (1988), 40 D.L.R. (4th) 435; *R. v. Morgentaler* (1988), 44 D.L.R. (4th) 385; see also *Irwin Toy v. Quebec* (1989), 58 D.L.R. (4th) 577.

deference and balancing should be applied. In a case like *Edwards Books*, for example, the judges were badly divided on how the competing interests that were affected by Ontario's Sunday closing law should be weighed in the balance.[13] That case also shows how different their instincts were in deciding when it was appropriate for the Court to defer to a legislature's will. It reminds us that judges like William McIntyre and Gerard La Forest were quite different from Bertha Wilson in thinking that there was a wide range of social and economic policies against which the Court should be reluctant to exercise its powers of review and on which legislators and policy makers should be given the benefit of every doubt.[14]

Legislative involvement in the appointment process confronts this unambiguous and unavoidable range of judicial discretion and law making power directly.[15] It forges a link through which those who are given authority to rule on the constitutionality of law are made accountable to those who will be governed by the decisions which result. Before a person is entrusted with the powers of review, the public is given an opportunity to evaluate his or her understanding of what the judicial role requires and to satisfy itself that this is the kind of person to whom it wants to entrust such legal authority. Because considerations of judicial independence make public review of a judge's performance on the Bench inappropriate in all but the most extreme cases, candidates are made accountable to the people through their elected representatives, *before* they are appointed, by being obliged to explain how they will exercise their powers of review. In the Canadian context, this would mean they could be questioned about their understanding of and commitment to the principles of review set out in *Oakes* and/or whether they think there are any other standards or criteria against which the constitutionality of laws should be measured. Within the model itself, candidates could be made to divulge their attitude toward the burdens of proof that have to be met by challengers and Government supporters, as well as the values and sources of reasoning they will turn to in applying principles such as deference and balancing. Before being given the legal authority to rule on the constitutionality of Canada's next abortion law, or the Sunday closing law in some province, a prospective judge would have to be willing to disclose the way in which and the basis on which he or she would rank the interests (of women, foetuses, workers, and members of religious minorities, etc.) that are involved in those cases.

In practical terms, legislative control of the appointment process would

---

13 *Edwards Books v. R.* (1987), 35 D.L.R. (4th) 1. See Part One, Chapter 3, pp. 60-61.
14 See Part One, Chapter 3, pp. 59-60.
15 G. Brinkmann, "The West German Federal Constitutional Court", *supra*, note 3, at 84, 91, writing about the German method of appointment, puts it simply: "Each house elects half of the members. Thus the [Federal Constitutional Court] is democratically legitimate."

permit the people to insist that only those who are "committed to the unremitting protection of human rights" should be appointed to the Bench if that is the kind of Court they wanted to create. It would mean that the public could withhold its consent, for example, from people whose value systems had tolerated racial discrimination in the past,[16] or who thought that a case like *Oakes* was wrongly decided,[17] or who believed that the Court should defer to the other two branches of government even when they have passed a law which quite unnecessarily impinges on somebody's constitutional guarantees. In personal terms, consent by the legislature means that ultimately it is for the people to decide whether, when the next vacancy occurs, they want to appoint a clone of William McIntyre or Bertha Wilson to the Court.

The logic of passing the appointment of judges to a country's highest court over to the legislative branch seems so obvious and compelling, and its practice is so widespread that, rather than questioning its justification, it is likely many reviewers would be wondering why Canada has not seen fit to embrace it before now. Historically the answer is that, originally, in deciding to vest control of all judicial appointments in the hands of the executive, Canada was simply following the method used in Britain and indeed all over the world at the time. When the practice of executive appointment was made part of Canada's legal system, it was conventional wisdom that, for the most part, the judicial role was a very mechanical one in which life's events were organized and classified according to a myriad of very particular and very detailed legal rules. Doing law was much like being a letter sorter in days gone by. The judge's task was seen to involve reading or listening to a case and filing it according to the proper legal category (contract, tort, crime) or rule (mitigation, negligence, murder). Within this predominant understanding of the function which judges performed, most of the concern was to ensure that those who knew and best understood all of the classifications and principles contained in the law, and how they should be applied, were appointed to the Bench. To the extent there was any writing about reforming the process by which judges were appointed to Canada's highest court, it generally favoured trying to immunize, not expose it to the pressures and vicissitudes of public life. Even today, legal academics and members of the professional bar continue to call for the creation of nominating commissions, heavily staffed

---

16 Questions concerning the extent to which nominees have been associated with racial discrimination have, not surprisingly, been important considerations in the confirmation hearings of several nominees for the U.S. Supreme Court. See L. Tribe, *God Save This Honorable Court*; and P. Freund, "Appointment of Justices", *supra*, note 7.

17 It should be recalled that of the original nine, William McIntyre and Willard Estey declined to embrace the model without qualification when the Court first spelled out its contours in *Oakes*.

with experts in law and judging, as the most effective reform that could be undertaken to ensure the best people end up on the Bench.[18] The call has generally been to further professionalize, not popularize, the process of appointment. Bureaucratization, not democratization, is where the logic of the traditional thinking about law and what function judges perform naturally led. With notable exceptions,[19] to the extent that legislative involvement in the appointment process has been discussed at all, it usually has been cast in a very shady, if not negative, light.

Being able to explain why Canada remains one of the few countries in the free and democratic world that has failed to recognize any role for its legislatures in the appointment of judges to its highest court does not, of course, provide any reason why this state of affairs should be allowed to endure any longer. Quite the contrary. In this day and age, after the entrenchment of the Charter and since the general recognition of the law-making powers that judges possess, there is no longer any basis on which the monopoly enjoyed by the executive branch can be defended. Canada stands at one extreme in the extent to which the executive branch controls appointments to the Bench.[20] Even those who historically have been quite unsympathetic to the idea of legislatures being involved in the appointment of judges have recognized that, with the entrenchment of the Charter, the role of the judges has changed to such a degree as to put in question the continued validity of the traditional approach.[21] The claim that the selection of judges is a purely professional question, based on a person's knowledge and understanding of intricate legal categories and rules, and having nothing to do with his or her values and ideological orientation, is the product of another time in which the dominant understanding of law was completely at odds with what it is today.[22] With the recognition

---

18 The most recent recommendations of the Canadian Bar Association and Canadian Law Teachers Association concerning judicial appointments are summarized in J. Ziegel, "Federal Judicial Appointments in Canada: The Time is Ripe for Change" (1987), 37 U.T.L.J. 1. See also L. Smith, "Judicial Independence and Accountability: The Institutional Ethics", paper prepared for the Ontario Law Reform Commission, Sept. 14, 1989, Kingston.

19 Academic commentators who have called for more democratic appointment procedures include Paul Weiler, *In the Last Resort, supra*, note 11, at 22 (ratification model); S.I. Bushnell, "The Appointment of Judges to the Supreme Court of Canada: Past, Present and Future", in *Judicial Selection in Canada: Discussion Papers and Reports* (Canadian Association of Law Teachers, 1987) (ratification model); and W.R. Lederman, "Current Proposals for Reform of Supreme Court of Canada" (1979), 57 Can. Bar Rev. 687.

20 See E. McWhinney, *Supreme Courts, supra*, note 1, at 46; P. Russell, *The Judiciary in Canada* (Toronto: McGraw-Hill, 1987), p. 114.

21 See J. Ziegel, "Federal Judicial Appointments in Canada", *supra*, note 18.

22 Though born of another era, the idea still seems to have its adherents today, including John Sopinka, the person chosen to fill the seat vacated by the resignation of Willard

that judges retain considerable discretion in applying the rules they use to decide whether a Government is acting constitutionally or not, our tradition of democracy and commitment to popular rule requires that the legislature must be involved and ultimately consent to how this law-making power will be used.

As well as being the product of an outmoded and largely discredited view of law and the role that judges perform, as a factual matter the idea that there is an irreconcilable tension between professionalism and merit on the one hand and democracy and the involvement of the legislature on the other is difficult, if not impossible, to sustain. Empirically there is just no evidence to support such a connection. If anything, the evidence points to exactly the opposite conclusion. The collective record and acclaimed performances of individual justices of the U.S. Supreme Court or German Constitutional Court, for example, make a mockery of the assertion that securing the consent of the legislative branch will compromise the quality of appointments. On any criteria, the performance of the members of these Courts is every bit as strong as the one the reviewer witnessed in the first part of this book.[23]

Logically, there is no reason why the traditional concerns about merit and the professional qualifications of the judges would be ignored or jeopardized by the democratization of the appointment process. There is, after all, nothing inherently inconsistent between the two ideas. Nominating councils could even be integrated into a more democratic appointment process if it was thought they were the best way of ensuring the appointment of the most qualified people. Rather than such councils forwarding their recommendations to the executive branch, they could send them to the legislature instead.

Estey. See John Sopinka, "Limited Value in Confirmation Ritual", *Financial Post*, August 15, 1988. See also L. Smith, "Judicial Independence and Accountability: The Institutional Ethics", prepared for the Ontario Law Reform Commission, Sept. 14, 1989, Kingston.

For a description of the early appointment practices in Canada, see W. Angus, "Judicial Selection in Canada: The Historical Perspective" (1969), J. of Cdn. L.S. 220; P. Russell, *The Supreme Court of Canada as a Bilingual and Bicultural Institution* (Ottawa: Queen's Printer, 1969); P. Russell, *The Judiciary in Canada: The Third Branch of Government* (Toronto: McGraw-Hill, 1987); and I. Bushnell, "The Appointment of Judges to the Supreme Court of Canada", *supra*, note 19.

23 Compare the assessments of the performance of judges in Canada, Germany and Spain by E.A. Tollefson, "The System of Judicial Appointments: A Collateral Issue" (1971), 21 U.T.L.J. 162; D. Kommers, *Judicial Politics in West Germany* (Sage, 1976), Chapter 4, p. 155; Hahn, "Trends in Interpretation of the German Constitution", 26 Am. J. Comp. L. 631; Eibert, "The Spanish Constitutional Tribunal", *supra*, note 6. To substantiate the claim that the democratization of the appointment process will prejudice the quality of the Court, supporters of the existing system would not only have to cite concrete examples, they would also have to show that the kinds of evaluations which these essays contain are wrong.

It is, however, highly unlikely that nominating councils would ever be seen as the preferred method by which the merits of each appointment could be guaranteed.[24] No country which entrusts judges with the power to review the constitutionality of its laws uses nominating councils, dominated by members of the legal or judicial elite, to participate in the appointment of the members of their highest court. Even in the United States, where the idea of appointing judges in this way was first developed, it has never been thought appropriate for the selection of judges to that country's Supreme Court. Although it may produce a more qualified judiciary in lower courts,[25] it is less certain whether it would make the kind of outstanding appointments which a court with final authority to rule on constitutional questions really needs.[26] More seriously, it suffers from delegating, to a legal and judicial elite, the most important power the people have in choosing those who will define the constitutional limits of governmental power.[27] As the experience of other countries shows, there are ways a legislature can guarantee the professional quality of its appointments without abdicating its authority so completely.

Of the various ways in which a legislature can be involved in the appointment process, many reviewers will instinctively be attracted to the kind of system which the West Germans have devised. The German model goes furthest in securing the democratic legitimacy of constitutional review, without any apparent sacrifice in the qualifications of those appointed to its Court. By involving the legislature throughout the entire process of every appointment, from the initial canvassing of candidates to the selection of a final choice, the control of the public and their representatives over how the Court's powers will be exercised, is maximized.

By contrast, the ratification model, such as exists in the United States, denies the legislative branch any power to initiate. Its only function is to react. It has no direct input into the selection and nomination of a candidate and, as the experience in Washington confirms, although the Senate may be able to resist one or two nominations, it will almost never be able to

---

24 Unless of course the Committee was made up exclusively of legislators. Such a proposal was advanced by one of Canada's leading scholars of constitutional law, W. Lederman, "Current Proposals for Reform of the Supreme Court of Canada", *supra*, note 19. In effect, this is the system used in West Germany. See D. Kommers, *Judicial Politics in West Germany*, *supra*, note 3, Chapter 4.

25 A review of the literature on the strengths and weaknesses of nominating commissions in the United States is contained in C. Baar, "Judicial Appointments and the Quality of Adjudication", 1986 R.J. Thèmis 1.

26 E. McWhinney, *Supreme Courts*, *supra*, note 1, at 46; P. Russell, *The Judiciary in Canada*, *supra*, note 20, at 134.

27 A point stressed by Paul Weiler, *In the Last Resort*, *supra*, note 11, at 21-22, and the *Royal Commission on the Economic Union* (MacDonald Commission), 1985, Minister of Supply and Services, in Vol. 3, Part VI, Chapter 23, p. 322.

deny an Executive which is determined to have its way. As Larry Tribe, a leading scholar of American constitutional law puts it, history shows that every American President "with any skill and a little luck can . . . with fair success, build the Court of his dreams".[28] Clearly more in keeping with our tradition of democratic government, the German system ensures that individuals of demonstrated ability will be appointed by building in, through practice and prescription, rigorous standards of professional competence and qualification.[29]

Depending on whether the provisions of the Meech Lake Accord dealing with the Supreme Court will ever be revived, the German model could be integrated at the federal level or the provincial level or both. If the Accord never gains the approval of all ten provincial legislatures, the West German model could either be transplanted in its entirety, or adapted as required, to the federal scene. A committee of the House of Commons, for example, could easily be struck to undertake the search, screening, and selection of candidates for appointment to the Court. From the reviewer's perspective, however, in order to maximize the democratic integrity of the Court, it would clearly be preferable if this part of the Accord was salvaged and the provinces were involved directly in the appointment of the members of the Court. The fact the judges review the constitutionality of provincial as well as federal law means that the members of provincial assemblies have just as legitimate a claim to participate in the appointment process as do members of the House of Commons. Even if Canada's regional mosaic is not a relevant criterion in choosing between individual candidates for the Court,[30] it is of decisive importance in the design of the appointment process itself. The federal

---

28 Tribe, *God Save This Honorable Court, supra*, note 7, at 76. In his book, Tribe also explodes the myth that Presidents are often surprised by how their choices turn out. As Tribe explains, when Presidents have been caught off guard it is usually because they have not paid sufficient, if any, attention to the nominees' ideas about constitutional law.

   The dominant role played by the nominator in the ratification model is also revealed in the experience of the European Court of Human Rights. The recent selection of the Swedish judge was one of the few occasions on which the Council of Europe did not select the first choice of the nominating Government.

29 By prescription, six of the sixteen judges must be chosen from one of the country's highest appellate courts. By practice many of the other members are drawn from the ranks of academe. See D. Kommers, *Judicial Politics in West Germany, supra*, note 3. For similar calls in Canada, see L. Weinrib, "Appointing Judges to the Supreme Court of Canada", prepared for Ontario Law Reform Commission, Sept. 14, 1989, Kingston; P. Russell, "Meech Lake and the Supreme Court", in K. Swinton and Carol Rogerson, *Competing Constitutional Visions* (Toronto: Carswell, 1988), p. 108.

30 P. Russell, "Constitutional Reform of the Judicial Branch", *supra*, note 9, at 237-238; MacDonald Commission, *supra*, note 27, Chapter 23, p. 320; E. McWhinney, *Supreme Courts, supra*, note 1, at 68; cf. W. Lederman, "Current Proposals for Reform of Supreme Court of Canada", *supra*, note 19, at 693.

character of countries like the United States, Switzerland and West Germany is reflected in their appointment processes through the participation of a second chamber in their national legislatures, which is organized to reflect the regional interests of these states. Without a democratically legitimate Senate in our own Parliament, the Meech Lake Accord provided Canada with an alternative way of giving expression to its regional character and of maximizing the democratic legitimacy of its Court.[31]

On the assumption that the provisions dealing with Supreme Court appointments in the Meech Lake Accord eventually secure the necessary consent for their entrenchment in the Constitution, and each province or region struck an appropriate committee to exercise its powers of nomination, a subsidiary question would be whether the recommendations of each provincial assembly should be made to the executive or legislative branch in Ottawa.[32] From the reviewer's perspective, the latter would obviously be the preferred choice. Again, the more opportunities the public have to participate in the appointment of those who will be judging the constitutionality of their laws the better. With each additional opportunity

---

31 A variation on this theme is Bill Lederman's proposal of a nominating Commission made up of members of both the federal Parliament and provincial legislatures. See "Current Proposals for Reform of Supreme Court of Canada", *supra*, note 19. Though sceptical of making regional background a qualification of appointments, Peter Russell also supports the idea of provincial involvement in the appointment process. See "Meech Lake and the Supreme Court", *supra*, note 29, at 104-105. Public participation through the provincial legislatures would also go some way to meet the concern of whether a single appointment process can adequately reflect both the federalism and human rights functions of the Court. See K. Banting, "Federalism and the Supreme Court of Canada", a paper prepared for the Ontario Law Reform Commission, Sept. 15, 1989, Kingston.

32 That Meech Lake provided a new framework within which appointments to the Supreme Court can be grounded more firmly in the democratic and federal tradition of the Canadian state does not mean that it supplied all of the answers. Still at issue were such questions as whether provinces should be required to submit a list of names rather than a single nominee (as is the case in appointments to the European Court of Human Rights) and how deadlocks between the federal and provincial levels of government should be resolved. For an analysis of the Meech Lake proposals see P. Russell, "Meech Lake and the Supreme Court", in K. Swinton and C. Rogerson (eds.), *Competing Constitutional Visions: The Meech Lake Accord* (Toronto: Carswell, 1988), p. 104.

An even more important area left unexplored by the Meech Lake Accord is what personal and professional qualifications candidates for appointment to the Court should have. For example, a very basic question would be whether it is necessary or desirable that everyone on the Court be trained in law. If, on the model in *Oakes*, the essence of the Court's function in reviewing the constitutionality of challenged laws is to make use of conventional tools (principles) of policy analysis and social well-being, the monopolization of lawyers seems hard to justify. Paul Weiler's recommendation to appoint non-lawyers to the Court would seem even more compelling today than it was when he first made it over fifteen years ago. See P. Weiler, *In the Last Resort*, *supra*, note 11.

for involvement by different individuals and groups across the country, the stronger the democratic integrity of the Court will be.

Ratification or confirmation of provincial nominations, by an all-party committee of the House of Commons, would also allow for the possibility of using public hearings in a way executive appointment, at least as it has traditionally been practised, does not. Although, as recent American experience makes clear, there is always a danger that the bounds of civility can be transgressed in public discussion and debate,[33] no one today seriously questions that they also add considerably to the democratic legitimacy of any court.[34] Conducted properly,[35] ratification hearings can provide the people with an effective way of informing and re-educating themselves about the role the Court has or should play in our system of government. Given the need to preserve the independence of the Court, they are perhaps the only way individual justices and the Court as a whole can be held directly accountable to the people whose lives are directly affected by the rulings they make. Public hearings can be a vehicle through which individuals and groups can deliver their own review of the Court's performance whenever a vacancy arises. They provide private citizens and interest groups with an opportunity to bring to light and comment publicly on matters which bear on the professional qualifications and personal attributes of a candidate to do the job. They are a forum in which those willing to serve on the Court can be made to declare and commit themselves to the principles and values they will rely on in the exercise of their powers of review. As well, as recent American constitutional history also confirms, open hearings and the glare of publicity can play an important role in preventing the appointment of people whose intellectual capacities, moral character and/or understanding of the Constitution do not meet the standards which are deemed to be necessary for appointment to the Court.[36]

Against this, it is sometimes argued that whatever their contribution to the democratic integrity of the Court, highly politicized and publicized

---

33 For a series of essays reviewing the Bork appointment, see "Essays on the Supreme Court Appointment Process" (1988), 101 Harv. L. Rev. 1146; see especially N. Totenberg, "The Confirmation Process and the Public: To Know or Not to Know", at p. 1213. For a more exhaustive treatment, see E. Bronner, *Battling Justice* (Norton & Co., 1989). For Bork's own account, see R. Bork, *The Tempting of America* (New York: Free Press, 1990).
34 For a strong statement in support of vigorous public hearings see Tribe, *God Save this Honorable Court, supra,* note 7. For two earlier but widely cited voices opposed to even the private questioning of nominees, see P. Freund, *Appointment of Justices, supra,* note 7, at 1159-60. See also S. Carter, "The Confirmation Mess", 101 Harv. L. Rev. 1185.
35 For a discussion of the kinds of considerations which may properly be explored with a candidate, see L. Tribe, *God Save This Honorable Court, supra,* note 7, Chapter 6.
36 See Tribe, *God Save This Honorable Court, supra,* note 7, Chapter 5, for a review of the nominations rejected in recent years by the United States Senate, including those of Messrs. Ginsberg, Bork, Haynesworth, and Carswell.

hearings, in which a candidate is grilled about his or her professional and personal past, are both inappropriate and counter-productive. Inappropriate, it is said, either because elected politicians will not or cannot be expected to understand the complexities of constitutional law or, even more basically, because it is ethically wrong for a candidate to be asked his or her views on matters which may subsequently come before the Court.[37] Public hearings are said to be counter-productive because, worse than being futile, the spotlights of the media may actually deter many otherwise highly-qualified people from even allowing their names to be considered.[38]

As empirical claims, concerns of this kind are completely groundless. There is no evidence to suggest that people have been, or would be, deterred from accepting an appointment to the Court on account of their objection to being questioned about their personal and professional views.[39] Nor, to my knowledge, has anyone ever tried to establish that, as a group, politicians are mentally incapable of understanding the basic principles and methods of constitutional law. More seriously, as normative claims about how one of the most important institutions in our system of government should be organized, these claims are based on political ideas and values which are completely at odds with the Charter and our commitment to responsible and accountable government. It is accepted practice in all free and democratic societies that those in the legislative and executive branches of Government, who are entrusted with law-making powers, should have reflected on the principles and ideas they will rely on in the exercise of that authority and, before their appointment, to account to the people for their views. Judges in the Supreme Court of Canada, with their final authority to rule on the limits of Government and the constitutionality of all law, can be no different in this respect.

The first argument, that the people and their elected representatives

---

In Canada, public hearings would also minimize, if not eliminate, the possibility of a deadlock occurring between the provincial and federal levels of government. Legislative hearings would oblige both levels of government to justify publicly the choices they made.

37 See, e.g., S. Carter, "The Confirmation Mess", 101 Harv. L. Rev. 1188-1195; H. Laski, "The Technique of Judicial Appointments" (1926), 24 Mich. L. Rev. 529. See also P. Freund, "Appointment of Justices", *supra*, note 7, at 1162, quoting Felix Frankfurter and Abraham Lincoln as holding similar opinions.

38 This view was recently expressed by John Sopinka, one of the newest members appointed to the Court. See note 22.

39 This is not literally true. In at least one case in U.S. constitutional history, a nominee — Sherman Minton — did refuse to appear at confirmation hearings before the Senate. Whether he would have withdrawn his name had the Senate insisted on his presence is not known, however, because in the end the Senate was prepared to ratify his nomination without requiring him to appear. See P. Freund, *"Appointment of Justices"*, *supra*, note 7, at 1161.

are incapable of carrying on such a sophisticated dialogue about a candidate's professional competence and understanding of the principles of constitutional law is clearly the most offensive to our tradition of responsible government and would not likely detain any reviewer for very long. Though it has been espoused from time to time by otherwise respected members of academe,[40] its elite, paternalistic premise is completely antagonistic to the democratic ideals of popular sovereignty and personal autonomy on which the Charter and our whole system of government is based. Nor does it accord with our ideas of democracy to suggest that there is something unethical in questioning a prospective judge openly and in a public forum about his or her understanding of and expectations for the role for which he or she is being considered. There is no legitimate basis on which anyone who was otherwise qualified for the job could take offense at the possibility of such a public inquiry and refuse to allow their nominations to stand.

The public is entitled to know candidates' philosophical views about the principles and values which distinguish the process of constitutional review, their position on important cases[41] and even their personal experiences which are relevant to the way in which they will perform the judicial role.[42] Candidates who are unwilling to respond to inquiries of this kind demonstrate their unsuitability for the job. Although it would be perfectly proper for a candidate to refuse to predict how he or she might rule on a specific case on its way to the Court[43], a broader unwillingness to talk about one's theories and ideas of judicial review and the Court's role in our system of government would signal either a flat rejection of the people's right to govern themselves or, alternatively, a complete misunderstanding about what the whole process is all about. At the point in time at which a person is being considered for appointment to the Court, as to any high office of State, it would be expected he or she would be fully informed about all matters relevant to constitutional law and his or her abilities to do the job. Larry Tribe put it as well as one can. At the point of nomination, he writes, "a blank slate is not the

---

40 *Supra*, note 37.

41 For example, a candidate might be asked whether, he or she agreed with the Court's definition of equality and, in particular, with its rejection of the similarly situated test (see Part One, Chapter 4, note 6), or how its rulings in cases like *B.C.G.U.E. v. A.G. B.C.* (1988), 53 D.L.R. (4th) 1, and *Slaight Communications v. Davidson* (1989), 59 D.L.R. (4th) 516, can be reconciled with its earlier ruling in *Dolphin Delivery v. R.W.D.S.U.* (1987), 33 D.L.R. (4th) 174. See Part One, Chapter 4, *supra*, note 61.

42 *Supra*, note 18.

43 A point even the strongest supporters of public hearings concedes. See L. Tribe, *God Save This Honorable Court, supra*, note 7, at 101.

sign of an open mind, but of an empty one — of immaturity and inexperience and perhaps even of indifference".[44]

2. TERMINATION

So it turns out that a reviewer can hold on to the democracy theme without much difficulty at all. A simple transfer of power in the appointment process, which would bring Canada in line with most other free and democratic societies with written bills of rights, would do the trick. Although amending the appointment process would be sufficient to repair the anti-democratic foundation of the existing Court, we might pause briefly to note that this is not the only reform a reviewer could recommend. From a comparative assessment of how constitutional review is practised elsewhere in the world, the reviewer will have encountered at least two other, equally simple structural adjustments that could be made to the institutional framework of the Court that would strengthen its democratic legitimacy even further.

The first of these involves imposing a strict limit on the period of time anyone is allowed to sit on a country's highest court. A fixed term appointment is a second, very simple lesson reviewers will learn from their research into comparative constitutional law. To maximize public control over how legal authority is exercised, most countries insist that anyone who is given the final say about the constitutionality of law must relinquish their powers after a specific number of years. By law in most countries, and by practice in the rest, appointments to a nation's highest court invariably terminate after somewhere between nine and twelve years and without any possibility for a further appointment or extension of the term.[45] Members of the Spanish and Italian Constitutional Courts, for example, hold their appointments for a period of nine years.[46] In Germany, it is twelve.[47]

Given the substantial powers that these individuals wield, it makes obvious sense, both theoretically and practically, to limit how long they will be able to monopolise such powerful positions of legal authority.

---

44 *Ibid.*
45 The convergence is noted in E. McWhinney, *Supreme Courts, supra*, note 1, at 57. The major exceptions would be Austria, which has a compulsory retirement rule at age seventy, and Switzerland, where members of the Tribunal Federal are elected for six-year renewable terms. The judges on the European Court of Human Rights are also eligible for reappointment to a second term — of nine years. The American Supreme Court stands alone in the practice of allowing its members to retain their legal powers as long as they wish.
46 *Supra*, notes 5 and 6.
47 *Supra*, note 3.

Theoretically, fixed term appointments ensure there will be a constant rejuvenation and re-assessment within the Court as to how its powers should be applied. Regular and systematic turnover protects against discredited and/or outworn principles and analytical approaches being applied indefinitely and, in so doing, further strengthens the democratic legitimacy of the Court. Practically, an appointment for a fixed term of years makes sense as well. It seems to accord with the experience of Messrs. Beetz, McIntyre, Estey and Le Dain all of whom left the Court after exercising the powers of constitutional review for a period of five years. When one takes account of the time they spent on the Court prior to the entrenchment of the Charter, appointments of nine to twelve years seems to match the physical and intellectual strength of people in their middle years, who are most likely to have that combination of wisdom and experience which is required in the job.

3. DECISION-MAKING PROCEDURES

In addition to making simple changes in the way the judges are appointed to and removed from the Court, a third technique, which other countries have used to ensure the powers of review are exercised in the most responsible and accountable way, is to design the procedure that the judges follow to arrive at their decisions in a way which emphasizes the collegial character of the Court. In comparison with other systems used around the world, the Canadian system once again stands at one extreme.[48] The decision-making process on the Canadian Supreme Court is highly individualistic and emphasizes the separate personality of each judge. Currently, each member of the Court is able to formulate his or her opinion as to whether a law is constitutional without ever having to defend it before the other judges. Under the present system, after a case has been argued orally, the judges meet in conference and, almost immediately, stake out preliminary positions as to how each of them thinks the case should be resolved.[49] Even though no one will have fully researched and analysed the case at this point, the judges more or less commit themselves to the final positions they will take. Only after announcing their opinions on the merits of a case are draft judgments researched, written and circulated to the other members of the Court. Although written memoranda and preliminary drafts may be exchanged, and issues joined indirectly and impersonally, there is no opportunity, and certainly no requirement, for the judges to collectively debate the relative merits of the various opinions circulating in the Court.

---

48 Peter Russell, *The Judiciary in Canada, supra,* note 20, at 349ff.
49 B. Wilson, "Decision Making on the Supreme Court" (1986), 36 U.T.L.J. 236.

In other countries with systems of judicial review, more effort is made to find the collective will of the Court; to see if there is one answer which is more compelling than any other and which can attract everyone's support.[50] More use is made of conferences and decision-making structures which build on the collegial character of the Court. Once again, it is the European communities, not our American neighbours, who turn out to be the most fruitful source of comparison.[51] In Germany, for example, a process of decision-making is used which provides a strong check that the judges will only use their powers of review in a way which can withstand the scrutiny of the other members of the Court. Every complaint which is received by the Constitutional Court is assigned in the first instance to one of its members who acts as a kind of rapporteur for the case. That person has the responsibility of doing the research, preparing a memorandum of the relevant issues and arguments, and of making a recommendation of what he or she thinks the ultimate disposition of the case should be. Once the dossier on the case is completed, copies are circulated to the other members of the Court. Only after all of the judges have had an opportunity to read the file and reflect on the case, is it discussed by the Court as a whole. Only then is each judge asked to state his or her opinion as to whether there has been a violation of the Constitution.[52]

The advantages of emphasizing the collegial character of the Court, in the processes by which its decisions are made, are manifold. In assigning one person the primary responsibility for the initial researching and writing up of a case, a collegial system is obviously highly efficient. As a practical matter it will minimize the waste and duplication that plagues the current system in which, on occasion, three and even four different judges might have the same research done on a case.[53] In addition to their efficiency, collegial systems of decision-making are likely to be highly effective as well. Making one person responsible for providing all of the judges with a comprehensive memorandum of the case, before any positions or opinions are staked out, should reduce the number of occasions on which mistakes will be made. In terms of the principle of alternative means, one could

---

50 E. McWhinney, *Supreme Courts, supra*, note 1, Chapter 2.

51 For a popular exposé on the decidedly unprincipled method of decision-making used by the American Supreme Court, see B. Woodward and S. Armstrong, *The Brethren* (New York: Avon Books, 1979).

52 For a more detailed description of the decision-making procedures in the German Constitutional Court, see D. Kommers, *Judicial Politics in West Germany, supra*, note 3, Chapter 5, pp. 175ff.

53 The efficacy of the German system can be sensed from the caseload it handles each year, ranging between 3,500 and 4,000 complaints. Although, admittedly only half its size, the Canadian Supreme Court handles a maximum of 600 cases, of which the vast majority are applications for leave which are treated perfunctorily and disposed of without issuing reasons of any kind.

say collegial decision-making maximizes the possibility that the Court will realize its ultimate objective, as "guardian of the Constitution", of rendering sound judgments in as many cases as it can. Minds are made up only after, not before, everyone has had an opportunity for considered reflection of every relevant aspect of a case.

And, beyond these considerations of efficiency and effectiveness, collegial decision-making is much more in keeping with the theory of constitutional review which underlies the model in *Oakes*. By encouraging the members of the Court to speak in a single voice,[54] the collegial approach provides another powerful check against those entrusted with the power of review using it improperly and in ways which conflict with the principles and values on which the Constitution is based. It is simply not as easy for an individual judge to stake out a position that cannot be justified within the Court's accepted framework of analysis if he or she must defend it before his or her colleagues on the Court. In the style of a faculty seminar, if a particular judge cannot sustain a position with the other members of the Court there will be considerable pressure to rethink his or her views.[55] In Canada, the failure to provide any opportunity for a full and informed debate among the members of the Court, *after* a case has been thoroughly researched and fully analysed, no doubt contributed to the highly indi- vidualistic and subjective style of decision-making we saw exhibited by the Court in the years immediately following its decision in *Oakes*. Had the judges been required to confront and account for their different methods and styles of review, it is likely that some, though perhaps not all, of the mistakes the reviewer identified in Part One might have been avoided.[56]

Examining comparative systems of constitutional review, and the different institutions and processes which they employ, should reassure a reviewer that her faith in the democratic legitimacy of written bills of rights

---

54 For a highly acclaimed critique of the institutional voice employed by the American Supreme Court, see J. Vining, *The Authoritative and the Authoritarian* (Chicago: University of Chicago Press, 1986).

55 So much so that in Germany it can happen that the other members on the Court will reject the rapporteur's recommendation and he will have to write a new judgment even though he may still believe his initial recommendation was correct.

56 Together with a more open and searching appointment process, a more collegial system of decision-making should be responsive to the concerns of those, like Paul Weiler, who have (usually with good reason) been highly critical of the reasoning and justification offered by the judges in explaining why they have decided a law is constitutional or not. See P. Weiler, "The Charter at Work: Reflections on the Constitutionalizing of Labour and Employment Law", 40 U.T.L.I. 117.

The fact the members of the Court were able to operate so independently also raises important questions about the role of a Chief Justice and the extent to which he or she should promote the collegial or collective character of the Court. See E. McWhinney, *Supreme Courts, supra,* note 1, at 74.

is justified. It shows that the anti-democratic character of the current Canadian regime is not something immutable or even difficult to change. The model itself is essentially sound. The defect is very much one of institutional design and, it turns out, a relatively minor one at that. The widespread experience of other free and democratic societies, which have incorporated similar systems of judicial review into their structure of government, shows the democratic legitimacy of the Supreme Court of Canada could be guaranteed with very simple adjustments to the way the judges are appointed to and terminated from the Court and to the processes by which their decisions are made. Without compromising their independence in any way, each of these institutional adaptations would make the judges more accountable to the people who are governed by the rulings they "hand down". In theatrical terms, simply by borrowing the common wisdom on matters of set design, those (politicians and judges) responsible for the production and direction of the show could do much to make it more certain that successful performances will be put on by the Court for years to come.

11

The Accessibility of the Court

Comparative constitutional law teaches a very similar lesson on how to deal with the prohibitive cost of maintaining a constitutional challenge as it did on how the judges could be made more accountable and the whole process more democratic. In particular, a review of the major European systems of judicial review[1] shows again that there are very simple and straightforward structural changes that could make the Canadian Supreme Court considerably more accessible and much less regressive than it presently is. Currently, access to the Supreme Court is governed by "rules of standing" (devised by the Court) which state when an individual is entitled to challenge the constitutionality of any law and take it through the courts. Canada's standing rules are very liberal. In fact they are amongst the most accommodating in the world.[2] In all of the European systems we have referred to, similar rules of standing stipulate when an ordinary citizen can start a case. Where the European systems differ from our own

---

1 In view of our attention throughout the book to the relevance of American constitutional law for the Canadian scene, it is worth noting that Canadian commentators seem virtually unanimous that American solutions to questions of access and standing offer no helpful guidance for Canadian policy makers and courts. See W.A. Bogart, "Standing and the Charter: Rights and Identity", in R. Sharpe (ed.), *Charter Litigation* (Toronto: Butterworths, 1987); C.J. Wydrzynski, "The Relevance of the Concept of Standing in the United States for Canadian Law", a study prepared for the Ontario Law Reform Commission, dated April 1984.

2 E. McWhinney, *Supreme Courts and Judicial Law Making* (Martinus-Nijhoff Publishers, 1986), p. 101. The Canadian rules were developed in a trilogy of cases: *Thorson v. A.G. Canada* (1958), 43 D.L.R. (3d) 1; *N.S. Board of Censors v. McNeil* (1978), 84 D.L.R. (3d) 1; and *Minister of Justice (Can.) v. Borowski* (1982), 130 D.L.R. (3d) 588. In *R. v. Big M Drug Mart*, Dickson indicated that standing to bring public interest challenges to the constitutionality of any law would be governed by these rules as well; see *R. v. Big M Drug Mart* (1985), 18 D.L.R. (4th) 321, 336; see also *Borowski v. A.G. Canada* (1989), 57 D.L.R. (4th) 231.

is in providing additional routes by which constitutional challenges can be brought to their country's highest courts. For the reviewer's purposes, what is most appealing about these alternative procedures is that not only do they make it easier to get a final ruling on the constitutionality of any law, they make it a whole lot cheaper as well.

Two devices stand out from the rest.[3] Both address the question of access and cost by shortening the process through which a challenge must pass before it can be referred to a country's highest court. One procedure, known as "indirect" or "concrete norm control", improves access and reduces cost by eliminating the requirement that every case be heard by an intermediate Court of Appeal before it reaches the country's highest court. When the constitutionality of a law which governs how an ordinary lawsuit will be resolved is put in issue, this procedure allows — indeed requires — the trial court judge to refer it immediately to the court with the final authority to rule on the Constitution. The second device is called "direct" or "abstract norm control" and it is even more attentive to questions of access and cost than the first. Abstract norm control allows references about the constitutionality of any law to be made directly to those with the final say and in a way which effectively transfers all of the costs from the individual citizen to the public purse.

"Indirect" or "concrete" norm control is an important part of the systems of constitutional review in Germany, Switzerland, Austria, Spain and Italy.[4] Norm control is just a shorthand way of describing the Court's role of measuring a law against the terms of the Constitution. The norms are simply the entitlements, principles, and values embedded in the constitutional text. "Indirect" or "concrete" norm control refers to the fact that the Court's evaluation of the law arises indirectly, in the context of an actual legal dispute. In all of these countries the procedure works, with

---

3 One should also make mention of another institutional variation in the German system that enhances access to the Court of rich and poor alike. As part of the committee system, which screens all individual complaints before they are heard by the full Court, it is the rule that if one member of the Committee thinks a case should be heard by the full Court, it is referred to all of the judges for consideration. If one additional judge on the full Court thinks the case raises an important issue, the case must be decided by the full Court. In Canada, access is restricted to persons who can persuade two of the three judges who sit on the leave application that their case is worthy of review by the full Court. See M. Singer, "The Constitutional Court of the German Federal Republic", 31 International and Comparative L.Q. 331, 338. In the U.S., the rule is if any member of the Supreme Court thinks a case is important enough to be heard he or she must secure the agreement of three other justices. See H. Abraham, *The Judicial Process: An Introductory Analysis of the Courts of the United States* (New York: Oxford University Press, 1980), pp. 182-89; P. Russell, *The Judiciary in Canada: The Third Branch of Government* (Toronto: McGraw-Hill, 1987), p. 346.

4 See Chapter 10, notes 3-8, *supra*.

local variations, more or less the same way. Whenever a trial judge is hearing a case in which he or she doubts the constitutionality of a law which is relevant to how the case will be decided, he or she must refer the constitutional issue directly to the country's highest or Constitutional Court. In such cases there is no requirement to pass through an intermediate level of appeal.

The advantage of having a method by which cases can be moved directly to a country's supreme or final court, after an opinion on the merits has been obtained from a lower court, is obvious. One level of appeals is much faster and cheaper than two (or three). In all events, the litigants should save a third of their costs, and if they are successful in their challenge, the amount could be even higher than that.[5] Moreover, forcing people to take their case through a second level of appeal is particularly hard on the poor and those with limited means.[6] Had a comparable rule been made a part of the Canadian process of judicial review from the beginning, prisoners like Badger and Grondin and working people like Lavigne, would have been among its first beneficiaries.

A procedure like concrete or indirect norm control would also fit easily into the Canadian scene. Indeed, until 1974 when all rights of appeal to the Supreme Court in civil cases were abolished, and access was made conditional on getting "leave" from the Court, Canada had a very similar process itself. From its inception, the Act that established the Supreme Court and regulated its affairs, contained a section that allowed provincial trial court judges to refer constitutional questions directly to the Supreme Court for its deliberation if they thought the issue was material to the case. Indeed, in the beginning, the process was thought to be an extremely important one[7] and as recently as 1964 it was singled out by one commentator as one of the three most outstanding characteristics of the Canadian method of judicial review.[8] Although it is true that the device was by and large a dormant one,[9] it would certainly not constitute a radical

---

5 If they are successful, they will also be spared the cost of having to repeat any alternative non-constitutional arguments that were pertinent to the case.

6 A point recognized by at least one member of the Court. See Willard Estey in S.I. Bushnell's "Leave to Appeal Applications to the Supreme Court of Canada: A Matter of Public Importance", 3 S. Ct. L. Rev. 479, 486.

7 See P. Russell, "The Jurisdiction of the Supreme Court of Canada: Present Policies and A Programme for Reform" (1968), 6 O.H.L.J. 1, 7-8.

8 J. Grant, "Judicial Review in Canada: Procedural Aspects", 42 Can. Bar Rev. 195, 222-224.

9 P. Russell, "The Jurisdiction of the Supreme Court", *supra*, note 7, at 8. See also G. Le Dain, "Concerning the Proposed Constitutional and Civil Law Specialization at the Supreme Court Level" (1967), R. Juridique Thémis 107.

break with Canada's legal tradition to reactivate a similar procedure for challenges under the Charter.

In the past, some concern has been expressed by a number of commentators who feared that such a procedure could substantially interfere with the Court's ability to control its own schedule and decide what cases it will hear.[10] It has been said that there is a danger that the Court would be swamped with cases it did not want to hear and which it felt were not important enough to warrant allocating any of its valuable time. Such concerns have no basis in theory or in fact. The reality is that, in the European experience, although these cases frequently raise important questions of constitutional law, quantitatively they represent less than 10% of the Court's docket. Moreover, as we have seen, its antecedent had essentially been a dead letter in Canadian law. In Germany, with a population more than twice the size of Canada's and having a reputation of being a very litigious society[11] these cases average between 30 and 60 per year.[12]

If there were concerns that Canada's experience under the Charter might prove different than its own past, or that of others, it would be a simple matter for Parliament to minimize the risk of the Court being deluged with cases. In Europe, the solution has been to draw the parameters of the procedure quite narrowly. In the first place, it is generally only members of the judiciary (rather than administrators or members of the bureaucracy) who are allowed to make use of the procedure.[13] This is not a mechanism like the one which existed in Canada until 1974, in which individual litigants were able to refer cases as well. Moreover, a case can only be referred under this procedure when the lower court judge has decided not only that the constitutionality of the law in question is doubtful, but also that there is no other way of deciding the case without addressing the constitutional question. If a judge can read the challenged law in a way that accords with the Constitution, or can decide the case on other than constitutional grounds, he or she must do so, and any attempt to refer

---

10 P. Russell, *ibid.*; Le Dain, *ibid.*, at 121.

11 See G. Brinkmann, *The West German Federal Constitutional Court* (1981), Public Law 83, 92; and see generally Kommers, *Judicial Politics in West Germany* (Sage, 1976).

12 See H. Rupp, "*Judicial Review in the Federal Republic of Germany*", 9 A.J.C.L. 29, 33; J. Ipsen, "Constitutional Review of Laws", in *Main Principles of the German Basic Law* (Baden Baden: Namos Verlagsgesellschaft, 1983), p. 115, and see generally D. Kommers, *Judicial Politics in West Germany* (Sage, 1976).

13 In Canada a parallel question is whether administrative tribunals have the authority to decide whether the law they have been empowered to regulate is constitutional or not. The issue will shortly be decided in a case called *Cuddy Chicks Ltd. v. Ontario Labour Relations Board* (1990), 62 D.L.R. (4th) 125 (Ont. C.A.). For an argument in favour of recognizing such a power, see D. Gibson, *The Law of the Charter: General Principles* (Toronto: Carswell, 1986), pp. 279ff.

the constitutional question to the final Court would be turned down. As well, the procedure is usually restricted to challenges to statutes, regulations, and the like and is not available to dispute the constitutionality of some administrative or bureaucratic act. Finally, all of these systems leave it open to the Constitutional Court to reject the lower court judge's decision that the constitutional issue was essential to the outcome of the case. In the final analysis the Court retains effective control of what cases will fill out its docket.[14]

Designed along the lines of the European systems of indirect or concrete norm control there is little risk that the Canadian Supreme Court would receive a radically higher number of referrals than what the European courts have experienced. If, out of an abundance of caution, Parliament wanted to, it could reduce the threat even further by favouring the more conservative variations of concrete normal control that exist in Europe today. It could, for example, follow the lead of the Federal Republic of Germany and permit a lower court judge to remove a case to the Constitutional Court only when his or her doubts about the constitutionality of the law he or she was considering were "serious" or "compelling".[15] Or, it could further restrict the persons who had the power to remove cases directly to the highest court to those who were members of the country's superior courts as Austria has done.[16]

However it is designed, a process like the European procedure of "indirect" or "concrete" norm control would improve access to the Court for cases which have been independently assessed as involving serious questions of constitutionality. It provides a way of directing the Court's attention to the most pressing constitutional issues in as simple and expeditious a way as possible. Reintroducing this procedure into the *Supreme Court Act* would make the process of constitutional review in Canada more accessible and less regressive than it currently is. In several European countries, however, this is not the only, or even the most important, procedure by which constitutional questions can be referred expeditiously to their highest courts. In Spain, Austria and Germany, indirect or concrete norm control works alongside a parallel procedure

---

14 See H. Rupp, *supra*, note 12, at 32; J. Ipsen, *supra*, note 12, at 115 and 131.

15 D. Kommers, *Judicial Politics in West Germany* (Sage, 1976), p. 106, and "Free Speech", 53 So. Cal. L. Rev. 657, 663.

16 See M. Cappelletti and J. Adams, "Judicial Review of Legislation: European Antecedents and Adaptations" 79 Harv. L. Rev. 1207, 1220; K. Heller, *Outline of Austrian Constitutional Law* (Kluwer, 1989). It might be noted that in *R. v. Mills* (1986), 29 D.L.R. (4th) 161, when the Court considered a related issue, it divided along the familiar liberal-conservative lines. William McIntyre held that provincial court judges in preliminary inquiries are not courts of competent jurisdiction, in contrast with Lamer and Dickson, who thought they could be in certain instances and for some purposes.

known as abstract or direct norm control.

Abstract norm control is a second procedure by which a constitutional question can be brought before a country's highest court in an expedited fashion. It differs from the referral process we have been considering in two respects. First, the party activating the procedure is not a member of an administrative tribunal or a judge in a lower court. Abstract norm control provides a means of access for the other two branches of government. It is a procedure by which Governments and/or a specified number of legislators can refer a constitutional question to the Court. In Germany and Austria it takes one-third of their legislatures to initiate a challenge; in Spain, fifty legislators have the power to put a question to their constitutional tribunal. Only the executive, or a specified number of legislators, can make use of this procedural device.[17] The other difference between abstract and concrete norm control is that the former is even faster and cheaper than the latter. With abstract norm control, a constitutional question can be referred directly to the highest court without any requirement of first having to file a complaint with some administrative agency or lower court.

Once again, the attractiveness of a process like abstract norm control is so obvious as to make unnecessary any extensive comment. For reviewers, it will be seen to provide another useful tool to alleviate the problems of access and cost which afflict the current system. Though it cannot solve these problems on its own, it does provide an effective means by which the most disputed and urgent cases can be put before the Court quickly and it does this in a way which relieves the individual of having to pay for any of the costs of the case. It would mean, for example, that the individuals and church groups who, under the present system, have been forced to divert hundreds of thousands of dollars to pay for the cost of challenging Canada's new refugee laws could have spent their money directly on the humanitarian causes they are organized to assist.

Abstract norm control also dovetails very nicely with the reviewer's democratic ambitions. Like the involvement of the legislature in the appointment process, this procedure provides another point of contact between the people, their elected representatives, and the process of judicial review. As a practical matter it especially enhances the involvement of members of opposition and minority parties in the process by which social policy is transformed into law. Effectively it gives them, rather than the

---

17   In exceptional circumstances, when a statute is self-executing and merely declaratory, it is theoretically possible for an individual to refer a constitutional question directly to the Court. In practice, these cases are rare and seem to parallel the kind of challenge *Thorson* brought to Canada's *Official Languages Act, supra*, note 2. See H. Rupp, "Judicial Review in the Federal Republic of Germany", *supra*, note 12, at 56-57.

Attorney-General, the responsibility for ensuring that Governments pay scrupulous attention to the requirements of the Charter. And, it can be expected they will do a more vigorous job. Unlike Attorney-Generals, who will often be inclined to subordinate their views to the wishes of their colleagues in the Cabinet when disputes about the Charter arise,[18] members of the Opposition will be highly motivated to make use of this power whenever they have serious doubts about the constitutionality of any policy which the Government proposes to enact into law. In a sense, by empowering the members of the Opposition in this way, abstract norm review redresses the privileged position the executive branch has traditionally enjoyed in its relations with the Court. It ensures ordinary legislators will have similar opportunities to seek a ruling from the Court as the other two branches of government.

Like each of the other features of the European systems of constitutional review that the reviewer has examined so far, abstract norm control is a procedure which could be expected to adapt without difficulty to the Canadian scene. In fact, it is the logical counterpart to the reference procedure which has always been available for disputes about the division of powers between the federal and provincial governments.[19] Abstract norm control really is just a reference procedure for Charter challenges. The only difference is that the party referring the question of constitutionality is the legislative branch rather than the Government itself.

Apart from that difference, the parallels between the two processes are striking. Both procedures are important, not so much because of the number of cases they process, but rather because of the kinds of disputes which they refer to the Court. Quantitatively neither the reference procedure in Canada,[20] nor abstract norm control in Western Europe, generate many cases at all.[21] In West Germany these cases average between five and ten a year. Neither process represents any threat to a court's ability to control its own docket. The real significance of both procedures lies in the fact that, though few in number, the cases it does handle are generally

---

18 See I. Scott, "The Role of the Attorney General and the Charter of Rights", in G. Beaudoin (ed.), *Charter Cases* (Yvon Blais, 1987); and "The Attorney-General: Law and Government", University of Toronto Faculty of Law, Goodman Lecture, 1988. Cf. J. Edwards, "The Attorney General and the Charter of Rights", in R. Sharpe (ed.), *Charter Litigation* (Toronto: Butterworths, 1987).

19 For a description and analysis of the use of the reference procedure for federalism questions, see P. Hogg, *Constitutional Law of Canada*, 2nd ed. (Toronto: Carswell, 1985), pp. 177ff.

20 See P. Weiler, "The Supreme Court and the Law of Canadian Federalism", 23 U.T.L.J. 307, 367; B. Strayer, *The Canadian Constitution and the Courts*, 2nd ed. (Toronto: Butterworths, 1983), Chapter 7.

21 J. Ipsen, "Constitutional Review", *supra*, note 12, at 115; H. Rupp, "Judicial Review", *supra*, note 12, at 36.

of the highest public interest and concern.[22] These are cases in which there is a serious disagreement in the political arena as to where the limits of government and legal authority lie.

Functionally, the two procedures share a common purpose as well. In its inception, the reference procedure was primarily thought of as the fairest way of settling disputes about the limits of government power and in particular, whether and/or when the federal power of disallowing provincial legislation should be used.[23] The reference procedure was included in the original *Supreme Court Act* largely as a way of ensuring that disputes about the constitutionality of any provincial law were settled by an impartial and independent body, like the Supreme Court, rather than allowing one of the interested parties to make the decision on its own. Abstract norm control works in exactly the same way. It has resort to the same neutral, objective process to decide whether Government action bears too heavily on the constitutional freedoms of those it affects. Like the reference procedure, it provides a way to ensure that disputes about the limits of government power are settled by an independent third party rather than by the Government itself. Moreover, it does this in a way which is free of the afflictions that historically have been thought to compromise the effectiveness of the reference procedure.

Traditionally there have been two major criticisms of the procedures by which abstract questions of constitutionality were referred directly to a country's highest court. First, it was said that in the absence of any "case or controversy" (to use the American legal jargon) within which a constitutional question can be put, a court will be less able to render informed and sound judgments.[24] Without two adversarial parties disputing the particulars of a specific case, the argument is that there is a risk the Court will not be supplied with the kind of factual evidence it needs to know what the consequences of its decision are likely to be. In addition, in Canada at least, the integrity of references has been challenged on the ground that, in these cases, the Court's rulings are really purely policy

---

22 Amongst others, the procedure of abstract norm control was used to test Germany's abortion laws and election funding laws. See J. Ipsen, *ibid*, at 122.

23 P. Russell, *The Supreme Court of Canada as a Bilingual and Bicultural Institution*, Royal Commission on Bilingualism and Biculturalism (Ottawa: Queen's Printer, 1969).

24 This is a criticism which is accepted as conventional wisdom by many leading figures in American constitutional law. See P. Freund, "The Supreme Court in a Federation", 53 Col. L. Rev. 597; A. Bickel, *The Least Dangerous Branch* (New Haven: Yale University Press, 1963); F. Frankfurter, "Comment" (1924), 37 Harv. L. Rev. 1002. For references in the Canadian literature, see T. Cromwell, *Locus Standi* (Toronto: Carswell, 1986), p. 10; S. Blake, "Standing to Litigate Constitutional Rights and Freedoms in Canada and the United States", 16 U. of Ottawa L. Rev. 66. For a criticism of the argument, see Australia Law Reform Commission, *Standing in Public Interest Litigation*, 1985, pp. 115-117, 122-123.

decisions and not legal judgments based on objective criteria and rules.

As criticisms of how the reference procedure has worked in the past, when it was concerned with controversies over the division of powers between the federal and provincial levels of government, these charges are not without merit. Legal academics can and have pointed to cases which manifest either or both of these flaws.[25] However, on closer analysis, it is apparent that whatever deficiencies have compromised the integrity of the Court's decisions in the past, these were not due to any inherent weakness in the reference procedure itself. Certainly there was no legal impediment or restriction on what kind of evidence the Court could hear. In every reference case, the Court was empowered to solicit whatever assistance it wanted from the parties.[26] Even before the entrenchment of the Charter, the Court had made it clear that it would be receptive to a wide range of material that was relevant to any constitutional question it had been asked to resolve.[27] As well, it also had the power, which it frequently used, to add other parties and participants to a reference whenever it thought their views and contributions would inform their deliberations.[28] In reality, to the extent that the Court's decisions in earlier references can fairly be criticized for lacking an adequate factual foundation, it is clear that the fault lay with either the parties or the Court rather than with the procedure itself. Either the parties failed to provide the Court with the necessary factual material[29] or, alternatively, the Court itself was open to criticism either for not taking seriously evidence which the parties did put in front of it[30] or for not even permitting all of the relevant evidence to be heard.[31]

If anything is clear in the brief experience we have had with the Charter so far, it is that there is little danger that either of these mistakes will be repeated in the future. In the first place, as we have seen, right from

---

25 B. Strayer, *The Canadian Constitution and the Courts*, 2nd ed. (Toronto: Butterworths, 1983), pp. 194-199; P. Weiler, *In the Last Resort* (Toronto: Carswell, 1974); P. Hogg, "Proof of Facts", 26 U.T.L.J. 390.

26 *Supreme Court Act*, R.S.C. 1985, c. S-26, s. 53(4), (5), (6), (7).

27 *Ref. re Anti-Inflation Act* (1976), 68 D.L.R. (3d) 452; *Ref. re Ontario Residential Tenancies* (1981), 123 D.L.R. (3d) 354.

28 See J. Welch, "No Room at the Top" (1985), 43 U.T. Fac. of L. Rev. 204; K. Swan, "Intervention and Amicus Curiae Status in Charter Litigation", in Sharpe (ed.), *Charter Litigation* (Toronto: Butterworths, 1987) ; E. Morgan, "Proof of Facts in Charter Litigation", in R. Sharpe (ed.), *Charter Litigation*; P. Hogg, "Proof of Facts in Constitutional Cases", 26 U.T.L.J. 386, 398; J. Grant, "Judicial Review in Canada", 42 Can. Bar Rev. 195, 207; V. MacDonald, "Constitutional Law and Extrinsic Evidence", 17 Can. Bar Rev. 77.

29 P. Weiler, *In the Last Resort, supra*, note 25, Chapter 6.

30 See, e.g., P. Hogg, "Proof of Facts", *supra*, note 28.

31 K. Swan, "Intervention and Amicus Curiae", *supra*, note 28.

the beginning the Court showed it was acutely sensitive to the importance of the litigants supplying it with the kind of social science evidence on which Charter cases inevitably turn. Early and often, the members of the Court made it clear they were eager and willing to receive any and all material counsel thought relevant to the case.[32]

And, by and large, the legal profession has been responsive to that call. Academic and practising lawyers were quick to supply a series of essays on how counsel might go about collecting and presenting such evidence, the purposes to which it could be put, and the attitude the Court should adopt in reviewing it.[33] In addition, lawyers have endeavoured to supply the Court with as much evidence bearing on their claims as they could find. Solicited, expert opinions, as well as all manner of academic and informal comment, relevant to the ends and means of a challenged law, have become the standard way of "proving" whether a law was constitutional or not.[34] The "Brandeis brief", incorporating all of this evidence quickly became as central a part of constitutional challenges in Canada as in the United States where this tool of advocacy was invented. Indeed, here as there, it is largely as a result of the importance that written evidence and argument of this kind has assumed, that the oral tradition has become much less important in presenting constitutional cases than ever before.

There is no reason to think that this positive attitude of both counsel and the Court to social science evidence would be any different if a case was initiated by members of the legislature rather than arising in a piece of concrete litigation. Certainly that has not been the experience in Germany where the Court possesses the same wide and flexible powers to call for evidence and allow for the intervention of interested individuals

---

32 See, e.g., *Skapinker v. Law Society of Upper Canada* (1984), 9 D.L.R. (4th) 161; *Singh v. M.E.I.* (1985), 17 D.L.R. (4th) 422; *R. v. Oakes* (1986), 28 D.L.R. (4th) 200. Similar calls were made by Brian Dickson in a speech to the Canadian Bar Association on February 2, 1985 (Edmonton); and by Bertha Wilson, "Decision Making", Chapter 10, *supra*, note 49.

33 Several of these essays are collected in R. Sharpe (ed.), *Charter Litigation*, *supra*, note 28; see, e.g., J. Hagan, "Can Social Science Save Us? The Problems and Prospects of Social Science Evidence in Constitutional Litigation", p. 214; B. Morgan, "Proof of Facts in Charter Litigation", p. 159; K. Swinton, "What Do The Courts Want from the Social Sciences", p. 187. Another collection of essays can be found in G. Beaudoin (ed.), *Charter Cases* (Yvon Blais, 1987), Part III; see, e.g., M. Manning, "Proof of Facts in Constitutional Cases", p. 271; C. Beckton, "Non Legal Evidence in Charter Cases", p. 331. See also P. Hogg, "Proof of Facts", *supra*, note 28; Y. Fricot, "The Challenge of Legislation By Means of the Charter: Evidentiary Issues", 16 U. of Ottawa L. Rev. 565.

34 See, e.g., *Ford v. Quebec* (1989), 54 D.L.R. (4th) 577; *Irwin Toy v. Quebec* (1989), 58 D.L.R. (4th) 577.

and groups as the Canadian Supreme Court enjoys.[35] In every case there still will be rival and antagonistic positions on the constitutionality of the challenged law.[36] Members of the opposition parties should be every bit as vigilant as any private citizen in ensuring the Court is fully apprised of all of the relevant evidence which gives rise to their doubts about the constitutionality of any law they may challenge. Indeed, with their access to a well-financed and sophisticated research staff it would be expected that the quality of evidence which would be made available to the Court would in all probability improve. In addition to being the fastest and cheapest way to decide if a law is constitutional or not, abstract norm control seems likely to be the most effective and rigorous way such issues can be presented to the Court.

Virtually the same comments can be made about the objection that, in reference cases, there are no objective criteria to guide the Court as the criticism that they are made in a factual vacuum. Unquestionably, there is a good deal of evidence to support such a claim in many of the Court's earlier division of powers decisions. There is simply no denying that frequently the Court would develop a set of contradictory principles, which "marched in pairs",[37] so to speak, and from which each judge could choose according to whichever outcome he or she wanted to reach. Regrettably, abstract jurisprudence and interpretative semantics do distinguish (and destroy the legitimacy of) many of the Court's most important decisions concerning the division of powers between the federal and provincial levels of government.[38] But abstract review of Charter challenges should not fall prey to similar reasoning so long as the judges stick to the model in *Oakes*. *Oakes*, as we know from our analysis in Part Two, is the very antithesis of the kind of arid, conceptual, definitional wrangling that has gone on in so many federalism cases. With *Oakes*, the whole emphasis is on the question of justification not interpretation; on two principles of proportionality and not on what range of interests and activities a particular right or freedom protects. On the model in *Oakes*, judicial review is all about alternative means and, as our analysis in Part Two has shown, alternate means is just the name lawyers use to describe a very conventional measure of social well-being.

Designing a process of direct or abstract constitutional review (norm control) under the Charter seems so attractive, it is almost certainly

---

35 G. Brinkmann, "The West German Constitutional Court" (1981), Public Law 83.
36 Note that this was also the Supreme Court's own experience in *Borowski v. A.G. Canada, supra*, note 2, where even though there was no concrete dispute, the Court was satisfied the litigants had fully canvassed and addressed all of the relevant issues.
37 P. Weiler, "Supreme Court and Law of Canadian Federalism" (1973), 23 U.T.L.J. 307.
38 B. Strayer, *The Canadian Constitution and the Courts, supra*, note 20.

something many reviewers would want to highlight at the end of their reviews. It would, simultaneously, promote the democratic character of the review process, by making it more accessible and less costly to individual Canadians, and it would do this without being afflicted with any of the deficiencies which have compromised the effectiveness of the reference process in the past. With its enhancement of the democratic and progressive character of the Court, it is a natural for reviewers to endorse. Together with alterations in the rules controlling how people are moved on and off the Court, it would represent another simple adjustment to the set design which the reviewer could recommend at the end of the review.

Indeed the advantages of a process like abstract norm control seem so compelling that some reviewers might be tempted to propose that it be made available to any individual citizen who thinks his or her constitutional rights have been violated. Though not part of the European practice of constitutional review,[39] a reviewer might think that creating a kind of automatic power of citizen review was the next logical step to take. On reflection however, it is unlikely that a reviewer will be attracted by such an idea for very long. Fairly quickly it should become apparent why such a procedure has never been favoured in any European system and why it would be inappropriate in Canada as well. Quite simply, the Court could be swamped if every individual with a constitutional complaint could come to it directly and without having to pass through any courts or tribunals of first instance. Even in the German system, in which individuals are required to exhaust all their non-constitutional remedies before they can petition the Constitutional Court, the evidence shows the justices find these cases of individual complaints burdensome and time consuming.[40] They have consistently made up over 95% of the Court's caseload and currently are running at a rate of 3500-4000 a year.

Traditionally, "floodgates" arguments, against liberalizing the rules of how constitutional challenges can be raised, have not made much impression on either commentators or courts.[41] Resistance to the floodgates argument, however, has largely been based on the premise that the high cost of taking a challenge through all of the initial and intermediate stages of review, before being able to get to the final court of appeal, would

---

39 Though Switzerland comes very close. For an overview of the Swiss system, see J.F. Aubert, *Traité de Droit Constitutionnel Suisse* (Neuchatel, 1982).

40 D. Kommers, *Judicial Politics in West Germany*, *supra*, note 15, at 167.

41 T. Cromwell, *Locus Standi*, *supra*, note 24, at 168; B. Strayer, *The Canadian Constitution and the Courts*, *supra*, note 25, at 135, 176; J. Johnson, "Locus Standi in Constitutional Cases After *Thorson*", [1975] Pub. Law 137, 152; W. Bogart, "Standing and the Charter: Rights and Identity", in R. Sharpe, *Charter Litigation*, *supra*, note 28; Australia Law Reform Commission, *Standing in Public Interest Litigation*, 1985, p. 105; cf. G. Le Dain in *Ministry of Finance v. Finlay* (1987), 33 D.L.R. (4th) 321, 340.

keep the numbers down. In the procedure we are now considering, however, that constraint obviously would not exist. If each citizen could petition the Supreme Court directly there would be a real risk that these personal complaints could overwhelm the resources of the Court. At a minimum, the judges would be obliged to spend a disproportionate amount of their time just sorting out which cases they wanted to hear. It would mean that the Court would lose control of its docket only very shortly after it had acquired some substantial powers in this regard.[42] Indeed, it would put the Court in an even worse position than it was prior to 1974, when it was obliged to hear any appeal from a judgment of a provincial Court of Appeal in which $10,000 or more was at stake.

Limiting abstract (and indeed concrete) review to members of the legislative (and judicial) branch, by contrast, provides a very effective method of screening and ordering cases so that those which the community thinks are most pressing and controversial and in need of resolution will be given the immediate attention of the Court. As a practical matter, procedures like abstract and concrete norm control make members of legislatures and lower court judges responsible for deciding which cases should be given the highest priority and have access to what is a very fast and cheap track to the Court. Through their supervision, less momentous cases, as well as those which can be settled on non-constitutional grounds, are prevented from diverting the Court from more important and urgent tasks.

Being screened out of the expedited procedure would not mean an individual challenge could never be brought to the Supreme Court. It would simply mean the challenger would have to follow the same procedure used by any other lawsuit or piece of litigation. A person who had been unsuccessful in persuading the requisite number of legislators or some lower judicial official that their constitutional rights had been violated would still be able to press their claims in the normal way. As we have already noted, Canada's "standing rules" are acknowledged to be amongst the most liberal in the world. Even if these rules could still be improved,[43] no one who had been unsuccessful in persuading the legislative and/or judicial branches to refer their challenge to the Court would have any difficulty in meeting the current rules governing who is allowed to initiate a constitutional case.

---

42   P. Russell, *The Judiciary in Canada, supra*, note 3, at 344; I. Bushnell, "Leave To Appeal", *supra*, note 6, at 479, 484.

43   Bogart, "Standing and the Charter", in R. Sharpe (ed.), *Charter Litigation, supra*, note 28; D. Mullan and A. Roman, "*Ministry of Justice v. Borowski*: The Extent of the Citizen's Right to Litigate the Lawfulness of Government Action" (1984), 4 Windsor Yearbook of Access to Justice 303.

Moreover, if the challenger were poor, he or she would almost always be eligible for some form of legal aid. Although this legal assistance will generally (though not invariably) not be enough to attract the most experienced and expert counsel in the field, in most cases it will be adequate to ensure that even those who are most disadvantaged will be able to hire a competent lawyer to press his or her case through to the end. Although a reviewer might wish to advert to ways in which public support for constitutional litigation can be enriched and extended in new ways,[44] these are really matters that go beyond the immediate focus of her review. For most reviewers, it will be sufficient to ensure that the procedural and institutional arrangements of the review process itself are made just as democratic and progressive as they can possibly be.

In the end then, it turns out that writing a review for a non-legal audience is not likely to affect either its substance or style very much. The reviewer will be able to stick with the descriptive and analytical framework that she used in Part One. All she needs to do is add a paragraph or two at the end explaining how, by re-introducing one long-standing procedure of constitutional law, and extending another, the institutional framework within the Court can be easily modified to ensure that all of the benefits that constitutional review theoretically provides will actually have an impact on the everyday lives of Canadians.

Ending with a series of positive, structural and institutional recommendations would certainly appeal to most reviewers whose instincts were to applaud the performance of the Court. In the first place, concluding in this way would allow the reviewer to highlight for a final time the strength and objectivity of the principle of alternative means. After all, in recommending various institutional and procedural modifications to the way the Supremes go about performing on stage, the reviewer would really be applying this second proportionality principle to the organizational character of the Court. In terms of the model in *Oakes*, the most important lesson of comparative constitutional law may well be in identifying the alternate ways in which the procedural and institutional framework of the Court can be organized so as to give maximum effect to the Charter.[45]

---

44 See K. Roberts, *Public Interest Advocacy in Canada*, 1984, Dept. of Justice, Ottawa.

45 Comparisons of the substantive outcomes which different Constitutional or Supreme Courts around the world have fashioned on common cases (e.g., abortion) may have much less practical significance. On the model in *Oakes*, the core function of judicial review involves an analysis of the ends for which and the means by which those empowered with legal authority exercise their powers. The different purposes pursued by various Governments will unavoidably affect the reasoning and the conclusions of the Courts. Moreover, the final stage of the process will be heavily influenced by the culture, traditions, values, etc. of the communities in which it takes place. In particular the evaluation of the balance that is struck between the purposes (objectives) and effects (consequences)

Having spent so much of the review emphasizing the importance of the principle of alternative means in the Court's own work with the Charter, it would be fitting to conclude with a final example of how it can also enhance the procedural and structural aspects of judicial review as much as the substantive rules and social policies that it yields.

Perhaps even more satisfying for the reviewer would be the fact that in finishing up the review in this way, she would finally be able to address some remarks to the politicians who, after all, are really the producers of the whole show. Having talked to and about the performers throughout the review, focusing on these structural and procedural recommendations would allow the reviewer an opportunity to remind the politicians that they share responsibility with the members of the Court to ensure a continuity of consistently first rate performances. She could stress that no matter how faithful the judges are to the principles and framework of analysis in *Oakes*, if the politicians fail to redress the most undemocratic and regressive features of the present system, its integrity and legitimacy will continue to be open to dispute. In the final analysis it is the legislature and not the judiciary that has the power (and responsibility) to respond to the criticisms of the sceptics and to ensure that Canada's system of judicial review does not become the exclusive domain and plaything of those (judges and litigators) who are already very powerful and richly endowed.[46]

Wrapping up the review by focusing on the responsibilities of the political officials would be especially appealing because in the end it would allow the reviewer to turn the tables and put the sceptics' beliefs to the test.[47] If the latter's confidence in the integrity of the political process is well-founded, the legitimacy of the reviewer's applause for the Court's performance will be secure. If the sceptics' faith in the processes of politics

---

of a challenged law will be strongly influenced by local conditions and values and so can be expected to yield different results in each country. See E. McWhinney, "The Canadian Charter of Rights and Freedoms: The Lessons of Comparative Jurisprudence", 61 Can. Bar Rev. 55; E. McWhinney, *Supreme Courts, supra*, note 2; D. Kommers, "Abortion and Constitution: United States and West Germany", 25 Am. J. Comp. L. 255.

46 See B. Slattery, "A Theory of the Charter", 25 Osgoode Hall L.J. 701, for a much more expansive treatment of the responsibility that the Charter assigns to the legislative and executive branches of government.

47 This would not be true of the most radical sceptics who have no such beliefs and who have as serious misgivings about the political process as they do about law. Some, like Michael Mandel, would not have much, if any, higher expectations for the political process than they would for the Court. Mandel claims that judicial review is discredited because, for the most part, it serves only to legitimate Government and a political process that is itself unjust and generally very oppressive. See *The Charter of Rights and the Legalization of Politics in Canada* (Toronto: Wall & Thompson, 1989).

is right, the politicians will not want to miss the opportunity to do their part.[48] Indeed, for everyone who believes in Parliament and is committed to popular rule, if the politicians do not do what it takes to guarantee the democratic and progressive character of the Court, we have only ourselves to blame.

---

48 It is at this stage of the review that the critic's character as romantic or pragmatist will have to be revealed. The most sceptical reviewers would doubt whether politicians could be persuaded to initiate the kinds of procedural and institutional reforms they might recommend. An extreme sceptic, such as Michael Mandel, would likely say the political system is so imperfect and unjust that it would be naive to think that politicians would make any structural changes to the Court.

More sanguine reviewers would hope politicians would see the Court in its proper light and make the organizational changes which are necessary for it to play its role to the full. Substantively, they would expect Government to see these initiatives as enabling the Court to perform its role in a way which is supportive of the other two branches of government and of our tradition of democratic and progressive government. Practically, they would hope Government would perceive the legislative programme that is required to put the changes into effect as a relatively modest and straightforward task.

Index